Palgrave Macmillan Asian Business Series

Series Editor: **Harukiyo Hasegawa** is Professor at Doshisha Business School, Kyoto, Japan, and Honourable Research Fellow at the University of Sheffield's School of East Asian Studies, where he was formerly Director of the Centre for Japanese Studies.

The *Palgrave Macmillan Asian Business Series* seeks to publish theoretical and empirical studies that contribute forward-looking social perspectives on the study of management issues not just in Asia, but by implication elsewhere. The series specifically aims at the development of new frontiers in the scope, themes and methods of business and management studies in Asia, a region which is seen as key to studies of modern management, organisation, strategies, human resources and technologies.

The series invites practitioners, policy-makers and academic researchers to join us at the cutting edge of constructive perspectives on Asian management, seeking to contribute towards the development of civil societies in Asia and further afield.

Titles include:

Claes-G. Alvstam, Harald Dolles and Patrik Ström (*editors*)
ASIAN INWARD AND OUTWARD FDI
New Challenges in the Global Economy

Glenn D. Hook and Harukiyo Hasegawa (*editors*)
JAPANESE RESPONSES TO GLOBALIZATION IN THE 21st CENTURY
Politics, Security, Economics and Business

David Marutschke
CONTINUOUS IMPROVEMENT STRATEGIES
Japanese Convenience Store Systems

Hiroaki Miyoshi and Yoshifumi Nakata (*editors*)
HAVE JAPANESE FIRMS CHANGED?
The Lost Decade

Hiroaki Miyoshi and Masanobu Kii (*editors*)
TECHNOLOGICAL INNOVATION AND PUBLIC POLICY
The Automotive Industry

Carlos Noronha (*editor*)
CORPORATE SOCIAL DISCLOSURE
Critical Perspectives in China and Japan

Diane Rosemary Sharpe and Harukiyo Hasegawa (*editors*)
NEW HORIZONS IN ASIAN MANAGEMENT
Emerging Issues and Critical Perspectives

Sten Söderman (*editor*)
EMERGING MULTIPLICITY
Integration and Responsiveness in Asian Business Development

Chikako Usui (*editor*)
COMPARATIVE ENTREPRENEURSHIP INITIATIVES
Studies in China, Japan and the USA

Oliver H.M. Yau and Raymond P.M. Chow (*editors*)
HARMONY VERSUS CONFLICT IN ASIAN BUSINESS
Managing in a Turbulent Era

Tan Yi
THE OIL AND GAS SERVICE INDUSTRY IN ASIA
A Comparison of Business Strategies

Palgrave Macmillan Asian Business Series
Series Standing Order ISBN 978–1–403–99841–5
(*outside North America only*)

You can receive future titles in this series as they are published by placing a standing order. Please contact your bookseller or, in case of difficulty, write to us at the address below with your name and address, the title of the series and the ISBN quoted above.

Customer Services Department, Macmillan Distribution Ltd, Houndmills, Basingstoke, Hampshire RG21 6XS, England

---

Corporate Social Disclosure

Critical Perspectives in China and Japan

Edited by

Carlos Noronha
University of Macau, China

palgrave
macmillan

First published 2015 by
PALGRAVE MACMILLAN

Palgrave Macmillan in the UK is an imprint of Macmillan Publishers Limited, registered in England, company number 785998, of Houndmills, Basingstoke, Hampshire RG21 6XS.

Palgrave Macmillan in the US is a division of St Martin's Press LLC, 175 Fifth Avenue, New York, NY 10010.

Palgrave Macmillan is the global academic imprint of the above companies and has companies and representatives throughout the world.

Palgrave® and Macmillan® are registered trademarks in the United States, the United Kingdom, Europe and other countries.

ISBN 978–1–137–41467–0

This book is printed on paper suitable for recycling and made from fully managed and sustained forest sources. Logging, pulping and manufacturing processes are expected to conform to the environmental regulations of the country of origin.

A catalogue record for this book is available from the British Library.

Library of Congress Cataloging-in-Publication Data
Corporate social disclosure : critical perspectives in China and Japan / edited by Carlos Noronha, University of Macau, China.
pages cm
Includes bibliographical references.
ISBN 978–1–137–41467–0
1. Social accounting—China. 2. Social accounting—Japan. 3. Social responsibility of business—China. 4. Social responsibility of business—Japan. 5. Disclosure of information—China. 6. Disclosure of information—Japan. I. Noronha, Carlos.
HD60.5.C6C67 2014
658.4'080951—dc23 2014026283

Contents

Figures and Tables

Figures

Tables

Contributors

Mohobbot Ali is Assistant Professor at the Faculty of Business, Government and Law, Discipline of Information Systems and Accounting, University of Canberra, Australia.

Philippe Debroux is Professor at the Faculty of Business Administration, Soka University, Tokyo, Japan.

Jenny J.Q. Guan is Lecturer of Accounting at the Faculty of Business Administration, Department of Accounting and Information Management, University of Macau, China.

Mohammad Badrul Haider is Associate Professor at the Institute of Business and Accounting, Kwansei Gakuin University, Japan.

Mohammad Tazul Islam is a PhD candidate at the Graduate School of Business Administration, Kobe University, Japan.

Katsuhiko Kokubu is Professor of Social and Environmental Accounting at the Graduate School of Business Administration, Kobe University, Japan.

Mari Kondo is Professor and Program Dean of Global MBA at the Doshisha Business School, Doshisha University, Kyoto, Japan.

Katy W.P. Kong is at the Human Resources Office, University of Macau, China.

Tiffany C.H. Leung is a PhD candidate at the School of Management, University of St Andrews, United Kingdom.

Carlos Noronha is Associate Professor of Accounting at the Faculty of Business Administration, Department of Accounting and Information Management, University of Macau, China.

Gustavo Tanaka is Associate Professor at the Doshisha Business School, Doshisha University, Kyoto, Japan.

Cynthia M.I. Si Tou is Senior Officer at the Finance Services Bureau, Macau, China.

Stefanie X. Wang is at the Lianyun District Financial Bureau of Lianyungang city, Jiangsu Province, China.

1
Corporate Social Disclosure in China and Japan: An Introduction

Carlos Noronha

Introduction

Corporate social disclosure (CSD), an important branch of social accounting (Gray, 2002), has been widely examined since the 1970s. Gray et al. (1996: 3) define social accounting as "the process of communicating the social and environmental effects of organisations' economic actions to particular interest groups within society and to society at large". During that time, managers were under pressure to disclose the wider consequences that corporate activities may have on the environment, human resources and consumer policies (McKie, 1974). Rapid globalization in the 1980s and 1990s forced corporations to realize that their operations and activities do not take place in a vacuum but have immense consequences both locally and globally (Macintosh et al., 2000). Consumers started to have an increased awareness of corporate social responsibility (CSR) and expected more transparency in corporate affairs. The disclosure of CSR information became very much in demand by various stakeholder groups, including governmental agencies and pressure groups. This was especially the case after the 2001 US accounting scandals of Enron and Arthur Andersen when CSD and reputation risk were seen to be related (Bebbington et al., 2008). Nowadays, CSD is still voluntary in most countries, although some European countries have mandatory requirements on environmental disclosure (Oxfam Hong Kong, 2010). Even so, given the fierce competition among global business players and the increased knowledge and demands of the various stakeholders, in order to continue to obtain their legitimate license (Deegan, 2002) to operate in society companies cannot avoid CSD.

China and Japan: Marathon runners

This volume has chosen China and Japan as two countries in which to observe the latest CSD issues. The first reason is that it allows comparison as if in a linear marathon. Japan has a rather mature approach to CSD as its development started quite early, together with its Western counterparts. Environmental pollution issues in the 1960s and 1970s were the primary trigger for corporate Japan's engagement in social responsibility (Takagaki, 2010). Further affected by the burst of the economic bubble in the 1990s, which was followed by the so-called "lost decade", a series of shocking corporate scandals were revealed to the public. These included food poisoning of Snow Brand milk products, concealed product recall at Mitsubishi Motor Company, the bankruptcy of Sogo department store and deceptive food product labeling at Nippon Ham (Kawamura, 2005). All these scandals led the Keizai Doyukai (Japan Association of Corporate Executives) to issue the new Corporate Evaluation Standards 2003. The objective was to restore trust in corporate Japan and to instill ethics and morality in business operations; to turn corporate scandals into corporate ethics and to transform the company-centered approach to a stakeholders-focused approach (Kawamura, 2005). The timing of this was crucial, as it coincided with the Enron and WorldCom incidents in the US, which brought global attention to bear on corporate business ethics and social responsibility. These experiences have caused many changes in the governance of Japanese firms, in essence changing it from a relational-based system to a more market-oriented system (Colpan et al., 2007). As such, the year 2003 was often labeled as the "CSR *gannen*" (the first year of CSR) (Fukukawa & Teramoto, 2009). Therefore we can state that Japan's CSR development started roughly 50 years ago. According to KPMG (2005), in 2005, 90% of the companies in Japan were already participating in voluntary CSD, outdoing the UK (71%) and the US (32%). China, on the other hand, is in the initial stages of CSR and CSD (Noronha et al., 2013) but the speed at which it has been catching up with developed countries during the past few years is quite surprising: there has been full support and directives from central government and other agencies, such as the Shanghai and Shenzhen Stock Exchanges. According to KPMG (2011a), the number of CSR reports issued by listed companies in China increased from one in 2001 to 663 in 2010. Therefore, these countries provide us with two vivid cases for comparative analysis.

China and Japan: Pragmatism versus idealism

The second reason for looking into China and Japan is inspired by prior literature about the cultural influence on corporate financial disclosure. A number of studies have employed Hofstede's (1980) four cultural dimensions to explain different countries' accounting practices, including their levels of disclosure of accounting information. For example, Gray's (1988) accounting subculture model suggested an important dimension related to the disclosure issue, that is the "secrecy versus transparency" continuum. Subsequent research found that Hofstede's cultural dimensions had an important influence on voluntary disclosure (Gray & Vint, 1995; Salter & Niswander, 1995). Building on the basis of these studies, Chow et al. (1995) indicated that China's disclosure practices appeared to tend toward the secrecy side of the continuum. Nevertheless, coupled with the development of China in recent years, some incremental improvements could be seen in terms of voluntary disclosure of, for example, certain corporate governance issues (Qu & Leung, 2006). Given China's large power distance (80), low uncertainty avoidance (30), high collectivism (individualism 20), masculinity (66) and long-term orientation (118), its disclosure tends toward secrecy. On the other hand, Japan's comparatively smaller power distance (54), lower collectivism (individualism 46), very much higher masculinity (95), extremely high uncertainty avoidance (92) and lower long-term orientation (80) (http://geert-hofstede.com) appear to put Japan more on the transparent side of the continuum.[1] If this relationship holds for voluntary disclosure of financial information, does it equally apply to CSD in these two countries? For Japan, we can say so yes without too much doubt, given the country's leading position in CSD worldwide. In China, there has been a rapid increase in the number of CSR reports during the last ten years. Is the country really improving this quickly, and emerging from the secrecy side of the disclosure continuum? This volume takes a critical perspective, and attempts to use the dichotomy of "pragmatism (sometimes the rejection of moral principles) versus idealism (adoption of moral principles)" to explain the phenomenon of China's exponential increase in CSD. As will be seen in the chapters revealing China's situation, the heavy influence by political motivation and the unique institutional factors in this socialist country with market characteristics are the major driving forces of CSR and CSD development. From this perspective, though, Japan serves as a proper counterpart for the purpose of comparison, in terms of the level of advancement in CSD, the cultural influences on accounting disclosure, or the institutional and legal factors surrounding the decision to disclose social information or not and the kind of information that is disclosed. Through the discussions in the chapters that follow, the reader will see how different CSD is viewed and utilized as a corporate tool in order to achieve various ends in these two countries, based on differences in the above-mentioned factors.

China and Japan: Corporate scandals

The third reason for comparing the two countries in this volume is that despite Japan's maturity in CSR and CSD and China's emergence in these issues, both countries in recent years have shocked the world with very serious business scandals. In China, the 2008 melamine-tainted milk powder incident which killed six infants and poisoned over 29,000 others was criticized by the World Health Organization as one of the biggest health scandals in history (Zaobao, 2008). In Japan, the 2011 Olympus accounting scandal was described as one of the biggest and most durable loss-concealing scams in the history of corporate Japan (*The Wall Street Journal*, 2011). Are we seeing Japan coming to its "final year of CSR" and awaiting another cycle, another "CSR *gannen*"? These incidents have triggered the use of a critical lens to examine the latest evolution of CSR and CSD in these two countries, and to address the recent challenges to morality and ethics under different institutional backgrounds. We also hope to shed light on the performance-disclosure gap in these two countries, where distinct social and political environments and, in particular, different degrees of the execution power of law and judicial independence prevail.

CSD in China: A research lacuna

The final reason for comparing these two countries is in order to help to fill a significant research lacuna in the CSR and CSD agenda. As mentioned at the beginning, CSD has been examined extensively in Western developed countries during the past decades, notwithstanding continued interest in the areas of CSR, sustainability development, and social and environmental accounting. However, CSD has only been studied quite recently in developing countries. Belal and Momin (2009) identified 41 articles related to CSR studies in developing countries or emerging regions that were published during 1983–2008 in English language journals. Surprisingly, none of these articles related to China, the largest in terms of size and strongest in terms of economic power of all developing nations. During the past two years or so, CSR and CSD studies about China have started to emerge gradually in English-speaking academia (e.g. Li & Zhang, 2010; Moon & Shen, 2010; Kuo et al., 2012; Luethge & Han, 2012). Nevertheless, there is much more to be done concerning this second largest economy of the world. Research about CSR and CSD in China is urgently called for (Belal, 2008; Guan & Noronha, 2013).

The present volume consists of 12 chapters written by scholars who specialize in CSR issues in these two countries, and they address the most recent observations of CSD in general and in different industries, based on their latest research findings.

Theoretical lens: Legitimacy

The theoretical lens used by most of the chapters in this volume is based on the legitimacy theory. Gray et al. (1995) pointed out that most studies in social accounting have drawn on social and political theory, in particular "stakeholder theory", "legitimacy theory" and "political economy theory". Many people see these as competing, but Gray et al. (1995) suggested that stakeholder theory and legitimacy theory should be viewed as two overlapping theories set within a framework of assumptions about political economy. Under political economy theory, the economic domain cannot be studied in isolation from the political, social and institutional framework within which economic activity takes place (Gray et al., 1995: 52). Political economy theory is therefore consistent with the pluralistic characteristics of CSR, in which the Triple Bottom Line (TBL) dimensions, namely the economic, social and environmental (Elkington, 1998), must coexist and be considered holistically.

Gray et al. (1995: 53) cited the perspective of Roberts (1992), where a corporation's continued existence requires the support of the stakeholders, and their approval must be sought and the activities of the corporation must be adjusted in order to gain the stakeholders' approval. In a similar vein, legitimacy theory can also be seen in the same light. Thus, as a variant of stakeholder theory, legitimacy theory argues that organizations can only continue to exist if the society in which they are based perceives the organization to be operating to a value system that is commensurate with the society's own value system (Gray et al., 2010: 28). This perspective stems from Lindblom's (1993) analysis of the relationship between the corporation and the "relevant publics", which depicts the strategies that the corporation uses in order to gain such a state of legitimacy.

Legitimacy can also be understood from a resource-based view (Tilling & Tilt, 2010). Congruent with the resource-dependence theory (Pfeffer & Salancik, 1978), legitimacy can be seen as an organizational resource that is held by other organizations and stakeholders. Thus the corporation and the stakeholders wrestle over the interplay of power for the conferment, loss and re-conferment of legitimacy.

At the organizational level, CSD has been used by the corporation to gain support from the relevant publics and to close any "legitimacy gap" (Sethi, 1978; Lindblom, 1993) through communicating positive organizational behavior information (e.g. Patten, 1992; Deegan et al., 2000; 2002; Milne & Patten, 2002; Campbell et al., 2003; Moerman & Van der Laan, 2005). In this volume, we will see different examples in which CSD is used as a strategy to improve corporate image after a severe industrial incident (e.g. Chapter 4, where milk companies increased CSD after a poisonous milk powder scandal), as well as using CSD as a kind of "greenwashing" technique to "wash away" undesirable information (e.g. Chapter 3, where the company only disclosed positive information and did not disclose the employee suicide incidents which were widely exposed by the public media, and Chapter 11, where the company was blacklisted on environmental violations and used CSD as a strategy to redirect attention). These cases demonstrate vividly the notion of strategic legitimacy theory or instrumental legitimacy theory (Ashford & Gibbs, 1990; Suchman, 1995).

The legitimacy theory can also be applied at the macro or institutional level (Suchman, 1995; Tilling & Tilt, 2010), where emphasis is placed on the industry, the government or the entire field of organization life, what DiMaggio and Powell (1983) termed "collective structuration". In this volume, cases encompassing the overall CSD of Chinese listed enterprises in relation to the Central Government's national policies (e.g. Chapter 2) and the unique institutional characteristics of state-owned enterprises that result in CSR engagement and disclosure which are heavily dependent on political directives (e.g. Chapter 5) are illustrated in detail.

Methodology: Content analysis

All the chapters are original works produced for this volume. Most of them are reports of empirical results of CSD studies carried out using content analysis. Content analysis (Holsti, 1969; Krippendorff, 1985) is a research technique widely employed in social accounting studies (Guthrie & Parker, 1990; Gray et al., 1995). Holsti (1969: 14) defines it as "any technique for making inferences by objectively and systematically identifying specified characteristics of messages". Content analysis is used to determine the presence of certain words, concepts, themes, phrases, characters or sentences within texts. The text is coded into manageable categories at a variety of levels (Busch et al., 2012), and these are evaluated using both quantitative and qualitative methods. The former emphasizes the frequency of certain words, sentences or phrases (conceptual analysis), while the latter focuses on the meaning of the stories hidden within the lines (relational analysis). In short, content analysis involves counting and comparing keywords and contents, followed by the interpretation of the underlying context. The results are then used to make inferences about the messages within the texts.

In this volume, content analysis of annual reports, CSR reports and official websites of enterprises was applied as a major data collection and analysis method. In brief, quantitative content analysis can be used to measure the quantity of disclosure in terms of various CSR dimensions, as well as the coverage of CSR topics. Qualitative content analysis can be used to investigate the reporting entity's motivations for voluntary disclosure, and to facilitate any speculation on the factors that constrain or encourage disclosure. International CSR reporting guidelines have been referred to while conducting the analyses, especially in the selection of keywords and categories. These include, among others, the GRI (G3) (e.g. Chapters 2 and 3), ISO26000 (e.g. Chapter 4) and the State-owned Assets Supervision and Administrative Commission Guideline (e.g. Chapter 5).

CSD in China

The volume is divided into two parts, namely CSD in China and CSD in Japan. In Chapter 2, Si Tou and Noronha examine the trend of CSD in mainland China over a longitudinal observation. While China has become a world economic superpower, CSR is still a relatively new concept in the country. The aim of this study is to investigate CSR development in China in recent years and to assess its level, with particular reference to companies listed on the Chinese stock markets. The disclosed information was examined around four main dimensions, namely marketplace, workplace, environment and community. The study shows that Chinese listed companies are still in the early stages of CSR reporting in terms of the quantity and quality of the information disclosed. Nevertheless, the study confirms that there have been considerable improvements on the reporting format and data nature for the years 2007/2008 and 2010/2011.

In Chapter 3, Noronha and Wang present a case study of the disclosure and performance gap of Foxconn Technology Group, a Taiwanese multinational electronics manufacturing company, which has been caught in controversies regarding employee issues that relate to its Shenzhen factories in China. On the mainland, there exists a host of factories that ignore employees' welfare. They treat workers like machines and pay them meagerly. Needless to say, few or no related details can often be found in the reports disclosed by these companies. Therefore, this study has used content analysis to compare Foxconn's 2010 and 2011 CSR reports with information obtained outside Foxconn, such as news reports from the mass media and third-party investigation reports, about its social performance. To some extent, the result could indicate the reliability level of CSD as a measurement of CSR performance of the company.

It is widely known that the 2008 milk contamination scandal in China had a tremendous impact on global awareness of the food safety of China's exports. In Chapter 4, Noronha and Kong assess the response of four milk products enterprises to the 2008 milk scandal. Content analysis was used to examine the CSR reports and CSR-related activities of these four businesses before, during and after the milk scandal. These CSR activities were then compared with other external information sources in order to determine their significance. A very close relationship between the increase in CSR activities of the dairy enterprises and the massive media coverage of the scandal in China and worldwide was found. It was clear that the enterprises increased their CSD during the period when media coverage was intense. The findings also indicated that the greater the market share of the milk enterprise, the higher was its social commitment.

Even though China has similar CSR dimensions to other developed or developing countries, a certain level of uniqueness also exists, especially in the reporting practices of state-owned enterprises. For example, the provision of job opportunities by state-owned enterprises in order to ease national employment pressures is seen as a unique Chinese CSR dimension. However, this may not be viewed as such by other more developed countries. In Chapter 5, Guan analyzes the annual reports and CSR reports of a number of the largest Chinese state-owned enterprises from 2011 and 2012, in order to understand the CSD practices of these extremely important economic giants. The content analysis results were then corroborated with a comprehensive literature review of CSR studies and policy documents issued by the Chinese government. The findings demonstrate that the CSD behavior of state-owned enterprises is closely related to China's political and economic sustainability, and has a different pattern to other developing and developed countries. Basically, this unique phenomenon comes from the characteristics of the socialist market economy system developed in new China, which is very different from the socialist planned economy in old China.

In Chapter 6, Leung studies the CSD of the gambling industry. This industry's products and services are highly controversial, and have become a source of tension and conflict between economic benefits and social costs. Several prior CSD studies have concentrated on industries such as oil and mining (e.g. Deegan et al., 2002; Jenkins & Yankovleva, 2006; Clarkson et al., 2008; Beck & Toms, 2009). However, some controversial industries remain largely unexplored. Exploring CSD in a novel setting provides an opportunity to examine the complexity and subtlety of business and society. This study focuses on Macau (a Special Administrative Region of mainland China), whose gross gambling revenue has outstripped that of Las Vegas to become the world's largest gambling market. Content analysis was conducted on a sample of 18 annual reports of six companies over three years (2007–2009). The findings suggest that there is a relatively low volume of CSD and responsible gambling disclosure in Macau's gambling industry. The study introduces a necessary caution into further investigations concerning the scope and extent of CSD in this industry.

CSD in Japan

After the five chapters on CSD in China outlined above, we turn to CSD in Japan. The Japan Business Federation (Keidanren, 2013) emphasizes CSR and environmental reporting as a tool to link the market, consumers and investors with corporations, and encourages its member companies and groups to actively establish and disclose these reports (METI, 2012). According to KPMG (2011b), 99% of Japanese companies are reporting on their CSR. In terms of the disclosure of information, it is generally agreed that published annual reports remain the most important sources of information for many stakeholders. They comprehensively and compactly represent the views and concerns of individual firms (Bontis, 2003). Guthrie et al. (2004) suggest that annual reports also have the advantage of being regularly produced, thereby offering the opportunity for a comparative analysis of management attitudes and policies across reporting periods. They are also required by legislation in some countries and are produced on a regular basis by all companies. In Chapter 7, Ali, Haider and Islam conduct a content analysis to assess the CSD practices of the top 100 listed Japanese companies. The study also aims to reveal the corporate characteristics which may influence the level of disclosure.

Launched in 2000, the Global Compact has expanded throughout the world, providing global standards for sustainable and responsible reporting. In Japan, through the efforts of the Global Compact Japan Network, a local arm of the Global Compact, many top tier companies have become members of this international institution. In Chapter 8, Kondo discusses the experiences of Global Compact signatory corporations in Japan in terms of reporting, and by doing so, the chapter also illustrates the characteristics of sustainability reporting practices in Japan. The chapter also examines the roles of the Global Compact Japan Network, the impact of its globally standardized reporting requirements on Japanese corporations, and the real intention of Japanese corporations that sign up to the Global Compact.

While sustainability reporting (SR) has become a common phenomenon among the world's leading companies, a good number of companies also adopt assurance on such non-financial reporting, in order to enhance the credibility of information provided to stakeholders. In Japan there is an important opportunity to investigate this novel audit practice, as almost all the big companies publish SR. The adoption of assurance in SR in Japan was 26% in 2002, then increased to 31% before declining to 24% and 23% in 2008 and 2011, respectively (KPMG, 2008; 2011b). In Chapter 9, Haider and Kokubu explore the recent development of SR in Japan with emphasis on assurance practice. While the extant literature observes wide variations and ambiguities in the assurance statements of European companies, the practice of Japan is still unknown. Content analysis of the assurance statements of the top 100 companies was conducted to understand the quality of such voluntary audit services. The evaluative framework of this study is adapted from prior studies that were based on the ISAE3000, GRI guideline, AccountAbility 1000AS and J-SUS guideline.

While it took longer for Japanese companies than those in other regions, especially the US and Western Europe, over time the transparency around their policies and systems, and the alignment with international standards in terms of disclosure, have started to improve. This has coincided with key developments in corporate governance since the beginning of the 2000s that were backed by enhancements to regulatory frameworks. As a result, significant improvements have been seen to compliance mechanisms and reporting structures that require internal control systems to be reported and disclosed. For a long time Japanese companies have been well known for their leading position in environmental reporting; but they are considered to be very reluctant to disclose social activities that would require exchange of information, which could lead to conflicting relationships with some stakeholders, notably those representing civil society. Likewise, the very self-sustained and self-contained nature of Japanese corporate culture has made companies reluctant to engage with stakeholders about governance issues. However, there are signs that this is about to change. Policymakers and major Japanese corporations are increasingly recognizing the importance of being more proactive in managing their social risk exposure. As a result, the number of Japanese companies that provide disclosure about human and labor rights issues and anti-bribery practices has increased significantly over the last decade. The recent launch of several socially responsible investment (SRI) products by mainstream investors has been very popular despite a stagnant economy, and they seem to have tapped into a new market. Although some barriers to the development of CSD still exist, especially over language, different cultural and social values, perceptions and the state of the markets, a number of factors look set to encourage growth in the medium to long term. Therefore, in Chapter 10, Debroux examines the growing acceptance of global standards by Japanese firms and the implication of this in terms of CSD.

Japan is known for the high degree of accuracy of CSD practices in corporations. However, concerns have been raised about the practices of Japanese companies in the electronics industry, particularly among suppliers of Apple Inc. In Chapter 11, Tanaka aims to complement Chapter 3 by looking into a Japanese corporation that has operations in China, namely Meiko Electronics Company Limited. Content analysis was used to compare the CSR and environmental practices of the company disclosed in Meiko's CSR report and website with the perceptions of these practices by stakeholders. Publicly available data in three languages, namely Chinese, English and Japanese, were analyzed and interpreted. The research objective was to analyze the factors that influence this Japanese corporation's CSR policies and decisions on disclosure. The chapter also addresses how and in what ways stakeholders influence the company's CSR practices and disclosure, the existence of any gaps between actual CSR and environmental practices of the company and the perceptions of its stakeholders on these matters, and some improvement strategies.

Acknowledgments

I would like to thank all the contributors who have dedicated their research to this volume and the staff at Palgrave for making this project possible. Also, I must thank Professor Harukiyo Hasegawa, Honorary Fellow of the White Rose East Asian Center, University of Sheffield, for his constant support of our research endeavors.

Note

1. It must be mentioned here that in Gray's (1988) accounting subculture model, he positioned Japan more on the secrecy side because his focus was mainly on its extremely high uncertainty avoidance (92). However, if we compare holistically, based on the four country dimension scores cited above, and look into the actual development of CSD in Japan nowadays, the country should be repositioned more toward the transparency end. This can be substantiated by Yamagami and Kokubu (1991), who stated that for 1985 and 1986 Japanese companies disclosed environmental and community involvement issues far less than research and development activities. They concluded that Japan had been slow in developing the practice of CSD compared to the West at that time. Furthermore, this can be supported with the other three accounting subculture characteristics of Japan, which appear to be along the lines of being a good discloser, namely uniformity in terms of authority, statutory control in terms of enforcement, and conservatism in terms of measurement.

References

Ashford, B.E. & Gibbs, B.W. (1990). The double-edge of organizational legitimacy. *Organization Science*, 1, (2), 177–194.

Bebbington, J., Larrinaga, C. & Moneva, J.M. (2008). Corporate social reporting and reputation risk management. *Accounting, Auditing and Accountability Journal*, 21, (3), 337–361.

Beck, M. & Toms, S. (2009). Accounting disclosure and human rights in the oil industry. In Mallin, C. (ed.) *Corporate Social Responsibility: A Case Study Approach*. Cheltenham: Edward Elgar.

Belal, A. (2008). *Corporate Social Responsibility Reporting in Developing Countries: The Case of Bangladesh*. Aldershot: Ashgate Publishing Limited.

Belal, A. & Momin, M. (2009). Corporate social reporting (CSR) in emerging economies: A review and future directions. *Research in Accounting in Emerging Economies*, 9, 119–143.

Bontis, N. (2003). Intellectual capital in disclosures in Canadian corporations. *Journal of Human Resource Costing and Accounting*, 7, (1/2), 9–20.

Busch, C., De Maret, P.S., Flynn, T. Kellum, R., Le, S., Meyers, B., Saunders, M., White, R. & Palmquist, M. (2012). Content Analysis. Writing@CSU. Colorado State University. Available at http://writing.colostate.edu/guides/guide.cfm?guideid=61

Campbell, D., Craven, B. & Shrives, P. (2003). Voluntary reporting in three FTSE sectors: A comment on perception and legitimacy. *Accounting, Auditing and Accountability Journal*, 16, (4), 558–581.

Chow, L.M.Y., Chau, G.K.K. & Gray, S.J. (1995). Accounting reforms in China: Cultural constraints on implementation and development. *Accounting and Business Research*, 26, (1), 29–45.

Clarkson, M.P., Li, Y., Richardson, D.G. & Vasvari, P.F. (2008). Revisiting the relation between environmental performance and environmental disclosure: An empirical analysis. *Accounting, Organizations and Society*, 33, 303–327.

Colpan, A.M., Yoshikawa, T., Hikino, T. & Miyoshi, H. (2007). Japanese corporate governance: Structural change and financial performance. *Asian Business and Management*, 6, (S1), 89–113.

Deegan, C. (2002). The legitimating effect of social and environmental disclosures – A theoretical foundation. *Accounting, Auditing and Accountability Journal*, 15, (3), 282–311.

Deegan, C., Rankin, M. & Voght, P. (2000). Firms' disclosure reactions to major social incidents: Australian evidence. *Accounting Forum*, 24, (1), 101–130.

Deegan, C., Rankin, M. & Tobin, J. (2002). An examination of the corporate social and environmental disclosures of BHP from 1983–1997: A test of legitimacy theory. *Accounting, Auditing and Accountability Journal*, 15, (3), 312–343.

DiMaggio, P.J. & Powell, W.W. (1983). The iron cage revisited: Institutional isomorphism and collective rationality in organizational fields. *American Sociological Review*, 48, (2), 147–160.

Elkington, J. (1998). *Cannibals with Forks: The Triple Bottom Line of 21st Century Business*. Gabriola Island, BC: New Society Publishers.

Fukukawa, K. & Teramoto, Y. (2008). Understanding Japanese CSR: The reflection of managers in the field of global operations. *Journal of Business Ethics*, 85, 133–146.

Gray, R. (2002). The social accounting project and accounting organizations and society: Privileging engagement, imaginings, new accountings and pragmatism over critique? *Accounting, Organizations and Society*, 27, (7), 687–708.

Gray, R., Kouhy, R. & Lavers, S. (1995). Corporate social and environmental reporting: A review of the literature and a longitudinal study of UK disclosure. *Accounting, Auditing and Accountability Journal*, 8, (2), 47–77.

Gray, R.H., Owen, D.L. & Adams, C. (1996). *Accounting and Accountability: Changes and Challenges in Corporate Social and Environmental Reporting*. London: Prentice Hall.

Gray, R.H., Owen, D.L. & Adams, C. (2010). Some theories for social accounting? A review essay and a tentative pedagogic categorization of theorizations around social accounting. *Advances in Environmental Accounting and Management*, 4, 1–54.

Gray, S.J. (1988). Towards a theory of cultural influence on the development of accounting systems internationally. *Abacus*, 24, (1), 1–15.

Gray, S.J. & Vint, H.M. (1995). The impact of culture on accounting disclosure: *Asia Pacific Journal of Accounting*, 21, 33–44.

Guan, J. & Noronha, C. (2013). Corporate social responsibility reporting research in the Chinese academia: A critical review. *Social Responsibility Journal*, 9, (1), 33–55.

Guthrie, J.E. & Parker, L.D. (1990). Corporate social disclosure practice: A comparative international analysis. *Advances in Public Interest Accounting*, 3, 159–175.

Guthrie, J., Petty, R., Yongvanich, K. & Ricceri, F. (2004). Using content analysis as a research method to inquire into intellectual capital reporting. *Journal of Intellectual Capital*, 5, (2), 282–293.

Hofstede, G.H. (1980). *Culture's Consequences: International Differences in Work-Related Values*. Beverley Hills, CA: Sage.

Holsti, O.R. (1969). *Content Analysis for the Social Sciences and Humanities*. Reading, MA: Addison-Wesley.

Jenkins, H. & Yankovleva, N. (2006). Corporate social responsibility in the mining industry: Exploring trends in social and environmental disclosure. *Journal of Cleaner Production*, 14, 271–284.

Kawamura, M. (2005). The evolution of corporate social responsibility in Japan (part 2): How CSR "swells" have impacted corporate values. *NLI Research*. NLI Research Institute.

Keidanren (2013). Corporate social responsibility (CSR). Available at http://www.keidanren.or.jp/en/policy/csr.html

KPMG (2005). *KPMG International Survey of Corporate Responsibility Reporting 2005*. Amsterdam: KPMG Global Sustainability Services and University of Amsterdam.

KPMG (2008). *KPMG International Survey of Corporate Responsibility Reporting 2008*. KPMG International.

KPMG (2011a). *The Gift of a Sustainable Future, 2011 KPMG China Corporate Social Responsibility Report*.

KPMG (2011b). *KPMG International Survey of Corporate Responsibility Reporting 2011*. KPMG International.

Krippendorff, K. (1985). *Content Analysis: An Introduction to its Methodology*. Beverly Hills, CA: Sage.

Kuo, L., Yeh, C.C. & Yu, H.C. (2012). Disclosure of corporate social responsibility and environmental management: Evidence from China. *Corporate Social Responsibility and Environmental Management*, 19, (5), 273–287.

Li, W. & Zhang, R. (2010). Corporate social responsibility, ownership structure, and political interference: Evidence from China. *Journal of Business Ethics*, 96, (4), 631–645.

Lindblom, C. (1993). The implications of organizational legitimacy for corporate social performance disclosure. Paper presented at the Critical Perspectives on Accounting Conference, New York.

Luethge, D. & Han, G. (2012). Assessing corporate social and financial performance in China. *Social Responsibility Journal*, 8, (3), 389–403.

Macintosh, N.B., Shearer, T., Thornton, D.B. & Welker, M. (2000). Accounting as simulacrum and hyper-reality: Perspectives on income and capital. *Accounting Organizations and Society*, 25, (1), 13–50.

McKie, J.W. (ed.) (1974). *The Issues, Social Responsibility and the Business Predicament*. Washington, DC: The Brookings Institution.

METI (2012). *Japan's Policy for CSR*. Ministry of Economy, Trade and Industry.

Milne, M.J. & Patten, D.M. (2002). Securing organizational legitimacy. An experimental decision case examining the impact of environmental disclosure. *Accounting, Auditing and Accountability Journal*, 15, (3), 372–405.

Moerman, L. & Van der Laan, S.L. (2005). Social reporting in the tobacco industry: All smokes and mirrors? *Accounting, Auditing and Accountability Journal*, 13, (8), 374–389.

Moon, J. & Shen, X. (2010). CSR in China research: Salience, focus and nature. *Journal of Business Ethics*, 94, 613–629.

Noronha, C., Si Tou, M.I. & Guan, J. (2013). Corporate social responsibility reporting in China: An overview and comparison with major trends. *Corporate Social Responsibility and Environmental Management*, 20, (1), 29–42.

Oxfam Hong Kong (2010). *Corporate Social Responsibility Survey of Hang Seng Index Constituent Companies 2009*. Hong Kong: Oxfam Hong Kong.

Patten, D.M. (1992). Intra-industry environmental disclosures in response to the Alaskan oil spill: A note on legitimacy theory. *Accounting, Organizations and Society*, 17, (5), 471–475.

Pfeffer, J. & Salancik, G.R. (1978). *The External Control of Organizations: A Resource Dependence Perspective*. New York, NY: Harper and Row.

Qu, W. & Leung, P. (2006). Cultural impact on Chinese corporate disclosure – A corporate governance perspective. *Managerial Auditing Journal*, 21, (3), 241–246.

Salter, S.B. & Niswander, F. (1995). Cultural influences on the development of accounting systems internationally: A test of Gray (1988) theory. *Journal of International Business Studies*, 26, (2), 379–397.

Roberts, R.W. (1992). Determinants of corporate social responsibility disclosure. *Accounting, Organizations and Society*, 17, (6), 595–612.

Sethi, S.P. (1978). Advocacy advertising – The American experience. *California Management Review*, 21, (1), 55–67.

Suchman, M.C. (1995). Managing legitimacy: Strategic and institutional approaches. *Academy of Management Review*, 20, (3), 571–610.

Takagaki, Y. (2010). Japanese firms' environmental strategies: Examples from electronics-related industries. *Asian Business and Management*, 9, (2), 245–264.

The Wall Street Journal. (2011). Olympus president will do utmost to avoid delisting. 7 November 2011.

Tilling, M.V. & Tilt, C.A. (2010). The edge of legitimacy: Voluntary social and environmental reporting in Rothmans' 1956–1999 annual reports. *Accounting, Auditing and Accountability Journal*, 23, 1, 55–81.

Yamagami, T. & Kokubu, K. (1991). A note on corporate social disclosure in Japan. *Accounting, Auditing and Accountability Journal*, 4, (4), 32–39.

Zaobao (2008). *Special Report of Poisonous Milk Powder in China* (in Chinese). Available at http://www.zaobao.com/special/china/milk/milk.shtml

Part I

Corporate Social Disclosure in China

2

The Trend of Corporate Social Disclosure in Mainland Chinese Listed Companies: A Longitudinal Observation

Cynthia M.I. Si Tou and Carlos Noronha

Introduction

The Seventeenth National Congress of the Communist Party of China promulgated the edict of "Scientific Concept of Development and Harmonious Society", which aimed to put people first and maintain comprehensive, coordinated and sustainable development. China has a plan to strategically build a "Socialist Harmonious Society" by the year 2020, encompassing democracy and the rule of law, fairness and justice, integrity and fraternity, vitality, stability and order and harmony between men and nature. In February 2009, China Premier Wen Jiabao quoted Adam Smith's *Theory of Moral Sentiments* to emphasize the importance of Corporate Social Responsibility (CSR). That is, "corporations should not purely strive to maximize profits at the expense of other people's or even the public's interest. In fact, corporations should take up social responsibilities in their hearts and exercise moral in their business dealings." The Chinese government has begun to promote CSR as one key component of the "Harmonious Society" (Wong, 2009). See (2008) even coined the term "hCSR" for "Harmonious Corporate Social Responsibility" in China.

As ideal as that may seem, it is a far cry from the reality in China. In 2007, the recall of more than 100 pet food brands exported by China to North America and the withdrawal of more than 20 million made-in-China toys by Mattel have revealed the lack of control over production, as harmful ingredients such as melamine were found in the pet food and excessive lead was found in the toys (Ma, 2008).

Since then, shocking reports of terrible incidents in China have been exposed globally, increasing perception of the country as a notorious land of unethical business behavior. Some recent examples include the child slaves incident in Shanxi brick factories (Feng, 2007), the Sanlu Group milk scandal (Xinhua, 2008), the export of poisonous dumplings to Japan (McCurry, 2008), various workplace accidents such as the Heilongjiang coal mine explosions (Bradsher, 2009), and the Foxconn employee suicides (Clarke, 2010).

It has been over three decades since China's 1978 "Open Door" policy was launched. In that time the country has shifted away from agriculture to manufacturing as the dominant source of gross domestic product (GDP). Through economic reform, China has built up a socialist market economy, where the market plays a primary role in allocating resources under the government's macro-policy. China's GDP has increased from 3,645 (in 100 million RMB) in 1978 to 472,881 (in 100 million RMB) in 2011 while per capita GDP has grown from 381 RMB in 1978 to 35,181 RMB in 2011 (National Bureau of Statistics of China, 2012). It is widely known that China overtook Japan's position as the world's second biggest economy in the second quarter of 2010.

Generally speaking, economic growth increases the nation's total wealth and decreases poverty. However, it is often doubtful whether society really benefits from economic growth in the long run. Such a high rate of economic growth has caused over-consumption of natural resources which are needed by future generations. Furthermore, wealth distribution can cause social inequity. In the end, benefits from economic growth may not outweigh the social costs. After the scandals mentioned above, one can only cast doubt on how Chinese enterprises view social and moral responsibilities. There is a divergence between what the Chinese government promulgates and what business practices are in reality. An in-depth study of the current CSR activities of Chinese enterprises and how they report them will reflect on the discrepancy between reported behavior and the ideal which the government promulgates, with the aim of shaping China into a major economic superpower. It is through investigating this discrepancy that weaknesses in the system and prompt actions that should be taken may be duly identified.

Objectives

According to the World Business Council for Sustainable Development (WBCSD), CSR is "the continuing commitment by business to behave ethically and contribute to economic development while improving the quality of life of the workforce and their families as well as of the community and society at large" (WBCSD, 1999). Thus, CSR aims to integrate business activities with the environment, consumers, employees, communities, suppliers, government and all other members of society as a whole.

Voluntary CSR reporting, also referred to as corporate social disclosure (CSD), is common in many developed countries. CSD aims to communicate the social, ethical and environmental effects of the organization's economic actions toward particular interest groups and in society at large (Gray et al., 1987). There has been a relatively fast movement toward CSD throughout the world in recent years. According to KPMG (2008), in 2005 only 52% of all G250 companies issued stand-alone CSR reports. In 2008, the proportion had increased to 79%.

In his study of CSR reporting in Bangladesh, Belal (2008: 7) pointed out that given the presence of widespread poverty, corruption, inequality and social exploitation in developing countries, social accounting and reporting is believed to have the potential of promoting equality, social justice, transparency and accountability by holding business organizations to account. Turning back to the situation in China, it is clear that the country is facing a dilemma. On the one hand, the Chinese government is promoting the development of a harmonious society and CSR; on the other hand, reports of unethical business behavior are never in short supply. Therefore, we hope that the current study will help us to understand more about the situation of CSR and CSD in China, and, in particular, allow us to explore the following questions:

- What CSR issues are acknowledged by Chinese listed enterprises, and what are the drivers for them to engage in CSR?
- What is the level of CSD of Chinese listed enterprises in terms of quantity and quality?
- What standards and guidelines for CSD are used in China in comparison with the global picture?
- Which types of CSR issues receive the highest priority among Chinese enterprises?

The study addresses the CSR disclosure practices of Chinese listed enterprises around four main dimensions, namely marketplace, workplace, community and environment. Each dimension is separated into specific categories for analysis. Twenty-five Chinese enterprises from the widely used CSI 100 index (Hu Shen 100), which are listed either on the Shanghai Stock Exchange (SSE) or the Shenzhen Stock Exchange (SZSE), were taken as the study sample. The source data were retrieved from traditional company annual reports and stand-alone CSR reports available either at the China Securities Regulatory Commission (CSRC) official website (www.cninfo.com.cn) or at the companies' websites for the years 2007/2008 and 2010/2011. Content analysis was applied to reveal the level of CSD in terms of volume and quality, as well as to explore the trend of the disclosure pattern.

Prior studies of CSD in developing countries

Belal and Owen (2007) pointed out that prior CSR studies mainly concentrated on developed Western countries and only very few are available in the context of developing countries. In general, it is believed that accounting rules and regulations in developed countries can be replicated in developing countries. However, Briston (1984) indicated that the financial regulations of developed countries are investor-oriented, while in developing countries regulations are not well established and the stock exchange markets are relatively new. Visser et al. (2008) also suggested that CSR in developing countries is different from developed countries because of discrepancies in the socio-economic and cultural contexts.

In terms of emerging economies, Belal and Lubinin (2008) found that 90% of the 20 largest companies listed on the Russian stock exchange reported some form of CSR information, but the absence of independent external verification and the avoidance of negative news indicated the need for further improvement. Idowu and Filho (2009) reported that CSR practices in Brazil are still at a very preliminary stage, and there is an urgent need to develop a framework in order to promote equity, social justice and environmental stewardship. On the other hand, KPMG (2005) reported on CSR practices in India and found that most reporting was largely voluntary. Some companies published CSR reports based on the Global Reporting Initiative (GRI) guidelines, and mostly focused just on community issues. In a subsequent study (KPMG, 2008), an increasing trend of CSR reporting was found in South Africa. The percentage of the top 100 South African companies preparing CSR reports increased from 18% in 2005 to 26% in 2008. In the case of Bangladesh, Imam (2000) noted that social and environmental disclosures were relatively low in volume compared to corporate financial disclosures; also, listed companies did not follow global guidelines and standards in reporting CSR information. Furthermore, Belal (2001) explored the socio-political and economic contexts of CSR practices in Bangladesh, and pointed out that CSR reporting still falls below the global standard and format.

Apart from some multi-country comparative studies (e.g. Baughn et al., 2007; Alon et al., 2010), in-depth studies on CSR reporting in China are very limited, at least in the Western world. Indeed, in Belal and Momin's (2009) comprehensive survey of 41 CSR research articles in 14 emerging economies (including 23 articles in Asian countries), not one article was about China. A reference may be made to the study conducted by the United Nations (2007) in which the corporate governance practices of a random sample of 80 companies listed on the CSI 300 index (Hu Shen 300) were analyzed. Based on the International Standards of Accounting and Reporting (ISAR) benchmark of 53 disclosure items, the China data were compared with those of 105 enterprises included in the United Nations Conference on Trade and Development (UNCTAD) 2006 review. Of these 53 items, seven of them were under the category of "corporate responsibilities and compliance". The findings showed that the average level of reporting on CSR was relatively lower for Chinese enterprises than for all UNCTAD enterprises. For instance, out of the sampled enterprises, only 36% had disclosed policies and performance in connection with environmental and social responsibilities as compared to 91% of the UNCTAD enterprises. Only 16% of the sampled Chinese enterprises disclosed the impact of environmental and social responsibility policies on the sustainability of the company, compared to 72% of the UNCTAD samples. Furthermore, only 1% of the Chinese enterprises disclosed whistleblower protection policies while half of the UNCTAD samples reported such policies. These results provide a preliminary idea about the low level of CSD in Chinese enterprises. As Alon et al. (2010) pointed out, although India's GDP per capita is lower than that of China, its communication of CSR is more intensive than China's. This evidence points to the urgent need to study the practice of CSD in Chinese enterprises.

Research method

Gray (2000) suggested that the concept of social accounting should not only include financial information, but it should also combine quantified non-financial information and non-quantified information in a descriptive manner. As such, content analysis is in line with the aim of social accounting and it has been used to address the issue of social responsibility in non-financial information for a long time. Mayring (2000) defined content analysis as a "family of systematic, rule-guided techniques to analyze the informational contents of textual data". This study will adopt both qualitative and quantitative content analysis approaches to provide a comprehensive analysis of the data.

Sample

The subjects of the study included enterprises listed on the SZSE or the SSE regardless of ownership type, covering all 13 different industry classifications according to the "Guidelines on Industry Classification of Listed Companies in China" issued by the China Securities Regulatory Commission (CSRC). The 13 classifications were (a) agriculture, forestry, livestock farming and fishery, (b) mining, (c) manufacturing, (d) electric power, gas and water production and supply, (e) construction, (f) transport and storage, (g) information technology, (h) wholesale and retail trade, (i) finance and insurance, (j) real estate, (k) social service, (l) communication and cultural industry, and (m) comprehensive. Reference was firstly made to the CSI 100 index which, as mentioned, is a widely used benchmark for the financial performance of China's A-share market. It was intended that 25% of all CSI 100 index listed enterprises be included in this research, with comparative data for the years 2007/2008 and 2010/2011. Those enterprises with the largest market capitalization and the highest liquidity in each particular industry listed in the CSI 100 index were initially selected. However, the CSI 100 index may not include enterprises operating in certain industries, and therefore these enterprises have to be looked for in the CSI 300 index. Subsequently, 25 top enterprises which were listed within the CSI 100 or the CSI 300 indices, representing 13 different industries, were taken as the sample for this study. Information about the 25 enterprises is summarized in Table 2.1.

Data source

The main source of data was from the company annual reports. In line with previous studies, the annual report is widely accepted as the major source of information with regard to CSD (Gray et al. 1995a; 1995b). Annual reports of the years 2007/2008 and 2010/2011 were available at the time of data collection and were selected to be analyzed. The reports were collected from the CSRC official website (www.cninfo.com.cn).

However, Unerman (2000) argued that it is not appropriate to use annual reports as the exclusive source to understand overall CSR issues; other media should be considered so as to obtain richer information. Moreover, content analysis only captures the words and numbers but ignores other data formats. Consequently, this may result in an incomplete representation of the level of CSD in the reports. In order to

Table 2.1 Twenty-five enterprises taken from the Shenzhen and Shanghai stock exchanges

No.	Name	Industry	Type	Stock code
1	Heilongjiang Agriculture Company limited	A	State owned	SSE (600598)
2	China Shenhua Energy Company Limited	B	State owned	SSE (601088)
3	PetroChina Company Limited	B	State owned	SSE (601857)
4	Cofco Tunhe Company Limited	C	State owned	SSE (600737)
5	Wuliangye Yibin Company Limited	C	State owned	SZSE (000858)
6	Youngor Group Company Limited	C	Private	SSE (600177)
7*	Qinghai Salt Lake Industry Company Limited	C	Private	SZSE (000792)
8	TCL Corporation	C	Private	SZSE (000100)
9	Baoshan Iron & Steel Company Limited	C	State owned	SSE (600019)
10	SAIC Motor Corporation Limited	C	State owned	SSE (600104)
11^	Midea Group Company Limited	C	Private	SZSE (000333)
12	Yunnan Baiyao Group Company Limited	C	State owned	SZSE (000538)
13	China Yangtze Power Company Limited	D	State owned	SSE (600900)
14	China Railway Erju Company Limited (CREC)	E	State owned	SSE (600528)
15	China COSCO Holdings Company Limited	F	State owned	SSE (601919)
16	Air China Limited	F	State owned	SSE (601111)
17	China United Network Communications Limited	G	State owned	SSE (600050)
18	Tsinghua Tongfang Company Limited	G	Private	SSE (600100)
19	Sinochem International Corporation	H	State owned	SSE (600500)
20	China Merchants Bank Company Limited	I	State owned	SSE (600036)

Table 2.1 (Continued)

No	Name	Industry	Type	Stock code
21	China Life Insurance Company	I	State owned	SSE (601628)
22	China Vanke Company Limited	J	Private	SZSE (000002)
23	Dazhong Transportation (Group) Company Limited	K	Private	SSE (600611)
24	Beijing Gehua CATV Network Company Limited	L	State owned	SSE (600037)
25	Shanghai Oriental Pearl (Group) Company Limited	M	State owned	SSE (600832)

Remark:
(*) Qinghai Salt Lake Potash Company Limited changed its name to Qinghai Salt Lake Industry Company Limited on 9 May 2011.
(^) Midea Group Company Limited delisted the stock code 000527 and relisted the new code 000333 on 18 September 2013.

investigate the corporate culture and image and further CSR-related activities of the sampled companies, the current study has made reference to the corporate websites of these enterprises. Furthermore, besides the annual reports, stand-alone CSR reports were downloaded either from the CSRC official website or from the company websites of those enterprises which have issued this type of report.

Unerman (2000) pointed out that many scholars have studied the quantified disclosure of CSR practices by using content analysis with different measurement methods. He also suggested that there is no single criterion to justify which particular method can provide the highest reliability. Hence, the current study of CSD of Chinese listed enterprises based on annual reports and CSR reports has measured the volume of disclosure in terms of number of pages or number of lines, the frequency of the keywords or main issues mentioned, and so on. On the other hand, the qualitative approach was used to address meanings and implications behind the CSR contents.

Analytical framework and categorization

In building up the analytical framework, references were made to Triple Bottom Line (TBL) accounting (Elkington, 1998). The TBL concept includes economic, social and environmental issues. The analytical framework of this study has therefore embraced these three perspectives in four dimensions in order to align with the idea of TBL. These four dimensions are marketplace, workplace, community and environment. For the economic perspective, workplace and marketplace dimensions were used to indicate the enterprise's internal operational issues and external matters, respectively. For the social perspective, the community dimension was used to investigate the social issues and concerns that were being considered by the enterprise. For the environmental perspective, the corresponding dimension was used to reveal the environmental protection concerns that were addressed by the enterprise.

The first step in the data analysis process was to organize the data into four different dimensions. Under each dimension, a set of categories was used to address various CSR issues. Therefore, the data, after being classified to each dimension, were further separated according to their specific categories for further analysis. In developing the categories under each dimension, references were made to the GRI-G3 content index and its specific performance indicators on economic, social and environmental areas. Figure 2.1 illustrates the analytical framework. Moreover, references were also made to the United Nations' (2008) "Guidance on Corporate Responsibility Indicators in Annual Reports" and Oxfam Hong Kong's (2008) "Corporate Social Responsibility Survey of Hang Seng Index Constituent Companies". Although the classifications and categories were carefully considered, they were still not

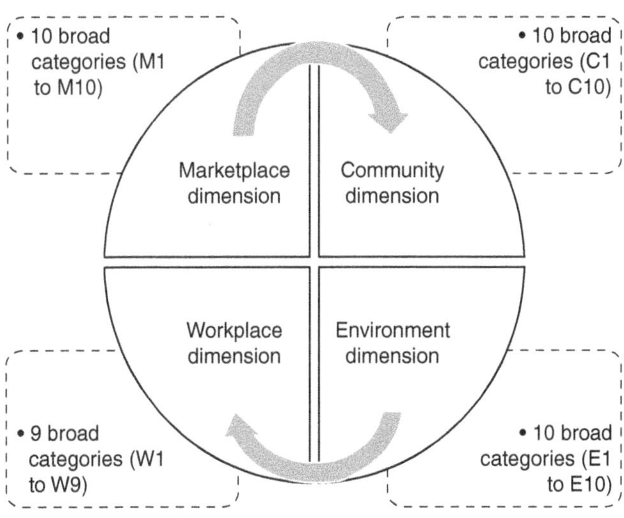

Figure 2.1 Data classification framework of CSD
Source: Authors.

exhaustive. A description of the dimensions with broad categories and their contents is provided in Appendix A.

Findings

General overview

As can be seen from Table 2.2, in 2007, up to 11 enterprises out of the total 25 samples chose to report their CSR information within the annual report. Only seven enterprises prepared the stand-alone report to disclose CSR information. In 2008, however, 22 enterprises made such disclosures. Along with the increasing number of enterprises disclosing CSR information, different types of reporting formats have also been developed. Some enterprises devoted a specific section or paragraph to CSR information disclosure, some mentioned CSR information across different sections within the annual reports, while others preferred to publish a stand-alone CSR report separate from the annual report, or enclosed the CSR report within the annual report. Moreover, some enterprises uploaded their stand-alone CSR report or provided a section in the company website to indicate the efforts they were making to communicate with stakeholders. In 2010 and 2011, up to 92% of the sampled enterprises issued stand-alone reports. Ten of them in 2010 and 12 in 2011 preferred not to disclose the CSR information in their annual reports; while 13 and 15 of them provided a section or paragraph to disclose CSR information in the same years. The study confirmed that enterprises prefer to disclose CSR information in separate stand-alone reports, and therefore none of them chose to mention the CSR information in different sections of the annual reports in 2010 and 2011.

Table 2.2 General overview of 25 Chinese listed enterprises

Number of enterprises	2007	2008	2010	2011
Without CSR information disclosure in annual report	5	1	10	12
Devoted a section/paragraph in annual report for CSR disclosure	11	3	15	13
CSR information spread across various sections of annual report	10	8	0	0
Stand-alone CSR report	7	22	23	23

Company website disclosure

The 25 sampled enterprises consisted of state-owned enterprises (72%) as well as those in private ownership (28%). The data suggested that 56% of the enterprises would disclose CSR information and 28% of them would also provide CSR reports on their company websites in 2007/2008; while in 2010/2011, 92% of the enterprises disclosed CSR information and 40% of them enclosed CSR reports on their company websites. In general, the enterprises reported more CSR information in Chinese than in English on their websites. Most of the sampled enterprises reported CSR information of a descriptive nature, and the volume of disclosure was rather limited on these websites (Table 2.3).

Annual report and stand-alone report disclosure

In terms of the presentation format, findings revealed that over a third of the 25 sampled enterprises preferred to disclose CSR information across different sections of their report in 2007/2008. However, the trend of spreading CSR information across within the annual report dramatically decreased in 2010/2011. Indeed, 92% of the enterprises preferred to prepare a stand-alone report in 2010/2011 compared to only 28% in 2007. The increased regulatory requirement imposed by local governments and both the SSE and SZSE might be a motivation. In 2008, the SSE mandated three types of enterprises to publish CSR reports, namely those which are simultaneously listed overseas, those which are listed in the SSE Corporate Governance Sector and financial companies. Since a large number of the listed enterprises on the CSI 100 index belonged to the SSE, many of the selected enterprises were also SSE listed. Moreover, the SSE started to promote some voluntary and mandatory guidelines in 2008, and thus more and more enterprises were mandated to publish stand-alone CSR reports. In 2011, CSRC Announcement No. 41 was issued to encourage listed enterprises to issue CSR reports, especially those in heavy polluting industries. Indeed, as evidence, seven

Table 2.3 Company websites of 25 enterprises and CSR information

Number of enterprises	2007/2008	In Percentage	2010/2011	In Percentage
CSR information	14	56	23	92
CSR report	7	28	10	40
Chinese website	25	100	25	100
English website	20	80	20	80

stand-alone CSR reports were published in 2007 compared to 22 in 2008 and 23 in 2010/2011.

Disclosure volume

The disclosure volume of CSR information in terms of each reporting type is shown in Appendices B1 and B2. The data indicated that in 2010/2011 most enterprises preferred to prepare stand-alone CSR reports which were separate from annual reports, in comparison with 2007/2008. Meanwhile, the enterprises began not to enclose stand-alone CSR reports within their annual reports in 2011. Different types of stand-alone CSR reports varied in terms of disclosure volume. Generally speaking, there has been a tendency to disclose more CSR information in 2010/2011 compared to 2007/2008. The upward trend was supported by an increasing number of pages in the stand-alone reports in 2010/2011. However, the data indicated a downward trend for CSR information carried in a devoted section or paragraph in the annual report, from three lines to six pages in 2007/2008 compared with three lines to less than two pages in 2010/2011. Meanwhile, there was also a decreasing trend in terms of the disclosure volume in stand-alone CSR reports enclosed within the annual reports in 2010/2011. Concerning the stand-alone report separated from the annual report or downloaded from company websites, the former reporting format showed a most remarkable increase in disclosure volume, from none in 2007 to 8–20 pages in 2008 and from 3–133 pages in 2010 to 4–187 pages in 2011. In 2007/2008, the disclosure volume in the stand-alone report available from the company website was 11–195 pages, compared to 23–187 pages in 2010/2011.

Key CSR wordings

In 2010/2011 the sampled enterprises mentioned many more key CSR wordings in their stand-alone reports than in 2007/2008 (see Figure 2.2). It was also noted that the enterprises mentioned key CSR wordings far more in the stand-alone reports than in the traditional annual reports. The data seemed to indicate that if the enterprises had published stand-alone reports, then they might not disclose as much CSR information in their annual reports. Key CSR wordings such as "social responsibility", "sustainable development" and "energy conservation" were the top three frequently mentioned in 2007/2008 and 2010/2011 in the stand-alone reports. In the 2007/2008 and 2010/2011 annual reports, key wordings such as "harmony", "energy conservation", "environment protection" and "emission reduction" decreased. This may further support the presumption that the enterprises emphasized stand-alone reports as the main medium of communication for

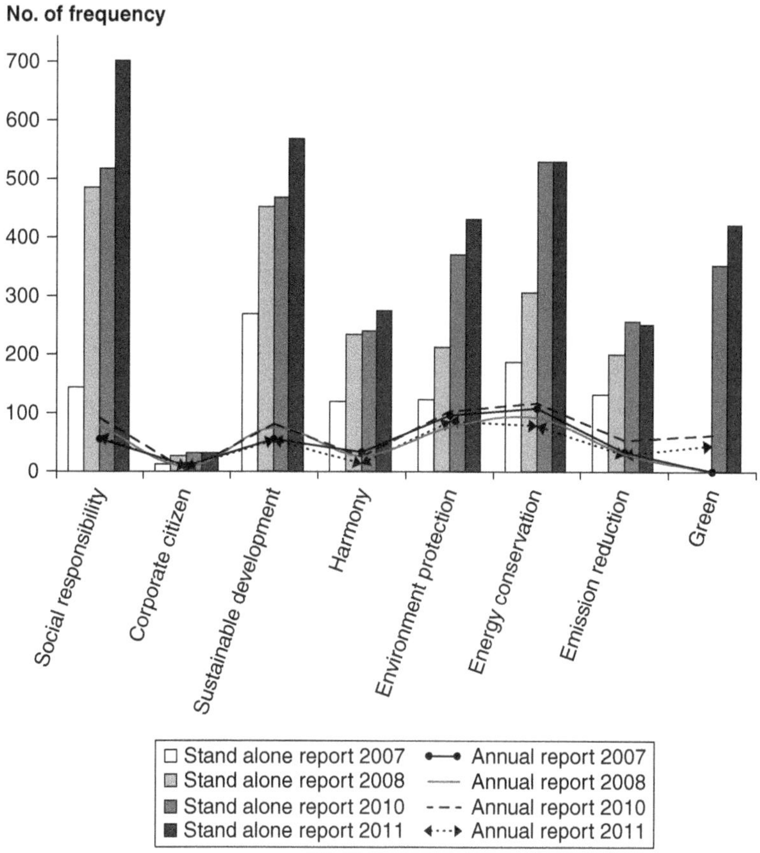

Figure 2.2 Key CSR wordings in 2007/2008 and 2010/2011

CSR-related information. Moreover, the least-mentioned CSR wording was "corporate citizen", both in annual reports and the stand-alone sections or reports in 2007/2008 and 2010/2011. In 2010/2011, the enterprises preferred to mention "green" policy or product, especially in the stand-alone report.

Listing, industry and ownership

The data appeared to indicate that the enterprises would most likely report CSR information in stand-alone reports if they had overseas listing. This is probably because they are subject to more regulations imposed by the overseas stock exchanges. Furthermore, as mentioned earlier, the SSE has mandated enterprises of this type to issue CSR reports. Two out of the six sampled enterprises listed on the SZSE issued stand-alone CSR reports in 2007. In 2008, 2010 and 2011 all the six enterprises issued stand-alone reports. Similarly, five out of the 19 enterprises listed on the SSE issued stand-alone CSR reports in 2007. In 2008, 16 of them issued stand-alone reports, while in both 2010 and 2011, 17 of them prepared stand-alone reports.

In terms of industry types, five industries seemed to report more CSR information then the others, namely (b) mining, (c) manufacturing, (f) transport and storage, (h) wholesale and retail trade, and (i) finance and insurance. Apart from financial companies, required by the SSE to issue CSR reports, the relatively higher volume of CSR information disclosure of these industries might be because of their more labor or environment intensive nature. Therefore, they had to disclose more information than the other industries.

As to ownership type, two out of the seven private enterprises issued stand-alone CSR reports in 2007, while in 2008, 2010 and 2011 all of them issued stand-alone reports. State-owned enterprises saw a similar increase, from five in 2007 to 16 in 2008, 2010 and 2011.

CSR reporting content

In this study, the contents of the reports were classified into three types of data. Numerical data refer to information concerning quantities; for example, how much money did the enterprise donate to disaster relief, how many times did the enterprise participate in charitable events and so on. Descriptive data refer to information describing an event; for example, the launch of a work safety promotion activity by an enterprise. Judgmental data refer to information containing personal judgment or values; for example, improvement of a working environment and therefore the morale of workers as a result of safety promotion activity.

For CSR information enclosed in a specific section or paragraph of the annual report, it was found that most of the sampled enterprises located the CSR section under the directors' report, and the data were mainly descriptive with some being numerical in nature. Also, most enterprises applied visual aids such as graphs and pictures to express their CSR concerns more frequently in the stand-alone reports in 2010/2011 than in 2007/2008.

Concerning the title of the stand-alone report, "Corporate Social Responsibility Report" was adopted by most enterprises in 2007. In 2008, the dominant name was "Social Responsibility Report"; this also pertained in 2010 and 2011. However, the stand-alone report downloaded from company websites preferred the title "Sustainable Development Report/Sustainability Report" in 2010 and 2011. The nature and quality of the reported CSR information and the names of the stand-alone reports in the other reporting formats are presented in Tables 2.4a and 2.4b.

In general, all stand-alone reports included data of judgmental, descriptive and numerical nature as well as providing some graphs or tables, or even pictures. Meanwhile, it was found that the stand-alone CSR reports from company websites seemed to have different data disclosures from the stand-alone reports enclosed within annual reports or separately published. It was also found that all types of stand-alone reports preferred to report CSR information in words rather than using visual aids.

CSR reporting guidelines and standards

Concerning the CSR reporting guidelines, it was found that most of the enterprises combined different guidelines and standards. Figure 2.3a shows that there has been a tremendous increase in the number of different guidelines or standards used by enterprises in order to prepare stand-alone CSR reports. Indeed, in 2007, only 12% of the sampled enterprises claimed to have adopted the local stock exchange instructions in preparing their reports, but in 2008, 56% claimed to have done so. Moreover, there has been an increasing trend to prepare stand-alone reports with regard to national regulations and international guidelines or standards. In addition, there has been a an up-down, but stable, trend for enterprises that do not follow any specific guidelines or standards in preparing their reports; from 20% of the sampled enterprises in 2007 to 32% in 2008 and down to 20% in 2011. For those that have followed guidelines, the most preferred local ones were the SSE and SZSE instructions to listed enterprises. As for international guidelines, the most preferred were the GRI and the UN Global Compact, as can be seen in Figure 2.3b.

However, the study also suggested that the reason why most of the enterprises would prefer to adopt local stock exchange guidelines was because of mandatory requirements since 2008. In terms of the mandatory guidelines for CSR reporting, it was found that six enterprises listed on the SZSE all belonged to the SZX 100 index in 2008, and thus they were mandated to prepare CSR reports. For those SSE listed enterprises in 2008, it was found that 16 belonged to those specific company types which should prepare mandatory CSR reports, while only three were not. That probably explains why the three with voluntary status did not prepare a CSR report.

Table 2.4a The nature and quality of CSR information disclosure

Number of sample	2007				2008				2010				2011			
Nature of information	#	<a>	<b>	<c>	#	<a>	<b>	<c>	#	<a>	<b>	<c>	#	<a>	<b>	<c>
Judgmental	4	0	0	6	2	11	4	7	0	1	16	10	0	0	18	10
Descriptive	11	0	1	6	2	13	6	6	9	2	21	10	9	0	23	10
Numerical	8	0	1	6	3	14	5	7	3	1	18	10	3	0	20	10
Visual aids	0	0	0	5	0	6	3	5	0	1	14	10	0	0	15	10
#Number of samples (with CSR information)	**12**	**0**	**1**	**6**	**3**	**14**	**6**	**7**	**9**	**2**	**21**	**10**	**9**	**0**	**23**	**10**

#Devoted section/paragraph in annual report, <a> Enclosed stand-alone report within annual report, <b> Published separately from annual report, <c> Downloadable from company website.

Table 2.4b Names of stand-alone CSR reports

Number of report	2007			2008			2010			2011			TOTAL		
Name of stand-alone report	<a>	<b>	<c>	<a>	<b>	<c>	<a>	<b>	<c>	<a>	<b>	<c>	<a>	<b>	<c>
Social Responsibility Report	0	1	1	12	6	0	1	15	4	0	15	4	**13**	**37**	**9**
Corporate Social Responsibility Report	0	0	3	1	0	5	0	2	1	0	3	1	**1**	**5**	**10**
Sustainable Development Report/Sustainability Report	0	0	1	1	0	1	1	3	4	0	3	4	**2**	**6**	**10**
Corporate Social Responsibility & Sustainability Report	0	0	0	0	0	0	0	1	1	0	2	1	**0**	**3**	**2**
Others (e.g. Green Book)	0	0	1	0	0	1	0	0	0	0	0	0	**0**	**0**	**2**

<a> Enclosed stand-alone report within annual report, <b> Published separately from annual report, <c> Downloadable from company website.

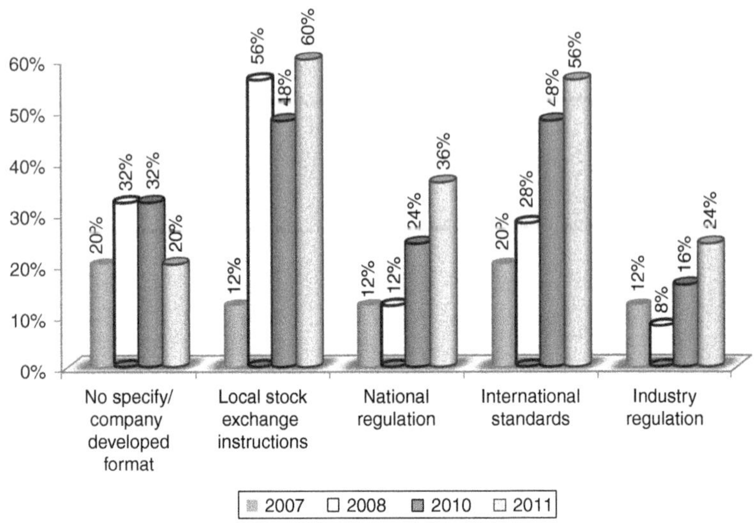

Figure 2.3a Reporting guidelines used by listed enterprises in stand-alone CSR reports

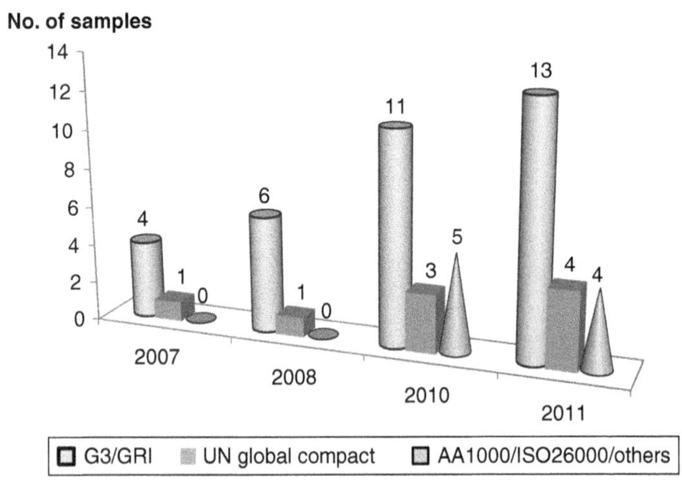

Figure 2.3b Breakdown of international guidelines used by listed enterprises

Verification of CSR reports

Concerning verification of the stand-alone CSR reports, it was found that in 2007 only two enterprises out of the 25 employed assurance services. In 2008, just three did so, while in 2010 and 2011, there were seven and eight enterprises, respectively. As to the choice of the verifier or assurance provider during 2007/2008 and 2010/2011, three enterprises were verified by a major professional accounting firm, seven were verified by internationally recognized organizations, nine were verified by local academicians who were specialists in CSR, while one was verified by self-assurance. The evidence revealed that the enterprises have become more willing to employ either internationally recognized organizations or local academicians to provide assurance services. However, the reliability of those reports which were not verified by independent third parties might be subject to doubt. It can be concluded that it is necessary to improve the credibility and reliability of Chinese listed enterprises' CSD, and more information should be disclosed concerning the assurance engagement process and the verification approach.

Recognition by international CSR bodies

The study also explored whether the sampled enterprises were related to some international organizations which promote non-financial reporting practices, such as GRI and AccountAbility. It was found that six of the sampled enterprises were signatories to the UN Global Compact. Two were registered members of the WBCSD. Moreover, in 2007 four enterprises had submitted their non-financial reports to the GRI and declared that they had used GRI (G3) as their reporting guidelines. In 2011, 13 enterprises declared that they had done so. However, only one enterprise's report (COSCO *Sustainable Development Report*) was verified by the GRI: this achieved a B+ level in 2007 and an A+ level in 2008, 2010 and 2011. One enterprise's report (Sinochem *Corporate Social Responsibility Report*) was self-declared to achieve A level in 2008. Shenhua *Social Responsibility Report* was declared to have achieved B+ level in 2011, while Baosteel and PetroChina did not declare what level of reporting had been achieved. All the other sampled enterprises did not engage as members of SA8000 or AA1000. It may be concluded that there is an urgent need for mainland Chinese enterprises to obtain international recognition in terms of their CSD practices.

Social contribution value per share

The study also assessed the sampled enterprises' reporting practice for the relatively new concept of social contribution value per share (SCVPS)[1] promoted by the SSE in 2008. The findings showed that five (26%) and nine (47%) out of the total 19 SSE listed enterprises had reported SCVPS in 2008 and 2011, respectively. The value varied from RMB 1.90 to RMB 5.229. As can be seen from Table 2.5 there has been an upward trend for SSE listed enterprises to disclose the SCVPS, while none of the SZSE listed enterprises voluntarily provided any SCVPS. In fact,

Table 2.5 SSE listed enterprises reporting SCVPS

Industry category	Short name	2007	2008	2010	2011
Mining	SHENHUA	N/A	RMB 2.960 (local standards) RMB 2.963 (international standards)	RMB 4.157 (local standards) RMB 4.205 (international standards)	RMB 5.186 (local standards) RMB 5.229 (international standards)
Manufacturing	BAOSTEEL	N/A	N/A	RMB1.713	RMB2.057
Manufacturing	SAIC	N/A	N/A	RMB5.376	RMB5.722
Construction	CREC	N/A	RMB 2.13	RMB3.20	RMB3.23
Transport and storage	COSCO	N/A	RMB 2.00	RMB1.44	RMB (1.90)
Transport and storage	AIRCHINA	N/A	N/A	N/A	RMB2.235
Information technology	TONGFANG	N/A	RMB 1.90	RMB 2.17 (adj. RMB1.09)	RMB1.31
Wholesale and retail trade	SINOCHEM	RMB 1.16	RMB 1.73	RMB1.44	RMB1.49
Finance and insurance	CMB	N/A	N/A	RMB3.80	RMB5.49

most of them did not provide detailed calculations of how to generate the value. Moreover, it was difficult to evaluate the SCVPS among different industries, since even today SCVPS is still a novel concept in China. Thus the benchmark value for any specific industry was not available at the time of data analysis.

Stakeholder issues

In addressing stakeholder issues, no explicit message was found embedded either in the annual reports or the stand-alone reports to indicate the drivers to report CSR issues. An interesting finding was that most of the enterprises mentioned that they issued CSR reports because they wanted to support government policies or regulations. One may speculate, therefore, that there were political pressures to report CSR issues. However, some enterprises mentioned that their top management perceived the ethical issues and thus published CSR reports, while a few of them had to prepare the reports because they were registered members of international reporting regulatory bodies, such as the UN Global Compact.

In analyzing the stand-alone CSR reports, it was found that the stakeholder groups mentioned with the highest frequency were

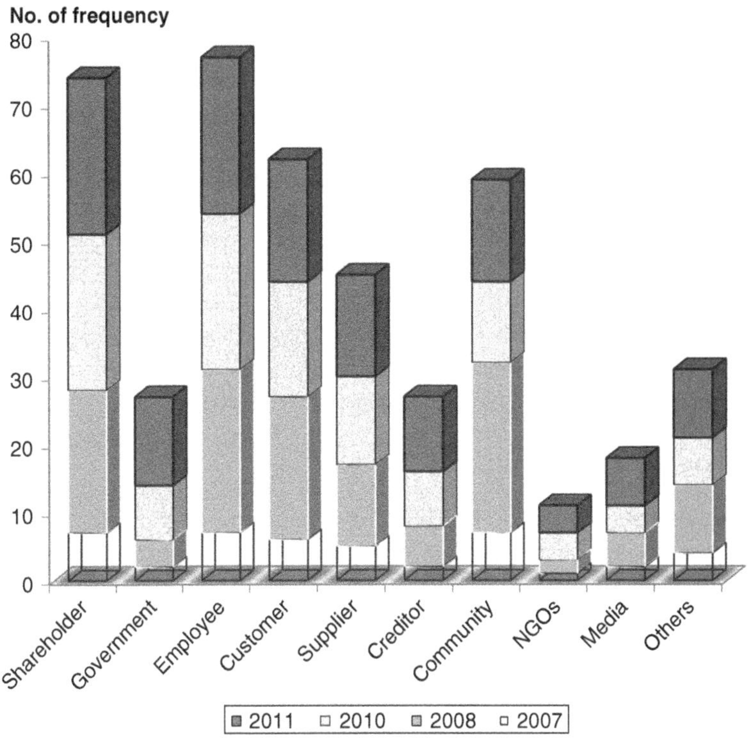

Figure 2.4 Frequency of stakeholder groups mentioned

"shareholders", "employees", "customers" and "community". The data showed that those four stakeholders were relatively important for the listed enterprises in the years 2007/2008 to 2010/2011 (see figure 2.4). In contrast, "creditor", "non-government organizations", "government" and "media" were seldom mentioned. Belal and Lubinin (2008) suggested that CSR practices were often geared mainly toward powerful stakeholders. In short, it was suggested that most enterprises considered the more important stakeholders as their first priority, since shareholders and employees were considered to be stakeholders with economic power.

As to the dialogue with key stakeholders, the enterprises mostly used annual shareholder meetings, annual reports and regular briefings and so on. A few enterprises used email, telephone or corporate websites to communicate with their shareholders. As to communicating with employees, the enterprises used internal means, such as staff magazines, direct reports to management, regular meetings with employees and corporate online forums and so on. As to the community, the enterprises made regular visits to the locality or held meetings with local organizations to understand their needs.

It was found that only one out of the 25 sampled enterprises included specific commentaries from stakeholders in the 2007 and 2008 stand-alone CSR reports, while six of them enclosed specific commentaries or contact methods both in 2010 and 2011. Two enterprises in 2007 and and four in 2008 invited the stakeholders to provide their comments on their stand-alone reports through an attached reader feedback sheet. A similar situation was also found in 2010 and 2011, with three and two enterprises, respectively, providing feedback sheets.

Analysis based on the four dimensions

It was mentioned earlier that the analytical framework of the contents of the CSR reports was based on the TBL accounting, incorporating four dimensions, namely marketplace, workplace, environment and community. Here the elements under each dimension are analyzed and explained.

Marketplace

Table 2.6 shows the key marketplace issues, such as CSR strategy and policy, honors and awards, stakeholder engagement and dialogue process, and so on, as contained in the stand-alone CSR reports. Topics centering on prevention of bribery and corruption, consumers' rights protection and product and service responsibilities were also captured in the reports. In principle, there was an increase in the number of enterprises disclosing this information from 2007 to 2011. However, the enterprises did not disclose much information concerning fair trade and competition issues in their stand-alone CSR reports. This may indicate that most Chinese listed enterprises do not frequently deal with these issues during their operations.

Under the category of CSR strategy and policy, most of the enterprises provided the CSR mission statement, vision and objectives and so on. However, the CSR strategy and policy were presented descriptively, which did not show a strong connection with the overall planning of the business. Most of the enterprises provided specific sections, from one paragraph to several pages, to list awards for their ethical behaviors, praise for their products and services, and so on. It appears that

Table 2.6 Number of enterprises disclosing marketplace issues in stand-alone reports

Category	Marketplace	2007	2008	2010	2011
M1	CSR strategy and policy	7	22	23	23
M2	Government incentives/subsidies	1	1	3	4
M3	Honors and awards	6	19	20	20
M4	Stakeholder engagement and dialogue	6	13	20	21
M5	Prevention for bribery and corruption	3	13	12	12
M6	Supply chain management	1	5	15	18
M7	Product and service responsibility	4	15	21	22
M8	Consumers' right protection	4	17	19	20
M9	Corporate Culture to promote CSR	1	3	5	4
M10	Fair trade/competition on CSR issues	1	1	2	4

honors and awards were used as promotional tools for the enhancement of business image. Furthermore, most of the enterprises included relatively more information when addressing their responsibilities for product quality and consumers' right protection, such as following the ISO requirements for quality control, setting up customer service hotlines and conducting customer satisfaction surveys to understand their needs. There was also an increasing trend for listed enterprises to address supplier chain policies and policies against corruption and bribery. However, they seldom disclosed any government incentives or subsidies for the implementation of CSR practices. Furthermore, not many enterprises promoted the CSR culture or the concept of fair trade within their business.

Workplace

As shown in Table 2.7, the issues of employee development policy, employee benefits and welfare, the environment and compliance with local labor law were still the critical issues among the sampled enterprises. There was also an upward trend for assessing staff remuneration and performance evaluation policy, health and safety policy (EHS) and recognition of work safety standards in the stand-alone CSR reports. There have been some serious accidents caused by illegal production in high-risk sectors, such as coal mining and hazardous chemical industries, in recent years, and this might be a motivation for listed enterprises to consider their work safety policies. Only a very few of them had addressed the issue of child labor. This may suggest that most Chinese listed enterprises focus more on employee training and fringe

Table 2.7 Number of enterprises disclosing workplace issues in stand-alone reports

Category	Workplace	2007	2008	2010	2011
W1	Employees' development policy	7	20	22	23
W2	Employees' benefits and welfare	7	20	22	23
W3	Staff remuneration and performance evaluation policy	4	13	15	17
W4	Employees' right and form of association	2	10	10	12
W5	Environment health and safety (EHS) policy	7	13	17	16
W6	Compliance with local labor law and regulation	4	15	20	21
W7	Non discriminate and diversity policy	4	6	12	15
W8	Recognition of work safety standards	0	2	18	21
W9	Prohibition of the use of child labor	2	1	3	3

benefits disclosure because of reporting requirements imposed by local regulatory bodies. As to the scant reporting of child labor issues, this might be because not many of the sampled enterprises were in labor intensive industries.

Under the employee development and employee welfare and benefits categories, issues included the basic employee structure of the company, training courses, insurance schemes and recreational activities provided to staff, financial support to poor employees and their families, performance evaluation policies and employee satisfaction surveys. Moreover, a few of the sampled enterprises not only included their internal EHS policies but also mentioned setting up EHS committees to monitor related issues.

Concerning anti-discrimination policies, the sampled enterprises reported that women had taken up senior management positions. The 2007 reports indicated that 3% of all the senior managers were female, while in 2008 this had increased to 25%. In 2010 and 2011 the average percentages were 15% and 17%, respectively.

Community

The study found that most of the sampled enterprises focused on philanthropic donations in the form of money and other kinds of support. Moreover, as shown in Table 2.8, the issues of educational support and investing in local community development were key concerns. There

Table 2.8 Number of enterprises disclosing community issues in stand-alone reports

Category	Community	2007	2008	2010	2011
C1	Philanthropic donation	5	22	20	20
C2	Support for education	2	16	15	17
C3	Investing and support for local community development	7	18	13	17
C4	Corporate foundation establishment	2	6	5	5
C5	Employee involvement for CSR activities	1	11	9	11
C6	Poverty alleviation	4	10	14	15
C7	Establishing community outreach council	2	2	1	1
C8	Job creation for community	0	13	6	12
C9	Contribution to national exchequer	3	7	7	7
C10	Community outreach program in knowledge sharing	4	7	2	2

was also an increasing trend to disclose issues such as the establishment of corporate foundations to support charitable organizations, employee volunteer programs, and poverty alleviation for remote regions in China, as well as job creation for the community. This may be because a number of the sampled enterprises were state owned, and government directives demanded that they had to provide more support to remote areas in China.

The most common entry in the philanthropic donation category was disaster relief contributions. In the educational support and local community support categories, popular issues included support for local school rebuilding, rural and infrastructure development for the local community, the establishment of medical organizations for local people and sponsorship for local community activities or other charitable organizations. Most enterprises also mentioned support for government development in terms of job creation and tax contribution. However, the community outreach program category and the establishment of community outreach councils were the least mentioned issues. This may reveal that not many enterprises intended to establish or provide business-related knowledge sharing programs for remote districts.

Environment

As shown in Table 2.9, issues relating to environmental protection, the recognition of environmental protection standards, investment in

Table 2.9 Number of enterprises disclosing environment issues in stand-alone reports

Category	Environment	2007	2008	2010	2011
E1	New technology investment/development for environmental protection	6	12	14	17
E2	Cost reduction in relation to energy efficiency	2	6	15	15
E3	Energy conservation and emission reduction	6	19	20	23
E4	Sewage disposal and waste recycling	5	11	10	11
E5	Green/Clean energy and renewable energy	5	8	15	17
E6	Issues on environment protection	6	20	15	17
E7	Biodiversity issues	4	6	6	8
E8	Recognition of environmental protection standards	3	8	18	20
E9	Climate change issues	2	2	6	5
E10	Environmental education for employees protection	1	3	10	12

new technology to avoid pollution, energy conservation and emission reduction were reported most frequently in the stand-alone CSR reports. Meanwhile, an increasing trend to report issues relating to sewage disposal and waste recycling, renewable energy and green energy development, cost reduction in relation to energy efficiency and education of employees in environmental protection was also found in the latest stand-alone CSR reports. Moreover, two topics not directly related to business operation, namely climate change and biodiversity of plantation and management of forests were also reported in the stand-alone reports. This implies that some enterprises have considered incorporating environmental protection concepts not just in their operations but also in wider society. This may be explained by the ever-increasing promotion and regulations imposed by the Chinese government on environmental protection in recent years. However, none of the sampled enterprises had committed to carbon disclosure projects (CDP).

Conclusion

Some relevant findings have been presented in the previous sections and can be used to respond to the research questions posed earlier. Firstly, the study has suggested that most of the sampled Chinese enterprises do have a basic concept of CSR. However, CSR should not be confined to donations and supporting community activities or contributing taxes to the government. Chinese businesses need to incorporate more CSR planning within their operations. Furthermore, it was found that most listed enterprises did not explicitly spell out their motivation to carry out CSR activities. Most of the enterprises mentioned that they would follow government regulations and promotion to engage in CSR issues. Thus, it can be inferred that the key driver that encourages Chinese businesses to address CSR issues is political pressure from regulatory bodies. However, it appears that the current status of CSR engagement by Chinese enterprises is still far from what central government has been promoting in terms of the concept of "Harmonious CSR"; indeed, it appears to be largely based on responses to political pressures, and lacks sustainability. The political characteristics in mainland China, where there are multi-level governments, state-owned enterprises and numerous state-involved businesses, even in the case of private enterprises, make it difficult for frontline business operators to really grasp the true edict of central government, which is promulgating the concept of hCSR. Proper education about CSR at various levels of the hierarchical society should be instilled so that CSR and CSD do not simply become window dressing or propaganda.

Secondly, the study has found that the overall disclosure level of the sampled enterprises appears to be far lower than the global standard in terms of information relevance, data objectivity and volume of disclosure. If we take the following criteria to judge whether an enterprise has achieved high-quality CSR reporting, namely (1) whether CSR information is contained in the company website, (2) whether there is a specific CSR section in the annual report, (3) whether there is a standalone CSR report, (4) whether combinations of different international reporting guidelines have been adopted, (5) whether the enterprise is a signatory of or has registered with an internationally recognized regulatory organization and (6) whether the CSR report has been verified by an independent third party, none of the 25 sampled enterprises can fulfill all six criteria. If criteria (2) and (3) were treated as either/or, then only two enterprises (Cosco and Sinochem) out of the 25 sampled can fulfill all criteria in 2007/2008 and 2010/2011.

Thirdly, the study has revealed that up to 20% of the sampled enterprises in 2007 and 56% in 2008 claimed to have followed different guidelines and standards in preparing their CSR reports; in 2010 and 2011 the percentages increased to 48% and 60%, respectively. In 2007 only 12% and in 2008 20% of the sampled enterprises had adopted the local guidelines and international standards. In 2010 and 2011, 60% and 56%, respectively, followed them. The trend to adopt national and industry regulations has been increasing. This is an encouraging phenomenon as China advances as a major player in the international arena.

To conclude, the study suggests that most Chinese listed enterprises are still at the initial stage of preparing CSR reports. Consequently, most of them interpret CSR according to their own understanding and present CSR information with varying contents and reporting formats. Indeed, there is no standardized CSR reporting format in China. In terms of data disclosure volume and quality, the study has suggested that the stand-alone CSR report seems to include higher quality and a larger volume of CSR information as compared to the traditional format of embedded CSR information in the annual reports. Moreover, the format of the stand-alone CSR report can also affect disclosure in terms of quantity and quality, because it was found that stand-alone CSR reports from company websites were superior to those enclosed within annual reports and those issued independently. Although all the sampled enterprises had their own company websites to promote CSR only half of them disclosed CSR information on their websites in 2007 and 2008. Nevertheless, 92% of the sampled enterprises started to disclose CSR information on their websites in 2010 and 2011. Finally, the enterprises disclose more CSR information on their company websites in Chinese than in English.

Implications and recommendations

Though CSR reporting is still weak, the study suggested that there has been a commendable improvement in terms of data volume and quality, as well as in the reporting format from the years 2007/2008 to 2010/2011 among the 25 sampled Chinese listed enterprises. Most enterprises report their non-financial information according to government policies and directives. In recent years there have been more and more initiatives from the government and stock exchanges in China to stimulate local enterprises to produce CSR reports. Belal (2008) argued that voluntary reporting does not always successfully achieve the objective of social accounting in terms of the quality and quantity of the disclosure. The findings from the current study have acknowledged Belal's argument, as the significant increase in CSR information disclosure from the years 2007/2008 to 2010/2011 was most likely thanks to government-imposed mandates for specific enterprises to publish CSR reports.

The study also found that most of the CSR information provided was good news; seldom did the enterprises address employee work accidents or report statistics on injury and death. In other words, most of the enterprises used the CSR report as a kind of company promotion material rather than a factual account of the organization's interactions with society, environment, employees, community, customers and other stakeholders, and the consequences of those interactions and activities (Gray, 2000). It must be stressed here that sound CSR reporting should include the consequences of such activities, and by consequences we mean both good news and bad news. For example, according to Greenpeace (2009), China Shenhua, PetroChina and Guangdong Midea were blacklisted on the Environmental Protection Department of China website for certain periods when their water pollutant exceeded the regular emission limit. However, this kind of adverse information or bad news was never mentioned in the CSR reports of the respective enterprises in our study. Therefore, there is doubt as to the level of data accuracy and reliability.

It is suggested that Chinese enterprises should employ more independent assurance service providers to verify the CSR information disclosed. Apart from third party assurance, local regulatory bodies and stock exchanges should also develop relevant regulations to verify the information, in addition to providing guidelines on the issues that should be reported. Specific organizations or government departments can be established to monitor CSR reporting in order to enhance data accuracy and reliability. On the other hand, legalizing certain reporting requirements is believed to be an effective way to monitor enterprises' CSR reporting. For example, the enterprises in our study seldom provided any information concerning the SSE requirement in 2008 for listed enterprises to provide "top management commitment on CSR information disclosed". Moreover, it is advised that standards should be established for the preparation of CSR reports, so as to achieve more uniformity and comparability among different enterprises. Specific standards should also be designed to guide those labor or environmentally intensive industries, as they are vulnerable to work accidents and other corporate scandals.

The study has revealed the current CSR engagement of Chinese listed enterprises and provided an up-to-date account of non-financial information disclosure practices in China. Moreover, this study has explored the status of CSD among Chinese enterprises in comparison with the global trend. Future studies should theorize CSR in China given its unique social, economic and political environment. The current reality is still quite a distance from the state of hCSR promulgated by the Chinese government. However, as more and more mandatory and voluntary guidelines are being promoted by the government and other regulatory bodies, and there is also an increasing demand for transparent reporting and ethical issues disclosure by various stakeholders, we are looking forward to seeing a switch from pressure-oriented to market-oriented reporting in China in the future.

Appendix A – Descriptions of broad categories within each dimension

Marketplace dimension (M1–M10)

M1: CSR strategy: Addresses the higher level company practices and approaches to CSR issues. In this part, the company should provide the overall CSR planning in terms of vision statement, objectives, policy statements and the commitments toward issues of environment, employee relations and products and services, and so on.

M2: Tax incentives or subsidies on CSR activities: Incentive programs or tangible benefits provided by the government to support the company's operations incorporating CSR practices.

M3: Honors and awards: Recognizing the company best practice in implementation of CSR programs or ethical behaviors related to CSR issues.

M4: Stakeholder engagement and dialogue: A systematic way of identifying the company stakeholders and communicating about the activities of the company. In the form of stakeholder engagement, it might involve planning how to manage different stakeholders' interests. Stakeholder dialogue usually takes the form of stakeholder statements, staff surveys, community panels and forums, annual general meetings, analyst presentations, direct interactions with customers, invitation for stakeholders' feedback on the report and publishing stakeholders' feedback, and so forth.

M5: Codes of conduct on prevention of bribery and anti-corruption: Policies and procedures against bribery and corrupt behavior, as well as how much the company elaborates on actual practice implementation in order to stamp out bribery and corruption.

M6: Supply chain management: Putting pressure on the supply chain management system rather than just taking corrective actions to remove the suppliers who are not in compliance with the company's code of conduct. The supply chain management system includes strategy and policies on supply chain, codes of conduct in supplier selection, supplier contracting and even supplier auditing, and so forth. Moreover, the specific operation procedures on various aspects are examined to find out if the supplier has followed the codes of conduct of the supply chain. For instance, the supplier should ensure the application of the responsibility agenda throughout the supply chain process. The scope of a responsibility agenda includes the protection of human rights, prohibition of child and forced labor, safe working conditions and environmental issues.

M7: Product and service responsibility: Engaging in various product and service responsibilities, which include product safety issues, the integration of ethical issues from product sourcing, production and packaging, product and service quality certification, R&D on improving product quality and safety, and so on.

M8: Consumers' right protection: Caring for consumers' health and safety when they use the company's products and services in the forms of consumers' right protection, including coordination with regulatory departments to fight against fake products, customers' compliant handling and hotline support service, customers' satisfaction survey, and so forth.

M9: Corporate Culture: Addresses the company's corporate culture in promoting CSR by setting up internal policies and guidelines, training courses for employees, ethical issues promoted by top management, and so on.

M10: Fair trade and Fair Competition: Introduction of organic food or fair trade certified products through the local sourcing initiatives to support local suppliers and businesses. Fair competition is concerned with anti-trust policies and procedures for business operation.

Workplace dimension (W1–W9)

W1: Employee development policy: Basic employee information, amount spent on training programs, percentage of learning programs to employees, job satisfaction surveys, enclosure of labor turnover ratios, policies on retaining talent, setting up of communication channels with employees, and so on.

W2: Employee benefits and welfare: Establishment of insurance and pension fund schemes as well as other kinds of subsidies for employees, different kinds of support for poor workers, recreational activities or programs for employees in order to balance work with life, and so on.

W3: Staff remuneration and performance evaluation policy: Establishment of a fair and reasonable compensation system and performance assessment policies for staff.

W4: Employee rights and formation of associations: Labor rights to form labor unions and to join related activities, establishment of labor unions for employees' negotiation rights and collective bargaining power.

W5: Environment, health and safety (EHS) policy: Commitment toenvironmental, health and safety stewardship, including the provision of prevention programs for work-related accidents and fatalities, safe workplace and living conditions in compliance with local labor law and regulations, disclosure of work accidents and injury frequencies, policy on minimizing adverse impact on environmental, health and safety concerns.

W6: Compliance with labor law and regulations: Whether the company has followed local, national or even international labor law and regulations on employee issues.

W7: Anti-discrimination and diversity policy: Provision of equal opportunities and workforce diversity, disclosure of the percentage of female, minorities or disabled staff in total labor force, labor diversity policies for equal opportunity issues.

W8: Recognition of work safety standards: Whether the company has followed various labor standards, such as SA8000 or ILO, and other recognitions for work safety.

W9: Prohibition of child labor: Whether the company has adopted the abolition of child labor and the prohibition of forced labor.

Community dimension (C1–C10)

C1: Philanthropic donation: Addressing monetary or other kinds of support to community or non-profit organizations and disaster relief, and so on.

C2: Support for education: Provision of education and training support to the community, in the forms of establishing schools and other educational institutions, establishing scholarships or subsidies for poor students, and so on.

C3: Investing in and support to local community development: Engaging in relationships with the community in the forms of sponsorship to local community programs or activities, spending on local infrastructure and rural development, consultancy services provided to the community, and so on.

C4: Corporate foundation establishment: Establishment of corporate foundations for community support or making charitable contributions to the disadvantaged.

C5: Employee involvement: Employees' contributions to community support, such as employee volunteer program, monetary donation and other kinds of support to disaster relief, and so on.

C6: Poverty alleviation: Contributions to remote districts in China, such as monetary support, regular visits, lower than market interest loans and guaranteed funding for the poor, helping the local people in knowledge and skills transfer, and so forth.

C7: Community outreach council: The overall organization of all CSR-related policies and programs as well as the establishment of community engagement and dialogue with stakeholders in the community. The formation of a CSR committee constituting various talents from different departments.

C8: Job creation: The volume of job opportunities provided by the company to support the local labor market and development.

C9: Contribution to the national exchequer: The tax contribution for the relevant period that is generated by the company and contributed to the government for national development.

C10: Community outreach program: Contributions in the forms of educational seminars and training, knowledge and skill sharing courses, establishment of recreational activities to the community, supporting services provided to the disadvantaged or minority groups.

Environment dimensions (E1–E10)

E1: New technology investment or development for environmental protection: Spending and research on new technology to improve energy efficiency, emission reduction and minimizing adverse impact on the environment.

E2: Cost reduction in relation to energy efficiency: Cost savings generated from the company's operations through saving energy, reducing water usage and minimizing paper consumption, and so on.

E3: Energy conservation and emission reduction: Setting up of reduction targets and relevant policies on energy conservation and emission reduction, including the issues of greenhouse gas emission reduction and forest carbon sequestration, and so on.

E4: Sewage disposal and waste recycling: Business policies or operational practices in removing contaminants from waste water and sewage. Recycling of waste water or used materials during the production process in order to reduce the consumption of fresh raw materials, savings on energy and avoiding water pollution.

E5: Green/Clean energy and renewable energy: Energy policies or planning so that the environment is not harmed during production or operation, clean and renewable energy in the form of wind power, hydropower or hydro-electricity, solar energy, biomass, biofuels and geothermal energy, and so on.

E6: Issues on environment protection: Operational policies and internal or external practices on environmental protection issues.

E7: Biodiversity issues: Company polices on protection of different life forms within a given ecosystem or biome, protection of biodiversity through sponsorship to support the protection of endangered and threatened species, supporting social forestry projects to plant trees along railway lines and roadsides or remote areas, spending on afforestation programs to prevent floods and other disasters, and so on.

E8: Recognition of environmental protection standards: Policies or practices which have been recognized by environmental protection agencies or certifiers.

E9: Climate change issues: Addressing issues of global warming and carbon disclosure projects (CDP), and so forth.

E10: Education for employees on environmental protection: Training programs provided to employees in order to understand environmental protection and to apply to business operations or even the employees' daily life.

Appendix B1 – CSR information presentation

No. of samples	2007	%	2008	%	2010	%	2011	%
Without CSR information disclosure in annual report	4	16	8	32	10	40	12	48
Devoted a section/paragraph in annual report for CSR disclosure	11	44	3	12	15	60	13	52
CSR information is spread across various sections of annual report	10	40	8	32	0	0	0	0
Stand-alone CSR report	7	28	22	88	23	92	23	92

Appendix B2 – CSR information disclosure volume

	Nature of industry	Devoted section/paragraph in annual report			
		2007	2008	2010	2011
A	Agriculture, forestry, livestock farming and fishery	–	6 lines	–	–
B	Mining	2 pages	–	6–8 lines	6–8 lines
C	Manufacturing	3 lines to 4 pages	–	3–15 lines	3–8 lines
D	Electric power, gas and water production and supply	6 pages	–	–	–
E	Construction	–	–	–	–
F	Transport and storage	–	–	–	–
G	Information Technology	14 lines	6 lines	–	–

(Continued)

	Nature of industry	Devoted section/paragraph in annual report			
		2007	2008	2010	2011
H	Wholesale and retail trade	–	–	–	–
I	Finance and insurance	9 lines to 1 page	2 pages	7 lines to 1.5 pages	9 lines to 1.5 pages
J	Real estate	3 pages	–	–	–
K	Social service	–	–	–	–
L	Communication and Cultural Industry	–	–	–	–
M	Comprehensive	7 lines	–	–	–
	Range of 25 samples	**3 lines to 6 pages**	**6 lines to 2 pages**	**3 lines to 1.5 pages**	**3 lines to 1.5 pages**

	Nature of industry	Enclosed stand-alone report within annual report			
		2007	2008	2010	2011
A	Agriculture, forestry, livestock farming and fishery	–	–	–	–
B	Mining	–	59 pages	–	–
C	Manufacturing	5 pages	3–38 pages	–	–
D	Electric power, gas and water production and supply	–	18 pages	–	–
E	Construction	–	14 pages	–	–
F	Transport and storage	–	7–14 pages	7 pages	–
G	Information Technology	–	6 pages	–	–
H	Wholesale and retail trade	–	10 pages	25 pages	–
I	Finance and insurance	–	48–52 pages	–	–

J	Real estate	–	–	–	–
K	Social service	–	5 pages	–	–
L	Communication and Cultural Industry	–	5 pages	–	–
M	Comprehensive	–	–	–	–
	Range of 25 samples	**5 pages**	**3–59 pages**	**7–25 pages**	**–**

	Nature of industry	Published stand-alone report separate from annual report			
		2007	2008	2010	2011
A	Agriculture, forestry, livestock farming and fishery	–	–	–	–
B	Mining	–	–	68–102 pages	68–102 pages
C	Manufacturing	–	10–20 pages	3–74 pages	14–80 pages
D	Electric power, gas and water production and supply	–	–	35 pages	39 pages
E	Construction	–	–	14 pages	23 pages
F	Transport and storage	–	–	58–133 pages	36–187 pages
G	Information Technology	–	–	5–70 pages	4–78 pages
H	Wholesale and retail trade	–	–	–	23 pages
I	Finance and insurance	–	–	40–49 pages	54–55 pages
J	Real estate	–	8 pages	52 pages	55 pages
K	Social service	–	–	9 pages	10 pages
L	Communication and Cultural Industry	–	–	5 pages	10 pages
M	Comprehensive	–	–	–	–
	Range of 25 samples	**–**	**8–20 pages**	**3–133 pages**	**4–187 pages**

(Continued)

	Nature of industry	Downloadable stand-alone report from company website			
		2007	2008	2010	2011
A	Agriculture, forestry, livestock farming and fishery	–	–	–	–
B	Mining	52–59 pages	59–77 pages	68–102 pages	68–102 pages
C	Manufacturing	116 pages	56 pages	62–74 pages	46–80 pages
D	Electric power, gas and water production and supply	–	–	–	–
E	Construction	–	–	–	–
F	Transport and storage	N/A*	195 pages	133 pages	187 pages
G	Information Technology	–	–	–	–
H	Wholesale and retail trade	46 pages	54 pages	64 pages	67 pages
I	Finance and insurance	–	52 pages	40 pages	54 pages
J	Real estate	20 pages	11 pages	28 pages	36 pages
K	Social service	–	–	–	–
L	Communication and Cultural Industry	–	–	–	–
M	Comprehensive	–	–	–	–
	Range of 25 samples	**20–116 pages**	**11–195 pages**	**28–133 pages**	**36–187 pages**

Note

1. According to Bank of China (2009), SCVPS = (Contribution value of economic performance + Contribution value of social performance – Social cost resulting from environmental pollution)/Total share capital, where Contribution value of economic performance = Annual net profit + Annual total tax payment + Total deposit interest paid to customers + Total remuneration of employees; Contribution value of social performance = Annual employee

welfare and gross social security expenditure + Annual total employee training costs + Annual total donations; Social cost resulted from environmental pollution by BOC was calculated as the sum of the effluent fees and the total fines for violating the regulations concerning environmental protection.

References

Alon, I., Latteman, C., Fetscherin, M., Li, S. & Schneider, A. (2010). Usage of public corporate communications of social responsibility in Brazil, Russia, India, China (BRIC). *International Journal of Emerging Markets*, 5, (1), 60–22.

Bank of China (2009). *CSR 2009: Building a Harmonious Society through Social Responsibilities*. Beijing: Bank of China.

Baughn, C., Bodie, N. & McIntosh, J. (2007). Corporate social and environmental responsibility in Asian countries and other geographical regions. *Corporate Social Responsibility and Environmental Management*, 14, (4), 189–205.

Belal, A. (2001). A study of corporate social disclosures in Bangladesh. *Managerial Auditing Journal*, 16, (5), 274–289.

Belal, A.R. (2008). *Corporate Social Responsibility Reporting in Developing Countries: The Case of Bangladesh*. Aldershot: Ashgate.

Belal, A.R. & Momin, M. (2009). Corporate social responsibility (CSR) reporting in emerging economies: A review and future direction. *Research in Accounting in Emerging Economies*, 9, 119–143.

Belal, A.R. & Owen, D. (2007). The view of corporate managers on the current state of, and future prospects for, social reporting in Bangladesh: An engagement based study. *Accounting, Auditing and Accountability Journal*, 20, (3), 472–494.

Belal, A.R. & Lubinin, V. (2008). Corporate social disclosures (CSD) in Russia. In Idowu, S.O. & Filho, W.L. (eds.) *Global Practices of Corporate Social Responsibility*. Berlin: Springer Verlag.

Bradsher, K. (2009). At least 92 die in Chinese coal mine explosion. *The New York Times*, 21 November 2009. Available at http://www.nytimes.com/2009/11/22/world/asia/22china.html

Briston, R.J. (1984). Accounting standards and host country control of multinational. *British Accounting Review*, 16, (1), 12–26.

Clarke, P. (2010). Another Foxconn employee commits suicide. *EE Times*, 14 May 2010. Available at http://www.eetimes.com/electronics-news/4199336/Report-Another-Foxconn-employee-commits-suicide

Elkington, J. (1998). *Cannibals with Forks: The Triple Bottom Line of 21st Century Business*. Gabriola Island, BC: New Society Publishers.

Feng, Y. (2007). Child slave labor in Chinese brick factories. *The Epoch Times*, 17 June 2007. Available at http://www.theepochtimes.com/news/7-6-17/56605.html

Gray, R.H., Owen, D.L. & Maunders, K.T. (1987). *Corporate Social Reporting: Accounting and Accountability*. Hemel Hempstead: Prentice Hall.

Gray, R., Kouhy, R. & Lavers, S. (1995a). Constructing a research database of social and environmental reporting by UK companies. *Accounting, Auditing and Accountability Journal*, 8, (2), 78–101.

Gray, R., Kouhy, R. & Lavers, S. (1995b). Corporate social and environmental reporting: A review of the literature and a longitudinal study of UK disclosure. *Accounting, Auditing and Accountability Journal*, 8, (2), 47–77.

Gray, R. (2000). Current developments and trends in social and environmental auditing. reporting and attestations. A review and comment. *International Journal of Auditing*, 4, 247–268.

Greenpeace (2009). Greenpeace water report for Chinese enterprises. Available at http://www.greenpeace.org/china/ch/

Idowu, S.O. & Filho, W.L. (eds.) (2009). *Global Practices of Corporate Social Responsibility*. Berlin: Springer Verlag.

Imam, S. (2000). Corporate social performance reporting in Bangladesh. *Managerial Auditing Journal*, 15, (3), 133–141.

KPMG (2005). *KPMG International Survey of Corporate Responsibility Reporting 2005*. Amsterdam: KPMG.

KPMG (2008). *KPMG International Survey of Corporate Responsibility Reporting 2008*. Amsterdam: KPMG.

Ma, J. (2008). Scandal will stoke fears of "Made in China" label. *South China Morning Post*, 13 September, A4.

Mayring, P. (2000). Qualitative content analysis. *Forum: Qualitative Social Research*, 1, (2). Available at http://www.qualitative-research.net/fqs-texte/2-00/2-00mayring-e.htm

McCurry, J. (2008). Chinese dumplings poison dozens in Japan. *The Guardian*, 31 January. Available at http://www.guardian.co.uk/world/2008/jan/31/japan.china

National Bureau of Statistics of China (2012). Statistical data. Available at http://www.stats.gov.cn/english/

Oxfam Hong Kong (2008). *Corporate Social Responsibility Survey of Hang Seng Index Constituent Companies*. Hong Kong: Oxfam Hong Kong.

Unerman, J. (2000). Methodological issues reflections on quantification in corporate social reporting content analysis. *Accounting Auditing and Accountability Journal*, 13, (5), 667–680.

United Nations (2007). *International accounting and reporting issues: 2007 review – chapter VIII-2007 review of the implementation status of corporate governance disclosures: Case study of China*. New York; Geneva: UN.

United Nations (2008). *Guidance on Corporate Responsibility Indicators in Annual Reports*. New York; Geneva: UN.

Visser, W., Matten, D., Pohl, M., Tolhurst, N., Bohmer, K., Ghebremariam, A., Hennigfeld, J. & Huble, S.S. (2008). *The A to Z of Corporate Social Responsibility: A Complete Reference Guide to Concepts, Codes and Organisations*. Chichester: Wiley.

WBCSD (1999). *Sustainable development reporting: Striking the balance*. World Business Council for Sustainable Development. Available at htttp://www.wbcsd.org

Wong, L. (2009). Corporate social responsibility in China: Between the market and the search for a sustainable growth development. *Asian Business and Management*, 8, (2), 129–148.

Xinhua (2008). China withdraws 8,300 tons of tainted milk products. *The China Daily*, 31 October. Available at http://www.chinadaily.com.cn/china/2008-10/31/content_7160357.htm

3

Corporate Social Disclosure and Performance Gap: Greenwashing Foxconn's Shenzhen Factories

Carlos Noronha and Stefanie X. Wang

Introduction

Companies are increasingly recognizing the importance of corporate social responsibility (CSR) reporting or corporate social disclosure (CSD), and realizing that in the long run, it may help them increase company value and promote business growth (KPMG, 2008). However, greater acknowledgment of the CSR agenda does not necessarily result in more responsible behaviors (Hess, 2008). As CSD is often used to measure actual performance (Ullmann, 1985), it is essential to assess the quality of CSD and identify if there is any discrepancy between corporate social reporting and actual performance.

Early studies cast doubts on the quality of social disclosure, for the results were mixed. Some studies concluded that there is no relationship between CSD and actual performance (Preston, 1978; Ingram & Frazier, 1980; Wiseman, 1982). Others had found either a positive relationship (Abbott & Monsen, 1979; Clarkson et al., 2008) or a negative relationship (Patten, 2002). Since the inconsistent relationships have been acknowledged, some scholars had developed theories that could be used to explain the discrepancies between CSD and actual performance. Voluntary disclosure theory, raised by Dye (1985) and Verrecchia (1983), predicts a positive relationship between social disclosure and performance. On the contrary, socio-political theory supported by Gray et al. (1995), Lindblom (1993) and Patten (1991; 2002) predicts a negative relationship between social disclosure and performance. In addition, Lyon and Maxwell (2011) recently conducted an economic analysis of the greenwashing theory (Greer & Bruno, 1996), which explains that both good performers and bad performers tend to disclose more positive information while hiding negative information.

As environmental issues are usually the first concern, previous studies mainly focused on the disclosure-performance gap regarding environmental issues. However, the disclosure-performance gap in employee issues has not been discussed in detail. Nevertheless, Font et al. (2012), in a study of the hotel industry, concluded that the disclosure-performance gap with regard to labor policies was small because of the constraint of legislation. However, in a setting like China, where the executive force of law is relatively weak, a considerable disclosure-performance gap can be expected, and many media reports of companies mistreating workers may be found.

In 2010, a string of employee suicides took place at Foxconn's Shenzhen factories, which drew the world's attention to working conditions in Chinese factories. A number of inappropriate managerial practices were reported by the mass media, including that at Foxconn, employees were forced to work an excessive amount of overtime, as long as 83.2 hours per month, while Chinese labor law stipulates a maximum of 36 hours per month. It was also reported that interns were exploited in order to save the cost of hiring regular employees (Chen, 2010; Duhigg & Barboza, 2012). Moreover, the media also reported harsh working conditions and other issues, such as the existence of various deadly health and safety hazards, overcrowded dormitories managed in military style and the exploitation of underage workers (Duhigg & Barboza, 2012).

These reports revealed the terrible working and living conditions in Foxconn, but the factories are often secluded and the public could hardly know what was happening until exposure in media reports. Foxconn is by far the world's largest electronics contract manufacturer and the world's tenth largest employer, with 1.2 million employees worldwide (Alexander, 2012). The tragedies that happened in its Chinese factories are regrettable. As conditions like this are not rare, these cases should be representative. Theoretically, CSR reporting mechanisms should work to prevent irresponsible behaviors. Therefore any discrepancy between disclosure and real performance would become a serious issue that warrants further investigation.

This chapter aims to provide evidence of the existence of a considerable disclosure-performance gap, especially in employee-related issues, in Foxconn. The company's CSR reports will be compared with sources from outside the company, including news and independent investigation reports available in the mass media. Deephouse and Suchman (2008) have indicated that the media is an important stakeholder of companies, providing sources of legitimacy. The findings will provide report users with implications about the credibility of CSR reports. Regulators will also benefit from the findings with regard to improving regulations and laws that protect employees. The results also underline the importance of incorporating stakeholders' engagement mechanisms into the CSD process.

In the following sections, we will first present a review of literature and then an analysis of Foxconn's CSR reports by comparing them with the Global Reporting Initiative (GRI) guidelines and other external information. Finally, conclusions are drawn and some suggestions are provided.

Literature review

Definition of CSR

As widely acknowledged, CSR is a broad topic which covers many concepts and ideas, resulting in many definitions. Until today, there has been no universal definition of CSR in both the corporate and the academic worlds (Dahlsrud, 2008).

According to Carroll (1999), the history of the CSR concept is long and varied, and can be traced back to the 1930s. Formal writings on social responsibility began to spring up in the 1950s, which can be marked as the beginning of the modern era of social responsibility. Carroll (1999) traced the evolution of the CSR construct; and according to him, Bowen's (1953) book *Social Responsibilities of the Businessman* was the landmark publication of the modern period of CSR literature. Bowen's definition was a broad one: "It [CSR] refers to the obligations of businessmen to pursue those policies, to make those decisions, or to follow those lines of action which are desirable in terms of the objectives and values of our society". Since then, various definitions of CSR started to emerge during the 1960s and began to proliferate and became more specific in the 1970s. A famous debate was raised after Friedman's (1970) publication of the article "The social responsibility of business is to increase its profits". He advocated the view that business has the responsibility to maximize shareholders' profits, which was in contrast with Bowen's ideology.

Carroll (1979) offered one of the best known and most often cited definitions: "The social responsibility of business encompasses the economic, legal, ethical, and discretionary expectations that society has of organizations at a given point in time". Dahlsrud (2008) found that the various CSR definitions are primarily congruent. Through an analysis of 37 CSR definitions, he developed five dimensions of CSR, and used the frequency counts from Google to explore how consistently these dimensions were invoked. The five dimensions are environmental, social, economic, stakeholder and voluntary. Among these five, social, stakeholder and economic dimensions were always included in the definitions according to the frequency counts, while the environmental dimension was least mentioned, maybe because this was not included in the earliest CSR definitions.

In conclusion, no matter how many definitions are there, it is certain that today businesses have responsibilities beyond legal requirements and economic considerations.

Recent development of CSD

CSD or CSR reporting has become increasingly prevalent since the mid-1980s. The duty to account for ethical, social and environmental impacts is being increasingly considered and captured by businesses, governments and legislators around the world.

With regard to CSD standards, there are a number of significant organizations involved at the international level. Amongst them, the GRI, formed in 1997, is one of the international, multi-stakeholder organizations that has great influence. The GRI is a non-profit organization that promotes economic, environmental and social sustainability. It provides organizations with a comprehensive reporting framework that is widely used around the world. The GRI reporting framework is intended to serve as a generally accepted framework for reporting on an organization's economic, environmental and social performance.[1] The GRI's Sustainability Reporting Guidelines were first published in 2000. The G4 guideline is currently the most updated version, after four generations of development. According to KPMG (2011), among the companies surveyed, more than 75% of the G250 (Global Fortune 250) companies and 70% of the N100 companies (top 100 companies in selected countries) used GRI guidelines for their reporting.

Furthermore, statistical data and reports on CSD development have been issued periodically. The GRI has issued the *Corporate Register Reporting Award (CRRA) Report* annually since 2008, in which it discloses reports that have won the CRRA and gives a brief analysis of the CSD trend. KPMG has, since 1993, been issuing a global survey of CSD entitled *KPMG International Survey of Corporate Responsibility Reporting*;

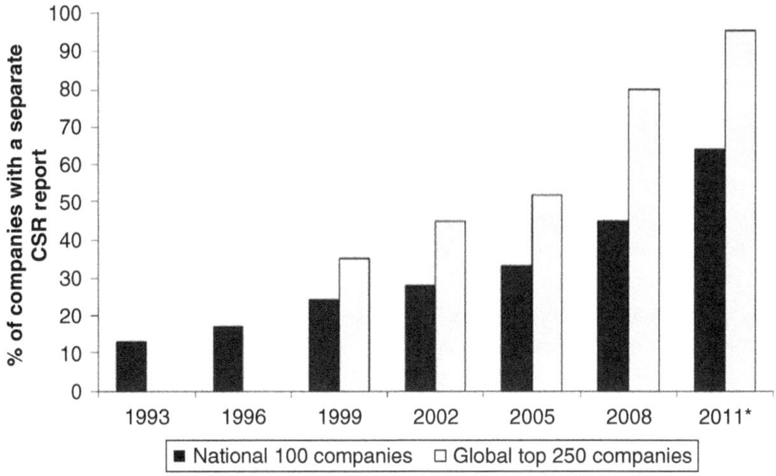

Figure 3.1 CSD trends among N100 and G250 companies (Adapted by authors from KPMG, 1993–2011 International Survey of Corporate Responsibility Reporting)

Note: Due to the increasing trend in integrating reporting, the figures published in 2011 represent total reports, separate and as part of annual reports.

this appears every three years. Two parallel surveys are carried out, one on the top global 250 corporations of Fortune 500 (top global 250) and another on the top 100 companies in selected countries (top national 100).

According to the statistics in KPMG's survey, CSD has been continuously growing ever since 1993, as shown in Figure 3.1.

One of the most significant findings of the surveys is the growth in the number of companies engaging in CSD since 2005, which has soared from about 50% (2005) to 95% (2011) of the top global 250. The top national 100 also almost doubled, from 35% (2005) to 64% (2011) of the total sample (KPMG, 2005; 2008; 2011). Besides, a growing number of companies are looking for external assurance to certify their CSR reports, so as to improve credibility and to deliver more value to management and stakeholders (KPMG, 2011).

Disclosure and performance gap

Regarding the relationship between companies' voluntary CSD and their actual CSR performance, some theories were developed by scholars in prior studies.

Voluntary disclosure theory

The voluntary disclosure theory, supported by Dye (1985) and Verrecchia (1983), predicts a positive relationship between environmental performance and discretionary disclosure. It indicates that companies with superior environmental performance tend to disclose more in order to differentiate themselves from those with inferior performance; while inferior performers tend to disclose less or remain silent. Dye (1985) and Verrecchia (1983) also indicated that superior environmental performers tend to disclose more to create their own "style", making the performance indicators difficult to mimic for inferior performers. Poor environmental performers tend to disclose less in their CSR reports because they want to stay in line with the average level companies and to avoid costs.

Socio-political theory

The socio-political theory (Patten, 1991; 2002) predicts a negative relationship between environmental performance and the level of discretionary disclosure. It indicates that those poor environmental performers with greater exposure to public pressure would be likely to disclose more information on environmental issues. Moreover, Gray et al. (1995) and Lindblom (1993) argued that companies whose social legitimacy is being threatened have more incentives to increase environmental disclosures. Through an empirical study on social disclosure in the annual reports of 128 companies, Patten (1991) found that social disclosures are more significantly related to public pressure measures than to profitability measures.

Greenwashing theory

Lyon and Maxwell (2011) have recently extended the concept of greenwashing by Greer and Bruno (1996), which indicates that no matter how a company performs, in order to create an overly positive corporate image, it tends to selectively disclose positive information but withhold negative information concerning its environmental and social performance. It is a washing away of undesirable information from the CSR report. Although the term is often used to relate to environmental disclosure, in this study we propose greenwashing to include other social issues beyond the environmental concern, including any disclosure strategies that paint a rosy picture of a company's CSR performance.

The above theories indicate that on the whole, discrepancies between disclosure and performance do exist, although there are mixed results in terms of their relationship. The disclosed information is often, to some extent, distorted and is not representative of a company's true performance. Disclosure becomes more of a tool to influence public opinion through the concealment of unpleasant facts, so as to help the company avoid criticism and punishment. This study testifies these theories and draws some conclusions about the reliability of CSD.

Disclosure and performance: Mixed results

Previous studies cast doubts on the quality of social disclosure, and the results were mixed.

Because most CSD are voluntary and unaudited, Ingram and Frazier (1980) used indices for pollution performance ranking devised by the Council on Economic Priorities (CEP) as surrogates of companies' performances. They found that, at best, there is only a weak association between disclosure content and social performance, which may be because of the lack of external monitoring of companies' social disclosures.

Through analyzing the completeness, length and items of information included in voluntary environmental disclosures, Wiseman (1982) checked the disclosed information for various US steel, oil, and paper and pulp companies and compared it with their environmental performance. The conclusion was that corporate environmental disclosure is not related to actual environmental performance.

Freedman and Wasley (1990) investigated 50 US companies in four industries (pulp and paper, steel, oil and electric utilities). The CEP rankings were used again as a surrogate for environmental performance. The results indicate that environmental disclosure is not indicative of the companies' actual environmental performance.

On the other hand, using a sample of 191 companies from the five most polluting industries in the US, Clarkson et al. (2008) found a positive association between environmental performance and the level of discretionary environmental disclosure, which indicates that the better a company performs, the more likely it is to disclose more.

In contrast, Patten (2002) examined the relationship between annual report environmental disclosure and the environmental performance of 131 US companies. The results indicated that, controlling for company size and industry classification, there is a significant negative relationship between performance and disclosure for the sampled companies.

Besides the above mixed results, it can be noticed that among the substantial body of literature on CSD, a special focus has been put on the disclosure of environmental issues (Font et al., 2012). Yet the disclosure of employee issues does not seem to gain enough attention either from the companies or the public.

Workers' working conditions in China

In China, most factories lack independent research and development ability, thus they survive as OEMs (original equipment manufacturers) for many Western developed countries. Being at the bottom of the global supply chain, low labor cost is the only advantage of these factories.

Numerous problems at Chinese factories have been well documented in the international media, such as factory fires, industrial explosions, poisoning from noxious chemicals and an uncountable number of maimings from unguarded industrial machinery (Chan, 1998). Chinese workers are forced to work for long hours for very low wages and are even mandated to sign "life and death" contracts with employers. The problem is particularly serious in the southeast coastal regions and in Taiwan- and South Korea-owned factories (Brown, 2002). There is also fierce competition from other low labor cost countries such as Vietnam and India. If Chinese manufacturers do not get more competitive through low labor costs, these countries will easily replace China in the global supply chain. After the highly publicized Foxconn suicides in 2010, the public is beginning to learn more about the low wages and substandard working conditions in China's electronics manufacturing industry (Price, 2010).

Research method

Objective

The main objective of this study is to identify whether there is any performance- disclosure gap in Foxconn's CSR reports and to assess how much users can rely on these reports. If a performance-disclosure gap exists, we would like to find out where the problem lies and to offer some suggestions.

Method

Since Foxconn issues CSR reports separately and not much related information was found in its annual reports, this study will concentrate on its CSR reports – the Corporate Social and Environmental Responsible (CSER) annual reports.

A content analysis was conducted to analyze Foxconn's CSER reports for the years 2010 and 2011. Content analysis seeks to analyze published information systematically, objectively and reliably. As a technique for gathering and analyzing data, it involves codifying qualitative and quantitative information into categories in order to find patterns in the presentation and reporting of information. (Guthrie & Parker, 1990). It is one of the most widely applied research methods in social accounting and has been found to be empirically valid (Guthrie & Parker, 1990; Gray et al., 1995). In similar studies about disclosure and performance relationship, content analysis was also frequently used as the primary methodology to measure the quality of social disclosure (Preston, 1978; Abbott & Monsen, 1979; Ingram & Frazier, 1980; Wiseman, 1982).

After analyzing the reports, two comparisons were conducted. The first compared Foxconn's CSER reports with the GRI G3.1 guidelines; and the other compared the reports with information obtained from outside Foxconn. The comparisons helped to provide evidence on the existence of a disclosure-performance gap.

As Foxconn's largest manufacturing site worldwide is in Shenzhen and the widely reported serial suicides also happened in factories there, the information collected outside Foxconn is mainly related to the Shenzhen factories. The non-Foxconn sources include media reports and independent investigation reports from various non-governmental organizations (NGOs). These reports delved into the employees' living and working conditions, compensation, health and safety, working hours, and workers' communication with management. For comparison, we focused on the external information of the same time period as that of the Foxconn CSER reports.

Background information on Foxconn

Before proceeding to the analysis, a brief introduction to Foxconn is necessary. Foxconn is a Taiwanese multinational electronics manufacturing company. It is the world's largest maker of electronic components and the largest exporter in Greater China.[2] It is also the world's 10th largest employer, with 1.2 million employees (Alexander, 2012). Foxconn has factories in Asia, Europe and South America, which together assemble around 40% of consumer electronic products globally (Charles & Bradsher, 2012).

According to news reports (Dean & Tsai, 2010; Lau, 2010; Pomfret et al., 2010), from January to November 2010, there were a total of 18 cases of suicidal accidents in Foxconn's Shenzhen factories, which caused 14 deaths and four injuries. These events were widely known as the "Foxconn suicides", and they raised wide public concern about working conditions in China; and Foxconn was labeled as a sweatshop.[3] Many regard the string of suicides as a national landmark event that would eventually promote workers' pay rises and working environment improvements in Chinese factories.

Foxconn started to disclose its CSER report annually from 2008. The information for the 2010 and 2011 reports was prepared and edited by the group's Global SER Committee in accordance with the GRI G3.1 standards. The reports were independently verified by the Longan Law Firm, to ensure proper disclosure in accordance with the standards (Foxconn CSER report, 2010; 2011).

Analysis and discussion

Analysis of Foxconn's CSR reports

2010 CSER report

The structure of Foxconn's 2010 CSER report is shown in Table 3.1.

Foxconn's 2010 CSER report is 76 pages long. It covers employee issues, environmental issues, community, and supply chain management. The 2010 report was released in September 2011. It primarily covers Foxconn's recent developments and the continued growth of the group's operations in Greater China with an overview of the various manufacturing sites worldwide. Except for the group overview and supply chain management sections, the report puts nearly equal weight on employee issues (26%), environmental issues (21%) and community (26%).

In the group overview section, Foxconn recognizes its main stakeholders as employees, customers, suppliers, the community, investors and NGOs. In describing its stakeholder engagement process, Foxconn lists its communication channels with employees, including hotline, forum, letter box, satisfaction survey and counseling. The

Table 3.1 Breakdown of the content of Foxconn's 2010 CSER report (including texts, pictures and graphics)

Content	2010 (pages)	Percentage
Message from the top management	1	1
Foxconn group overview	10	14
Our employees	20	26
Environmental sustainability	16	21
Community and culture	20	26
Supply chain management	8	11
Conclusion	1	1

24 hour counseling service is described to be effective in enhancing employees' health and mental well-being.

Regarding employee issues, Foxconn states that all hiring entities must follow rules that include respect for human rights and prohibition of child labor. It claims to adhere to people-oriented management and fair treatment in compensation, promotion and unemployment of employees. These aspects will be verified later through comparisons with external information.

In the section on employee welfare, Foxconn describes itself as striving to create a healthy and harmonious working atmosphere and putting employees' interest at heart. It lists many employee welfare services, such as free-of-charge laundry, uniforms, internet services and shuttle bus services. It also provides employees with facilities such as multi-purpose gyms, basketball courts, swimming pools and libraries. All kinds of associations related to sports and art are open to all employees. However, it should be noted that these facilities are not all free of charge.

In introducing the labor union, Foxconn does not mention the constitution of the union, workers' participation rate and so on, but only includes the entertainment activities that the union hosted during the year. Two pages of activity pictures might visually impress readers with a caring and responsible image. From the report, it appears that the labor union's main duty is to host entertainment activities and to provide mental health counseling services. These functions make it seem more like an administrative unit than a labor union.

In the section of occupational health and safety, Foxconn claims to have implemented preventive and diagnostic measures to protect employees' health. It is stated that periodic workplace inspections and physical examination for 75,000 employees, which in fact accounts for only 8% of total employees, have been conducted. Foxconn also claims to have conducted 17,000 periodic chemical inspections at locations where noise, dust and volatile organic compounds (VOCs) were likely to have an impact on employees.

Foxconn also appears to care deeply about employees' mental health. In 2010, the company established an employee care center and counseling clinics to provide professional advice and counseling services, to guarantee employees' mental health.

In accordance with the CEO's instructions, Foxconn mandates that all work injuries must be reported within two hours to ensure that adequate attention is given to them. It is stated that the scope of work injuries has been expanded to include all injuries suffered commuting to and from work. In 2010, the work injury ratio per million man hours was 1.48, and Foxconn claims to be striving for a lower ratio of around 1.0.

Generally, the report portrays a responsible company image by presenting a lot of positive pictures, such as employee entertainment activities, charitable activities and awards obtained, which all demonstrate that Foxconn is a company that cares about its employees and wider society. The company is described to be "humanistic" in management of its employees and performed well in its CSR practices. Not a single negative message is reported. Notwithstanding that the 2010 report should cover related events within that year, there is not a word about the 2010 "Foxconn suicides". This could be considered as seriously incomplete reporting, or intentionally withholding unpleasant information.

2011 CSER report

The structure of Foxconn's 2011 CSER report is shown in Table 3.2.

Foxconn's 2011 CSER report is 47 pages long. It covers employee issues, health and safety, community relations, environmental issues and supply chain management. The 2011 report was released in June 2012. The report is a summary of the actions taken by Foxconn during 2011 that relate to economic, social and environmental matters, and provides an overview of other Foxconn locations worldwide.

The 2011 CSER report (47 pages) is only about half the length of the 2010 report (76 pages). In the 2011 report, the sections on employees and health and safety have the most attention and occupy the highest proportion, 29.5% (21% and 8.5%, respectively), of the whole report, which is slightly more than in 2010 (26%). The second highest is community charity events (23%), while the environmental section drops from 21% in 2010 to 13%.

Table 3.2 Breakdown of the content of Foxconn's 2011 CSER report (including texts, pictures and graphics)

Content	2011(pages)	percentage
Message from the Chairman	1	2
About Foxconn Group	9	19
Employees	10	21
Health and safety	4	8.5
Community charity events	11	23
Green development/Low carbon strategy	6	13
Supply chain management	5	10.5
Conclusion	1	2

The reporting scope and content have not changed much from that of 2010, with a certain degree of improvement in clarity and conciseness. As may be seen from the content, Foxconn seems to have provided more welfare for employees than in 2010, as more recreational activities had been held throughout the year. Foxconn also reports the amount of money it spent on various areas of employee welfare. The efforts it put in are impressive, but the numbers are hard to verify.

One issue worthy of note is that the 2011 report discloses detailed information about the labor union. It is stated that during the year the labor union representative had extensive discussions and negotiations with Foxconn and signed a collective bargaining agreement which stipulated employees' wage increases for 2012.

Furthermore, the 2011 report adds a section on employee survey. It is stated that Foxconn conducted surveys which were aimed to gather employee opinions and to search for improvements in areas such as working conditions, living quarters and transportation. Foxconn also hosted regular discussion forums on various topics to guarantee that employees' voices could be heard and appropriate measures could be taken. But there is no disclosure on the survey results and what measures were taken as a result.

This report also does not mention any negative issues. It does not refer to the suicides during the year and an explosion which happened in May 2011, as revealed by the mass media. Concerning the disclosure of negative information, Foxconn does not do any better than in the 2010 report.

Generally, the 2011 content is more concise than that in the 2010 report, and there is more focus on employee welfare and rights. More related information is disclosed, compared with the lengthy descriptions and vague numbers in 2010. As with the 2010 report, the 2011 report does not disclose any negative information, which indicates that the problem of incomplete disclosure still exists.

Compliance level of Foxconn's CSER reports with the GRI guidelines

Compared with the GRI 3.1 guidelines, it is found that the 2010 and 2011 CSER reports are not strictly compliant, although Foxconn claimed to have followed them. The content compared is mainly on employee issues, as Foxconn had been most accused of neglecting this aspect. The non-compliance is shown in Tables 3.3 and 3.4.

According to previous analysis, Foxconn did not disclose any negative information in its CSER reports, which violated GRI's

Table 3.3 Non-compliance of Foxconn's CSER reports with the GRI principles

Reporting principles	Requirements	Non-compliance in Foxconn's CSER reports
Materiality	The information in a report should cover topics and indicators that reflect the organization's significant economic, environmental and social impacts or that would substantively influence the assessments and decisions of stakeholders.	The "Foxconn suicides" had been widely reported and caused very significant social impacts. Moreover, the company might have violated the Chinese labor law as external investigation reports had indicated. However, none of these were disclosed in the reports.
Stakeholder inclusiveness	The reporting organization should identify its stakeholders and explain in the report how it has responded to their reasonable expectations and interests.	No reflection of employees' expectations or responses to their expectations and interests were found in the reports.
Completeness	Coverage of the material topics and indicators and definition of the report boundary should be sufficient to reflect significant economic, environmental and social impacts and enable stakeholders to assess the reporting organization's performance in the reporting period.	No disclosure of negative information could be found although the "Foxconn suicides" had raised public attention and had badly damaged Foxconn's company image. Meanwhile, external investigation reports had indicated that Foxconn was at the risk of being accused of violating the Chinese labor law.
Balance	The report should reflect positive and negative aspects of the organization's performance to enable a reasoned assessment of overall performance.	No disclosure of negative information could be found. Only positive aspects were elaborated in detail.
Timeliness	Reporting occurs on a regular schedule and information is available in time for stakeholders to make informed decisions.	The 2010 report was issued in September of the next year and the 2011 report was issued in June of the next year, which was much later than the annual financial reports, prejudicing the usefulness of the reports.

Table 3.4 Non-compliance of Foxconn's CSER reports with the GRI performance indicators

Aspects	GRI G3.1 performance indicators	Compliance level of 2010 CSER report	Compliance level of 2011 CSER report
Human rights	HR3 Total hours of employee training on policies and procedures concerning aspects of human rights that are relevant to operations, including the percentage of employees trained.	The disclosed labor training courses were mostly work-related technical training. No training courses were on policies and procedures regarding human rights relevant to operations. Compliance level: Non-compliance	The disclosed training courses were even more varied than those of 2010. However, still there were no training courses on policies and procedures regarding human rights relevant to operations. Compliance level: Non-compliance
	HR5 Operations identified in which the right to exercise freedom of association and collective bargaining may be at significant risk, and actions taken to support these rights.	The report mentioned that the labor union had launched many activities, but there was no disclosure on the constitution of the union and operations that may harm the right of freedom of association and collective bargaining. There was also no disclosure of supporting activities. Compliance level: Non-compliance	The report disclosed the number of labor union organizations and the membership rate. But still there was no disclosure of operations that may harm the right of freedom of association and collective bargaining and that of any supporting activities. Compliance level: Non-compliance
Labor practices and decent work	LA7 Rates of injury, occupational diseases, lost days and absenteeism, and total number of work-related fatalities by region.	The report vaguely mentioned a number of reports of occupational hazards, but no details as required by the indicator could be found. Compliance level: Non-compliance	The report mentioned the percentage of work-related injury cases, but did not fully disclose the rates as required by the indicators. Compliance level: Non-compliance
	LA10 Average hours of training per year per employee by employee category.	The report disclosed the total training hours and the number of attendees of each type of courses, but did not disclose the average hours per employee by employee category. Compliance level: Partial compliance	The report disclosed the total training hours and the number of attendees, but still did not disclose the average hours per employee by employee category. Compliance level: Partial-compliance

principle of "balance", which requires that both positive and negative aspects of organizations' performance should be disclosed. Also, the principles of "materiality" and "completeness" state that the report should cover topics that reflect the organization's significant social impacts. Since the "Foxconn suicides" had caught wide public attention, which had already badly influenced the company's image, and Foxconn was also at risk of being accused of violating Chinese labor law, the non-disclosure of these aspects clearly violates the GRI principles.

Under the current reporting environment in China, CSD is not mandatory. Companies disclose their CSR information only voluntarily and the quality of CSR reports cannot be guaranteed. As the GRI reporting guidelines are to some extent flexible, Foxconn could choose different application levels according to the actual situation. Therefore, the reporting content depends to a large extent on management discretion. It is most likely that when there are negative events at the company, management would choose not to disclose such information.

In addition, it was claimed that both the 2010 and 2011 reports were independently verified by the Longan Law Firm, which assured that they were properly disclosed according to the GRI guidelines. Yet in this case, the deficiencies of the reports shows that third-party assurance of CSR reports does not work well, given the management's discretion as to what should be disclosed and what should not. Thus, even with third-party assurance, the quality of reports cannot be guaranteed. Furthermore, the third party may also have problems, such as a lack of independence and difficulty in verifying the completeness of reports.

Information obtained from external sources

The URG investigation reports (2010 & 2012)

After Foxconn's breaking news of suicide events, a research group consisting of more than 100 students and teachers from 20 universities in mainland China, Hong Kong and Taiwan, including Peking University, Tsinghua University, National Taiwan University and Chinese University of Hong Kong, voluntarily conducted an investigation on Foxconn's factories in mainland China from July 2010 to January 2012. The investigation group will be collectively called the URG (University Research Group) hereafter. The URG has released three reports: the 2010 and 2012 reports related to Foxconn's Shenzhen factories and are referred to in this study.

The field investigation involved Foxconn's 19 factories in 14 cities. Owing to Foxconn's unwillingness to cooperate, the investigation could not be carried out inside the factories, and thus was undertaken in communities outside the factories or in workers' homes. In these environments, workers could freely express their feelings without pressure from Foxconn. To gather data, the URG used questionnaires as well as interviews, obtaining 2,409 valid questionnaires (Shenzhen and Kunshan factories) and more than 500 interviews. Moreover, 20 investigation team members worked in the factories for a few days to experience life there, and acquired a lot of first-hand information. The reports can be downloaded from the internet.[4,5]

The FLA investigation report (2012)

The Fair Labor Association (FLA) is a collaborative group of universities, civil society organizations and socially responsible companies that are dedicated to protecting workers' rights around the world. It is an international organization with headquarters in Washington, DC.[6]

On 26 January 2012, a report in *The New York Times* entitled "In China, human costs are built into an iPad" sparked the media's interests in the sweatshops behind Apple. As a major supplier for Apple in China, Foxconn was called the "Fear Factory". Under great pressure from the public, Apple joined the FLA and agreed to allow the organization to conduct a thorough investigation of its suppliers, starting with Foxconn's three factories in China.

The FLA's nearly month-long investigation revealed serious and pressing non-compliance with the FLA's Workplace Code of Conduct as well as Chinese labor law. The FLA observed at least 50 issues related to the code of conduct and the labor law, including health and safety, worker integration and communication, and wages and working hours (FLA report, 2012).

The FLA investigation report was released in March 2012. Although the time period does not match Foxconn's CSER reports under study, the unprecedented inspection scale has a high reference value. The FLA report can be downloaded from the FLA's official website.[7]

The SACOM report (2011)

Students and Scholars against Corporate Misbehavior (SACOM) is an NGO based in Hong Kong. It was founded in June 2005 by students, who were later joined by other cultural and labor activists. The organization's main goal is to monitor and campaign against corporate misbehaviors that violate workers' rights, health, safety, welfare and dignity in China.[8]

From March to April 2011, SACOM researchers interviewed about 120 Foxconn workers in Shenzhen, Chengdu and Chongqing. The majority of the interviewees were frontline workers, and about ten of them were frontline supervisors and middle managers. A report entitled *Foxconn and Apple Fail to Fulfill Promises: Predicaments of Workers after the Suicides* was released on 6 May 2011. Another report, *iSlave behind the iPhone: Foxconn Workers in Central China*, was released on 24 September 2011. The reports can be downloaded from the internet.[9]

The CLW report (2011)

China Labor Watch (CLW) is a New York-based NGO that was founded in 2000. Through research, advocacy and legal assistance, CLW seeks to help China's workers to become more informed of their rights and more empowered to realize those rights.[10]

From October 2010 to June 2011, through an investigation of ten global brand supplier electronics factories, CLW discovered multiple violations of China's labor law. The ten electronics factories that CLW investigated were all located in Guangdong and Jiangsu provinces. In total, 408 workers were interviewed on-site and off-site. After the interviews in March 2011, CLW remained in communication with the workers and revisited the factories in April and May 2011 to conduct follow-up interviews. All of the workers interviewed reflected on the widespread problems throughout all the factories. The report was released on 12 July 2011 and can be downloaded from the internet.[11]

News reports

Besides the investigation reports, news reports also revealed many problems. *The Southern Weekend* sent an intern to work in a Foxconn factory for a month, and he wrote about the workers' lack of connection in such a giant factory, with its transient population:

> When the workers are desperate to improve their situation in life, they rarely know how to. There are hundreds of thousands of workers but they find that they come to resemble each other. Dormitory mates on different shifts barely get a chance to talk to each other, and even if you have slept in a dorm for a few months you might not know the name of your room mates.
>
> (Liu, 2010)

In 2011, there were news reports of an explosion caused by aluminum dust in the iPad assembly plant in Foxconn, which caused three deaths and 16 injuries (Areddy & Kane, 2011). A report in *The New York Times* also pointed out that workers in Apple's Chinese suppliers often labor in harsh conditions. They worked excessive overtime and child labor also existed (Duhigg & Barboza, 2012).

Comparing external reports with Foxconn's CSER reports

In this section, the problems most frequently mentioned by the external reports introduced above are listed. The relevant parts of Foxconn's 2010 and 2011 CSER reports are then selected and compared with those problems, so as to assess the credibility of these reports.

Excessive working hours

During peak production, the average number of working hours per month at Foxconn factories often exceeded the Chinese legal limit of number of overtime working hours per month. There were also periods in which some employees worked more than seven days in a row without the required minimum 24-hour break per week (FLA report, 2012). The total number of overtime working hours commonly exceeded 100 hours per month before the suicide events. Overtime hours were still as high as 80 per month after the events, which is much more than the 36-hour limit laid down in Chinese labor law (URG report, 2010). In Shenzhen, workers revealed that they usually have 50 to 80 hours of overtime a month, and the number of overtime hours was subject to the production plan. (SACOM report, 2011). All of the factories' overtime was between 36 and 160 hours per month. No factory was found to be in compliance with China's labor law, which states that overtime should not exceed 36 hours each month (CLW report, 2011).

Comparison with 2010 and 2011 CSER reports (overtime)

The 2010 CSER report introduced the company's employee welfare, training, and health and safety issues, but did not disclose any information on the excessive overtime problem. The discrepancy between disclosure and reported facts revealed that the company intentionally failed to disclose negative information. Similarly, the 2011 report did not disclose any related information about excessive overtime, even after the suicide events.

Health and safety problems

The assessors identified numerous issues related to inconsistent policies, procedures and practices. A considerable number of workers felt generally insecure regarding their health and safety. The issue of aluminum dust was of particular concern, as this was the cause of an explosion at the Chengdu factory (FLA report, 2012). In-depth interviews in hospitals with ten workers suffering from industrial injuries revealed that industrial injuries were often hidden and settled privately. This was because of Foxconn's regulation on "Three-level guilt by association" (if a work injury had been reported, from the responsible line supervisor up to the third level superior managers would be collectively punished). Industrial injuries were often concealed by grass-root management departments, and problems were often settled privately. In these circumstances, workers often could not get full compensation, as they should have (URG report, 2010). The workers commonly reflected on the severe environment in their plants, with the most mentioned issues including high temperature, loud noises, harmful gas and dust, not to mention the physical damage caused by intense work and fixed poses (URG report, 2010). In 2011, Foxconn had a deadly explosion in its Chengdu plant, which caused three deaths and 16 injuries. This may have resulted from combustible dust in a polishing workshop (Areddy & Kane, 2011). No face masks were provided. The workshop was extremely loud, but workers were not supplied with earplugs. Workers were likely to be exposed to significant radiation, as their skin was very dry and itchy. There were no first-aid kits in the workshop. Occupational injuries were very frequent (CLW report, 2011). One year after the suicides, conditions had not improved much. Workers still lacked protection, and they were not well informed about the chemicals in use (SACOM, 2011).

Comparison with 2010 and 2011 CSER reports (health and safety)

The 2010 report claimed that Foxconn had put much effort into implementing preventive and diagnostic measures at their factories in China, to ensure that the potential risks of disease were properly managed and employees' healthcare was preserved. It also continued to strengthen its policy on healthcare, having heightened the monitoring of radiation equipment and management by conducting periodic inspections and data collection. Foxconn had distributed 5,210 radiation dosage cards to employees, conducted 21,000 workplace inspections, provided physical examinations for 75,000 employees (8% of total workers), and achieved 100% on-the-job training on occupational health. No mention of the explosion was to be found in the 2011 report, although Foxconn declared that it always made safety a top priority. Six firefighting systems had been built and a lot of money had been invested in installing testing equipment necessary for conducting safety inspections. Foxconn's CEO even announced that the company's mission was to strive for "100% safety and zero accident".

Awful industrial relations

Workers were largely alienated, in fact or perception. Committees may not be representative of the workers, because management nominates candidates for election. As a result, committees did not represent those who needed representation, but were dominated by representatives of the management (FLA report, 2012). On 25 May 2010, Foxconn asked workers to sign a form in which they agreed to ask no more than legal compensation from the company for injuries not caused by the employer, including those from suicide attempts (Hille & Kwong, 2010). Some disciplinary practices for workers who made mistakes were subject to abuse and insult. Punitive measures included workers being required to write a report of at least 500 words and post the report with their photo on the wall, and workers being required to stand still for 30 minutes to four hours (CLW, 2011). After the series of suicide events, Foxconn quickly launched an employee caring center with a "24-hour reporting system". This caring center was officially a department that assisted employees who had emotional problems and provided counseling services. However, the investigation group found that the 24-hour hotline was actually used to report "problem workers". "Problem workers" were put under strict monitoring. Once they started to behave slightly unusually, they were usually forced to resign within 24 hours, so that the situation was brought back under control (URG, 2010). According to statistics, 27.9% of the workers reflected on the experience of being scolded by managers and security guards, and 34.7% had been insulted (for example, through a "daily check-up") by managers and security guards. In Foxconn, the management system was rigidly hierarchical and workers were severely oppressed, so that they bore the maximum pressure and the heaviest workload. Thus conflicts often happened at the bottom of the hierarchy and were concealed by the managers (URG, 2010).

Comparison between 2010 and 2011 CSER reports (industrial relations)

The 2010 report mentioned that Foxconn fostered a harmonious work environment that promoted "health, stability, and development", and that the company had provided many services for employees, frequently hosting various kinds of activities to ensure an enjoyable working environment and work-life balance. The 2011 report disclosed various recreational activities for employees that were hosted by Foxconn, and the money spent. Festive and birthday gifts were given to employees.

Inequitable compensation and social insurance

Though Foxconn's wages were above the Chinese average and legal minimum, the assessment found that 14% of the workers may not receive fair compensation for unscheduled overtime. The assessors discovered that this was only paid in 30-minute increments, which means that 29 minutes of overtime work resulted in no pay and 58 minutes resulted in only one unit of overtime pay (FLA report, 2012). Reports of increasing salaries were a lie. In Shenzhen factories, the basic salary was RMB 1,200, with an extra food and housing allowance paid separately. After Foxconn promised to raise the basic wage, these allowances were cancelled and were incorporated into the basic salary. The new salary of RMB 1,590 was actually the same amount that workers used to get, yet officially the basic wage had risen by 33%. Moreover, there were problems with miscalculation of wages (often underpayment) and delayed payslips (SACOM report, 2011). Formal resignation was hard for workers. During the probation period, workers were required to submit resignation requests three days in advance, with the authorized signature of their line leaders, directors and managers. After the probation period, a resignation request had to be submitted 30 days in advance in writing. It was very difficult to resign during the peak season because line leaders and managers intervened to prevent the completion of the process. If workers were unable to resign through the standard procedure, they were forced to quit without pay (CLW, 2011).

Comparison with 2010 and 2011 CSER reports (compensation)

The 2010 report claimed that Foxconn adhered to its policy of people-oriented management and fair treatment in the recruitment, promotion, compensation, training, unemployment and retirement of employees. No compensation-related issues were mentioned. Similarly, the 2011 report claimed that the company adhered to a policy of fair compensation and further disclosed the pay rise in 2011, mentioning that Foxconn had increased workers' compensation in mainland China, and since then had exceeded the minimum pay rate for each region.

Conclusion and suggestions

Conclusion

This chapter has presented a case study of Foxconn, aiming at providing evidence of the existence of disclosure-performance gap in the company's CSER reports, mainly on employee issues. Foxconn's 2010 and

2011 CSER reports were analyzed and were compared with the principles and indicators of GRI G3.1 as well as independent external reports and news reports obtained from the mass media. It could be concluded that Foxconn's CSR reporting did not match its actual performance.

In this study, the voluntary disclosure theory cannot be used as testimony, because the theory is about the behaviors of "good performers", while Foxconn is obviously not one of those. The socio-political theory might serve to explain the tiny improvement in Foxconn's 2011 CSER report compared with its 2010 report. Yet the improvement was not significant. According to the results, the greenwashing theory appears to be the best explanation of Foxconn's problems. The theory posits that no matter how a company performs, in order to create an overly positive corporate image, the company tends to selectively disclose positive information but withhold negative information of its environmental and social performance. Foxconn's behavior is consistent with this theory. Two major problems in the Foxconn CSER reports are listed below.

Incomplete disclosure

Problems such as excessive working hours, health and safety problems, awful industrial relations and inequitable compensation and social insurance as revealed by the external reports were either not disclosed or were glorified in Foxconn's CSER reports. The reports did not even disclose suicide events that had already caused material social impacts and had damaged the company's reputation. Foxconn did not disclose any negative information, while positive information was elaborated in great detail. And as external reports indicated, the company may have violated one or more Chinese laws. In view of the conservatism principle, Foxconn did not care to disclose these significant corporate hazards to its stakeholders at all.

Non-compliance with requirements of reporting guidelines

Although the reports had been verified by a third party, the content was not compliant with the reporting guidelines that were claimed to have been followed. The reports violated the principles of "materiality", "balance" and "competence", which contributed to the incomplete disclosure problem. The reports were also found not to disclose information as the performance indicators had required, leading to non-disclosure or vaguely disclosed sensitive information.

Suggestions

Adams (2004) stated that the main problem of the current disclosure-performance gap is the lack of competency. Foxconn is no exception. In China, the sophistication and the executive force of law leave much room for improvement. If the legal system is not transparent and strong in administration, labor abuse will continue to prevail. Directives from the central government to strictly comply with the law and to carry out CSR are the primary driving force to improve the situation.

It was mentioned earlier that it is now a given for both companies and the public that businesses have responsibilities beyond earning profits. Some scholars advocate that companies should disclose CSR information voluntarily. In mainland China, where the legal and institutional factors are not mature (Claessens & Fan, 2002), mandatory CSD would serve to improve reporting quality. Disclosure of certain issues and indices can be made compulsory by promulgating new laws and regulations. Penalty for violation should also be properly institutionalized, so as to prevent companies from hiding unsavory information.

Stakeholder engagement mechanism could be enhanced and incorporated into both the corporate governance system and the reporting process, so that the interests of stakeholders can be protected and their voices and appeals can be heard. Since the company itself is the reporting entity, the disclosed content should seek for stakeholders' approval in order to guarantee appropriateness and reliability.

Finally, third-party assurance should play a much more significant role. Proper principles for CSD audits should be developed to provide valid support for reliable assurance. The introduction of audit procedures and techniques from advanced international agencies, such as those from the "Big 4" audit firms and standards agencies such as SGS, is vital in ensuring valid and reliable assurance of CSR reports.

At the time of finalizing this chapter, the 2012 *Social and Environmental Responsibility (SER) Annual Report* was published, in July 2013. Consistent with past practices, Foxconn did not include any negative information in the report.

Appendix: Details of the "Foxconn suicides"

Between January and November 2010, a string of suicides took place at Foxconn's Chinese factories, with an estimation of 18 employees attempting suicide and resulting in 14 deaths. The clustered suicides attracted media attention and public concern about Foxconn's employment practices. The controversy brought about many controversies in China, with the media and police investigating the causes of the suicides. Foxconn's customers, Apple, Dell, HP and many more, were also under pressure to investigate the situation. This table shows the list of employees who committed suicide in 2010:

Name	Gender	Age	Suicide attempt date	Description	Status
Rong Bo	Male	19	8 January 2010	Jumped off building	Deceased
Ma Xiangqian	Male	19	23 January 2010	Jumped off building	Deceased
Li	Male	28	11 March 2010	Jumped off building	Deceased
Tian Yu	Female	17	17 March 2010	Jumped off building	Paralyzed
Li Wei	Male	23	23 March 2010	Jumped off building	Deceased
Lau	Male	23	29 March 2010	Jumped off building	Unknown
Rao Shuqin	Female	18	6 April 2010	Jumped off building	Survived
Ms. Ling	Female	18	7 April 2010	Jumped off building	Deceased
Lu Xin	Male	24	6 May 2010	Jumped off building	Deceased
Zhu Chenming	Female	24	11 May 2010	Jumped off building	Deceased
Liang Chao	Male	21	14 May 2010	Jumped off building	Deceased
Nan Gan	Male	21	21 May 2010	Jumped off building	Deceased
Li Hai	Male	19	25 May 2010	Jumped off building	Deceased
He	Male	23	26 May 2010	Jumped off building	Unknown
Chen	Male	25	27 May 2010	Suicide	Deceased
Liu	Male	18	20 July 2010	Jumped off building	Deceased
Liu	Female	23	23 August 2010	Jumped off building	Deceased
Unknown	Male	23	5 November 2010	Jumped off building	Deceased

Source: URG investigation reports 2010.

Notes

1. https://www.globalreporting.org/Information/about-gri/Pages/default.aspx
2. http://www.foxconn.com./GroupProfile_En/GroupProfile.html
3. Details available in the Appendix
4. http://it.sohu.com/20101009/n275489839.shtml
5. http://tech.sina.com.cn/it/2012-03-31/09356900441.shtml
6. http://www.fairlabor.org/about-us
7. http://www.fairlabor.org/report/foxconn-investigation-report
8. http://www.sacom.net/
9. http://sacom.hk/wp-content/uploads/2011/09/20110924-islave-behind-the-iphone.pdf
10. http://www.chinalaborwatch.org/
11. chinalaborwatch.org/pdf/20110712.pdf

References

Abbott, W.F. & Monsen, R.J. (1979). On the measurement of corporate social responsibility: Self-reported disclosure as a method of measuring corporate social involvement. *Academy of Management Journal*, 22, 501–515.

Adams, A.C. (2004). The ethical, social and environmental reporting-performance portrayal gap. *Accounting, Auditing and Accountability Journal*, 17, (5), 731–757.

Alexander, R. (2012). Which is the world's biggest employer? *BBC News*, 20 March. Available at http://www.bbc.co.uk/news/magazine-17429786

Areddy, J.T. & Kane, Y.I. (2011). Explosion kills 3 at Foxconn plant. *The Wall Street Journal*, 21 May. Available at http://online.wsj.com/article/SB10001424052748704816604576335262591187804.html

Bowen, H.R. (1953). *Social Responsibilities of the Businessman*. New York: Harper and Row.

Brown, G.D. (2002). The global threats to workers' health and safety on the job. *Social Justice*, 29, (3), 12–25.

Carroll, A.B. (1979). A three-dimensional conceptual model of corporate social performance. *Academy of Management Review*, 4, 497–505.

Carroll, A.B. (1999). Corporate social responsibility: Evolution of a definitional construction. *Business and Society*, 38, (3), 268–295.

Chan. A. (1998). Labor standards and human rights: The case of Chinese workers under market socialism. *Human Rights Quarterly*, 20, (4), 886–904.

Charles, D. & Bradsher, K. (2012). How the US lost out on iPhone work. *The New York Times*, 21 January. Available at http://www.nytimes.com/2012/01/22/business/apple-america-and-a-squeezed-middle-class.html?pagewanted=all&_r=0

Chen, H. (2010). Survey accuses Foxconn of more labor law violations. *China Daily*, 9 October. Available at http://www.chinadaily.com.cn/china/2010-10/09/content_11389573.htm

China Labor Watch. (2011). *Tragedies of Globalization: The Truth behind Electronics Sweatshops*. New York: China Labor Watch.

Claessens, S. & Fan, J.P.H. (2002). Corporate governance in Asia: A survey. *International Review of Finance*, 3, (2), 71–103.

Clarkson, M.P., Li, Y., Richardson, D.G. & Vasvari, P.F. (2008). Revisiting the relation between environmental performance and environmental disclosure: An empirical analysis. *Accounting, Organizations and Society*, 33, 303–327.

Dahlsrud, A. (2008). How corporate social responsibility is defined: An analysis of 37 definitions. *Corporate Social Responsibility and Environmental Management*, 15, (1), 1–13.

Dean, J. & Tsai, T.I. (2010). Apple, HP to examine Asian supplier after string of deaths at factory. *The Wall Street Journal*, 29 May. Available at http://online.wsj.com/article/SB10001424052748704026204575267603576594936.html

Deephouse, D.L. & Suchman, M. (2008). Legitimacy in organizational institutionalism. In: Greenwood, R., Oliver, C., Suddaby, R. & Salin-Andersson, K. (eds.) *The SAGE Handbook of Organizational Institutionalism*. London: Sage.

Duhigg, C. & Barboza, D. (2012). In China, human costs are built into an iPad. *The New York Times*, 25 January. Available at http://www.nytimes.com/2012/01/26/business/ieconomy-apples-ipad-and-the-human-costs-for-workers-in-china.html?pagewanted=all

Dye, R.A. (1985). Disclosure of nonproprietary information. *Journal of Accounting Research*, 23, 123–145.

Font, X., Walmsley, A., Cogotti, S., McCombes, L. & Häusler, N. (2012). Corporate social responsibility: The disclosure performance gap. *Tourism Management*, 33, 1544–1553.

Freedman, M. & Wasley, C. (1990). The association between environmental performance and environmental disclosure in annual reports and 10 Ks. *Advances in Public Interest Accounting*, 3, 183–193.

Friedman, M. (1970). The social responsibility of business is to increase its profits. *The New York Times Magazine*. September, 13, (32–33), 122, 126.

Gray, R., Kouhy, R. & Lavers, S. (1995). Corporate social and environmental reporting: A review of the literature and a longitudinal study of UK disclosure. *Accounting, Auditing and Accountability Journal*, 8, (2), 47–77.

Greer, J. & Bruno, K. (1996). *Greenwash: The Reality behind Corporate Environmentalism*. New York: Apex.

Guthrie, J. & Parker, L.D. (1990). Corporate social disclosure practice: A comparative international analysis. *Advances in Public Interest Accounting*, 3, 159–175.

Hess, D. (2008). The three pillars of corporate social reporting as new governance regulation: Disclosure, dialogue, and development. *Business Ethics Quarterly*, 18, (4), 447–487.

Hille, K. & Kwong, R. (2010). Apple, HP and Dell investigate Foxconn. *Financial Times*, 27 May. Available at http://www.ftchinese.com/story/001032811/en

Ingram, R.W. & Frazier, K.B. (1980). Environmental performance and corporate disclosure. *Journal of Accounting Research*, 18, 614–622.

KPMG (2005). *International Survey of Corporate Responsibility Reporting*. Amsterdam: KPMG.

KPMG (2008). *International Survey of Corporate Responsibility Reporting*. Amsterdam: KPMG.

KPMG (2011). *International Survey of Corporate Responsibility Reporting*. Amsterdam: KPMG.

Lau, M. (2010). Struggle for Foxconn girl who wanted to die. *South China Morning Post*, 19 July. Available at http://www.scmp.com/article/733389/struggle-foxconn-girl-who-wanted-die

Lindblom, C. (1993). The implications of organizational legitimacy for corporate social performance disclosure. Paper presented at the Critical Perspectives on Accounting Conference, New York.

Liu, Z.Y. (2010). Youth and fate accompanied with the machine: 28-day latent Foxconn notes (in Chinese). *Southern Weekend*, 25 May. Available at http://www.infzm.com/content/44881

Lyon, T.P. & Maxwell, J.W. (2011). Greenwash: Corporate environmental disclosure under threat of audit. *Journal of Economics and Management Strategy*, 20, (1), 3–41.

Patten, D.M. (1991). Exposure, legitimacy and social disclosure. *Journal of Accounting and Public Policy*, 10, 297–308.

Patten, D.M. (2002). The relation between environmental performance and environmental disclosure: A research note. *Accounting, Organizations and Society*, 27, 763–773.

Pomfret, J., Huang, Y. & Kelvin, S. (2010). Foxconn worker plunges to death at China plant: Report. *Reuters*, 5 Nov. Available at http://www.reuters.com/article/2010/11/05/us-china-foxconn-death-idUSTRE6A41M920101105

Preston, L.E. (1978). Analyzing corporate social performance: Methods and results. *Journal of Contemporary Business*, 7, 135–150.

Price, R. (2010). Chinese factory deaths and low wages: Who is to blame and how to fix the problems? *Human Rights Quarterly*, 20, (4), 886–904.

Ullmann, A.A. (1985). Data in search of a theory: A critical examination of the relationships among social performance, social disclosure and economic performance of US firms. *Academy of Management Review*, 10, (3), 540–557.

Verrecchia, R.E. (1983). Discretionary disclosure. *Journal of Accounting and Economics*, 5, 179–194.

Wiseman, J. (1982). An evaluation of environmental disclosures made in corporate annual reports. *Accounting, Organizations and Society*, 7, (1), 53–63.

4
Corporate Social Disclosure: The Case of China's Milk Product Industry

Carlos Noronha and Katy W.P. Kong

Introduction

China's milk production has undergone rapid growth over the past three decades. Several factors have contributed to this expansion. Firstly, the Chinese government has taken a variety of measures to promote dairy production and consumption. These included the introduction of a school lunch program that provided subsidized milk for schoolchildren, aiming to promote milk consumption and production in the rural areas; provision of technical and financial support to farmers, to improve dairy farming (Wang et al., 2010); and the introduction of the so-called Grassland Law, which was enacted to protect and make rational use of grasslands and to improve the ecological environment and biodiversity of animals (Muhammad et al., 2009). Secondly, urban residents have gradually developed a preference for dairy products, owing to a general increase in wealth and recognition of the nutritional value brought by such products (Wang & Zhang, 2004). In addition, China's dairy industry is dominated by over 500,000 farm households, with each family having one to five cows. More and more farm households are eager to profit from the supply of milk, leading to the expansion of the dairy farming business (Lohmar et al., 2009). Thirdly, international organizations, foreign governments and multinational enterprises have provided technical and financial investment to China in order to support the dairy industry. For instance, the European Union has helped to purchase dairy cows and enhance dairy processing plants in Gansu province (Crook, 1998). Finally, following China's participation in the

World Trade Organization in 2001, China's economy has grown considerably, with major policy changes for agricultural products. This has also led to a significant reduction in the number of barriers for foreign retailers who wish to commence or expand operations in China (Lohmar et al., 2009).

KPMG's (2008: 4) report on the milk and dairy market in China revealed that total dairy consumption in 2006 had reached 19 million tons, rising 10% annually from 14 million tons in 2003. The report forecasted that consumption would surpass 25 million tons by 2008 and 33 million tons by 2010.

Recent data from the Commonwealth Bank of Australia (2013) indicated that Chinese per capita consumption for fluid milk, butter and whole milk powder has grown 5% per year since 2010. China has also contributed 33% to global fresh milk consumption growth, 36% to global skim milk powder growth and 80% to whole milk powder growth since 2010.

According to KPMG (2008: 6), China's milk product market was dominated by four major dairy enterprises which represented 44% of the market in 2006, compared with 40% in 2003. These enterprises, namely Mengniu, Yili, Sanlu and Bright Dairy, held 16%, 15%, 8% and 5% market share in China, respectively. The remaining market share (56%) was divided among over 1,000 small-scale dairy companies, mostly run by low-income residents in rural and less developed areas.

China's melamine milk scandal in 2008

In September 2008, the contamination of Chinese dairy products with melamine was exposed after incidences of kidney problems among infants who had consumed Sanlu formula milk. After subsequent discoveries of melamine-contaminated exported powdered milk, the scandal had a tremendous impact on Chinese dairy exports. The Sanlu Group incident was initially revealed by the Chinese government and was followed by investigations of existing problems in 21 other enterprises (BBC News, 2010), including Mengniu and Yili. By December 2008, at least six infants had died and over 290,000 other victims had suffered from sickness (Zaobao, 2008). In spite of the different levels of criminal prosecutions of local government officials, China faced boycotts of its dairy product exports by at least 25 countries (ESCAP, 2009). The scandal alerted the world to the general food safety level of China's exports.

In 2000, the government had established the Inspection Exemption certification program in order to reduce the cost of monitoring food safety standards in China. Passing quality and safety inspections three consecutive times permitted enterprises to be certified with Inspection Exemption Status. As a result, the majority of high market share enterprises had escaped regular food safety inspections, thus increasing the risk of problems in this regard (Xinhua News Agency, 2008).

To recover from the international impact of these food scandals and to regain its reputation for food safety control, the Chinese government implemented a set of recovery actions (Dobson, 2008). These included reinforcing food product recall policies, offering free medication to affected infants and children, allowing transparency in cooperation with third-party countries for joint investigations, and inspections of food production lines and outlets, as well as establishing a series of safety standards, such as food safety certification programs, and tightening up inspection and testing (BBC News, 2010).

Corporate social disclosure and organizational legitimacy

According to Deegan (2002), legitimacy theory can be understood via the concept of social contract, which suggests that the society that provides resources to any organization will expect that benefits should be returned by such organizations to the society, and that more responsibilities beyond mere legal requirements should be assumed by them. The organizations are expected to proactively engage in social and environmental concerns in order to ensure their survival in society (Palazzo & Scherer, 2006).

Corporate social disclosure (CSD) refers to the provision of information about a particular organization that may embrace any subject in any medium to any parties, with the aim of providing improved accountability to a wide array of stakeholders on environmental and societal issues (Gray et al., 1995). CSD has been used by companies to gain organizational legitimacy and this has been investigated in the accounting literature. Companies have been employing CSD as a strategy to reduce the impact of negative media reports (Deegan et al., 2002), to alleviate corporate image (Deegan et al., 2000), to influence the government in implementing disadvantageous regulations (Moerman & Van der Laan, 2005) and to restore a company's legitimacy after a critical incident (Milne & Patten, 2002; Campbell et al., 2003). Furthermore, Patten (1992) indicated that when companies face threat to their organizational legitimacy, their level of CSD increases.

Objective

In fact, before the scandals, the Chinese government had not established any food safety laws (FSLs). There are also no mandatory requirements that govern the CSR system for the dairy industry in China. The existing CSR system practiced by enterprises is solely dependent on their own initiatives.

The objective of this study is to examine the CSR activities and CSD of China's four major dairy enterprises during the period when the 2008 milk scandals were disclosed to the public. The study aims to explore whether such enterprises disclosed more of their CSR activities in order to promote a positive image during the scandals and whether negative news was disclosed responsibly to the public. We are also interested in exploring how Chinese milk enterprises perceived and utilized CSD as a strategic means for achieving certain corporate objectives.

This study has employed a qualitative content analysis, by examining the CSR sections or related content in the annual reports, stand-alone CSR reports and CSD on the official websites of the four enterprises. The study was conducted for the period 2006–2012.

The coverage of CSR activities was also compared against news reports related to the scandals taken from selected media channels. The aim is to discover the significance of this news for these enterprises, and whether it may lead them to construct particular behavioral patterns in terms of CSD. We wish to assess whether these enterprises reported the facts of the news or increased their CSD. The disclosure patterns were analyzed according to two recognized international CSR frameworks, namely the Triple Bottom Line (TBL) and the ISO 26000.

In this study, it is shown that the milk enterprises may adopt strategies according to the legitimacy theory, such as delivering a desirable contribution to society in a socially responsible manner for the purpose of ensuring their survival and growth. Furthermore, in order to redirect the stakeholders' attention from the negativity of scandals, these enterprises may perform many other socially desirable actions beyond mere product safety and health issues. Thus, this study has included the whole package of dimensions under the TBL and ISO 26000 in order to provide a full picture of their socially responsible behaviors, such as employee welfare, code of ethics, innovations, energy-saving, education and philanthropy.

Next, an overview of recent CSR development in the China milk product industry is presented. Then, the methodology of the study is explained and results of the content analysis are compared with the TBL and ISO 26000 frameworks as well as with news reports. Finally, a discussion of the significance of such CSR actions in relation to the milk scandals is provided.

Overview of CSR

Definition of CSR

Gray et al. (1987: ix) define social accounting (including CSD) as the process of communicating the social and environmental effects of organizations' economic actions to particular interest groups within society and to society at large. Pratten and Mashat (2009: 312) indicate that CSR information should illustrate how an organization relates to its stakeholders and would commonly include environment and energy-related disclosure, community involvement-related disclosure; workplace-related information; product and consumer relations. Generally speaking, there are three complementary dimensions in CSR, namely the environment, human resources and community involvement or ethics. The environment dimension involves a corporation's effect on environmental improvement, consumption and discharge. The human resources dimension involves employee welfare, such as training and development opportunities, occupational health and safety and equal opportunities. The community involvement or ethics dimension involves codes of conduct and business ethics, human rights, charity work, sponsoring, product safety and investment policies.

CSR in China and the milk product industry

The concept of CSR is still at its rudimentary stage in China (Kuo et al., 2011; Noronha et al., 2013). The 1994 Company Law of the People's Republic of China was the first to promote the concept of CSR: although it was not explicitly mentioned, the concept was indirectly embedded in this law. The 1994 law was superseded by the 2006 Company Law, in which the term "social responsibility" was explicitly articulated and profit-seeking enterprises were required to include CSR in their business plans and activities. Since the 1990s, many other laws and regulations that promote CSR have been enacted in China. These laws cover the areas of product quality (1993), food hygiene (1995), the coal industry (1996), donations for public welfare (1999), prohibition of child labor (2002), production safety (2002), prevention and control of water pollution (2008), energy conservation (2008) and work safety incidents (2009) (Chen, 2011).

The milk scandal in 2008 forced the passing of China's FSL on 1 June 2009. The FSL, which superseded the 1995 Food Hygiene Law, provided standards of food safety and suggestions on how to improve monitoring and supervision. The law also included provisions for severe penalties and enhanced consumer rights (Chen, 2011).

The massive expansion of Sanlu's business led to insufficient milk sources. Anyone can be a dairy farmer or milk station collection agent without holding a license or undergoing training or background checks (Yan, 2011). These cow owners often do not have proper knowledge that enables them to optimize their rearing environment, thus affecting milk quality. The absence of tracking of sources and a lack of quality control in the supply chain ultimately resulted in Sanlu milk suppliers' contamination of their milk with melamine (Delaurentis, 2009; Yan, 2011). China's Food Safety Administration 2008 report stated that 99.1% of infant formula on the market had undergone food safety inspection just a few months before the scandal was exposed (Jiang, 2008). This revealed the lack of monitoring by China's administration and that the existing safety laws had not been enforced. By 2009, the new FSL emphasized the prevention of cover-ups by health authorities and the responsibility of officials to examine and certify additives in all processed food (Dellios et al., 2009).

The Chinese government established new sets of safety regulations in order to rebuild trust in the dairy industry (Euromonitor International, 2011). In March 2010, health authorities announced a new regulatory framework, which highlighted action points to improve current laws (Yan, 2011). Zhang and Yang (2011) pointed out that China's tremendous economic growth is facing various social issues, such as environmental deterioration, food safety scandals and sweatshops. Enterprises should maintain sustainable development and consider CSR when seeking profit maximization and business development. On the other hand, government entities should proactively enhance and implement the laws in line with social responsibility (Levine, 2008).

TBL and ISO 26000

The current study has employed the TBL and ISO 26000 as the framework for content analysis. Here we review some related concepts and the development of these two frameworks.

The development of the TBL theory is attributable to Elkington (1998), who suggested that corporations must weigh social, economic and environmental concerns equally in their business strategies. The traditional reporting framework has to be expanded by considering environmental and social performance in addition to financial performance. The framework can also be understood in terms of three pillars, namely people, planet and profit.

The people pillar (social performance) ensures business activities are beneficial to employees as well as to the community. This includes ensuring employee rights and the reduction of occupational health hazards. Positive ways to contribute to the community include organizing or participating in charitable activities and contributions, educational programs and donations.

The planet pillar (environmental performance) ensures business operations benefit the health of the planet by minimizing their ecological impact. Examples include reducing carbon emissions, responsible sourcing of materials, careful energy consumption, and minimizing wastes and toxic pollution.

The profit pillar (economic performance) represents financial performance, incorporating reducing costs and increasing revenues, targeting emerging markets and managing risk.

The TBL is widely adopted by enterprises that are under increasing pressure to manage their environmental, social and community, and economic impacts. The success of a company is based on the interrelation between corporate social responsibility, corporate financial responsibility and corporate environmental responsibility (Adldoot, 2012).

Companies with traditional financial systems will need an extensive readjustment of their operations when implementing TBL (Rogers & Ryan, 2001). Additional responsibilities may create extra workload and costs. In order to implement TBL effectively and to avoid self-serving bias, Painter-Morland (2006) suggested that a company can appoint an independent sustainability committee. All CSD following TBL standards and all TBL information should be thoroughly checked, considered and approved by this committee before being integrated into the annual report, CSR report or other publicly available communication channels. Moreover, such disclosures must be transparent and present clear and understandable messages to the public.

The three pillars of TBL can be viewed as a general conceptual framework, while ISO 26000 is a set of guidelines for enterprises aiming to operate in a socially responsible manner. ISO 26000 is built around seven core subjects of social responsibility.

ISO 26000, published in November 2010 by the International Organization for Standards, provides practical guidance to operationalize social responsibility and sustainable development. Different from ISO 9000 and ISO 14000, ISO 26000 is not a management system standard for certification purposes (ISO, 2010).

Soderberg (2012) cited the ISO National Member Bodies Survey 2012, and pointed out that the ISO 26000 guidelines help to increase the understanding of social responsibility and clarify the definitions, principles, core subjects, methods for integration, stakeholder engagement and communication. ISO 26000 is applicable to all companies, of different business natures, sizes and scopes. The seven core subjects of social responsibility are depicted in Table 4.1.

Table 4.1 The seven core subjects of the ISO 26000 (Adapted by authors from ISO, 2010)

ISO 26000 clauses	Explanation
Human rights	Government has the primary responsibility to ensure human rights, such as civil, political, economic, social and cultural rights.
Labor practices	This includes employment relationships, protection, health and safety, development and training.
The environment	An organization should contribute to sustainability in environmental protection by constructing green policies within its capacity.
Fair operating practices	Ethical cooperation between partners, industrial competitors, the government, the public and other stakeholders for fair trade.
Consumer issues	Consumer interest should be protected by way of maintaining fair marketing, communication of factual information with transparency, communications and dispute channel and opportunities.
Community involvement and development	Enterprise, as one of the members in the community, should contribute to the improvement, development and benefit of the society.
Integrating social responsibility throughout an organization	Socially responsible concepts should be encouraged and integrated into working environments, and employees should be provided with such awareness and incorporate this in the workplace.

According to Soderberg (2012), the ISO 26000 guidelines have been implemented in 74 countries (66 in 2011). Over half (59%; 44 countries) responded that they have made ISO 26000 into a national standard. ISO 26000 is available in 22 languages (17 in 2011).

The increases in adoption and the number of translations show the growing interest in the utilization of ISO 26000 at a worldwide level, with growth especially noticeable among developing countries. There is also a tendency for a rising number of companies to utilize the guidelines for self-assessment of their CSR performance.

Method

The current study examines the CSD of the four major milk enterprises in China in view of the milk scandals. The content disclosed in the CSR sections or passages in annual reports, stand-alone CSR reports and CSD on their official websites between 2006 and 2012 were analyzed.

The research method is based on a qualitative approach, namely by using content analysis (Krippendorff, 1985). This research technique is commonly used in social and environmental accounting (Ernst & Ernst, 1978; Abbott & Monsen, 1979; Guthrie & Matthews, 1985; Guthrie & Parker, 1990; Zeghal & Ahmed, 1990). The CSR content was then mapped with the elements of the framework used in this study, namely the indicators of the TBL and ISO 26000. Through this exercise, we hope to understand the focus of the enterprises' CSR activities, assess the level of CSR coverage during the milk scandals and examine the disclosure or non-disclosure of negativities by these enterprises.

The annual reports, CSR reports and other CSD were all collected from the four selected enterprises' official websites. News reports on the milk scandal were obtained by means of keyword search on the Google and *China Daily* websites during April to May 2013. Both English and Chinese news reports were collected. Altogether 334 news reports were obtained. The CSD of the four enterprises was then compared with the news reports to assess the enterprises' disclosure level during the scandal period. Tables 4.2 and 4.3 depict the TBL and ISO 26000 indicators that were used in the analysis.

Analysis

Analysis of disclosure formats

This section presents the four enterprises' CSD formats and the quantitative content analysis conducted.

Table 4.2 TBL indicators (Adapted by authors from Slaper & Hall, 2011)

TBL		
Profit pillar (Economic performance)		Risk management Cost saving Marketing positioning Innovation Opportunity
People pillar (Social performance)	On employee	Motivation mechanism Equal opportunity Training and development Code of ethics/ conduct Health and safety Benefit Support program Communication Work-life balance
	On community	Donation Sponsorship Education Volunteer program
Planet pillar (Environmental performance)		Energy Materials Water Recycling

Disclosure format of Mengniu

The data source for Mengniu was the 2006–2012 annual reports published on the enterprise's official website. Seven annual reports were included in the analysis, among which four (2006, 2007, 2008 and 2009) were published in English only, whereas the annual reports of 2010, 2011 and 2012 were published in both English and traditional Chinese. As the Chinese version of the 2006–2009 annual reports were not disclosed in Mengniu's official website, an enquiry was made to Mengniu's customer service department to request these reports; but unfortunately there was no response.

Firstly, CSR-related keywords contained in statements in the reports were identified, and were related to the TBL and ISO 26000 indicators as shown in Table 4.4. Both English and Chinese CSR-related statements were included in the content analysis. However, only the English keywords and statements are included in this chapter.

Table 4.3 ISO 26000 indicators (Adapted by authors from Pojasek, 2011)

ISO 26000 seven core subjects of social responsibility	
Clause	**Core subject**
Clause 6: Guidance on social responsibility core subjects	
6.3	**Human rights**
6.3.3	Due diligence
6.3.4	Human rights risk situations
6.3.5	Avoidance of complicity
6.3.6	Resolving grievances
6.3.7	Discrimination and vulnerable groups
6.3.8	Civil and political rights
6.3.9	Economic, social and cultural rights
6.3.10	Fundamental principles and rights at work
6.4	**Labor practices**
6.4.3	Employment and employment relationships
6.4.4	Conditions of work and social protection
6.4.5	Social dialogue
6.4.6	Health and safety at work
6.4.7	Human development and training in the workplace
6.5	**The environment**
6.5.3	Prevention of pollution
6.5.4	Sustainable resource use
6.5.5	Climate change mitigation and adaptation
6.5.6	Protection of the environment, biodiversity and restoration of natural habitats
6.6	**Fair operating practices**
6.6.3	Anti-corruption
6.6.4	Responsible political involvement
6.6.5	Fair competition
6.6.6	Promoting social responsibility in the value chain
6.6.7	Respect to property rights
6.7	**Consumer issues**
6.7.3	Fair marketing, factual and unbiased information and fair contractual practices
6.7.4	Protecting consumers' health and safety
6.7.5	Sustainable consumption
6.7.6	Consumer service, support, and complaint and dispute resolution
6.7.7	Consumer data protection and privacy
6.7.8	Access to essential services
6.7.9	Education and awareness
6.8	**Community involvement and development**
6.8.3	Community involvement
6.8.4	Education and culture
6.8.5	Employment creation and skills development
6.8.6	Technology development and access

Table 4.3 (Continued)

Clause	Core subject
6.8.7	Wealth and income creation
6.8.8	Health
6.8.9	Social investment
Clause 7: Integrating social responsibility throughout an organization	
7.2	**The relationship of an organization's characteristics to social responsibility**
7.3	**Understanding the social responsibility of the organization**
7.3.1	Due diligence
7.3.2	Determining relevance and significance of core subjects and issues to an organization
7.3.3	An organization's sphere of influence
7.3.4	Establishing priorities for addressing issues
7.4	**Practices for integrating social responsibility throughout an organization**
7.4.1	Raising awareness and building competency for social responsibility
7.4.2	Setting the direction of an organization for social responsibility
7.4.3	Building social responsibility into an organization's governance systems and procedures
7.5	**Communication on social responsibility**
7.5.1	The role of communication in social responsibility
7.5.2	Characteristics of information related to social responsibility
7.5.3	Types of communication on social responsibility
7.5.4	Stakeholder dialogue on communication about social responsibility
7.6	**Enhancing credibility regarding social responsibility**
7.6.1	Methods of enhancing credibility
7.6.2	Enhancing the credibility of reports and claims about social responsibility
7.6.3	Resolving conflicts or disagreements between an organization and its stakeholders
7.7	**Reviewing and improving an organization's actions and practices related to social responsibility**
7.7.1	General
7.7.2	Monitoring activities on social responsibility
7.7.3	Reviewing an organization's progress and performance on social responsibility
7.7.4	Enhancing the reliability of data and information collection and management
7.7.5	Improving performance
7.8	**Voluntary initiatives for social responsibility**

Table 4.4 Determination of CSR-related keywords in statements based on the TBL and ISO 26000 indicators

Source	Keywords in CSR-related statements	Related TBL indicators	Related ISO 26000 indicators
Annual reports and official websites	Branding and marketing/ Marketing positioning	Risk management/ Marketing Positioning/ Cost saving Opportunity	
	Health/ Food quality/ Safety/ Control/ Inspection/ Consumer protection	Health and safety	Health and safety at work/ Protecting consumer health and safety
	Social responsibilities/ Corporate social responsibilities/ Social involvement/ Communication/ Equal opportunities	Support program/ Code of ethics/ Equal opportunities	Human rights/ Community involvement/ Social investment/ Wealth & income creation/ Promoting social responsibility in the value chain
	Research/ Development/ Technology/ Innovation/ Training/ Education	Innovation/ Training and development/ Education	Technology development and access/ Education and culture
	Human resources/ Remuneration/ Employee benefits	Benefits/ Work-life balance/ Communication	Employment and employment relationships/ Conditions of work and social protection/ Human development and training in the workplace
	Charity/ Donation/ Care/ Love/ Volunteer	Donation/ Sponsorship/ Volunteer program	
	Environmental protection/ Save the Earth/ Green/ Recycling/ Water/ Energy/ Material/ Ecological/ Low-carbon	Energy/ Materials/ Water/ Recycling	Prevention of pollution Sustainable resource Protection of environment
CSR reports	All statements in the CSR reports are regarded as CSR-related statements		

Next, an attempt was made to search for any stand-alone CSR report issued by Mengniu. Only one stand-alone CSR report, entitled the "*Social Responsibility of Business Report*" and issued on 25 February 2008, was identified. This report covered the whole period 1999–2007 and was written in both simplified Chinese and English. It contained 93 pages, half in simplified Chinese and half in English. The content of both languages was included in the analysis.

The CSR-related information on the company website was then identified. The press releases published on Mengniu Corporation's three official websites[1] were found to contain CSR-related information. Such information was published only in simplified Chinese. News for the period 2006–2012 was selected for analysis in this study. Table 4.5 summarizes quantitatively the CSD of Mengniu for the period 2006–2011based on information contained in the annual reports, the stand-alone CSR report and official websites.

The change in language pattern from English only for the 2006–2009 annual reports to both English and traditional Chinese thereafter may indicate that the enterprise had gradually recognized the importance of both its stakeholders and the general public understanding its CSR practices and activities. Therefore, by publishing bilingual reports, Mengniu's CSR image could be promoted in a more proactive and positive way. This could increase the attention level of the public and ensure information was thoroughly transmitted to stakeholders in a straightforward manner.

Next, for the content in the annual reports, we compared the total amount of CSR-related statements with the total number of statements in each annual report. The percentage of CSR coverage was then generated in order to find out the ratio of CSR content. As seen in Table 4.5, the percentage of CSR coverage showed a gradual increase from 2006 to 2007 (+0.23%), but a significant increase in 2008 (+0.46%), 2009 (+0.55%) and 2010 (+4.47%) before a gradual decline again in 2011 (−2.98%) and 2012 (−2.74%). Figure 4.1 depicts the trend in a graphical manner.

As seen in Table 4.5, the average percentage of CSR-related statements in English annual reports between 2006 and 2012 was 1.69%, which was much higher than 2006 (0.47%) and 2012 (0.46%) individually. The average coverage in the traditional Chinese versions between 2010 and 2012 was 1.86%, which was approximately the mid-point of the three years (2.01% in 2010; 1.23% in 2012). This finding also implied that Mengniu had emphasized more CSR disclosures, especially in the wake of the milk scandals in 2008.

Table 4.5 Quantitative summary of the CSD of Mengniu

Mengniu			**Year**	**CSR statements**	**Total statements in report**	**CSR statements %**	**Variance in %**
1. Annual reports	Language	Traditional Chinese	2006		*(No Chinese language version available)*		
			2007				
			2008				
			2009				
			2010	2,060	102,281	2.0	–
			2011	2,243	99,052	2.26	+0.25
			2012	1,064	86,837	1.23	−1.03
Subtotal				**5,367**	**288,170**		
		English	2006	175	37,548	0.47	
			2007	268	38,174	0.70	+0.23
			2008	497	42,740	1.16	**+0.4**
			2009	823	48,095	1.71	**+0.55**
			2010	1,598	25,842	6.18	**+4.47**
			2011	1,111	34,748	3.20	−2.98
			2012	244	52,696	0.46	−2.74
Subtotal			**4,716**	**279,843**	**1.69**	–	
Total CSR statements				**10,083**	**568,013**	**1.78**	–

Table 4.5 (Continued)

2. CSR report	Stand-alone report		Year	CSR Statements	Total statements in report	CSR statements %	Variance in statements
	Language	Simplified Chinese	1999–2007	13,288	–	–	–
		English		7,984	–	–	–
Total CSR statements				**21,272**	–	–	–
3. Official websites	**News/ Press releases**		**Year**	**CSR statements**	**Total statements on websites**	**CSR statements %**	**Variance in statements**
	Language	Traditional Chinese	2006	560	–	–	
			2007	2,223	–	–	+1,663
			2008	612	–	–	−1,611
			2009	–	–	–	−612
			2010	1,755	–	–	–
			2011	19	–	–	−1,736
			2012	7,208	–	–	−7,189
Total CSR statements				**12,377**	–	–	–
Grand Total CSR statements				**43,732**	**568,013**	**7.70%**	–

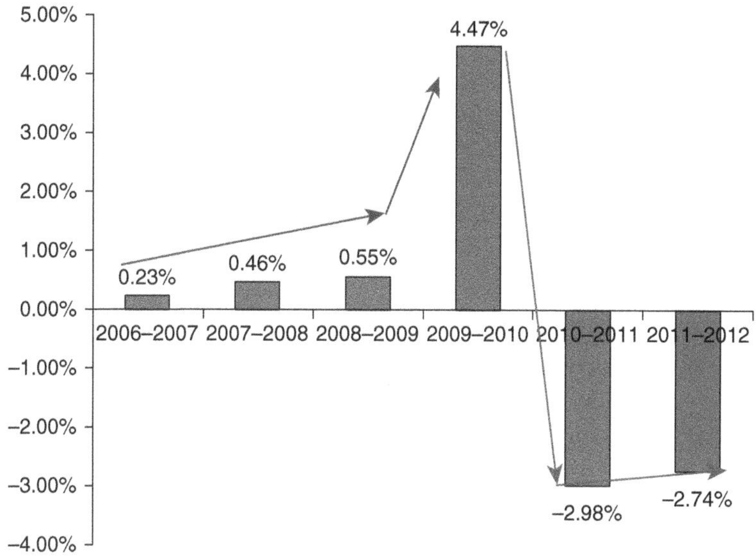

Figure 4.1 The trend of CSD in Mengniu's annual reports

As for Mengniu's stand-alone CSR report, as seen in Table 4.5, 13,288 statements were accounted for in the simplified Chinese version and 7,984 statements in the English version, over the eight years from 1999 to 2007. As this report was first issued in February 2008, it was assumed that the reason for issuing it was unrelated to the milk scandals in 2008.

As to Mengniu's official websites, as seen in Table 4.5, there was a decrease in CSR-related statements from 2007 to 2008 (−1,611) and from 2008 to 2009 (−612). Compared with its annual report of the same period, more CSR-related statements were included (+0.46% from 2007 to 2008; +0.55% from 2008 to 2009). This finding may imply that Mengniu had emphasized its CSR coverage in its stand-alone CSR report and its bilingual annual reports, and simultaneously maintained an average level of CSD through its official website.

Disclosure format of Yili

For Yili, four stand-alone CSR reports were identified on its official website[2] which covered the years 2006, 2007–2008, 2009–2010 and 2011, respectively. All reports were in simplified Chinese. No CSR report for 2012 was published.

Yili's annual reports from 2007 to 2012 were accessed on the Morningstar website[3] instead of on Yili's official website. These reports included the first quarter, third quarter, semi-annual and annual reports for each year. As no CSR-related statements were found in these reports, they were not included in the analysis.

Online information was published in simplified Chinese only and was assumed to relate to the year in which it was published. Since news reports were published between 2008 and 2012, only these five years were included in the analysis. Table 4.6 depicts a quantitative summary for the CSD of Yili from 2006 to 2012.

Judging by the number of pages, the 2006 CSR report was longest (68 pages) compared with the other three reports (2007–2008: 67 pages; 2009–2010: 67 pages; 2011: 62 pages). From 2007 to 2010, these CSR reports were issued on a biannual basis (2007–2008, 2008–2009, 2009–2010) compared with the annual versions in 2006, 2011 and 2012. Nevertheless, they had a similar extent, ranging between 62 and 67 pages.

In terms of the number of statements, as seen in Table 4.6, the 2006 report included the most CSR statements. The 2007–2008 report covered only half (49.86%) of the CSR statements made in the 2006 CSR report; while the 2009–2010 report was close to the 2006 level. This increase of coverage was reasonable given the outbreak of the 2008 milk scandals. The 2011 CSR report recorded a tremendously low number of CSR statements compared with 2009–2010 (−59.09%). It was understandable for Yili to decrease its coverage after the milk scandal impact had cooled down.

In terms of coverage on its official website, as in Table 4.6, Yili reduced its CSR coverage in 2009 (−83%). However, this can be compared with the increase in coverage in its CSR report during the same period (+99.18%). Similarly, the increase in coverage on the website from 2010 onwards (2010 +916%) can also be compared with the drop in coverage in its CSR report in 2011 (−59.09%). This has indicated that Yili was emphasizing different disclosure channels during different periods to communicate with its stakeholders.

Disclosure format of Sanlu

Sanlu was the protagonist of the 2008 milk scandals that affected over 290,000 Chinese infants. The official investigation found that intense competition had forced the enterprise to loosen its quality inspections and control (Gong & Liu, 2008). In fact, Sanlu was the first enterprise to receive complaints that its products were making infants sick, and

Table 4.6 Quantitative summary of the CSD of Yili

1. CSR report	Stand-alone report		Year	CSR statements	Total statements in report	CSR statements %	Variance in statements
a.	Language	Simplified Chinese	2006	21,196	–	–	–
a.			2007–2008	10,629	–	–	−10,567/−49.86
a.			2009–2010	21,171	–	–	**+10,543/+99.18**
a.			2011	8,660	–	–	−12,511/−59.09
			2012		*(No CSR report was published)*		
Total				**61,656**	–	–	–
2. Official website	**Press release**		**Year**	**CSR statements**	**Total statements on website**	**CSR statements %**	**Variance in statements**
	Language	Simplified Chinese	2006		*(No CSD on its official website)*		
			2007				
			2008	4,141	–	–	–
			2009	687	–	–	−3,454/−83
			2010	6,982	–	–	**+6,295/916**
			2011	7,004	–	–	+22/32
			2012	7,572	–	–	+568/8
Total				**26,386**	–	–	–
Grand total				**88,042**	–	–	–

this was followed by an increase in other reported cases. Sanlu was then taken over by another enterprise, namely Sanyuan Group, a state-owned group of companies based on agriculture and animal husbandry in China.

Upon its filing for bankruptcy on 23 December 2008 (BBC News, 2010), Sanlu's official website was closed down and no annual reports, CSR reports or other CSD were available. Therefore, attempts were made to search from related listed companies' websites for records relating to its annual reports and CSR reports; however, no results were found. In addition, a general search was made with keywords such as "Sanlu annual reports" and "Sanlu corporate social responsibility reports"; but many news reports related to the 2008 milk scandals were found instead of the annual and CSR reports. Some of Sanlu's social responsibility activities according to external press releases are listed in Table 4.7. Since no further CSD information of Sanlu could be identified, it had to be excluded from the analysis.

Table 4.7 Past CSR activities of Sanlu (Adapted by authors from various sources)

Date	CSR activities
1999	Donation of 1,500 dairy products to old people.
1998	Donation of 1,000,000 boxes of dairy products to Yangtze River, Hubei, Hunan, Jinxi, which were massively affected by flood disasters.
April 2001	Donation of RMB 100,000 to special needs schools.
June 2002	Donation of RMB 7,320 to sponsor charitable children's day.
April, May 2003	Donation of RMB 2,300,000 and 1,000,000 boxes of dairy products to physicians and nurses who assisted in the SARS outbreak.
December 2003	Donation of one-year consumption of Sanlu infant formula and baby clothing (worth RMB 8,000).
May 2008	Donation of dairy products of RMB 1,000,000 to the Wen Chuan earthquake; cooperated with other manufacturing partners to donate RMB 5,000,000. Another donation of RMB 8,800,000 infant formula dairy products.
July 2003	Sponsored 36 students' school fees.
January 2004	Donation of daily necessities to 20 families in the Xin Hua district.
April 2004	Donation of 300,000 infant formula dairy products.

Disclosure format of Bright Dairy

Bright Dairy's annual reports were published on its official website from 2006 to 2012. Bright Dairy published its CSR reports in a dedicated section of its annual reports in 2008, 2009 and 2010.[4] These reports were published in simplified Chinese and were included in the analysis. For 2011 and 2012,[5] Bright Dairy separated its CSR section in the annual report and published a separate CSR report in simplified Chinese. These two CSR reports were also included in the analysis. As to press releases, they were obtained from Bright Dairy's official website.[6] Such information was published in simplified Chinese. Table 4.8 depicts a quantitative summary of Bright Dairy's CSD.

The CSR section in the 2008 annual report that directly focused on the milk scandal of 2008 included two counts of mentioning with 442 statements, which occupied 4.36% of the CSR section in the 2008 annual report. Comparing the number of CSR statements made in the CSR section of the 2010 annual report (4,374) and in the 2011 CSR report (12,665), the increase in CSR coverage in 2011 was almost 200% over that in 2010. In addition, the number of CSR statements in the 2012 CSR report (11,954) had only a slight reduction of 5.6% compared with that of 2011.

Based on the foregoing, it was clear that Bright Dairy did not provide as many years of CSR reports as Mengniu and Yili did. The reporting format was also not as legibly demonstrated as those of Mengniu and Yili, which attracted a higher level of attention of the stakeholders. Since Bright Dairy was not as dominant in the industry as Mengniu and Yili, the company was only at the beginning stages of incorporating CSR into its business strategy. This may imply that the more market dominating the enterprise is, the more its CSD is facilitated, since more attention will be paid by various stakeholders and its social impacts will be much greater.

Analysis of the TBL framework

A quantitative content analysis based on the three pillars of TBL was conducted on the CSD of the three enterprises. The results are in Table 4.9. The following paragraphs briefly summarize the quantitative results and readings of the CSD of the three enterprises.

For Mengniu, social performance was its core concern, with a coverage ratio of over 50% relative to total performance. Mengniu had valued employee quality and the importance of employee training and

Table 4.8 Quantitative summary of the CSD of Bright Dairy

1. Annual reports	CSR section		Year	CSR statements	Total statements in report	CSR statements %	Variance in %
	Language	Simplified Chinese	2006		*(No CSR section was available)*		
			2007				
			2008	10,139	70,927	14.30	–
			2009	4,032	78,966	5.11	–9.18
			2010	4,374	65,464	6.68	–1.57
Total				**18,545**	215,357	**8.61**	
2. CSR reports	**Stand-alone report**		**Year**	**CSR statements**	**Total statements in report**	**CSR statements %**	**Variance in statements**
	Language	Simplified Chinese	2011	12,665	–	–	+8.291**
			2012	11,954	–	–	–711***
Total				**24,619**	–	–	–
3. Official website	**CSD**		**Year**	**CSR statements**	**Total statements in report**	**CSR statements %**	**Variance in % and statements**
	Language	Simplified Chinese	2006		*(No CSR disclosures were published on the official website)*		
			2007				
			2008	2,937	–	–	–
			2009	51	–	–	–98.26/–2,886
			2010	0	–	–	–
			2011	0	–	–	–
			2012	0	–	–	–
Total				**2,988**	–	–	–
Grand Total				**46,152**			

Table 4.9 CSD of three enterprises based on the TBL framework

1. Profit pillar (Economic performance)		**Mengniu**		**Yili**		**Bright Dairy**	
		Traditional Chinese	**English**	**Simplified Chinese**	**English**	**Simplified Chinese**	**English**
Economic	Risk management	627	0	3,174	–	**10,566**	–
	Cost saving	0	0	1,322	–	1,775	–
	Marketing positioning	**4,358**	**2,271**	11,933	–	6,897	–
	Innovation	2,664	1044	**12,808**	–	3,540	–
	Opportunity	1,115	372	11,662	–	4,534	–
Total CSR statements		**8,764**	**3,687**	**40,899**	–	**27,312**	–
2. People pillar (Social performance)		**Mengniu**		**Yili**		**Bright Dairy**	
		Traditional Chinese	**English**	**Simplified Chinese**	**English**	**Simplified Chinese**	**English**
Employee	Motivation	0	0	1,162	–	4,214	–
	Equal opportunity	818	312	2,410	–	2,826	–
	Training and development	1,058	558	**5,421**	–	**5,574**	–
	Code of ethics/ conduct	**2,596**	**1,009**	2,853	–	0	–
	Health and safety	1,296	332	4,095	–	993	–
	Benefit	216	50	1,837	–	2,628	–
	Support program	1,553	390	320	–	2,041	–
	Communication	95	20	1,010	–	1,551	–
	Work-life balance	0	0	620	–	2,631	–
	Subtotal	**7,632**	**2,671**	**19,928**	–	**22,458**	–

Table 4.9 (Continued)

Community	Donation	1,396	270	**10,744**	–	2,130	–
	Sponsorship	1,324	665	4,590	–	2,412	–
	Education	**5,481**	**2,189**	1,128	–	2,630	–
	Volunteer	32	18	0	–	1,531	–
	Program	693	235	3,734	–	**3,773**	–
	Subtotal	**8,926**	**3,377**	**20,196**	–	**12,476**	–
Total CSR statements		**16,358**	**5,848**	**40,124**	–	**34,934**	–

3. Planet pillar (Environment performance)		**Mengniu**		**Yili**		**Bright Dairy**	
		Traditional Chinese	**English**	**Simplified Chinese**	**English**	**Simplified Chinese**	**English**
Environment	Energy	**3,493**	**1,022**	**5,044**	–	**2,398**	–
	Materials	713	286	2,093	–	1,987	–
	Water	1,072	420	0	–	999	–
	Recycling	1,489	580	1,421	–	1,920	–
Total CSR statements		**6,767**	**2,308**	**8,558**	–	**7,304**	–
Grand total		**31,889**	**11,843**	**89,581**	–	**69,550**	–

advancement for business development. Moreover, health and safety was another element promoted by Mengniu.

Yili was concerned about both its economic and social performances (over 90% of total disclosure). It had strived hard to stabilize its dominant market position with the support of the Chinese government. For example, it had enhanced its technology and innovation aspects in terms of milk supplies in order to improve quality and safety and built long-standing partnerships with its milk suppliers. Environmental concerns only accounted for just below 10% of total disclosure.

For Bright Dairy, its coverage focused mainly on the people pillar (around 50% of total disclosure), understanding the importance of maintaining good and motivating business relationships with its employees and its work partners. Social activities and contributions in the local community were also its core concerns.

Analysis of the ISO 26000 framework

Similar to the above, a quantitative content analysis was conducted on the CSD of the three enterprises based on the ISO 26000 framework indicators. The results are in Table 4.10. Both Mengniu and Yili emphasized the category of community involvement and development (46% (8,494 CSR statements) and 55% (39,791) of their total CSR statements, respectively). Yili had a comparatively higher number of CSR statements, as it had issued more CSR reports (2006 to 2012), whereas Mengniu had issued only one CSR report which covered the period 1999–2007. Furthermore, Mengniu and Yili had attempted to be good citizens by contributing to community development and proactively cooperating with other business sectors in socially responsible activities. By contrast, Bright Dairy was only in the early stages of integrating CSR into its business model.

Comparison with news reports

News articles about the milk scandals published between September 2008 and December 2009 in China-based and international media were collected using the Google search engine and the *China Daily* and the China Central Television (CCTV) websites. A total of 334 news articles from over 20 media entities were collected, as shown in Table 4.11. This included 196 articles from China-based outlets and 138 articles from international outlets. Among these articles, 272 were in English and 62 in simplified Chinese.

Table 4.10 CSD of three enterprises based on the ISO 26000 framework

Clause	Core subject	Mengniu		Yili		Bright Dairy	
		Simplified Chinese	English	Simplified Chinese	English	Simplified Chinese	English
Clause 6: Guidance on social responsibility core subjects							
6.3	**Human rights**						
6.3.3	Due diligence	0	0	0	–	0	–
6.3.4	Human rights risk situations	0	0	0	–	0	–
6.3.5	Avoidance of complicity	0	0	0	–	0	–
6.3.6	Resolving grievances	0	0	0	–	0	–
6.3.7	Discrimination and vulnerable groups	1,729	0	503	–	0	–
6.3.8	Civil and political rights	0	0	0	–	0	–
6.3.9	Economic, social and cultural rights	0	0	0	–	0	–
6.3.10	Fundamental principles and rights at work	0	0	0	–	0	–
Total		**1,729**	**0**	**503**	–	**0**	–
6.4	**Labor practices**						
6.4.3	Employment and employment relationships	0	0	1,557	–	**2,522**	–
6.4.4	Conditions of work and social protection	189	144	1,686	–	2,397	–
6.4.5	Social dialogue	0	0	420	–	0	–
6.4.6	Health and safety at work	544	0	1,551	–	493	–
6.4.7	Human development and training in workplace	904	461	462	–	3,349	–
Total		**1,637**	**605**	**5,676**	–	**8,761**	–
6.5	**The environment**						
6.5.3	Prevention of pollution	207	0	825	–	1,372	–
6.5.4	Sustainable resource use	**3,851**	1,437	2,866	–	**3,495**	–
6.5.5	Climate change mitigation and adaptation	0	0	0	–	0	–
6.5.6	Protection of the environment, biodiversity and restoration of natural habitats	591	360	3,585	–	**2,753**	–
Total		**4,649**	**1,797**	**7,276**	–	**7,620**	–

6.6	**Fair operating practices**						
6.6.3	Anti-corruption	0	0	0	–	0	
6.6.4	Responsible political involvement	120	89	1,183	–	0	
6.6.5	Fair competition	0	0	759	–	**1,299**	
6.6.6	Promoting social responsibility in the value chain	255	128	180	–	0	
6.6.7	Respect of property rights	0	0	0	–	0	–
Total		**375**	**217**	**2,122**	–	**1,299**	–
6.7	**Consumer issues**						
6.7.3	Fair marketing, factual and unbiased information and fair contractual practices	0	0	0	–	235	–
6.7.4	Protecting consumer health and safety	706	210	**4,389**	–	**5,915**	–
6.7.5	Sustainable consumption	0	0	0	–	0	–
6.7.6	Consumer service, support, complaint and dispute resolution	0	0	954	–	**2,558**	–
6.7.7	Consumer data protection and privacy	0	0	0	–	0	–
6.7.8	Access to essential services	448	72	0	–	0	–
6.7.9	Education and awareness	724	0	2,100	–	0	–
Total		**1,878**	**282**	**7,443**	–	**8,708**	–
6.8	**Community involvement and development**						
6.8.3	Community involvement	3,461	774	11,064	–	**2,367**	–
6.8.4	Education and culture	1,383	321	6,418	–	530	–
6.8.5	Employment creation and skills development	110	0	0	–	0	–
6.8.6	Technology development and access	**1,709**	742	**14,844**	–	**1,711**	–
6.8.7	Wealth and income creation	692	514	1,771	–	286	–
6.8.8	Health	653	345	3,266	–	73	–
6.8.9	Social investment	486	240	2,428	–	312	–
Total		**8,494**	**2,936**	**39,791**	–	**5,279**	–

Table 4.10 (Continued)

Clause	Core subject	Mengniu		Yili		Bright Dairy	
		Simplified Chinese	**English**	**Simplified Chinese**	**English**	**Simplified Chinese**	**English**
Clause 7: Integrating social responsibility throughout an organization							
7.2	Relationship of an organization's characteristics to social responsibility	0	0	4,361	–	0	–
7.3	Understanding social responsibility of organization	288	270	5,613	–	229	–
7.4	Practices for integrating social responsibility throughout an organization	**1,842**	1,255	1823	–	**2,857**	–
7.5	Communication on social responsibility	946	594	3,334	–	**3,653**	–
7.6	Enhancing credibility regarding social responsibility	126	0	52	–	**2,386**	–
7.7	Reviewing and improving an organization's actions and practices related to social responsibility	242	0	1,521	–	1,982	–
7.8	Voluntary initiatives for social responsibility	0	0	0	–	142	–
Total		**3,444**	**2,119**	**167,04**	–	**11,249**	–
Grand Total		22,206	7,956	72,239	–	43,706	–

Table 4.11 News articles collected

Rank	Media outlet	Media type	Number of news articles
News articles in English			
1	*China Daily*	China-based	116
2	Xinhua	China-based	18
3	*The Telegraph*	International	15
4	BBC News	International	12
5	*The Guardian*	International	10
6	Reuters	International	8
7	Bloomberg	International	6
8	*Los Angeles Times*	International	4
9	Time World	International	2
10	*USA Today*	International	3
11	CNN	International	3
12	*The New York Times*	International	3
13	NBC News	International	2
14	*The Wall Street Journal*	International	2
15	*Washington Post*	International	1
16	20+ other media	International	67
News articles in simplified Chinese			
1	CCTV	China-based	62
Total China-based news articles			**196**
Total international news articles			**138**
Total articles in English			**272**
Total articles in simplified Chinese			**62**
Total news articles collected			**334**

On 16 July 2008, Gansu Province reported to the Ministry of Health that a local hospital had identified an increase in cases of infants' kidney problems. Most of them had ingested Sanlu's milk products. The first news report about 14 infants falling ill after taking the same brand of milk product was exposed by the *Lanzhou Morning Post* in Gansu Province on 9 September 2008. Two days later, Sanlu was suspected to be responsible for the melamine contamination, and admitted melamine contamination the next day (Caijing Staff, 2008). Very soon more dairy enterprises were reported to be involved in the contamination, including Mengniu and Yili. By January 2009, 296,000 children were reported to have fallen ill after consuming the tainted milk products (BBC News, 2010).

Sanlu paid RMB 200,000 to the parents of the first infant who had died owing to the contamination; however, over 200 more families appealed to the court for justice and compensation (BBC News, 2010). This further aroused the attention of the international media toward China's food safety. China's dairy exports were boycotted by both developed and developing countries, and warnings about China's food safety were given (ESCAP, 2009). Thereafter, the news coverage reduced gradually after the court's decisions on the punishment of the involved parties, including two death sentences, had been reported in January 2009 (BBC News, 2010). Figure 4.2 illustrates the trend of the collected news reports during the period under study.

Figures 4.3, 4.4 and 4.5 show the percentage of CSR-related coverage of the three enterprises. It is noticed that all three enterprises strengthened their CSR activities and disclosure for the period 2008–2009 in the wake of the milk scandal crisis. This is in line with the traditional view held by Patten (1992) that CSD increases as an organization faces threats to its legitimacy. Furthermore, CSD was used here as a strategy to defend organizational legitimacy (Ashford & Gibbs, 1990). Nevertheless, it is clear from the figures that Bright Dairy began its CSR activities about two years later than Mengniu and Yili.

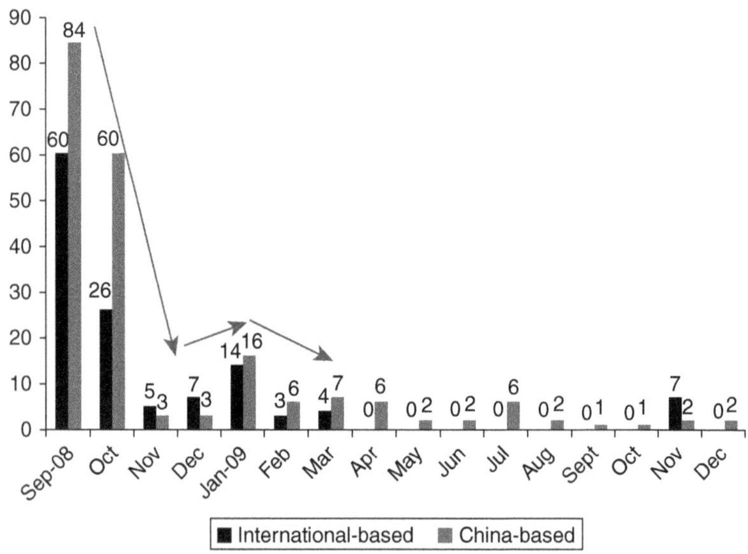

Figure 4.2 Trend of news reports from September 2008 to December 2009

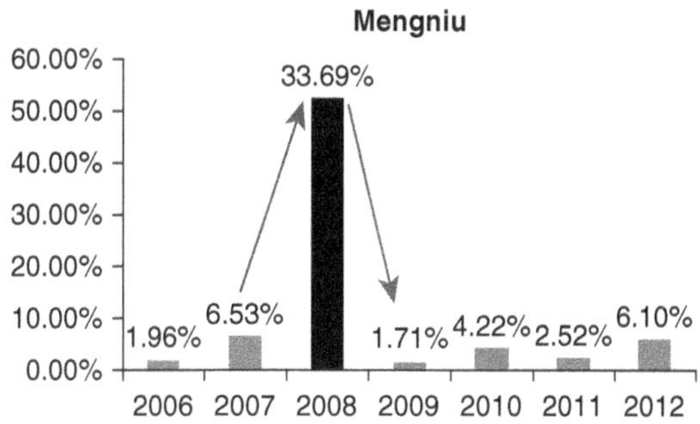

Figure 4.3 Percentage of CSD by Mengniu (2006–2012)

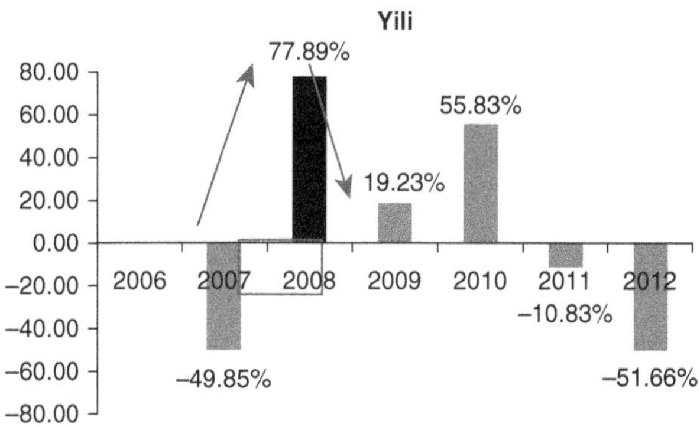

Figure 4.4 Percentage of CSD by Yili (2006–2012)

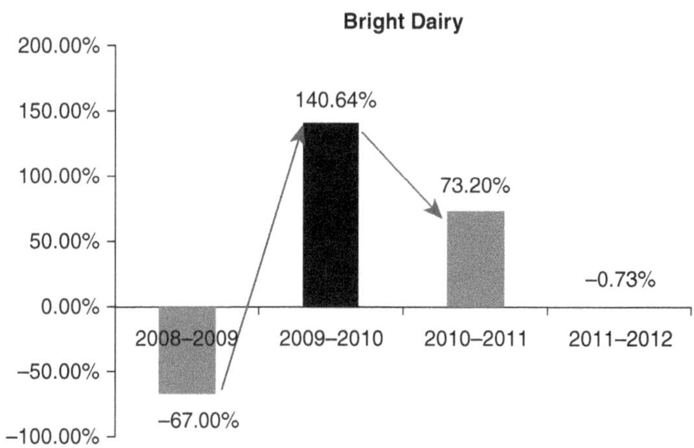

Figure 4.5 Percentage of CSD by Bright Dairy (2006–2012)

Conclusion

The easier it is to search for CSR information for a company, the greater is its CSR awareness in the public domain. If more CSR statements and phrases appear in voluntary disclosures, it indicates that more details are being revealed to society (Amran & Susela Devi, 2007). From the analysis presented above, we can draw the following conclusions.

Willingness of the enterprises to disclose

Mengniu, Yili and Bright Dairy all have established CSR systems. However, while Mengniu and Yili started to provide CSR information in 2006 by including it in their annual reports and CSR reports, Bright Dairy only started to do so in 2008. This finding shows that the willingness to establish CSR topics and the levels of disclosure are different for Mengniu and Yili as opposed to Bright Dairy. The former two enterprises are dominant in the milk product market, while Bright Dairy has a lower market share. It also shows that larger enterprises tend to demonstrate a higher degree of proactive CSD. Well-known enterprises may need to devote more resources to CSR activities and disclosures in order to gain business benefits, such as improved corporate image and customer loyalty. In this respect, the voluntary disclosure theory supported by Dye (1985) and Verrecchia (1983) appears to be applicable to Mengniu and Yili. The theory posits that companies with superior performance tend to disclose more in order to differentiate themselves from poor performers.

Biased disclosures

From the reading of the CSD of the three enterprises, it was found that negative news and related information, such as that about the milk scandals, was not reported or was reported in limited contexts or in a biased way. The news articles on the scandal were actually all found in the mass media outlets. Such news was not disclosed or was disclosed in a limited and filtered way by the three enterprises. For example, Mengniu strategically switched from a negative approach (no disclosure at all) to a positive approach (recovery and improvement actions to respond to the outbreak) after the milk scandal in 2008, aiming to bring about a positive response from the public.

Mengniu's CEO Niu Gensheng mentioned in the 2008 annual report, under the heading "CEO Statement", that

> The Chinese dairy industry had a tough and difficult time in 2008. In the past few years, the industry boomed and achieved rapid growth

> until September 2008. The milk contamination incident revealed that the development of operation practices such as raw materials procurement and transportation lagged behind the industry development. The incident also aroused the Chinese dairy industry's concerns over product safety....The group promptly responded to the government and promised to recall the relevant products. It also installed additional inspection equipment and included additional new testing items for products without delay. Undertakings for quality raw milk were obtained from raw milk collection centers to ensure the provision of safe milk....As a responsible enterprise, the Group will enhance its quality control and inspection to assure consumer confidence. I strongly believe that the lesson learned last year prepares the Chinese dairy industry for a brighter future and a better tomorrow.

In contrast to Mengniu, Yili did not disclose any information regarding the milk scandals in its 2007–2008 and 2009–2010 CSR reports. It could have reported the scandals and its corrective and preventive actions, but it chose not to do so. The voluntary disclosure theory applies partially in this sense, given the dragon head position of Mengniu.

As for Bright Dairy, it disclosed the milk scandals in the CSR sections of its 2008 annual report. Bright Dairy also mentioned its proactive preventive measures in the report. Unlike the voluntary disclosure theory, some (e.g. Patten, 1991) suggest that poor performers may tend to disclose because they are under pressure from the public, and therefore in order to continue to operate legitimately, they have to disclose more CSR information. In this case, Bright Dairy was at that time new to CSR activities and CSD and had a very low market share compared with Mengniu and Yili. Furthermore, the 2008 annual report indicated that Bright Dairy actually suffered from a loss of RMB 319,543,911, compared with a profit of RMB 273,255,760 in 2007, a significant 216.93% decrease in profitability. Given all these pressures, Bright Dairy had to recover its corporate reputation in all possible ways, including the disclosure of bad news, such as the milk scandals, and its preventive measures.

Increase in initiatives and voluntary implementation of CSR

Mengniu and Yili more broadly adopted ISO 26000, which has specified requirements on people factors, such as human rights (including rights at work), labor practices (employer–employee relationships, health and safety of employees, development and training), fair operating practices (among competitors, suppliers, buyers, the public, government, employees), consumers' needs and rights, and the integration of social responsibility into organizations. To this end, both Mengniu and Yili covered not only the three pillars of TBL, but also aimed to reach a higher standard of social responsibility than Bright Dairy. The voluntary disclosure theory applies in this case again.

To sum up, the study has presented a quantitative content analysis of the CSD of three enterprises in the China milk product industry during the milk scandal crisis period. It can be seen that disclosure was used as a tool not only to communicate corporate affairs to stakeholders, but also as a strategy to respond to corporate or industrial crises. Leaders of the market know how to strategically maneuver through thousands of pieces of social information and to present to stakeholders the desirable ones in a satisfactory fashion, thus building up a responsible and legitimate corporate image. However, very often these enterprises violated the main principles of CSD, such as completeness in disclosure. Enterprises may claim that they have disclosed the information when running down a checklist, but users of CSR reports are recommended always to compare and triangulate such reported information with what has been reported by the mass media; as in the case of the milk scandals in this study. Disclosure should not be seen as binary (0 or 1, no or yes). The depth of disclosure is the key point. Given the ever-increasing demand from stakeholders, access to international media and the global advancement of CSR and CSD, those enterprises in China which choose not to disclose bad news or remain opaque in their operations will eventually not be competitive.

Notes

1. http://www.mengniu.com.cn/duty/ http://www.mengniu.com.cn/ http://www.nmg.xinhuanet.com/nmgwq/mn/
2. http://www.yili.com/peopleduty/qygmbg/5_1.html
3. http://quicktake.morningstar.com/stocknet/secdocuments.aspx?symbol=600887&country=chn
4. http://www.brightdairy.com/UploadFile/file/2008.pdf http://www.brightdairy.com/UploadFile/file/2009.pdf http://www.brightdairy.com/UploadFile/file/2010.pdf
5. http://www.csr-china.net/templates/report/index.aspx?nodeid=ac59cbef-70ff-4947-bfda-fe06f2e2b093&page=contentpage&contentid=b255151b-03b5-4235-931b-2ca3f7b418b0 http://quotes.money.163.com/f10/ggmx_600597_1067913.html
6. http://www.brightdairy.com/home.php

References

Abbott, W.F. & Monsen, R.J. (1979). On the measurement of corporate social responsibility: Self reported disclosures as a method of measuring corporate social involvement. *Academy of Management Journal*, 22, (3), 510–515.

Adldoot, M. (2012). *Communication of CSR Activities – A Case Study in the Dairy Sector.* Master's thesis. Swedish University of Agricultural Sciences.

Amran, A & Susela Devi, S. (2007). Corporate social reporting in Malaysia: A political theory perspective. *Malaysian Accounting Review*, 6, (1), 19–44.

Ashford, B.E. & Gibbs, B.W. (1990). The double-edge of organizational legitimacy. *Organization Science*, 1, (2), 177–194.

BBC News (2010). Timeline: China milk scandal. 25 January. Available at http://news.bbc.co.uk/2/hi/7720404.stm

Caijing Staff (2008). Timeline of China's tainted milk scandal. *Caijing Magazine*, 31 December 2008. Available at http://english.caijing.com.cn/2008-12-31/110044273.html

Campbell, D., Craven, B. & Shrives, P. (2003). Voluntary reporting in three FTSE sectors: A comment on perception and legitimacy. *Accounting, Auditing and Accountability Journal*, 16, (4), 558–581.

Chen, Y. (2011). Corporate social responsibility from the Chinese perspective. *Indiana International and Comparative Law Review*, 21, (3), 419–434.

Commonwealth Bank of Australia (2013). *Global Market Research. Commodities: Agri Updates.* 26 February.

Crook, F.W. (1998). China's economy slows; livestock sector posts long-term growth. *International Agricultural and Trade Report.* Washington DC: Economic Research Service, US Department of Agriculture.

Deegan, C. (2002). The legitimizing effect of social and environmental disclosures – A theoretical foundation. *Accounting, Auditing, and Accountability Journal*, 15, (3), 282–311.

Deegan, C., Rankin, M. & Tobin, J. (2002). An examination of the corporate social and environmental disclosures of BHP from 1983–1997: A test of legitimacy theory. *Accounting, Auditing and Accountability Journal*, 15, (3), 312–343.

Deegan, C., Rankin, M. & Voght, P. (2000). Firms' disclosure reactions to major social incidents: Australian evidence. *Accounting Forum*, 24, (1), 101–130.

Delaurentis, T. (2009). Ethical supply chain management. *China Business Review*, 36, (3), 38–41.

Dellios, R., Yang, X.H. & Yilmaz, N.K. (2009). Food safety and the role of the government: Implications for CSR policies in China, *iBusiness*, 1, (2), 74–84.

Dobson, W.D. (2008). Milk contamination problems in China: Implications for international dairy businesses. Babcock Institute Discussion Paper no. 2008-4. Madison, WI: The Babcock Institute for International Dairy Research and Development.

Dye, R.A. (1985). Disclosure of nonproprietary information. *Journal of Accounting Research*, 23, 123–145.

Elkington, J. (1998). *Cannibals with Forks: The Triple Bottom Line of 21st Century Business.* Gabriola Island, BC: New Society Publishers.

Ernst and Ernst. (1978). *Social Responsibility Disclosure: Survey of Fortune 500 Annual Reports.* Cleveland, OH: Ernst and Ernst.

ESCAP (2009). Creating business and social value: The Asian way to integrate CSR into business strategies. *Studies in Trade and Investment 68*, Bangkok: Economic and Social Commission for Asia and the Pacific, United Nations.

Euromonitor International (2011). Stricter Chinese regulatory framework gives international dairy companies opportunity to thrive. 21 January.

Gong, J. & Liu, J.J. (2008). Spilling the blame for China's milk crisis (in Chinese). *Caijing Magazine*. Available at http://english.caijing.com.cn/2008-10-10/110019183.html

Gray, R., Owen, D. & Maunders, K.T. (1987). *Corporate Social Reporting, Accounting and Accountability*. Hemel Hempstead: Prentice Hall.

Gray, R., Kouhy, R. & Lavers, S. (1995). Corporate social and environmental reporting: A review of the literature and a longitudinal study of UK disclosure. *Accounting, Auditing and Accountability Journal*, 8, (2), 47–77.

Guthrie, J., & Matthews, M. R. (1985). Corporate social accounting in Australasia. *Research in Corporate Social Performance and Policy*, 7, 251–277.

Guthrie, J.E. & Parker, L.D. (1990). Corporate social disclosure practice: A comparative international analysis. *Advances in Public Interest Accounting*, 3, 159–175.

ISO (2010). ISO 26000 – Social Responsibility. Available at http://www.iso.org/iso/home/standards/iso26000.htm

Jiang, J. (2008). China's rage over toxic baby milk. *Time*, 19 September. Available at http://www.time.com/time/world/article/0,8599,1842727,00.html

KPMG (2008). *The Milk and Dairy Market in China*. Available at http://www.kpmg.com/CN/en/IssuesAndInsights/ArticlesPublications/Documents/milk-dairy-mkt-china-0806.pdf

Krippendorff, K. (1985). *Content Analysis: An Introduction to its Methodology*. Beverly Hills, CA: Sage.

Kuo, L., Yeh, C.C. & Yu, H.C. (2011). Disclosure of corporate social responsibility and environmental management: Evidence from China. *Corporate Social Responsibility and Environmental Management*, 25, (5), 54–87.

Levine, M.A. (2008). China's CSR expectations mature. *China Business Review*, November-December, 50–53.

Lohmar, B., Gale, F., Tuan, F., & Hansen, J. (2009). China's ongoing agricultural modernization: challenges remain after 30 years of reform. Economic Information Bulletin No. 51 (EIB-51), Washington, DC: Economic Research Service, US Department of Agriculture.

Milne, M.J. & Patten, D.M. (2002). Securing organizational legitimacy. An experimental decision case examining the impact of environmental disclosure. *Accounting, Auditing and Accountability Journal*, 15, (3), 372–405.

Muhammad, A., Jones, K.G. & Blayney, D.P. (2009). Asian dairy markets: A focus on production, consumption and trade. In Bellini Leite, J.L., Siqueira, K.B. & Carvalho, G.R. (eds). *Comércio Internacional de Lacteos*. Segunda edição. Juiz de Fora, Brazil: Embrapa Gado de Leite.

Moerman, L. & Van der Laan, S.L. (2005). Social reporting in the tobacco industry: All smokes and mirrors? *Accounting, Auditing and Accountability Journal*, 13, (8), 374–389.

Noronha, C., Si Tou, M.I. & Guan, J. (2013). Corporate social responsibility reporting in China: An overview and comparison with major trends. *Corporate Social Responsibility and Environmental Management*, 20, (1), 29–42.

Painter-Morland, M. (2006). Triple bottom-line reporting as social grammar: Integrating corporate social responsibility and corporate codes of conduct. *Business Ethics: A European Review*, 15, (4), 352–364.

Palazzo, G. & Scherer, A.G. (2006). Corporate legitimacy as deliberation: A communicative framework. *Journal of Business Ethics*, 66, 71–88.

Patten, D.M. (1991). Exposure, legitimacy and social disclosure. *Journal of Accounting and Public Policy*, 10, 297–308.

Patten, D.M. (1992). Intra-industry environmental disclosures in response to the Alaskan oil spill: A note on legitimacy theory. *Accounting, Organizations and Society*, 17, (5), 471–475.

Pojasek, R.B. (2011). ISO 26000 guidance on social responsibility, *Environmental Quality Management*, 20, (3), 85–93.

Pratten, J. D. & Mashat, A.A. (2009). Corporate social disclosure in Libya. *Social Responsibility Journal*, 5, (3), 311–327.

Rogers, M. & Ryan, R. (2001). The triple bottom line for sustainable community development. *Local Environment*, 6, (3), 279–289.

Slaper, T.F. & Hall, T.J. (2011). The triple bottom line: What is it and how does it work? *Indiana Business Review*, Spring, 4–8.

Soderberg, S. (2012). ISO 26000 – Guidance on Social Responsibility Status. Available at http://www.slideshare.net/StaffanS/iso-26000-social-responsbility-status-dec-2012

Verrecchia, R.E. (1983). Discretionary disclosure. *Journal of Accounting and Economics*, 5, 179–194.

Wang, Q.B. & Zhang, W. (2004). China's potato industry and potential impacts on the global market. *American Journal of Potato Research*, 81, 101–109.

Wang, Q.B., Parsons, R. & Zhang, G. (2010). China's dairy markets: Trends, disparities and implications for trade. *China Agricultural Economic Review*, 2, (3), 356–371.

Xinhua News Agency (2008). Food safety draft law reviewed following tainted dairy products scandal. 24 October. Available at http://www.npc.gov.cn/englishnpc/news/Legislation/2008-10/24/content_1454453.htm

Yan, J. (2011). *Fonterra in the San Lu Milk Scandal – A Case Study of a New Zealand Company in a Product-harm Crisis*. Bachelor of Commerce with Honors dissertation. Lincoln University.

Zaobao (2008). Special Report of Poisonous Milk Powder in China (In Chinese). Available at http://www.zaobao.com/special/china/milk/milk.shtml

Zhang, X.W. & Yang, M.C. (2011). Research on social responsibility and China's sustainable development based on ISO 26000. *M&D Forum*, 85–88. Available at http://www.seiofbluemountain.com/upload/product/201112/2011jscx0a17.pdf

Zeghal, D., & Ahmed, S. A. (1990). Comparison of social responsibility information disclosure media used by Canadian firms. *Accounting, Auditing and Accountability Journal*, 3, (1), 38–53.

5
How Do Chinese SOEs Integrate Economic Functions with Social Functions? A Viewpoint Based on the Analysis of Social Reporting Features

Jenny J.Q. Guan

Introduction

As a core component of the socialist market economy,[1] the state sector (SS) plays an important role in guiding the economic development of China and ensuring its economic function of retaining and increasing the value of national assets. However, securing economic stability and development is not the only responsibility taken by state-owned enterprises (SOEs) as stated by De (2012), "SOEs across the world serve multiple functions and have heterogeneous goals... judging their functions... on the basis of profitability or some other criterion of market-linked efficiency is futile". Nowadays, people expect more from the SS's social function. State-owned or state holding enterprises[2] (SOE) as a major component of the SS automatically undertake the dual function of economy and society. However, under many circumstances, these two functions are irreconcilable. Therefore, this study aims to investigate the SOEs' methods of integrating their economic functions with social functions from the perspective of corporate social responsibility (CSR) reporting.

Literature review

Research conducted by Chinese scholars has indicated the functions of SOEs. For example, Zhou and Guo (2009) conclude that improving national welfare is treated as an essential attribute and major objective of the SOEs. Bi (2006) emphasizes the union of economic and social attributes in SOEs. Wang (2008) lists nine responsibilities which should be taken by SOEs, such as economic responsibility, legal liability and environmental responsibility. Shen et al. (2008) and Long (2008) classify SOEs' social responsibilities by stakeholder groups such as employees, consumers, suppliers, creditors and governments. He also points out that SOEs should have responsibilities at different levels depending on their operational scale. In addition, based on the nature of SOEs, Huang and Yu (2006) emphasize that SOEs' social responsibility can be classified according to their economic and social objectives. However, most of the SOE papers written by Chinese scholars are descriptive in nature; related empirical research is largely absent in both Chinese and international academia. Furthermore, the difference between SOEs' social reporting style and international CSR reporting practice is still unknown. Therefore, this research intends to fill in the gaps through a qualitative content analysis of 100 social reports or sustainability reports issued by SOEs during 2011–2012.

Economic function difference between SOEs and the Chinese government

Regardless of ownership type, the primary objective of an enterprise is to generate profit in order to retain sufficient capital for long-term operation and development. Although SOE is a kind of organ controlled by state policies, it exists as an economic organization rather than an administrative organization. Thus, similar to other enterprises, SOEs also have profit-orientated attributes, as SOEs are owned by all Chinese people and need to retain or increase the value of national assets (Qiao & Liu, 2010). In addition, value created by SOE directly affects the construction of infrastructure and the living standards of Chinese people (Qu, 1997).

The economic features of SOEs lie in domestic politics determined by the Chinese government, which is considered as a political economic function (Xu, 2012). For some pillar industries (such as coal, mine, oil, natural gas, electricity, steel, banking and telecommunication), China has chosen to grow large SOEs and provide protected market positions for them, with preferential treatment and sufficient financial support. All these sectors are treated as "strategic" by the government because of two reasons: they are important to national security, which "includes internal political and social stability, external security and foreign relations"; and they contribute significantly to "the competitiveness of other sectors and the rest of the economy" (Hsueh, 2011: 34). Moreover, these SOEs play major roles in regional or industrial economies and often hold monopolistic or oligopolistic positions. In addition to flourishing within respective industries, these SOEs are also expected to advance Beijing's strategic and political objectives (Xu, 2012). As claimed by Liu, "the development of large, centrally controlled SOEs in the strategic sectors of China's economy offers an adaptive and efficacious strategy to maintain stability in financial systems, energy and natural resources supply, food supply, and transportation and communications systems" (Liu, 2009: 551).

Social function differences between SOEs and other types of enterprises

SOE is considered as an important medium through which government may participate in economic activities (Bi, 2006). The Chinese government has tightened control of the top Chinese industrial firms and at the same time has improved their economic performances since the "grasp the large, release the small" policy was adopted in 1996 (Pearson, 2007). However, owing to SOEs' special role, profit maximization cannot be set as the primary objective, because it is inconsistent with the goal of improving social welfare (Long, 2008). For example, the operation of an SOE leads to environmental problems, and unbalance of economic structure and industrial development. Therefore, to minimize the social cost, SOEs have to slow down production speed and retain profit when operating at low efficiency (Xu & Yang, 2007).

Upon making profits, SOEs also have many more social responsibilities than other enterprises. Nowadays, fulfilling social functions is treated as an important method by which enterprises can increase firm value and reputation. However, SOEs have their own special social functions, which are directly related to the nation's economy and the people's livelihood as well as the healthy development of a market economy (Huang, 2006).

First, under the socialist market economic system, the basic social responsibility of the SOEs is to optimize the allocation of different types of resources for society (Liu, 2008). The purpose is to maximize social welfare, ensure the people's interests and promote harmonious development of society.

At the second level, SOEs are a means for the government to adjust the economic environment through focusing on macro-economic objectives, such as developing science and technology, upgrading industry structure, balancing the development of regional economies, realizing the rational layout of national economies, securing employment, adjusting income allocation, eliminating polarization, and maintaining market discipline and fairness (Zhang & Liu, 2007).

In addition, SOEs play an important role in constructing basic infrastructure, improving people's living standards and creating a good social atmosphere. This includes the following activities (Zhou & Guo, 2009):

(1) Undertaking construction projects with high cost and a long payback period. However, the infrastructure should be able to provide basic services for economic development and improve the people's livelihood in the long run;
(2) Making a large investment in environmental protection and acting as a sustainability pioneer;
(3) Making a contribution to charity at a reasonable level.

Last but not least, SOEs are the economic lifeline of the state. For some industrial sectors, such as banking, railway, power and telecommunications, SOEs have to maintain a monopolistic position in order to ensure the stability of politics, the economy and the military.

As discussed above, SOEs have the dual function of maintaining the economy as well as society. Under many circumstances, these two functions have mutual exclusions (Qiao & Liu, 2010), such as production expansion versus environmental pollution, overcapacity versus employment security. In addition, Xu (2012: 2) states several potential conflicts between the economic function and the social function of SOEs:

> the uneven playing field between public (SOEs) and private enterprises in accessing finance or other political and economic resources the government can distribute; the steady decline in profitability and even losses of some SOEs, which are then paid for by the government and taxpayers; the slow process of introducing an effective corporate governance system in these public enterprises (SOEs) to ensure good performance as well as to prevent corruption. Finally, these state players have raised philosophical and ideological debates on the role of the state, the state versus markets, and "varieties of capitalism".

Although difficulties do exist in reconciling economic and social functions, Naughton (2010: 443) notes that "state control of the commanding heights of the economy allows the Chinese leadership to achieve social goals, while also protecting national security and preventing foreign dominance of the economy". Therefore, "how do SOEs integrate and make the union of both?" becomes an interesting question, and is investigated in the following sections.

Methodology

Content analysis

Content analysis has been applied to investigate SOEs' social reporting practices and classify their responsibilities from economic and social perspectives. Content analysis has been widely used in social accounting research (Guthrie & Parker, 1990; Gray et al., 1995; Milne & Adler, 1999; Parker, 2005; Kamla, 2007; Kamla & Rammal, 2013). Similar to these studies, the present research analyzes the quality of disclosure in social or sustainability reports, and the acknowledgment of certain words and themes within the text (Brennan, 2001; Beattie et al., 2004).The major purpose is to identify the SOEs' common CSR reporting features and style rather than evaluating their reporting framework according to international CSR initiatives. If more than 50% of the selected SOEs present specific features or specific topics, then the related information is deemed to be common disclosure (Franks, 2001; Marcuccio & Steccolini, 2009). Most of the extant literature related to Chinese SOEs enumerates the types of social responsibilities without in-depth analyses and empirical studies (Huang & Yu, 2006; Liu, 2007; Xu & Yang, 2007). For example, Huang and Yu (2006) mention the economic and non-economic objectives of SOEs in their study, but no classification was made according to the features of these objectives.

The analytical procedures are stated below:

Step 1: List the common reporting features identified in the CSR and sustainability reports of selected SOEs;

Step 2: Group the common reporting features into five dimensions, namely economic responsibility, legal liability, environmental responsibility, moral responsibility and political responsibility (Qiao & Liu, 2010; Xu & Yang, 2007; Long, 2008);

Step 3: Differentiate the reporting of political economic functions from social functions. Reference is made to the analytical framework developed by De (2012). De evaluates the performance of petroleum and natural gas SOEs and public sector enterprises in India from the perspectives of economic, political, social and international affairs. In this research, economic and political aspects were merged together and treated as political economic functions. For instance, price stability and employment are important for political, economic and social reasons; controlling monopolies and industrial policies are crucial at the political economic stage. Furthermore, international affairs are also considered as political economy issues in China; examples are energy security and technical cooperation.

Sample selection and period of observation

The SOEs were ranked in terms of revenue figures in 2011 and 2012, respectively. The top 50 SOEs with CSR or sustainability reports were selected for each year (see Table 5.1). Revenue figures and related data were obtained from the CEInet Statistics Database, state data center (db.cei.gov.cn). Social reports and sustainability reports were collected from the firms' websites, the Shanghai Stock Exchange (www.sse.com.cn) and the Shenzhen Stock Exchange (www.szse.cn).

The years 2011 and 2012 were selected as the period of observation because of the following critical issues:

(1) The Fifth Plenum of the 17th Central Committee of the Communist Party of China (CPC) was held on 18 October 2010. The plenum adopted the CPC Central Committee's Proposal for Formulating the 12th Five-Year Program for China's Economic and Social Development (2011–2015).
(2) The Eighteenth National Congress of the Communist Party of China was held on 8 November 2012. One of the major topics was to deepen the structural reform of SOEs.

The plenum and national congress are the most important national meetings, and are held every five years in order to learn from the past, look to the future and, more importantly, to set economic and social development policies and goals for the next five years. The SOEs are treated as actors that are able to implement these policies and objectives during their daily operations. This influence normally affects the SOEs' practices before and after the plenum and national congress. Owing to the incompleteness of the 2013 reports at the time of conducting this research, 2011 and 2012 were selected as two critical years for observation.

Table 5.1 Sample distribution

Industry	2011	2012
Basic Materials	12	12
Oil and Gas	4	4
Industrials	2	3
Airlines	3	3
Automobiles	2	2
Consumer Electronics	2	1
Retail	3	2
Financials	11	12
Technology	4	2
Telecommunications	3	3
Utility	2	2
Construction and Material	2	4
Total	50	50

Findings

Table 5.2 below lists the common CSR reporting features disclosed by selected SOEs. The overall reporting framework is in line with the main content of fulfilling CSR as required by the State-owned Assets Supervision and Administrative Commission (SASAC) in the Guideline (2008). For instance, the Guideline mentioned the following major CSR dimensions: " insisting on a legal and honest way in business operations", "improve corporate governance", "improve product quality and service", "try the best to meet the demand of consumers", "strengthen resource conservation and environmental protection", "promote independent innovation and technological advancement", "ensure production safety", "protecting legal rights of employees" and "participating in social public welfare programs". These dimensions cover more than 60% (at least 17 points out of the total of 28) of the features in Table 5.2. Moreover, the information disclosed is mainly driven by the SOEs' economic objectives and/or social objectives with economic, legal, environmental, moral and political aspects.

To investigate the SOEs' motivations for CSR disclosure, guidelines, communiqués and reports listed in Table 5.3 are the major supporting documents for content analysis. Before and after the important CPC's plenums and national congresses, SOEs study related policy documents intensively and integrate major contents into their CSR reports.

Table 5.2 Classification of common CSR reporting features and objectives

Step 2 Dimension (Responsibility)	Step 1 Common reporting features		% of SOEs disclosed	Step 3 Function (E/S/B)*
Economic	Self-development	1. Generate profit at reasonable level in order to ensure going concern and long-term development	68	E
		2. Independent innovation	94	
	Shareholder's interest and Creditor's interest	3. Retain and increase the value of national assets	83	E
		4. Corporate governance with high standards	100	
	Client's interest and consumer interest	5. Create value for client and cooperate for win-win situation	98	E
		6. Ensure the quality and safety of products and provide good service	100	E
		7. Product innovation for enhancing the influencing power of local or traditional products	93	B
		8. Meet consumer's need	77	S
	Employee's interest	9. Provide training and career development courses	89	S
		10. (1) Improve working environment, provide hygienic and safe conditions, (2) prevent occupational disease and protect legal rights of labor and staff.	(1) 76 (2) 52	S
		11. (1) Respect employee, create and develop good working atmosphere; (2) help employee in trouble or need	(1) 77 (2) 72	S

Table 5.2 (Continued)

Step 2 Dimension (Responsibility)	Step 1 Common reporting features	% of SOEs disclosed	Step 3 Function (E/S/B)*
Legal	12. Consciously accept oversight from government and public	67	B
	13. Observe discipline and abide by the law	100	B
	14. Pay tax in compliance with tax law and make contribution to fiscal income	64	E
Environmental	15. Energy saving and emission reduction; Low carbon concept	100	S
	16. Protect environment and abate pollution	100	
	17. Develop environmentally friendly technology and green manufacturing	88	
Moral	18. Accelerate development of a credit rating system	57	S
	19. Care for vulnerable groups	91	
	20. (1) Proactively participate in charitable activities and (2) make contribution to the construction of infrastructure	(1) 100 (2) 65	
	21. Support the construction of border areas and the development of education	86	
Political	22. Secure employment and adjust income distribution	88	S
	23. (1) Lead industrial innovation, (2) promote industrial reform and upgrade, (3) support the development of national and traditional industries	(1) 58 (2) 57 (3) 66	B
	24. Maintain the order of market economic system and keep a fair market	56	E
	25. Promote balanced development of regional economies and realize reasonable economic layout	83	E
	26. Safeguard national security in related areas	67	S
	27. Serve for national economic strategies and promote sustainable development of economy and society	97	B

*E denotes economic function; S denotes social function; B denotes both.

Table 5.3 List of important policy documents

	Documents	Date
Guideline, 2008	Guidelines to the State-owned Enterprises Directly under the Central Government on Fulfilling Corporate Social Responsibilities released by SASAC	4/1/2008
Communiqué, 2010	Communiqué of the Fifth Plenum of the 17th Central Committee of the Communist Party of China	18/10/ 2010
Report I, 2011	Report on the implementation of the central and local budgets for 2010 and on the draft central and local budgets for 2011, Fourth Session of the Eleventh National People's Congress	5/3/ 2011
Report II, 2011	Report on the implementation of the 2010 plan for national economic and social development and on the 2011 draft plan for national economic and social development, Fourth Session of the Eleventh National People's Congress	5/3/ 2011
Report III, 2011	Report on the work of the government, Fourth Session of the Eleventh National People's Congress	5/3/ 2011
Report I, 2012	Report on the implementation of central and local budgets for 2011 and on draft central and local budgets for 2012, Fifth Session of the Eleventh National People's Congress	5/3/2012
Report II, 2012	Report on the implementation of the 2011 plan for national economic and social development and on the 2012 draft plan for national economic and social development, Fifth Session of the Eleventh National People's Congress	5/3/2012
Report III, 2012	Work report of the standing committee of the Chinese People's Political Consultative Conference (CPPCC) national committee, the Fifth Plenary Session of the Eleventh CPPCC National Committee.	3/3/2012
Report IV, 2012	Report on the work of the government, the Fifth Session of the Eleventh National People's Congress	5/3/2012
Report V, 2012	Report to the Eighteenth National Congress of the Communist Party of China on 8 November 2012	8/11/2012

Economic responsibilities

When SOEs take economic responsibilities, they focus more on the economic function of sustainable development and retaining the value of national assets. Thus, more attention is paid to corporate reputation, staff development, technical innovation, brand image construction and so on. Some of these aspects also cover the SOEs' social function owing to their large operational scale and social position.

The result shows that 68% of SOEs mentioned "generate profit at reasonable level" in their social reports (Point 1, Table 5.2). The word "reasonable" is in accordance with the nature of SOEs, as profit maximization is not their primary goal. Instead, economic stability and sustainable development are more important as SOEs are required to "constantly improving ability of making sustainable profits" (Guideline, 2008). Clues can also be found in Report II (2011: 20), "Local governments should set their growth rates scientifically in line with their actual conditions and base on necessity and possibility. They absolutely should not seek rapid growth at all costs or complete for the fastest rate, still less raise targets at each administrative level…"

As shown below, R&D or innovation is one of the major focus points in the CPC plenums and national congresses held during 2010–2012:

> The plenum called for upgrading China's scientific innovation ability, improving the innovation system and accelerating educational reform and development…
>
> (Communique, 2010)

> …We will increase support for scientific and technological innovation and give impetus to the industrial application of scientific and technological results…
>
> (Report I, 2011: 22)

> …further increase investment in R&D; strive to promote independent innovation…
>
> (Report II, 2011: 20)

> …improving and upgrading the economic structure, we will continue to increase government spending on science and technology and further increase spending on R & D…
>
> (Report II, 2012: 19)

> …to support independent innovation and the development of strategic emerging industries…to develop strategic emerging industries and the plan to improve independent innovation capacity…
>
> (Report II, 2012: 28)

> ...we will vigorously boost innovation in science and technology...
>
> (Report IV, 2012: *Part II major task for 2012, section 5*)

> ...Implement the strategy of innovation-driven development...
>
> (Report V, 2012: *Part IV, Section 2*)

Responding to the government's call, 79% of the SOEs disclosed detailed information related to R&D and independent innovation in their social reports (Points 2 &7, Table 5.2). For example, as a representative of Chinese consumer electronics and the world's largest professional air-conditioning company, combining R&D, manufacturing and marketing as well as after sales service, Gree (Gree Electric Appliance, Inc. of Zhuhai) places special importance on technological innovation. Its ten innovations were elected as state science and technology projects, making Gree one of the companies that owns most state projects in the air-conditioning industry.

Although no direct or clear statement of "retaining the value of state-owned assets" (Point 3, Table 5.2) was mentioned in the communiqué and reports listed in Table 5.3, the following sentences reflect the importance of this point:

> ...We will continue to advance the strategic adjustment of the state sector of the economy and improve the mechanisms for redirecting investments of state capital to ensure its rational flow. We will improve the system for overseeing state-owned financial assets, non-operational state-owned assets and natural resource assets...
>
> (Report III, 2011: 33)

For the aspect of corporate governance (CG) (Point 4, Table 5.2), 100% of the observations provided related information, such as governance structure, board independence and a process to avoid conflicts of interests. It is not only because CG is a routine reporting section, but also because SOEs are required to improve CG and integrate CSR into the CG process (Guideline, 2008). In addition, "strengthening efforts to promote clean government and combat corruption" is emphasized in Report III (2011: 33). Therefore, anti-corruption and anti-bribery also become focal points in the CG section of the SOEs' social reports.

Value creation and win-win cooperation with clients (Point 5, Table 5.2) is another popular reporting aspect, reported by 98% of the

SOEs, which is also implied by the following sentences from Reports II and V:

> ...we will steadfastly implement the win-win strategy of opening up and expand international economic cooperation...
>
> (Report II, 2011: 37)

> ...we must implement a more proactive opening up strategy and improve the open economy so that it promotes mutual benefit and is diversified, balanced, secure and efficient...
>
> (Report V, 2012: *Section IV, Section 5*)

In recent years, several industrial scandals have damaged the brand image of products made in China, such as the poisonous milk powder in 2008 and clenbuterol pork in 2011. Therefore, "product quality or safety" and "consumers' needs" have become two major reporting topics in social reports (Points 6 & 8, Table 5.2). It is also required by the Guideline (2008) to

> Improve product quality and service...try to ensure the safety of products and quality of services, update product performance and service system aiming at providing well-qualified products and service to consumers...protect consumer interests, properly handle consumer complaints and suggestions and try their best to meet the demand of consumers...establish a good image in consumers.

All the observed enterprises provided very detailed information in this aspect. For example, the Shanghai Automotive Group Company performed well in the area of product quality management. The promotion of a "zero-defect" culture and the launching of 142 quality improvement programs have led the group to receive awards from the China Association for Quality and the Shanghai Municipal Bureau of Quality and Technical Supervision.

Employees' interest is the last focal section of economic responsibility, but ultimately is an element of an SOE's social function and objective. Indeed, 89% of the observed SOEs demonstrated their efforts by providing training and career development courses for their staff (Point 9, Table 5.2), which is in line with the target set in the following communiqué and report:

> ...we will make plans for training all types of personnel with the focus on high-level and highly skilled ones...
>
> (Communiqué, 2010)

> ...we will improve the mechanism for training, employing, evaluating, and giving incentives to talented personnel, and create a favorable social environment for them to come to the fore in large numbers and tap their full potential...
>
> (Report IV, 2012: *Part II, section 5*)

The disclosure of working environment (atmosphere), labor right and employee respects (Points 10 &11, Table 5.2) can be treated as an improvement in CSR reporting. In the 2011 and 2012 reports, more than 70% of observations proactively disclosed related information. For example, ZTE Corporation gave special importance to employee well-being by setting up an international Employee Assistance Program, which supports employees in various areas such as mental health and offered extended maternity leave for female staff, as well as special dining halls and rooms for mothers and new-born babies. To support work-life balance, ZTE also founded many internal associations, such as a photography club, dancing club and climbing club, and holds regular "family days" to help employees balance work and life. Another typical example is China Pacific Insurance (Group) Company Limited (CPCC), which mentioned human rights in its social report and integrated relevant practices into its operations. Furthermore, CPCC paid high attention to employee welfare and training, and provided detailed solutions to minimize hygiene and safety risks in the workplace. Obviously, in recent years, more focus is being placed on labor rights and employee welfare in China, which is mainly driven by the emphasis made in various policy documents as shown below:

> ...Safe and healthy working conditions and living environment are necessary to ensure the health of employees, prevent any harm of occupational and other diseases to employees...
>
> (Guideline, 2008)
>
> ...to promote employment and harmonious labor relations, to reasonably adjust income distribution...
>
> (Communiqué, 2010)
>
> ...we will accelerate the establishment of sound mechanisms for safe guarding people's rights and interests, and for evaluating the risks of administrative decisions and correcting wrong decisions...
>
> (Report III, 2011:32)

Legal responsibility

SOEs' legal responsibility is mainly classified as part of their economic function. Abiding law is the basic criterion during daily operations. It is also emphasized in the Eighteenth National Congress, "The rule of law is the basic way for running the country. We should make laws in a scientific way, enforce them strictly, administer justice impartially, and ensure that everyone abides by the law" (Report V, 2012: Part V, Section 4). Any acts violating laws and regulations will directly affect the realization of SOEs' economic functions and in turn will injure their financial benefits. Thus, all the SOEs disclosed information on this aspect (Point 13, Table 5.2). In addition, 67% of the selected SOEs expressed their willingness to accept oversight from government and the public. It is believed that the motivation of disclosure comes from the following statement in Report III (2011: *Part V, Section 6*):

> Improve the mechanism for conducting checks and oversight over the exercise of power... We should tighten intra-Party, democratic and legal oversight as well as oversight through public opinion to ensure that the people oversee the exercise of power and that power is exercised in a transparent manner...

Furthermore, tax contributed by SOEs is the major source of fiscal income: "paying tax in compliance with tax law" (Point 14, Table 5.2) is an inescapable economic mission of the SOEs, to support the construction of public infrastructure. They are required to "insist on a legal and honest way in business operation... to comply with regulations and laws, public ethnics and commercial conventions, and trade rules... also fulfill their tax obligations..." (Guideline, 2008)

Environmental responsibility

In recent years, the environment has been one of the major concerns of the Chinese people, because of a continuous sharp deterioration in air quality. It is also a focal topic in each plenum of CPC and national congresses (see Table 5.4).

In a similar situation, environmental disclosure (Points 15–17, Table 5.2) accounts for much of the SOEs' social reports and has the highest reporting rate of the CSR features listed in Table 5.2. Most of the enterprises, especially those from high-profile industries, disclosed definite figures to demonstrate their efforts in this area. For instance, SAIC Motor Corporation Limited introduced its new-energy

Table 5.4 Content of environmental issues in policy documents

Source	Content quoted
Communiqué, 2010	It is urged that the building of a resource-saving and environment-friendly society should be accelerated, and the ecological conservation culture should be promoted. More work should be done to proactively combat global climate change, increase environment protection, develop the recycling economy, improve resource conservation and management, speed up the construction of the ecological protection system and that of disaster prevention and reduction, and enhance the ability of maintaining sustainable development...
Report I, 2011:21	Funds allocated for capital construction investment in the central government budget will be used mainly to support... energy conservation, emission reductions, ecological conservation and environmental protection.... We will vigorously support energy conservation and emissions reductions, accelerate the creation of a mechanism to compensate for damage caused to the ecological environment, and comprehensively establish a mechanism for subsidizing and rewarding preservation of grassland ecological environments...
Report II, 2011: Section 2 & 3	...reduce energy consumption per unit of GDP by 3.5% compared to last year, reduce the intensity of carbon dioxide emissions by about 3.5%, and cut the four major pollutant indexes – chemical oxygen demand, total ammonia nitrogen and emissions of sulfur dioxide and nitrogen oxide... strengthen energy conservation, emissions reduction, and ecological and environmental... we will actively push for the transformation of the methods of energy production and use, and build a modern energy industrial system that is safe, stable, economical and clean... we will vigorously develop renewable energy sources and promote the development and use of new energy sources... will do a good job of breaking down the overall targets for energy conservation and emissions reductions in the Twelfth Five-Year Plan into local targets...
Report III, 2011:25	...we will strengthen energy conservation, environmental protection and ecological development, and actively respond to climate change....
Report II, 2012: 20 & 30	...intensify efforts to conserve energy and reduce emissions in order to reduce energy consumption per unit of GDP by about 3.5%, decrease the intensity of carbon dioxide emissions by a bigger percentage, cut

Table 5.4 (Continued)

Source	Content quoted
	chemical oxygen demand and emissions of sulfur dioxide both by 2% and total ammonia nitrogen by 1.5%, and stop the emissions of nitrogen oxide from increasing...we will work hard to advance energy conservation, emissions reduction and environmental protection, and accelerate the building of a resource-conserving and environmentally friendly society...
Report IV, 2012: Part II, Section 4	...we will conserve energy, reduce emissions, and protect the ecological environment...
Report V, 2012: Part III & VIII	Major progress should be made in building a resource-conserving and environmentally friendly society... We should remain committed to the basic state policy of conserving resources and protecting the environment as well as the principle of giving high priority to conserving resources, protecting the environment and promoting its natural restoration, and strive for green, circular and low-carbon development...

motors which could transport more than 75% of total visitors while saving around 2,811 tons of fuel and 8,854 tons of carbon. In addition, they invested nearly RMB 38.3 million in 23 energy-saving innovation projects, reducing coal usage by 7,162 tons. Baoshan Iron and Steel Company Limited has recycled more than 130,000 tons of waste equipment as of 2011, saving RMB 80 million. Sinopec Shanghai Petrochemical Company Limited stood out for its commitment to managing its resource use and the promotion of a recycling economy. Sinopec's investment in the environment amounted to RMB 4.1 billion in 2012.

Some other enterprises disclosed detailed information of their environmental protection programs. For example, China Southern Airlines introduced the Green Flight Program, which aims to reduce overall and per passenger carbon emissions, to which end, the company has set itself strict targets to be achieved in coming years; and China Construction Bank has launched the Green Credit Program to support renewable energy, corporate pollution prevention and energy saving measures. The scale of the Green Credit Program has been steadily increasing in the years since, totaling RMB 218 billion in 2012.

Moral responsibilities

Moral responsibilities mainly refer to credibility and charity. More than half of the observed SOEs indicated their attention to building credit systems with their clients and consumers (Point 18, Table 5.2), which is also emphasized by SASAC in the Guideline (2008), "insisting on a legal and honest way in business operation... keep business creditability, oppose improper competition and eradicate corruption in commercial activities".

Similar to environmental issues, charity is another aspect that occupies a significant space in SOEs' social reports. The disclosures are mainly focused on donation, caring vulnerable groups, supporting the construction of border areas or infrastructure and making contribution to education (Points 19–21, Table 5.2). For example, GREE donated RMB 3 million for community health projects, and a further RMB 1 million for reconstruction of a disaster area. Ping An Insurance (Group) Company of China, Limited has finished the set-up of 100 primary schools around China. At the same time, the company actively supports higher education, and has provided RMB 10.69 billion in scholarships and other awards to 3,080 students. China Mobile has supported the government focus on economic development in rural areas and agricultural modernization through the provision of new products and services. The company has set up a rural information network, which became a primary source of agricultural, market and business information in rural communities, established new pricing structures that were affordable in rural communities and expanded its network to the most remote areas of China. As shown in Table 5.5, helping the poor and needy, supporting education and construction of border areas were also widely discussed during plenums of CPC and national congresses, which motivates SOEs to disclose more on these issues.

Political responsibilities

Political responsibilities mainly reflect the SOEs' economic functions, such as t securing employment, adjusting income distribution, reforming and upgrading national or traditional industries, ordering market and economic systems, balancing regional development, safeguarding national security and ensuring sustainable development of economy and society.

As mentioned in the literature review section, profit maximization is not set as a primary objective by the SOEs. Instead, job creation and income distribution adjustment (Point 22, Table 5.2) are two major

Table 5.5 Content of charities in policy documents

Source	Content quoted
Communique, 2010	Poverty alleviation work that targets old revolutionary base areas, ethnic regions, border areas and poverty-stricken areas will be strengthened ... The plenum urged further enforcement of the strategy of rejuvenating the nation through science and education ...
Report I, 2011: Section II	Funds allocated for capital construction investment in the central government budget will be used mainly to support the construction of low-income housing projects and the development of agricultural infrastructure, particularly water conservancy, and education and health infrastructure ... give more support to old revolutionary areas, ethnic areas, border areas and impoverished areas ... increase education spending, and increase returns on the use of education funds ...
Report II, 2011: Section III	... governments at all levels will increase allowances to higher education and secondary vocational school students from poor families as well as subsidies to student cafeterias of such schools ... set up as soon as possible a sound mechanism for coordinating subsistence allowances and unemployment insurance benefits with price rises to guarantee the basic living conditions of low-income people ...
Report III, 2011: 26 & 29	... we will continue to give high priority to education. We will promote the scientific development of education programs, and provide people with more diverse, more equitable and higher-quality education ... we will also vigorously develop charity programs ...
Report I, 2012: 16	... we need to maintain a large scale of government spending so that we can increase expenditures on ensuring and improving living standards; direct more funds toward the primary level, rural and remote areas, and groups with financial difficulties ...
Report IV, Part II, 2012: Section 5	... we will continue to give high priority to develop education ...
Report V, 2012: Part VII, Section 1	... we should support special education, increase subsidies to students from poor families, and ensure that children of rural migrant workers in cities have equal access to education ...

economic functions. 88% of the observed SOEs made disclosure in this aspect, among which 67% disclosed headcount or an increasing number of new staff, and 78% treated "adjusting income distribution" as one of their major tasks. Related topics have often been mentioned in the policy documents:

> ...make adjustments in the distribution of national income...we will spur the adjustment of national income distribution...
>
> (Report I, 2011: *Section II*)

> ...we will increase urban employment by more than 9 million and keep the urban registered unemployment rate no higher than 4.6%...we need to give higher priority to properly solving major problems that concern the immediate interests of the people such as employment, income distribution and social security...we will steadfastly implement a more proactive employment policy...we will rationally adjust income distribution. We will conduct research and formulate a plan to reform income distribution, adjust the pattern of national income distribution, and narrow the income gap...
>
> (Report II, 2011*: Section II & III*)

> ...we will do everything in our power to expand employment. We will continue to implement a more proactive employment policy...we will put more effort into adjusting income distribution...
>
> (Report III, 2011: 28)

> ...we will deepen the reform of the income distribution system...
>
> (Report II, 2012: 34)

> ...we will make every effort to increase employment. Employment is of great importance of China's development and the people's wellbeing...we will deepen reform of the income distribution system...
>
> (Report IV, 2012*: Part II, section 6 & 8*)

> Deliver a better job in creating employment...We should improve the human resources market and employment services, and make unemployment insurance play a bigger role in promoting employment...
>
> (Report V, 2012*: Part VII, Section 2*)

Industrial innovation or reform and ordering a market economic system (Points 23 & 24, Table 5.2) are another two important economic functions. However, compared to other CSR features, the reporting rate of these two aspects is relatively low. This situation is consistent with the low frequency of discussion by the government. Each aspect was mentioned twice in the following reports:

> ... nurture and develop strategic emerging industries; promote the transformation and upgrading of traditional industries...
>
> (Report II, 2011: *Section II*)

> ... improving and upgrading the economic structure, we will continue to increase government spending on science and technology and further increase spending on R&D... we will transform and upgrade traditional industries...
>
> (Report II, 2012: *19 & 28*)

> ... need to continue to strengthen and improve macro control; more actively yet prudently handle the relationships between maintaining steady and rapid economic development... we will make regulation better targeted... establish a sound market monitoring and early warning system... improve contingency plans for regulating key commodity markets and prices...
>
> (Report II, 2012: *Section III*)

> ... we will tighten oversight and ensure market order...
>
> (Report IV, 2012: *Part II, Section 2*)

Similar to other developing countries, the wealth gap between the west and the east, coastland and inland is big in China. Thus, SOEs play an important role in balancing the development of regional economies and respond to the government's call, as shown below, to open manufacturing plants or branches in less developed regions:

> Balanced development between regions should be maintained... master strategy of regional development and the strategy of main functional regions will be implemented, and the urbanization pattern will be improved with enhanced urban management... Great importance should be attached to building a regional development pattern that enables regions to make their advantages complementary with main functions clearly defined, enables more efficient spatial use of the land, and achieves a harmonious relation between humans and nature...
>
> (Communique, 2010)

> ...we will promote balanced development between regions...
>
> (Report III, 2011: *24*)

> ...we need to promote economic restructuring and balanced regional development to spur faster transformation of the pattern of economic development...
>
> (Report I, 2012: *16*)

> ...we will enhance balanced economic development among regions...
>
> (Report IV, 2012: *Part II, section 4*)

In China, several industrial sectors are still monopolized by SOEs because of concerns about national security, such as telecommunications, the financial industry, highways and railways, power generation and so on. In the report of the Eighteenth National Congress, CPC outlines its plans to invest more state capital in major industries which are vital to national security (Report V, 2012: Part IV, Section 1). For this reason, over 60% of the observations made disclosed related information in the social reports. For example, China Mobile described their efforts to avoid the leakage of confidential national information, and Bank of China provided training courses for their staff to allow them to discern international commercial espionage, so they could help to protect national security.

Last but not least, 97% of selected SOEs expressed their loyalty to the country and their determination to promote the sustainable development of economy and society (Point 27, Table 5.2). This is also clearly required by the Guideline (2008), "SOEs should... thoroughly apply the scientific outlook on development, adhere to the demands of human-oriented policy and sustainable development strategy from the Central Government of China...".

Conflicts and challenges

In 2011, SASAC mandated that all SOEs should publish an annual CSR report in an effort to increase their competitiveness.[3] On the one hand, this has led to a very positive improvement, based on the content analysis presented in the previous section. Most reports are well designed and contain information that meets local standards, and they also make reference to international guidelines. On the other hand, many of the reports were produced just to meet SASAC requirements or policy documents, such as Guideline (2008), rather than to reshape a company's long-term business goals and sustainability strategy. Although the government's endorsement has reinforced the CSR reporting practice of SOEs sharply (the number of SOEs publishing CSR reports increased from 1,006 to 1,337 between October 2011 and 2012[4]), there are still several hidden preoccupations which are discussed in the following paragraphs.

Excessive government control on CSR

From the content analysis result, SOEs have taken the responsibility of looking after the social welfare of their current staffs, retired employees, their families and even the regional employment rate (see Table 5.2, employee interest and moral aspects). Enterprises from monopolized or oligopolized industries, such as coal, mining, steel and energy, actually run schools, utilities, entertainment spots, hospitals, cable television stations and many other types of public infrastructures. They have basically relieved the government's burden by delivering this social welfare and care. However, before engaging in CSR, SOEs need to balance their CSR functions with economic functions, and to ensure the resources are in place to carry out related CSR activities without impairing normal business operations. At present, the problem is that many SOEs invest a lot in CSR activities in response to the government's call (see Table 5.2), but fail to perform well in business because of budget constraints, shortages of skilled workers, and unclear or undefined responsibilities and scope. As suggested by the shareholders of General Motors, forcing a firm to take social functions is an "efficient" way to lead to its bankruptcy and to leave a lot of people without social safety in the long run (Glac, 2010). Therefore, the Chinese government should in fact set lower CSR performance expectations on those SOEs which are suffering from financial difficulties. The focus of these enterprises needs to be on survival and competitiveness. They need to fulfill their economic functions in the first place rather than planting forests, building schools or working on other CSR activities (see Table 5.2). Only in this way can real sustainable development be achieved in the long run.

Form more than content

Regardless of SOE's economic functions, their social disclosure has in many aspects followed a pathway that may be likened to recent international experience. According to the content analysis (see Table 5.2), SOEs often engage in sponsorship of local educational facilities, tree planting, and environmental and community efforts, which are the major sustainability contents discussed in the international community.

Nowadays, the CSR of SOEs is considered as China's own global brand and its way of doing business internationally. From the analysis in the Findings section, obviously, China has begun to emphasize sustainability on the leadership agenda and on the international economic and policy stage. It cannot be denied that SOEs represent the state's will. They support, guide, drive and control the development of China's economic system and internationalization process. From this perspective, currently, SOE's economic responsibilities are supported by CSR.

However, insufficient CSR effort is put on other substantive matters, such as the inequality between enterprises and consumers. The business scope of SOEs mainly covers industries of national security, natural resources, public infrastructure, energy and some other pillar industries. This special position leads to serious inequality between enterprises and consumers which, in turn, impairs consumers' rights and violates SOEs' "manifestos", which are disclosed in their social reports. It is mainly reflected by asymmetry or disparity in after-sale service, in monopolized prices and so on. For example, the prices of air tickets are sliding, according to market demand and supply; but in contrast, the price of railway tickets increases year by year. No discount is granted even when occupancy rate is low, such as in the case of the high-speed railway. This problem is caused by centralization and monopolization, which finally affects SOEs' economic functions.

Excessive uniformity of CSR reporting

After reviewing the social reports, it can be strongly felt that donation, emission control, environmental protection, and helping the poor and needy have become the major CSR issues, implying the Chinese meaning of CSR. Furthermore, the related disclosures have very similar words and expressions to the content quoted from policy documents. Indeed, SOEs also need to consider developing a medium and long-term strategy to engage with a wider stakeholder group, such as local communities, employees, business units and suppliers. They need to educate their staff to solve sustainability issues through training, sharing and peer learning among management to ensure long-term success. More importantly, what appears to be missing in the reports is how SOEs have demonstrated engagement with stakeholders, or an assessment of their strategy and the integration of those topics most important to their business model, such as supply chain management, product quality and human rights.

All in all, CSR has become a key part of the government's approach. Government policy is seen as a key reason for SOEs to take

CSR seriously. A survey report indicated that raising an enterprise's profile and supporting government policy were the most often cited reasons for CSR reporting in China (SynTao, 2008); this is in line with our content analysis findings. In addition, a survey on the opinions of citizens in 16 major cities by Liao Wang[5] found that 66% of the participants viewed government as the major driving force for CSR in China.

Conclusion

This study shows that SOEs give focus to CSR issues which directly impact their economic and social functions. Conversely, areas outside their functions are given less priority, such as supply chain and biodiversity. SOEs still see social responsibility merely as corporate philanthropy and guided by instruction from the government. The Chinese government is playing an active role in pushing for a better integration of CSR among SOEs by issuing and imposing CSR guidelines and policy documents. For example, 2011 and 2012 are the first two years of China's Twelfth Five-Year Plan, and mapping our content analysis criteria to the Five-Year Plan resulted in around 67% subcriteria matches. This result shows that to some extent, CSR objectives in policy documents serve as a guideline for SOEs in determining their CSR strategy, which is backed up by the following quotation from the Guideline (2008):

> SOEs should ... enhance their awareness of social responsibility and sustainable development, make overall planning with due consideration of every aspect. They should actively embody their responsibilities and set up good examples for other enterprises in fulfilling CSR so as to promote the construction of a harmonious and well-off society ...

Along the same lines, the Guideline (2008) issued by SASAC has become one of the standard guidelines in CSR reporting. Other industry standards such as China's Industrial Enterprise and Industrial Association Social Responsibility Guideline and China Banking and Financial Institutions Enterprise Social Responsibility Guideline are followed by almost all SOEs in the relevant industries. SOEs are facing increasing scrutiny from the government and industry associations to standardize CSR activities. This top-down process is boosting CSR performance in China.

On the other hand, the Shanghai Stock Exchange and the Shenzhen Stock Exchange have released compulsory guidelines toward CSR disclosure, thus expecting their constituents to follow strict requirements for their CSR reports. The proactive reaction is that 76% of the observed SOEs publishing a CSR report follow either the Shanghai or Shenzhen Stock Exchange Guidelines; 63% of them also integrate the Global Reporting Initiative and ISO 26000. With the ongoing rapid internationalization process, SOEs are expected to improve their CSR reporting framework and to proactively disclose CSR information in all manners for various stakeholder groups in the future.

Notes

1. Building a "socialist market economy" is the key theme of Jiang Zemin's political report to the 14th Congress of the Chinese Communist Party, held on 12–18 October 1992,

   > The objective of economic restructuring is to develop a socialist market economy, keeping the public sector as the dominant one and remuneration according to one's work as the principal mode of distribution, supplemented by other sectors and other modes... The socialist market economy is a component part of the basic system of socialism. So far as the ownership structure is concerned, for a long time to come we should allow diverse sectors of the economy to develop side by side. The public sector, which includes enterprises owned by the whole people and enterprises owned by collectives, is to remain predominant, with the private sector, which includes individually owned and foreign-owned enterprises, as a supplement. Different sectors of the economy can operate jointly in different ways on a voluntary basis. Enterprises owned by the whole people should play the leading role when they compete with others in the market on an equal footing.
   >
   > (*Source: Central Compilation and Translation Bureau*)

2. State-owned and state-holding enterprises include state-owned enterprises plus those firms whose majority shares belong to the government or other SOE. (This latter category, also referred to as state-controlled enterprises, can also include firms in which the state-or SOE-owned share is less than 50% as long as the state or SOE has controlling influence over management and operation (WTO, 2010).
3. Source: http://www.china.org.cn/business/2011-04/01/content_22275584.htm
4. A survey report released by leading Chinese news site Renmin Online in August 2011, available at http://news.xinhuanet.com/politics/2011-08/22/c_121892728.htm
5. A weekly magazine under the supervision of Xinhua News Agency. The survey result is available at http://news.xinhuanet.com/politics/2011-08/22/c_121892728.htm

References

Beattie, V., McInnes, W. & Fearnley, S. (2004). A methodology for analyzing and evaluating narratives in annual reports. A comprehensive descriptive profile and metrics for disclosure quality attributes. *Accounting Forum*, 28, (3), 205–236.

Bi, Z.Q. (2006). *Dual attribute and reform of the state-owned enterprises*. Thesis of Management College of Business Administration Enterprise Management, Capital University of Economics and Business (In Chinese).

Brennan, N. (2001). Reporting intellectual capital in annual reports: Evidence from Ireland. *Accounting, Auditing and Accountability Journal*, 14, (4), 423–436.

Communique (2010). *Communique of the Fifth Plenum of the 17th Central Committee of the Communist Party of China*. edu.sina.com.cn/en/2010-10-20/105258100.shtml.

De, S. (2012). Old jewels in new boxes? India's major public sector petroleum and natural gas exploration and production enterprises, In Xu, Y. (ed.) *The Political Economy of State-owned Enterprises in China and India*. Basingstoke: Palgrave Macmillan.

Franks, A. (2001). How goes the night watchman? An overview of the first annual clinical governance reports (1999/2000) from acute trusts in an English NHS region. *Journal of Management in Medicine*, 15, (3), 220–226.

Glac, K. (2010). The influence of shareholders on corporate social responsibility, History of corporate responsibility project, *Working Paper No.2, Center for Ethical Business Cultures*.

Gray, R., Walters, D., Bebbington, J. & Thompson, I. (1995). The greening of enterprise: An exploration of the (non) role of environmental accounting and environmental accountants in organizational change. *Critical Perspectives on Accounting*, 6, 211–239.

Guideline (2008). *Guidelines to the State-owned Enterprises Directly under the Central Government on Fulfilling Corporate Social Responsibilities released by SASAC*. Available at www.sasac.gov.cn/n2963340/n2964712/4891623.html

Guthrie, J. & Parker, L.D. (1990). Corporate social disclosure practice: A comparative international analysis. *Advances in Public Interest Accounting*, 3, 159–175.

Hsueh, R. (2011). *China's Regulatory State*. Ithaca NY: Cornell University Press.

Huang, S.J. (2006). The nature, objectives and social responsibility of state-owned enterprises. *China Industrial Economy*, 2, 68–76 (In Chinese).

Huang, S.Y. & Yu, J. (2006). The nature, objectives and social responsibility of state-owned enterprises. *China Industrial Economy*, 215, (2), 68–76 (In Chinese).

Kamla, R. (2007). Critically appreciating social accounting and reporting in the Arab Middle East: A postcolonial perspective. *Advances in International Accounting*, 20, 105–177.

Kamla, R. & Rammal, H. G. (2013). Social reporting by Islamic banks: Does social justice matter? *Accounting, Auditing and Accountability Journal*, 26, (6), 911–945.

Liu, L. (2007). CSR research of state-owned enterprises: The framework based on the relationship among enterprise, government and society. *Theory Horizon*, 9, 95–96. (In Chinese).

Liu, J.P. (2008). Ponder over social responsibility of state-owned business. *Journal of Hubei Radio and Television University*, 28, (2), 5–7 (In Chinese).

Liu, Y. (2009). A comparison of China's state-owned enterprises and their counterparts in the United States: Performance and regulatory policy. *Public Administration Review*, 69, 46–52.

Long, X. (2008). On social responsibility of state-owned enterprises in the light of stakeholder theory. *Journal of East China Institute of Technology* (Social Science), 27, (3), 216–220 (In Chinese).

Marcuccio M. & Steccolini, I. (2009). Patterns of voluntary extended performance reporting in Italian local authorities. *International Journal of Public Sector Management*, 22, (2), 146–167.

Milne, M. & Adler, R. (1999). Exploring the reliability of social and environmental disclosures content analysis. *Accounting, Auditing and Accountability Journal*, 12, (2), 237–256.

Naughton, B. (2010). China's distinctive system: can it be a model for others? *Journal of Contemporary China*, 19, (65), 437–460.

Parker, L. (2005). Social and environmental accountability research: A view from the commentary box. *Accounting, Auditing and Accountability Journal*, 18, (6), 842–860.

Pearson, M. (2007). Governing the Chinese economy: Regulatory reform in the service of the state. *Public Administration Review*, 67, 4, 718–730.

Qiao, M.Z. & Liu, F.C. (2010). A study of Chinese state-owned enterprises' CSR on perspective of nature and function. *East China Economic Management*, 24, 3, 86–90 (In Chinese).

Qu, W.B. (1997). Functions of state-owned enterprises. *Research on Financial and Economic Issues*, 8, 24–26 (In Chinese).

Report I. (2011). *Report on the implementation of the central and local budgets for 2010 and on the draft central and local budgets for 2011, Fourth Session of the Eleventh National People's Congress*. Available at www.cctb.net/bygz/wxfy/201103/W020110314374131020688.pdf

Report II. (2011). *Report on the implementation of the 2010 plan for national economic and social development and on the 2011 draft plan for national economic and social development, Fourth Session of the Eleventh National People's Congress*. Available at www.cctb.net/bygz/wxfy/201103/W020110314387180086255.pdf

Report III. (2011). *Report on the work of the government, Fourth Session of the Eleventh National People's Congress*. Available at www.cctb.net/bygz/wxfy/201103/W020110314394380394940.pdf

Report I. (2012). *Report on the implementation of central and local budgets for 2011 and on draft central and local budgets for 2012, Fifth Session of the Eleventh National People's Congress*. Available at www.cctb.net/bygz/wxfy/201203/t20120319_285297.htm

Report II. (2012). *Report on the implementation of the 2011 plan for national economic and social development and on the 2012 draft plan for national economic and social development, Fifth Session of the Eleventh National People's Congress*. Available at www.cctb.net/bygz/wxfy/201203/t20120319_285302.htm

Report III. (2012). *Work report of the standing committee of the Chinese people's political consultative conference (CPPCC) national committee, the Fifth Plenary Session of the Eleventh CPPCC National Committee*. Available at www.cctb.net/bygz/wxfy/201203/t20120319_285307.htm

Report IV. (2012). *Report on the work of the government, the Fifth Session of the Eleventh National People's Congress*. Available at www.cctb.net/bygz/wxfy/201203/t20120319_285310.htm

Report V. (2012). *Report to the Eighteenth National Congress of the Communist Party of China*, news.xinhuanet.com/english/special/18cpcnc/2012-11/17/c_131981259.htm

Shen, Z.Y., Liu, X.G. & Zhou, X.H. (2008). A study on the reform of state-owned enterprises based on social responsibility. *China Industrial Economics*, 9, 141–129 (In Chinese).

SynTao (2008). Journey to Discover Values. Available at www.syntao.com

Wang, X. (2008). Inductive analysis on CSR definitions of SOE in harmonious society. *The Third China Management Annual Meeting*. November 11–12, 2008, Chang Sa, China (In Chinese).

WTO (2010). *Trade Policy Review: China (Revised)*. Geneva: WTO.

Xu, S.K. & Yang, R.D. (2007). A conclusive analysis within the conceptive scope of corporate social responsibility, *China Industrial Economics*, 5, 71–79 (In Chinese).

Xu, Y. (2012). *The Political Economy of State-owned Enterprises in China and India*. Basingstoke: Palgrave Macmillan.

Zhang, C.M. & Liu, W.J. (2007). An analysis of SOEs' social responsibility based on the nature of SOEs. *Forward Position*, 12, 80–84 (In Chinese).

Zhou, B. & Guo, L.C. (2009). On function orientation of national ownership enterprise. *Finance and Economics*, 250, (1), 73–79 (In Chinese).

6
An Initial Exploration of Corporate Social Disclosure and Responsible a Gambling Disclosure in Macau's Gambling Industry

Tiffany C.H. Leung

Introduction

Corporate social responsibility[1] (CSR) has been widely discussed, and this term has been growing in importance in various fields of business studies, for example accounting (Gray et al., 1995a). In particular, CSR is often associated with the gradual increase in corporate reporting of social and environmental policies and practices. According to KPMG's (2011) survey, 95% of the largest global 250 companies in the world report on their CSR, and this activity is often known as corporate social disclosure (CSD). Prior CSD studies have paid relatively little attention to controversial industries (see Campbell et al., 2003; Moerman & Van Der Laan, 2005; Tilling & Tilt, 2010).

Controversial industries have been defined as those which are often linked to "products, services or concepts that for reasons of delicacy, decency, morality, or even fear, elicit reactions of distaste, disgust, offence or outrage when mentioned or when openly presented" (Wilson & West, 1981: 92). Miller and Michelson (2012: 601) further explain that all objects and actions classified as controversial "can generate strong dissensus among societal members". Controversial industries are mostly characterized by social taboos and moral debates, and these industries include both sinful industries (tobacco, alcohol, gambling and pornography) and industries largely associated with emerging environmental, social or ethical issues (weapons, nuclear and biotech) (Cai et al., 2012). Nevertheless, the classification of these industries can change according to time, culture and social norms (Campbell, 2007; Waller et al., 2005; Jo & Na, 2012).

A number of CSD studies have investigated a range of controversial industries, for example the oil industry (US) (Patten, 1992; Unerman, 2000), the mining industry (Australia) (Guthrie & Parker, 1989; Deegan, 2002) and the clothing and retail industry (Bangladesh) (Islam & Deegan, 2008; 2010). Several CSD studies have examined addictive industries such as tobacco (Campbell et al., 2003; Moerman & Van Der Laan, 2005; Tilling & Tilt, 2010) and brewing (Campbell et al., 2006). The gambling industry, a further example of a controversial industry, remains largely unexplored in the CSD literature (Jones et al., 2009 is one of the few). Gambling appears to be a source of tension and conflict between CSR and profit-making organizations. The gambling industry may provide a different context, setting and background (Cai et al., 2012; Soriano et al., 2012). In particular, the industry has been facing a number of challenges, notably "problem gambling". Thus, gambling operators attempt to incorporate an ethical concern known as a responsible gambling (RG) initiative (Blaszczynski et al., 2011).

This chapter attempts to respond to the call for more CSD studies in a specific controversial industry (see Deegan & Blomquist, 2006). The previous CSD literature has not had an extended focus on the gambling industry (see Literature Review). With this novel setting, this chapter opens an opportunity to examine how the gambling industry might employ CSD and responsible gambling disclosure (RGD) (see Reast et al., 2012). Furthermore, this chapter attempts to explore the gambling industry in the Asian context, particularly in a developing economy, where there is a weak institution and poor governance (see Matten & Moon, 2008). This chapter will focus on Macau, a Special Administrative Region of China, where its gross gambling revenue is six times more than that of the Las Vegas Strip, making it the world's largest gambling market (*The Economist*, 2013). This chapter attempts to investigate a main research question – to what extent does Macau's gambling industry disclose CSR-related information? This question seeks to provide an initial exploration of CSD and RGD in Macau's gambling industry.

This chapter is structured as follows. The next section presents a general background summary of the gambling industry in the world and Macau's gambling industry. A brief literature review of CSR, CSD and RG and the theory used are then provided. These are followed by the research design and a presentation of the descriptive findings based on content analysis. A discussion and conclusion wrap up the chapter.

Background

Gambling is said to have a long history and is likely to be related to different aspects of human nature, such as ethics, rationality and faith (Reith, 2007). Gambling is often viewed as a social phenomenon, although it varies across different cultures, values and beliefs (Raylu & Oei, 2004). The industry consists of different forms of betting and gaming, including casino table games, lotteries, sport betting, bingo and online gambling (MarketLine, 2013a).

The gambling industry has provided a number of benefits. From an economic perspective, legalized gambling can be seen as a major source of tax revenue to provide public goods (e.g. education, pension and health service) (Christiansen, 1998; Blaszczynski et al., 2004; Beem & Mikler, 2011) and national infrastructure, employment and tourism (Felsenstein et al., 1999; Korn & Shaffer, 1999; Collins & Lapsley, 2003). However, these benefits heavily depend on the degree of the government's political transparency, fairness and integrity (Cheng, 2009). On the other hand, the gambling industry faces several drawbacks. Owing to the dramatic growth of commercial gambling, this industry creates several socially undesirable externalities in the generation of gaming revenue. Gambling may cause a psychological health crisis (Quinn, 2001) and induce "problem gambling" (McMillen, 1996). Gamblers will enhance the risk of suicide, family violence and social disruption (McMillen, 1996; Korn & Shaffer, 1999).

In order to provide a general overview of the global gambling industry, the size of this sector will be discussed. MarketLine (2013a) shows that this sector had a total revenue of US$456 billion in 2012. This figure reflects the fact that the growing global gambling industry is smaller than the global oil and gas sector (US$3,065.7 billion), but considerably bigger than the banking and brokerage sector (US$63.2 billion) (MarketLine, 2013c; 2013d). More importantly, this global gambling sector grew by 9.2% in 2012, while the Asia-Pacific and European gambling sectors grew by 9.5% and 3.9%, respectively (MarketLine, 2013a). The gambling sector is expected to grow at a rate of 7% from 2012 to 2017 (MarketLine, 2013a).

Table 6.1 shows the global casinos and gaming sectors in five geographical regions, namely Asia-Pacific, America, Europe, Middle East and Africa and the rest of the world (MarketLine, 2013a). Asia-Pacific

Table 6.1 Global casinos and gaming sector geography segmentation

Geography	Total revenue in US$ billion (2012)	Percentage
Asia-Pacific	222.2	48.7
– China	115.6	51.6
– Japan	53.9	24.3
– Australia	21.3	9.8
– South Korea	12.3	5.5
– India	5.7	3.0
– Rest of Asia-Pacific	19.6	5.8
America	98.4	21.6
Europe	97.7	21.4
Middle East	2.7	0.6
Rest of world	37.8	8.3
Total	456	100

Source: Global Casinos and Gaming, MarketLine (2013a; 2013b).

accounts for 48.7% of the global gambling sector, followed by America (21.6%) and Europe (21.4%) (MarketLine, 2013a). The casinos and gaming sectors in the Asia-Pacific region include China, Japan, Australia, South Korea, India and the rest of the region (MarketLine, 2013a; 2013b). The Asian-Pacific casinos and gaming sector value of China, Japan and Australia account for 51.6%, 24.3% and 9.8%, respectively. However, most forms of gambling in China are strictly prohibited. The exception is Macau, where gambling activities are permitted, and Hong Kong, where horse racing, sports betting and lotteries are authorized (see MarketLine, 2013b).

This chapter primarily focuses on Macau (a Special Administrative Region in mainland China), where the gambling industry is the leading industry. Notably, Macau's gross gambling revenue has replaced the Las Vegas Strip as the world's largest gambling market (Eadington & Siu, 2007). Macau, a Portuguese colony for over 400 years, has a unique mixture of Asian and Portuguese cultures (Hannigan, 2007; Fallows, 2009). Macau has been experiencing legalized gambling for more than 150 years and is the only legal place where it is possible to gamble in casinos in mainland China (Vong, 2004; BBC, 2009; MarketLine, 2013b). Tai Heng Company held the monopoly on the industry from the 1930s to 1960s (Hobson, 1995); then, Stanley Ho purchased the gambling license in 1961 and held it for four decades (Gaylord, 2008). The liberalization of Macau's gambling industry was in 2002, when it was opened to international gambling companies (Fallows, 2009). The government of Macau was allowed to increase the number of concessions from three to six (Fallows, 2009). Macau's Special Administrative Region Gaming Inspection and Coordination Bureau (2013) reports that there are six major licensed gambling operators, with one domestic company (SJM Holdings Limited), one Hong Kong company (Galaxy International Development Limited), and four international gambling companies (Wynn Resorts Limited, Las Vegas Sands Corporation, MGM Mirage and Melco International Development Limited). The number of casinos has increased from 15 in 2004 to 35 in 2013. Importantly, two gambling concession contracts will be valid until 2020, while the others will be valid until 2022.

In 2011, Macau attracted more than 28 million tourists, which is 50 times greater than its population (Government of Macau SAR Statistics and Census Service, 2012a). Importantly, 50% of the gaming profit was from VIP rooms (*The Economist*, 2013). In addition, all gambling operators should contribute 35% of their gross gaming revenue to the government of Macau as a gambling tax and an additional 4% for other social and cultural activities (The Government Information Bureau, 2010).

In spite of Macau's gambling industry's significant economic contribution to the local community, the industry creates socially undesirable externalities, notably problem gambling. This is increasing amongst those between 15 and 64 years old, from 4.3% to 6.0% between 2003 and 2007 (The Institute for the Study of Commercial Gaming, 2009). In particular, the prevalence rate of problem gambling in Macau is greater than that in Hong Kong with 4.5%, Australia with 1.5% and some places in China between 2.5% and 4.0% (LaPlante et al., 2008; Loo et al., 2008; The Institute for the Study of Commercial Gaming, 2009; Miller & Michelson, 2012).

According to Fong et al.'s (2011: 46 & 48) study, the social cost[2] of gambling, which includes treatment costs, prevention costs, family or friends' physical and psychological costs, legal costs, rent-seeking costs, regulatory expenses and public cost of training, and promotion and research in Macau, rose from US$40 million in 2003 to US$106 million in 2007 and has serious social impact on neighboring countries, such as mainland China (Fong et al., 2011). Importantly, nearly 90% of the clientele is from mainland China, rather than from Macau (The Government Information Bureau, 2010). Starting from 2003, the Free Individual Traveler Scheme (FITS) has permitted a large number of Chinese visitors to stay and travel in Macau for a week (Gu & Tam, 2011).

Literature review

CSD can be regarded as one of the management tactics in CSR. Gray et al. (1996: 3) define CSD or social and environmental accounting" (SEA) as "the process of communicating the social and environmental effects of organizations' economic actions to particular interest groups within society and to society at large. As such it involves extending the accountability of organizations (particularly companies), beyond the traditional role of providing a financial account to the owners of capital, in particular shareholders". Owing to a dramatic increase in economic, social and environmental reporting practices over the last decades, KPMG (2005) shows that 50% of the largest global 250 companies in the world used CSD to report on what might be thought as their claim of corporate responsibility activities. This trend grew considerably from 80% in 2008 to 95% in 2011 (KPMG, 2008; 2011). These phenomena are due to several common drivers, such as managing legitimacy (Deegan et al., 2002; Patten, 2002) and stakeholder demands (Islam & Deegan, 2010).

A number of CSR studies have attempted to compare the gambling industry with other controversial industries in terms of financial performance, firm value and firm risk (Lee & Park, 2009; Cai et al., 2012; Jo & Na, 2012). Other CSR studies have analyzed a single aspect, for example the relationship between consumers' perception of gambling and CSR (Li et al., 2011; Soriano et al., 2012). However, relatively few studies have investigated CSR in the gambling industry in developing countries, with some notable exceptions, such as China's sports lottery industry (Li et al., 2011).

Since the social consequences of gambling can be harmful, gambling operators incorporate ethical concerns in their business operations, so-called RG initiatives (Blaszczynski et al., 2004; 2011). These initiatives have been introduced in certain Western countries, notably Australia, Canada, New Zealand, the UK and the US; however, the legislation and voluntary RG codes vary greatly across countries. Several studies have concentrated on casino employees' perspectives of RG and were conducted in the US (LaPlante et al., 2011), Canada (Giroux et al., 2008) and Australia (Breen et al., 2005; Hing & Nuske, 2011). Yet a few RG studies have focused on developing countries. Tyawa's (2012) study provides a general introduction to gambling and RG in South Africa, while Vong (2010) explores students' and teachers' perceptions of CSR and RG in Macau.

Regarding CSD in the gambling industry, there is little exploration and investigation in this context. Jones et al.'s (2009) study is one of the few that examines CSR reports posted on the website of gambling companies in the UK. Their study examines CSR issues by using online reporting among 16 companies. Their results show that four sampled companies published CSR reports, nine companies provided limited CSR information confined to RG issues and three companies did not explicitly mention CSR. CSR issues are related to the marketplace, the workplace, the environment and the community. Their findings indicate that there is no coercive force in the legislation to ensure CSD.

In particular, a few prior CSD studies have applied legitimacy theory in the context of the tobacco industry. Campbell et al. (2003) conducted a longitudinal study of voluntary social disclosure of companies in the tobacco, brewing and retailing industries in the UK, and the findings show that the volume of social disclosure in the annual reports varies across sectors. When corporations are faced with a threat, they increase the volume of social disclosure as a legitimizing strategy; however, British American Tobacco (BAT)'s social disclosure declined over time, and the findings do not support the traditional view (Campbell et al., 2003). Moerman and Van Der Laan (2005) conducted another study of the tobacco industry, and they explored BAT's 2001/2002 social report. Their findings indicate that managing the perceptions of society through social reporting appears to forestall the introduction of stringent laws, privileging certain issues and deflecting poor social performance (Moerman & Van Der Laan, 2005). Another study was conducted by Tilling and Tilt (2010). The authors provide a longitudinal study (1955–1999) of CSD in the annual reports of the Rothmans Limited (an Australian-based tobacco company). Their findings indicate that voluntary social and environmental disclosures may have been provided with a view to counteracting the negative information and the organizational legitimacy of the smoking and health debate (Tilling & Tilt, 2010). Their results support the traditional view that when corporations face a threat, they engage in legitimizing strategies, such as increasing the volume of disclosure. However, their quantitative analysis did not support this (Tilling & Tilt, 2010).

In conclusion, several CSR and RG studies have attempted to investigate issues in the gambling industry. However, relatively few prior CSD studies have concentrated on the gambling industry. This study investigates to what extent organizations in Macau's gambling industry disclose CSR-related information. It will explore CSD primarily in the annual reports from six gambling companies in Macau. The selected sample includes 17 annual reports over three years from 2007 to 2009.

Legitimacy theory

A controversial industry can be regarded as contested. The level of cognitive beliefs about the product or service helps to constitute product acceptability and reconfigure a controversial industry's legitimacy (Galvin et al., 2004–2005). In this chapter, it will be argued that the construction of legitimacy in the gambling industry can be complex owing to both laws and societal norms.

First, there is the dichotomy of free market-based regulations and gambling prohibition, "which does not seem to advance us very far as both positions in pure and simple form are rather marginal in mainstream debate" (Borrell, 2008: 267). From an industry perspective, some gambling regulations are suitable owing to an increase in lucrative profit (Borrell, 2008). Much debate exists around which type of gambling activities should be legalized. However, Galvin et al. (2004–2005: 69) argue that "the struggles over industry legitimacy are less about the activity of gambling per se, and much more about the authorized organizations and locations in which these activities take place". Thus, it is subject to significant regulations and control by government (Miller & Michelson, 2012). Some developed countries, for example the US, the UK and Australia, have legalized the gambling industry for urban regeneration, tax revenue and tourism development (Austrin & West, 2005). In this vein, the legitimacy of the gambling industry can ensure the stability of businesses and investors (Borrell, 2008). The gambling industry therefore responds to any accusations by providing official arguments and legal justifications for its actions (see also Spar & La Mure, 2003).

Second, gambling tends to be socially constructed as illegitimate owing to its historical background (Reith, 2007). However, the evolution of gambling can be characterized as a movement from an illegitimate form to a legitimated form of socially undesirable behavior of recreation and consumption because of economic, political, and cultural changes in Western society (Reith, 2007). Hence, the legitimacy of gambling is susceptible to reinterpretation and change over time (see Johnson & Holub, 2003). For these two reasons, legitimacy theory can offer a starting point and provides a useful lens for investigating CSD in the gambling industry.

Legitimacy theory, derived from political economy theories (Deegan, 2007), explains why corporations undertake certain actions (Deegan,

2007). Legitimacy theory has been widely employed in management studies and the CSR and CSD literature; however, this theory needs further development (Neu et al., 1998; Deegan, 2007; Tilling & Tilt, 2010).

Suchman (1995: 574) provides a generic definition of legitimacy as "a generalized perception or assumption that the actions of an entity are desirable, proper or appropriate within some socially constructed systems of norms, values, beliefs and definition". Legitimacy can be understood as actors' perceptions of the organization, as a judgment regarding the organization, or as the "behavioral consequences of perception and judgment" so as to reveal actors' actions, particularly "acceptance" and "endorsement" (Bitektine, 2011: 152).

Suchman (1995) suggests that there are two main streams of organizational legitimacy: strategic and institutional legitimacy. Strategic legitimacy takes a micro level of analysis by referring to "a managerial perspective [which] emphasizes the ways in which organizations instrumentally manipulate and deploy evocative symbols in order to garner societal support" (Suchman, 1995: 572). This approach assumes that managers have a high degree of control over the legitimacy process (Dowling & Pfeffer, 1975; Ashforth & Gibbs, 1990; Lindblom, 1993). Ashforth and Gibbs (1990) suggest legitimation practices and Suchman (1995) further explores three distinct purposes of legitimacy: gaining, maintaining and repairing legitimacy. The choice of legitimation tactics often depends on the aims of any organizational response (O'Donovan, 2002: 349).

Organizational legitimacy suggests strategic initiatives for organizations seeking or gaining legitimacy in controversial industries (Campbell et al., 2003; Deegan & Blomquist, 2006; Tilling & Tilt, 2010; Reast et al., 2012). In particular, the tobacco industry has often faced ongoing threats to its legitimacy: smoking and health issues (Tilling & Tilt, 2010). Thus, this industry appears to adopt proactive strategies in gaining legitimacy, rather than taking reactive strategies to repair legitimacy in order to respond to an unforeseen crisis. Similarly, legitimacy theory can be employed in the context of the gambling industry, which tends to have a similar contested nature to controversial industries (see introduction).

According to strategic legitimacy, the gambling industry has been facing ongoing threats to its legitimacy, notably in the form of gambling addiction and health-related issues. The legitimacy threat can create a significant legitimacy gap (Sethi, 1978), which is used to describe a situation where there is a lack of correspondence between the actual or perceived behavior of an organization and social values and norms.

This main reason provides an important motivation for organizational legitimation within the gambling industry.

The gambling industry might endeavor to reduce this gap through identifying some symbols of social legitimacy, particularly CSD. Organizations in the gambling industry are expected to deploy legitimating disclosure more strongly (see Campbell et al., 2003; Moerman & Van Der Laan, 2005; Tilling & Tilt, 2010), particularly RGD (e.g. gambling addiction and health-related information) to minimize the legitimacy gap.

Dowling and Pfeffer (1975: 127) suggest three ways in which corporations can face legitimacy threats: (1) the organization can adapt its output, goals and methods of operation to conform to prevailing definitions of legitimacy; (2) the organization can attempt, through communication, to alter the definition of social legitimacy so that it conforms to the organization's present practices, output and value; and (3) the organization can attempt, again through communication, to become identified with symbols, values or institutions which have a strong base of social legitimacy.

Consistent with Dowling and Pfeffer's communication strategy, Lindblom (1993) states that legitimacy is a dynamic concept. Lindblom (1993) argues that a distinction between legitimacy and legitimation needs to be considered. Legitimacy is a status or condition, whereas legitimation is the process of obtaining states or conditions. When organizations face different legitimacy threats, they tend to adopt four common legitimation strategies, which overlap with Dowling and Pfeffer's (1975) work. Lindblom (1993) identified four legitimation strategies: (1) an attempt to educate its stakeholders about the organization's intentions to improve that performance; (2) an attempt to change stakeholders' perceptions of the event (but without changing its actual performance); (3) an attempt to distract (manipulate) attention from the perceived problem areas (concentrate on some positive activities not necessarily related to the failure itself); (4) an attempt to change external expectations about its performance. Dowling and Pfeffer's (1975) and Lindblom's (1993) legitimacy strategies have been extensively employed in CSD studies, which in turn limit legitimacy to a superficial level of examining a set of strategies, rather than examining a deeper level of discussing the concept of legitimacy itself.

On the other hand, institutional legitimacy takes a macro level of analysis and tends to focus on how organizations adopt an institutional environment to manage legitimacy (DiMaggio & Powell, 1983; Meyer & Rowan, 1991). DiMaggio and Powell (1983) propose that three important processes are employed to maintain institutional legitimacy:

coercive isomorphism, mimetic processes and normative pressures. Organizations in the gambling industry are expected to be shaped by or to conform to the institutional environment, such as national authorities, industry associations and local governments.

Coercive isomorphism refers to organizations becoming similar "not through adaptation to an external or technically demanding environment or through weeding out of technical and social misfits, but through adaptation to a socially constructed environment" (Boxenbaum & Jonsson, 2008: 80). This institutional environment refers to organizational behavior which may be controlled by institutional pressure rather than by managers who produce an "iron cage" and follow isomorphism in the organizational domain (DiMaggio & Powell, 1983). However, these pressures may be complex, pervasive and powerful, and explain why and how organizations should exist and behave (Milne & Patten, 2002). Coercive isomorphism includes both formal and informal rules for organizations. Formal rules are considered as hard law and forms of regulative pressures from governmental regulation (Scherer & Palazzo, 2011), while informal rules are regarded as "soft law"[3], voluntary actions and self-regulation of companies without governmental power. Self-regulation can be viewed as the "new institutionalism" in CSR, which includes codified rules, norms and regulations assigning legitimacy to new management practices (Matten & Moon, 2008; Moon et al., 2011). The new institution can be divided into four main types: responsible global business institutions within companies, responsible global business institution among companies, multi-stakeholder institutions involving responsible global business and international government-led institutions for responsible business (Moon et al., 2010).

Mimetic pressures arise mostly from uncertainties in the business environment, for example changes in consumer preferences, absence of government regulations or negative publicity (Bondy et al., 2012). Organizations are likely to imitate peers that are perceived as influential or successful (Haveman, 1993), and sometimes managers seem to consider practices from industry peers, for example total quality management, as "best practices" (Matten & Moon, 2008).

Normative pressures refer to what is generally considered a proper moral duty (Suchman, 1995). Such pressures are usually related to an external source, such as education and professional authorities which, directly or indirectly, set standards for legitimate organizational practices (Matten & Moon, 2008). Importantly, professional power is usually assigned by the state (DiMaggio & Powell, 1983). Such authorities can standardize the "skills and cognitive base" for members of education and professional authorities so as to develop the "legitimacy for their occupational autonomy" (Bondy et al., 2012: 283). Therefore, universities and professional training bodies are the main centers for the development of organizational norms for managers and their staff (DiMaggio & Power, 1983). There are signals from the organizational environment that adoption of a certain practice or structure is a proper action (Boxenbaum & Jonsson, 2008).

The limitation of institutional legitimacy needs to be considered. DiMaggio and Powell's (1983) theoretical framework is ambiguous, therefore leading empirical researchers to develop their own methods (Oliver, 1988). Isomorphic pressure has been found in relation to competitive pressure, space and time (Dacin, 1997; Ruef & Scott, 1998). Mimetic pressure has received the most attention among the three isomorphic pressures (Mizruchi & Fein, 1999). It is more widely employed than coercive and normative pressures in North American social sciences, while coercive and normative pressures are usually used in certain institutional literature, such as the European institutional school (Mizruchi & Fein, 1999). In addition, mimetic pressure is easier than coercive and normative pressures to examine with quantitative methods, while it is more difficult to collect data in quantitative studies with coercive and normative pressures than with mimetic pressure (Mizruchi & Fein, 1999). DiMaggio and Powell's (1983) study seems to ignore the connection between institutional processes and elite interests (Tolbert & Zucker, 1983). The political consequences of institutional process can generally be lost in organization theory (see Stern & Barley, 1996).

Research Design

This study uses a conventional content analysis[4] to examine the data and to discern the pattern, salience and trend of CSR-related information in Macau's gambling industry. Content analysis has been widely employed in the CSD literature (see Gray et al., 1995a; Hackston & Milne, 1996; Williams & Pei, 1999).

Content analysis has three main advantages: (1) it has clear coding rules and procedures to ensure replications and transparency; (2) it does not involve any participants; (3) it is flexible because it uses different media (Bryman & Bell, 2011). On the other hand, this method has a number of limitations: (1) errors in setting a coding rule or manual; (2) difficulties in asking why questions; (3) problem of getting authentic documents (Bryman & Bell, 2007; Beattie et al., 2004).

Macau was chosen in this study because of the restriction of most forms of gambling in mainland China. All six licensed gambling companies, namely SJM Holdings Limited, Galaxy Entertainment Group Limited, Melco International Development Limited, Las Vegas Sands Corporation, Wynn Resorts Limited and MGM Mirage, were selected in the sample. The data were taken for three years[5] in order to provide a general understanding of CSD in Macau's gambling industry.

There are shortages of CSR reports, stand-alone reports and integrated reports on Macau's gambling industry. Only Melco International Development Limited and MGM Mirage provided CSR reports, while other sampled companies did not. Additionally, the sampled companies provide neither stand-alone reports nor integrated reports. However, all of them provide CSR information on their corporate websites. Thus, the websites were used for any updated CSR-related information. In order to have a systematic data set, annual reports download from the corporate website were selected as the sampling units.

There are a number of reasons for selecting annual reports as sampling units: (1) a higher degree of credibility than other types of reports to shareholders and stakeholders (Tilt, 1994; Deegan & Rankin, 1997; Buhr, 1998; Neu et al., 1998); (2) they represent a way of communication and social construction (Hines, 1988; Neimark, 1992); (3) a statutory form of mandatory and voluntary reporting (Hackston & Milne, 1996; Wilmshurst & Frost, 2000); (4) more easily accessible via corporate websites than other corporate reports (Adams & Harte, 1998; Wilmshurst & Frost, 2000). However, annual reports cannot provide a full picture of CSR policies (Roberts, 1992) and can be viewed as superficial disclosures of CSR information (Gray & Bebbington, 2001). Other functions are frequently published in separate reports rather than in annual reports (Gray, 2001).

The choice of the enumeration was made in order to capture the CSR-related information. The enumeration units usually include words (Deegan & Gordon, 1996; Deegan & Rankin, 1996; Wilmshurst & Frost, 2000), sentences (Hackston & Milne, 1996, Patten & Crampton, 2004) and pages (Guthrie & Parker, 1990, Gray et al., 1995b; Unerman, 2000), frequency of disclosure (Cowen et al., 1987) or high/low disclosure rating (Patten, 1991). This study chose the proportion of pages devoted to CSR information as the unit of analysis for several reasons. Pages can not only overcome grammatical differences, but also cover non-narrative disclosure, such as photographs, charts and figures, which are more powerful than narrative disclosure (words or sentences) as stakeholders may not have time to read all the details in annual reports (Unerman, 2000).

Measuring the proportion of pages will thus provide potentially immediate and effective methods of communication (Beattie & Jones, 1992; 1994; Graves et al., 1996; Preston et al, 1996). However, the use of pages has some difficulties, for example measuring font size, some problems of comparability when using a grid, difficulty in capturing boldness and color in both non-narrative and narrative disclosures (Ng, 1995 cited in Hackston & Milne, 1996; Wilmshurst & Frost, 2000; Beattie & Thomson, 2007). Milne and Adler (1999) show that counts of sentences give similar results to proportions of pages. Thus, the volume of pages seems to be the best method for use in this study.

The categories and subcategories were based on those established categories, including environment, consumer/product, community, employees, directors, corporate governance and other information (Gray et al., 1995a; 1995b; CSEAR, 2011). However, adjustments were made owing to cultural differences (e.g. the context of Macau), emerging issues from the literature (e.g. economic performance) and the context of the gambling industry (e.g. responsible gambling). CSD was divided into eight categories: economic, environment, consumers (+ responsible gambling), community, employees, directors, corporate governance and other disclosures (see Appendix 6.1[6]).

Further analysis will be divided into mandatory and voluntary disclosure (see Table 6.2 and Appendix 6.2). This classification can depict legislative disclosure (minimum disclosure) and voluntary disclosure beyond minimum requirement (see Adams et al., 1995; Gray et al., 1995a). The sampled companies are listed on the Hong Kong Stock Exchange, so these organizations comply with the reporting legislation of such regulatory bodies or authorities, for example Hong Kong Accounting Standards, International Financial Reporting Standards and International Accounting Standards. This compliance can be viewed as mandatory disclosure. However, other scholars have not divided disclosure into mandatory and voluntary disclosure (Patten, 1991; Hackston &

Table 6.2 Difference between mandatory and voluntary disclosure

Type of disclosure	Definition	Explanation
Mandatory disclosure	Legislative disclosure (minimum disclosure)	Corporations need to comply with reporting requirements in local authorities.
Voluntary disclosure	Disclosure beyond minimum requirement	Corporations report information beyond the local authorities.

Milne, 1996). Patten (1991) argues that a distinction between two types of disclosures is not useful owing to the low level of mandatory disclosure. The distinction between the two types of disclosures can arguably be considered, to observe whether corporations follow the minimum disclosure standards.

The author conducted a pilot study before the formal study was carried out. The classification scheme is designed to be reliable, consistent and robust so that different people coding the same text can get similar results (Weber, 1990). The author coded the text at different times and invited four colleagues from the research department (School of Management, University of St Andrews) to code the same text in order to adjust and refine the coding schedule, to increase intra-coder and inter-coder reliability and to limit inconsistency.

The results of this pilot study suggested that Gray et al.'s (1995b) categories were largely appropriate. First, economic development seemed to be a main factor in developing countries; thus this subcategory was added. Second, the subcategory of stakeholder engagement disclosure was added in the community category, which emerged from the KPMG reports (2005; 2008). Third, the subcategory of RGD was also added in the consumer category owing to the large number of times it is mentioned in the sampled annual reports. The final sample of this study includes 17 annual reports over three years. The next section discusses the descriptive results and provides some explanations.

Descriptive findings

Trends in total CSD

Figure 6.1 is a comparison of CSD in Macau's gambling industry. The highest volume of disclosure over three years is from Melco International Development Limited, followed by Galaxy Entertainment Group Limited and SJM Holdings Limited. Surprisingly, the volume of disclosure of the international gambling companies, namely Las Vegas Sands Corporation, Wynn Resorts Limited and MGM Mirage appears to be lower than the other companies. Further analysis will be discussed in the following sections.

Themes analysis in Macau's gambling industry

Figure 6.2 provides a general overview of different types of disclosure across six gambling companies in Macau. First, both director and employee disclosures dominated the annual reports. This finding is in line with those of the prior CSD literature and indicates the importance

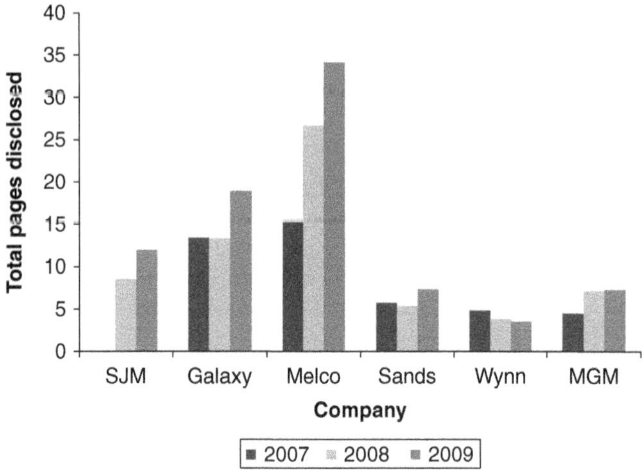

Figure 6.1 Average volume of total, voluntary and mandatory CSD in Macau's gambling industry (2007–2009)

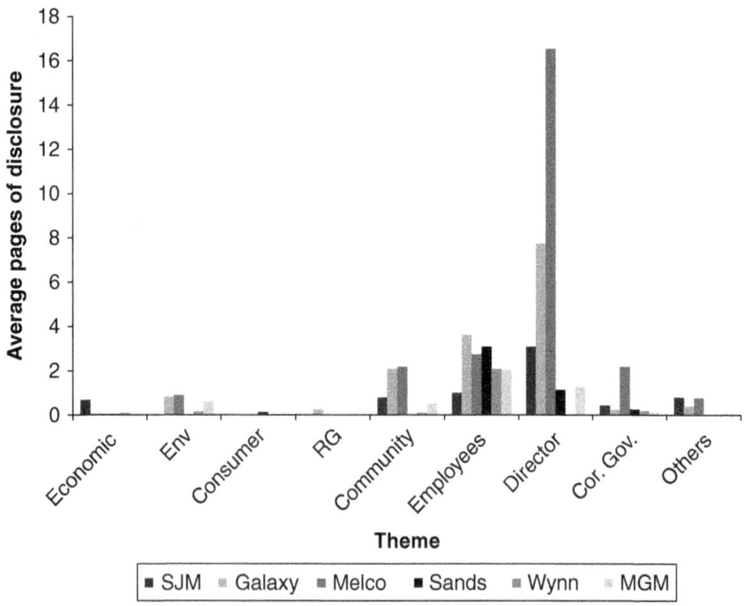

Figure 6.2 Total pages of CSD across six companies in Macau's gambling industry (2007–2009)

of mandatory disclosure (Gray et al., 1995a; Parker, 2008/2009). Second, the volume of voluntary disclosure appears to be very low in general. This is because there is no soft regulation of voluntary disclosure. This means the effectiveness of soft regulations depends to a large extent on "the extent to which the inherent norms are understood and spread among business" (Moon et al., 2011). Third, environmental disclosure in the sampled companies tends to be very low on average. These findings concerning Macau's gambling industry are inconsistent with those of previous studies (KPMG, 2005; 2008), which found that companies in various sectors (in developed countries) tend to disclose environmental information. Fourth, little economic disclosure, which includes economic performance, market presence and indirect economic impact, is disclosed. However, SJM Holdings Limited's volume of disclosure is relatively higher than that of the other sampled companies. Since SJM Holdings Limited has been operating since the 1960s, this company tends to claim that it plays a significant economic contribution to the local community in terms of job creation and local infrastructure development. Finally, one unique theme pertaining to this industry is often RGD. However, this is very unsatisfactory, with a low volume of disclosure or almost no disclosure (see Figure 6.5). In particular, SJM Holdings Limited and Galaxy Entertainment Group Limited provide a relatively higher volume of RGD than the other sampled companies, which offer no disclosure.

Mandatory disclosure

Figure 6.3 shows that mandatory disclosure in Macau's gambling companies can be mainly divided into director disclosure, mandatory employee disclosure and corporate governance disclosure. The average volume of director disclosure is 4.96 pages higher than that of other types of disclosure, which is less than one page (see Table 6.2).

Director disclosure

Figure 6.3 illustrates that director disclosure is the highest in the volume of mandatory disclosure. These findings are in line with prior CSD studies, which suggest that the volume of director disclosure appears to be an important mandatory disclosure (see Parker, 2008/2009). In particular, director disclosure is dominated by that from one company, Melco International Development Limited, followed by Galaxy Entertainment Group Limited. The former company has the highest volume

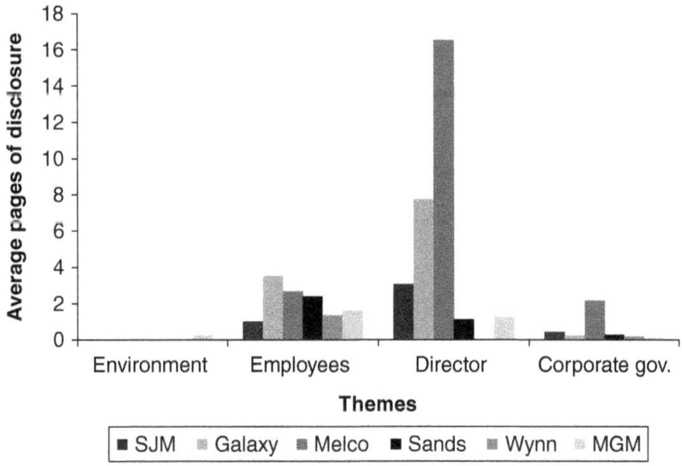

Figure 6.3 Average volume of mandatory disclosure among six companies in Macau (2007–2009)

of director disclosure with a maximum of 16.54 pages between 2007 and 2009, while the latter company has a volume of director disclosure of approximately 7.75 pages over the three-year period. All of the gambling companies are listed on the Hong Kong Stock Exchange. However, four of the sampled companies, namely Wynn Resorts Limited, Las Vegas Sands Corporation, MGM Mirage and Melco International Development Limited, are international gaming companies which are not only listed on the Hong Kong Stock Exchange, but are also listed on the National Association of Securities Dealers Automated Quotations (NASDAQ). These companies comply with all requirements under Section 404 of the Sarbanes-Oxley Act for US-listed companies. These organizations require mandatory disclosure concerning directors' information, such as directors' emoluments, remuneration and short-term benefits. The following text is extracted from one of the sampled annual reports.

Emoluments of Directors

> The emoluments of the Directors are determined with regard to the performance of individuals, the Company's operating results and market standards. During the year, the Remuneration Committee has considered and approved bonus payments to employees of the Group, salary increase for general employees, salary cut arrangement

for some of the senior staff of the Group, share options and restricted shares granted to the Directors and management of the Group.

(Macau, Melco International Development Limited, 2008: 50)

Mandatory employee disclosure

Employee disclosure can be divided into two types: mandatory and voluntary employee disclosures (Figures 6.3 and 6.4). This section mainly concentrates on the former. This type of disclosure can be seen as a statutory item in the annual reports (Day & Woodward, 2004). These findings are in line with those of previous CSD studies, which found that employee disclosure was the most common disclosure in annual reports (Guthrie & Parker, 1990; Roberts, 1992; Adams et al., 1995; Gray et al., 1995a; Hackston & Milne, 1996; Adams et al., 1998; Parker, 2008/2009). All of the gambling companies are listed on the Hong Kong

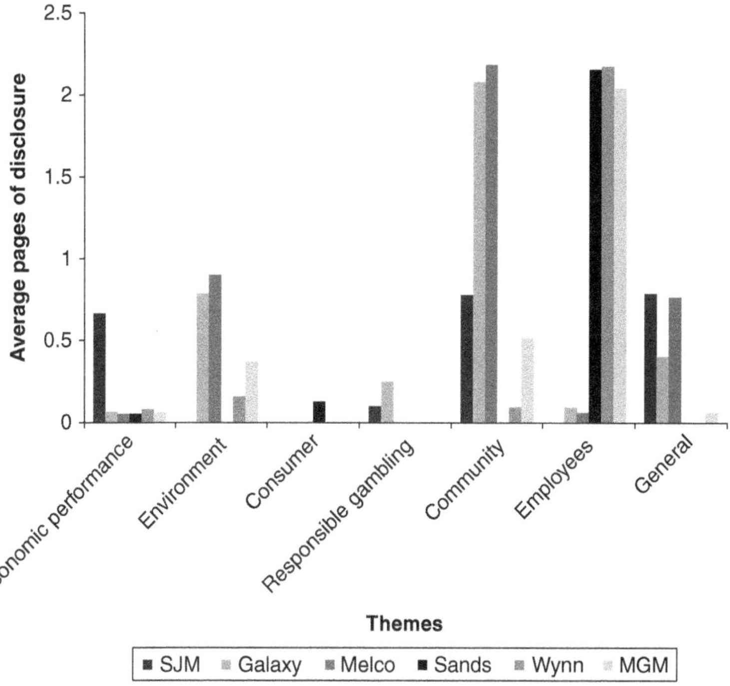

Figure 6.4 Average volume of voluntary disclosure among six companies in Macau (2007–2009)

Stock Exchange, which has legislation to disclose this type of information concerning employees, which is based on, for example, Hong Kong Accounting Standard 26 (HKAS 26) (employee pensions), International Financial Reporting Standard 2 (IFRS 2) (employee share-based payments) and International Accounting Standard 19 (IAS 19) (employee short term benefits). The following text is one of the examples:

Share-Based Compensation

> "The Company established the 2002 Stock Incentive Plan (the "Stock Plan") to provide for the grant of (i) incentive stock options, (ii) compensatory (i.e. nonqualified) stock options, and (iii) non-vested shares of Common Stock of Wynn Resorts, Limited.
>
> (Macau, Wynn Resort Limited, 2008: 88)

Corporate governance disclosure

The volume of corporate governance disclosure provides on average 0.56 pages across six gambling companies in Macau (see Table 6.3), except in Melco International Development Limited. This company appears to disclose more information concerning corporate governance disclosure. In particular, this company tends to make disclosures concerning "Corporate Governance Asia Annual Recognition Awards from the Corporate Asia Magazine" (Melco International Development Limited, 2007: 36) and promotion of corporate governance practices. The other gambling companies indicate compliance in relation to legislative requirement in corporate governance; however, in their annual reports, these sampled companies tend to disclose only general information in terms of corporate governance. SJM Holdings Limited is one of the examples.

Corporate Governance Practices

> SJM Holdings Limited (the "Company") is committed to the establishment of good corporate governance practices and procedures. The Company has adopted its own code of corporate governance based on the principles and code provisions as set out in the Code on Corporate Governance Practices (the "Corporate Governance Code") as stated in Appendix 14 of the Rules Governing the Listing of Securities (the "Listing Rules") on The Stock Exchange of Hong Kong Limited (the "Stock Exchange").
>
> (Macau, SJM Holdings Limited, 2009: 47)

Table 6.3 Average volume of CSD 2007–2009 in Macau's gambling industry

	2007	2008	2009	Mean (07–09)	Max (07–09)	Min (07–09)	Median (07–09)	Disclosure	No Disclosure
Total CSR	6.87	9.97	12.81	9.88	41.30	0	5.18	17 (100%)	0 (0%)
Voluntary CSD	2.02	3.03	3.30	2.78	5.10	0	0.82	17 (100%)	0 (0%)
Mandatory CSD	4.85	6.94	9.51	7.10	36.20	0	4.36	17 (100%)	0 (0%)
Economic	0.03	0.38	0.08	0.16	2.00	0.00	0.05	10/17 (59%)	7/17(41%)
Environment	0.32	0.58	0.35	0.42	2.26	0.00	0.22	11/17 (65%)	6/17 (35%)
Consumers	0.02	0.02	0.02	0.02	0.14	0.00	0.00	3/17 (18%)	14/17 (82%)
Responsible Gambling	0.00	0.02	0.11	0.04	0.64	0.00	0.00	3/17 (18%)	14/17 (82%)
Community	0.93	0.77	1.13	0.94	2.66	0.00	0.40	12/17 (71%)	5/17 (29%)
Employees	2.24	2.32	2.72	2.43	4.16	0.00	2.48	17/17 (100%)	0/17 (0%)
Directors	2.89	4.70	7.30	4.96	24.08	0.00	1.69	14/17 (82%)	3/17 (18%)
Corporate Governance	0.30	0.64	0.77	0.57	3.28	0.00	0.24	16/17 (94%)	1/17 (6%)
Others	0.14	0.54	0.33	0.34	2.08	0.00	0.10	9/17 (53%)	8/17 (47%)

Note 1: The numbers show the average volume of pages in the annual reports of the sample in each category.
Note 2: The figures in % indicate the percentage of companies in the sample disclosing in the relevant category.
Note 3: Max, Min, Median are from the year 2007–2009.

Voluntary disclosure

Figure 6.4 indicates the average volume of voluntary disclosure in Macau's gambling companies. This type of disclosure can be divided into seven categories, namely economic, environmental, consumer (+ responsible gambling), community, voluntary employee and other forms (see Appendix 6.2). The following sections will discuss community disclosure, employee disclosure and consumer disclosure in detail.

Community disclosure

Figure 6.4 shows that Melco International Development Limited and Galaxy Entertainment Group Limited have the highest average volume of community disclosure, with a maximum of two pages, followed by SJM Holdings Limited with 0.78 pages. By contrast, the international gambling companies, namely Las Vegas Sands Corporation, Wynn Resorts Limited and MGM Mirage, have a far lower volume of disclosure of less than 0.52 pages. The reason for this is not obvious, but it may relate to the types of reports. The annual reports of these international organizations were in 10-K form because the New York Stock Exchange had special disclosure requirements. Surprisingly, these findings are not consistent with those of prior studies. These found that community disclosure is a higher priority than other types of disclosures in the annual reports of the higher profile industries[7] (e.g. retailers, brewers, petrochemicals) which interact directly with consumers than in the annual reports of lower profile industries[8] (e.g. chemicals, intermediates and aggregates) (Campbell, 2000; Campbell et al., 2006). Here is one of the examples.

Corporate Sponsorships

> We fully support the sports development of Macau. In year 2008, Galaxy served as the title sponsor of the following major sports events: 2008 Macau Galaxy Entertainment FIVB World Grand Prix and 2008 Macau Galaxy Entertainment International Marathon
>
> (Macau, Galaxy, 2008: 28)

Voluntary employee disclosure

This section concentrates on voluntary employee disclosure. Figure 6.4 shows that the international gambling companies, Las Vegas Sands Corporation, Wynn Resorts Limited and MGM Mirage, provided a relatively higher volume of voluntary employee disclosure than SJM Holdings

Limited, Galaxy Entertainment Group Limited and Melco International Development Limited. The voluntary employee disclosure includes employee information, such as Employee Disability, Employee Equal Opportunity and Employee Others. Wynn Macau shows an example of Employees Others, which claims that the company reduced employee bonus owing to financial crisis and visa restrictions in 2009.

> These initiatives include reductions in pay for certain salaried employees, reduced work weeks for full-time hourly employees, a reduction of certain 2009 bonus accruals and a suspension of the employer match to the 401(k) plan. We continually review the cost structure of our operating properties and corporate offices to identify further opportunities to reduce costs.
>
> (Macau, Wynn, 2009: 8)

Consumer (responsible gambling) disclosure

Figure 6.5 illustrates the average volume of RGD with a comparison of consumer disclosure. After taking a pilot study of content analysis and reviewing the RG literature, RG appears to be important to the gambling industry. The concept of RG can be regarded as a subset of the wider field of CSR (Hing, 2003). RG appears to incorporate the concept of consumers and a range of stakeholders (See Blaszczynski et al., 2004). Thus, RGD was added as a subcategory of consumer disclosure. This category shows how the gambling companies attempt to manage their social impacts.

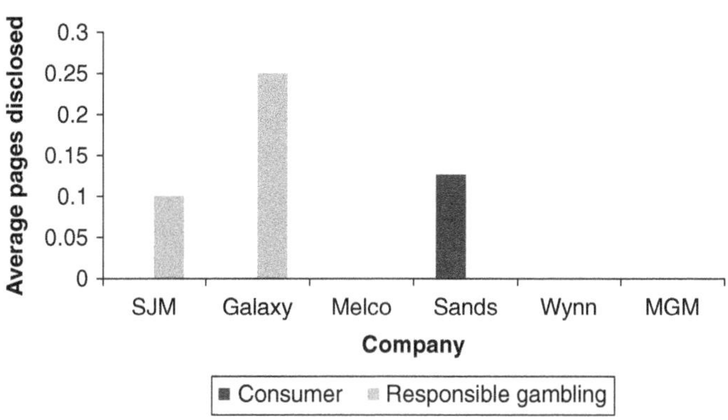

Figure 6.5 Average volume of consumer (responsible gambling) disclosure

The nature of the industry can be viewed as an important factor affecting the level of CSD. Companies operating in sensitive industries tend to disclose more CSD information (Adams et al., 1998). In the case of the gambling industry, organizations have been facing an ongoing threat to their legitimacy, in the form of gambling problems and health-related issues as discussed above. The legitimacy threat can create a significant legitimacy gap. Thus, these organizations might engage in efforts to minimize this gap through deploying CSD more strongly (see Campbell et al., 2003). These organizations can be expected to disclose high volume of RGD concerning customers. Unexpectedly, the findings show that the volume of consumer disclosure and RGD is the lowest among all voluntary disclosures during the period 2007–2009 (See Figure 6.5). However, these organizations began to engage in RG promotion after the introduction of RG policies, which started in 2009. These organizations appeared to publish more information concerning RG engagement in 2010 than before. Further research could extend the sample period and could offer an objective representation of CSD in Macau's gambling industry.

Figure 6.5 shows the difference between the volume of consumer disclosure and RGD. Only Las Vegas Sands Corporation provides a volume of consumer disclosure with an average of 0.13 pages; while other companies showed no disclosure. By contrast, SJM Holdings Limited and Galaxy Entertainment Group Limited show an average of 0.1 and 0.25 pages, respectively, while other companies show no disclosure. The reason for no disclosure among the sampled companies is not clear, but it might be related to the selection of the sampled annual reports. First, Wynn Resorts Limited, Las Vegas Sands Corporation and MGM Mirage are originally from the US. The annual reports were selected from the parent companies (the country of origin), rather than the subsidiary companies in Macau. Second, for Macau's gambling market, Wynn Macau Limited and Sands China Limited[9] both published their annual reports for the year ending 31 December 2009; while MGM China Holdings Limited published annual reports for the year ended 31 December 2011 (Wynn Macau Limited, 2010; Sands China Limited, 2010; MGM China Holdings Limited, 2012). The researcher started to collect all the annual reports at the end of 2009 and examined them at the beginning of 2010. It was not possible to obtain a subsidiary annual report for the whole period from 2009 to 2011 for companies such as Wynn Macau Limited and Sands China Limited. Furthermore, MGM China Holdings Limited did not publish their subsidiary annual report until 2011. Hence, the annual reports from parent companies were utilized in this study.

Another possible explanation is that this industry appears to disclose RG information concerning voluntary employee disclosure and community disclosure, rather than customer disclosure. Remarkably, RGD tends to highlight employee training programs in recognizing high risk behaviors on site and educating employees to develop RG awareness. Such disclosures are primarily declarative and are classified as "Employee Others", rather than "Consumer" disclosure. The tone and orientation of RGD accorded closely with Lindblom's (1993) third legitimation strategy. Gambling companies appear to distract attention away from the customer protection toward employee protection with satisfactory performance within RG. Here is one example of highlighting RG for employees.

Responsible Gaming

> Placed new Responsible Gaming materials including brochures and posters, at the main entrances and back-of house areas at StarWorld Hotel & Casino and the four City Club Casinos to alert both the public and our staff members of the importance of responsible gaming
>
> Established Macau's first and only Responsible Gaming Support and Counselling Hotline to provide staff members with twenty-four hours, seven days a week telephone counselling. Individual face-to-face counselling and online counselling are also provided as needed
>
> (Macau, Galaxy Entertainment Group Limited, 2009: 29)

With the sampled companies, the role of RG is unique in this study. In the sampled companies RGD is almost negligible, with a range of 0.01 pages and 0.25 pages, respectively. In particular, two out of six gambling companies in Macau disclosed RG information, while three out of 17 annual reports in the sample disclosed RG information.

The relationship between corporate size and volume of CSD

The previous CSD studies suggest that corporate size can be viewed as a contributing factor and as an important explanatory variable affecting the volume of disclosure (Cowen et al., 1987; Patten, 1991; 1992; 2002; Roberts, 1992; Gray et al., 1995a; Deegan & Gordon, 1996; Hackston & Milne, 1996; Adams et al., 1998; Cormier & Magnan, 2003; Cho et al., 2010). The CSD literature suggests that larger corporations appear to disclose more social and environmental information than smaller corporations (Andrews et al., 1989; Williams, 1999; Gao et al., 2005). Furthermore, prior CSD studies conducted in Asia-Pacific nations[10] found the same result. However, a number of previous CSD studies have shown an inverse relationship between corporate size and volume of disclosure, which found that there is no size effect in the US sample (Roberts, 1992), in the Hong Kong sample (Lynn, 1992) and the US and Belgium sample (Bouten et al., 2012). This section examines whether the relationship also holds for Macau's gambling industry.

In prior CSD studies, corporate size has been measured by different factors, namely market capitalization (Guthrie & Parker, 1990; Hackston & Milne, 1996; Newson & Deegan, 2002), number of employees (Abbott & Monsen, 1979), turnover (Deegan & Gordon, 1996; Adams et al., 1998; Gao et al., 2005) and total assets (Trotman & Bradley, 1981; Brammer & Pavelin, 2004; Cho et al., 2010). Market capitalization was selected to examine corporate size. This selection attempts to provide consistency with previous CSD studies that make international comparisons (Guthrie & Parker, 1990; Hackston & Milne, 1996). Although the sample is limited to Macau, the sampled companies are mixed with domestic companies and international companies. Market capitalization was collected from the Thomson Reuters DataStream.

Table 6.4 presents the relationship between corporate size and volume of CSD among Macau's gambling companies. Market capitalization in the sampled companies ranges from US$18,420,075 million to US$975,373 million from 2007 to 2009. The total average disclosure can be divided into total average mandatory disclosure and total average voluntary disclosure. The column of market capitalization and the three types of disclosure columns are connected to rank columns. The findings indicate that there is no apparent relationship between corporate

Table 6.4 Comparison between corporate size and volume of disclosure

Enterprise	Market Capitalization US$ (million) 2007–2009	Rank	Total average disclosure 2007–2009 (pages)	Rank	Total average mandatory disclosure 2007–2009 (pages)	Rank	Total average voluntary disclosure 2007–2009 (pages)	Rank
Sands	18,420,075	1	6.15	5	4.37	3	1.91	5
MGM	10,510,465	2	6.33	4	2.53	5	2.91	3
Wynn	9,564,216	3	4.05	6	1.73	6	2.67	4
Galaxy	1,873,285	4	15.22	2	11.93	2	3.32	2
SJM	1,305,073	5	6.84	3	3.08	4	0.92	6
Melco	975,373	6	25.36	1	18.17	1	3.37	1

size and the three types of disclosure. There are two examples to support this argument. The first example is Las Vegas Sands Corporation, which ranks first in market capitalization. However, this company ranks fifth in total average disclosure, third in total average mandatory disclosure and fifth in total average voluntary disclosure. The second example is Melco International Development Limited, which ranks sixth in market capitalization. However, it ranks first in total average disclosure, first in total average mandatory disclosure and first in total average voluntary disclosure. Surprisingly, the findings in this study are inconsistent with the findings of previous CSD studies (Andrews et al., 1989; Williams, 1999; Gao et al., 2005), which found that larger gambling corporations generally tend to disclose more CSD than smaller gambling corporations.

Table 6.5 shows a simple Spearman rank correlation coefficient for Macau gambling companies in order to enhance the previous argument. The findings indicate that the sampled companies show a significant negative correlation between corporate size and the volume of disclosure regardless of its nature (mandatory or voluntary). In Macau, smaller gambling companies appear to disclose more CSD than larger gambling companies. However, caution should be applied owing to the limited sample in this study. The reason for this phenomenon is not apparent, but it might be related to the composition of the sample (see Bouten et al., 2012). The sample of prior CSD studies consists of companies from both environmentally sensitive industries (e.g. oil, mining and airlines) and non-environmentally sensitive industries (e.g. food, retailers

Table 6.5 Spearman rank correlation coefficient for Macau sampled companies (2007–2009)

Macau	**Spearman**			
	Size	**Total average disclosure**	**Total average mandatory**	**Total average voluntary**
Size	1			
Total average disclosure	−0.8162* 0.0001	1		
Total average mandatory	−0.7181* 0.0012	0.9559* 0	1	
Total average voluntary	−0.7941* 0.0001	0.7475* 0.0006	0.5686 0.0172	1

and banks), which are traditionally very large (see Bouten et al., 2012). The sample in this study is composed of only one industry. This might explain the inconsistent findings.

Discussion

This study helps scholars who are studying CSD understand the ways in which the construction of legitimacy is undertaken in the gambling industry. Given the contested nature of this industry, organizations "which are considered to be more sinful than others will be expected to disclose more social information than those which are considered to be less sinful" (Campbell et al., 2003: 561). These organizations have been facing an ongoing threat to their legitimacy, in the form of problem gambling and health-related issues. This threat can create a significant legitimacy gap, and thus these organizations can be expected to minimize this gap through deploying CSD more strongly (See Campbell et al., 2003). However, the CSD provided by all the sampled gambling companies appeared to be relatively low, ranging from none to two pages. More importantly, the role of RGD, related to promoting consumer protection, appears not to be a major issue in the annual reports. Surprisingly, the volume of RGD is the lowest among voluntary disclosure as discussed above. These findings are somewhat similar to Jones et al.'s (2009), which found that major gambling operators in the UK focus narrowly on what they define as RG, while other gambling operators publish limited information or no information in relation to RG. The reason might be related to inadequate industry RG reporting requirements (Blaszczynski et al., 2011). An alternative explanation could be drawn from the sample period 2007 to 2009. The introduction of RG polices was implemented in 2009, so these organizations appear to disclose more information concerning RG engagement. However, RGD appears to be voluntary. Perhaps a legal requirement for some form of RGD is necessary in the gambling industry. More disclosure concerning customer protection, public education and public health care can be undertaken. These organizations can maintain legitimacy to improve integrity, transparency and fairness of their operations.

Strategic legitimacy

The construction of legitimacy in the gambling industry is contested for two reasons. The gambling industry may or may not be a legalized industry and gambling may or may not be a legitimate form of activity

(Reith, 2007). However, this industry has been associated with illegal activities, for example drugs, prostitution and crime, and thus it was perceived to be negative.

More pertinently, organizations in Macau's gambling industry attempt to identify symbols of social legitimacy, namely CSD and RGD, to signify falsely that their organizational performance has already changed. However, these organizations endeavored to bolster their position as legitimate without really changing their operations. The legitimizing activity could benefit the interests of the owners of the gambling industry, rather than the interests of consumers. It could be argued that CSD is seen as potentially quite harmful to certain stakeholders if the industry's adoption of CSD fails to act in the interests of customers (gamblers) within society.

In addition, the findings suggest that negligible or low RGD concerning gambling addiction and health-related issues can perhaps be considered as a proactive legitimizing strategy (see O'Donovan, 2002). Prominently, these organizations seldom publish information on the nature or the extent of the gambling problem concerning customers and public health in their annual reports. These findings are in line with those of Campbell et al. (2003) for the UK's tobacco industry, Tilling and Tilt (2010) for the Australian tobacco industry and De Villiers and van Staden (2006) for the South African mining industry, which found that reducing disclosure can be viewed as a legitimizing strategy. These findings are consistent with O'Donovan (2002), who found that the lower the perceived legitimacy of the organization, the less likely it was to bother providing CSD (e.g. RGD in the gambling industry).

However, these findings for Macau's gambling industry are totally different from previous CSD studies on unforeseen crises, which found that organizations facing an expected disaster will try to repair and maintain legitimacy (Patten, 1992; 2002; Elsbach & Sutton, 1992; Elsbach, 1994; Deegan et al., 2000). Organizations in the gambling industry attempting to build legitimacy might feel that the costs of disclosure are higher than the benefits, and thus the best strategy is simply to remain silent (Campbell et al., 2003). These organizations can possibly restrict negative information, such as problem gambling, gambling addiction, and health-related issues, as long as possible (see O'Donovan, 2002). These organizations can be socially constructed as illegitimate so that social disclosure would be of "no effective value" (Campbell et al., 2003). Hence, these organizations appear not to develop some symbols of social legitimacy, for example CSD and RGD, to build their social legitimacy.

In other words, disclosing CSR and RGD-related information or not seems to make no difference to these organizations.

Institutional legitimacy

The findings relating to organizations in Macau's gambling industry are somewhat similar to those in the institutional legitimacy literature, which suggest that these organizations are shaped by and entirely conform to the institutional environment. This study has contributed to the institutional legitimacy literature, as the gambling industry tends to lack institutional pressures, including coercive, mimetic and normative pressures.

Coercive pressures can be divided into those at a global, industry or regional level. On account of the unexpected weak coercive pressure from international organizations, there was insufficient pressure to regulate this industry. Indeed, the gambling industry is entirely different from other industries, such as the Australian mineral industry, which has some guidelines for Sustainable Development (KPMG, 2005), and the tobacco industry, which has international standards[11] such as the Framework Convention on Tobacco Control (FCTC) developed by the World Health Organization (Moerman & Van Der Laan, 2005). In the case of the gambling industry, an international governing organization could set standards on such issues as gambling addiction prevention, advertising and anti-money laundering. Such an enforcement mechanism could possibly also promote ethically responsible practices.

At industry level, the sampled companies apparently do not follow any industry-based standard of RG practices. Each company tends to apply voluntary codes of RG practices proposed by a local authority, the government of Macau, rather than international or industry authorities. However, the sampled companies sometimes make references to a third party, such as the University of Macau, in their annual report. These organizations appear to adopt minimum RG requirements for customers and employees rather than a wide range of key stakeholders (see Table 6.6). These organizations appear to widely adopt the voluntary RG initiatives. However, the international gambling companies are likely to engage in RG rather than the Chinese and domestic gambling companies. Obviously, without the incentive of mandatory RG, some organizations did not follow RG guidelines. The government of Macau can perhaps learn from developed countries, such as Australia, Canada and the UK (Breen et al., 2005; Miers, 2008; Smith, 2009; Delfabbro & King,

Table 6.6 RG polices adopted by the gambling operators in Macau

Stakeholders	SJM	Galaxy	Melco	Sands	Wynn	MGM
Employees	RG training	RG training	RG training, brochures, signage, video	Re-induction, RG training, employee assistance program, sponsor employees to be RG counselor	Re-induction, RG training, signage, video	RG training (including, rejection of underage, problem gambling symptoms, employee assistance program)
Customers	RG promotion	RG information	RG information, Voluntary self-exclusion, RG ambassador, Third-party exclusion program	Voluntary Self-exclusion	RG information, voluntary self-exclusion, removal from GP list at patron's request	RG signage, RG including corporate policy, limit credit borrowing
Government		RGAW		RGAW	RG information	
University		RGAW		Donation for research		
Social Service organizations				Donation	RG information	
Others				Attending problem gambling conference		

Source: The Institute for the Study of Commercial Gaming, University of Macau (2011: 20–25) Note: RG refers to Responsible Gambling; RGAW refers to Responsible Gambling Awareness Week.

2012), which suggest that RG practices are mandatory rather than voluntary (such as voluntary self-exclusion programs, age restrictions and financial transaction policies).

At the local level, organizations in Macau's gambling industry seem to employ both regional and international reporting practices as a point of reference in their annual reports. All the sampled companies are listed on the Hong Kong Stock Exchange, and these organizations tend to follow Hong Kong reporting standards, such as Hong Kong Accounting Standards (HKAS), International Financial Reporting Standards (IFRS) and International Accounting Standards (IAS). However, four of the sampled companies are also listed on the New York Stock Exchange. These companies comply with all requirements of NASDAQ, the United States Securities Exchange Commission (SEC) and the Financial Accounting Standard Board (FASB). However, these sampled organizations did not generally apply or follow any global reporting guidelines, such as the AA 1000 guideline,[12] Global Compact and the Global Reporting Initiative (GRI) Sustainability Guidelines in their annual reports. Thus, these findings are not in line with those of the CSD literature (see Campbell et al., 2003) and mainstream reporting practices (Kolk, 2003; KPMG, 2008; 2011).

Regarding mimetic pressure in Macau's gambling industry, there is some evidence that a weak mimetic process is working on the CSR and RG initiatives in the international gambling companies, but not in the non-international gambling companies. CSR and RG initiatives seem to come from international gambling organizations, particularly those from the US, via their parent companies. The subsidiaries of international gambling companies operating in Macau are, in most cases, highly reliant on the parent companies for accessing critical resources, with particular reference to CSR and RG knowledge and philosophy so as to develop CSR and RG initiatives. Additionally, these findings are in line with the resource dependency theory (Pfeffer & Salancik, 1978). However, CSR and RG initiatives in a subsidiary gambling company in Macau are not always entirely the same as those in the US parent company and should be adapted to local economic, social and political situations, and more importantly the local culture. The findings are similar to Chapple and Moon's (2005) study, which found that multinational corporations are more likely to adopt CSR than those operating in their home countries, but that the profile of their CSR is likely to reflect the country of operation rather than the country of origin. In Macau, the mimetic process from industry peers appears to be weak. This interpretation is supported by the fact that CSR and RG polices were widely discussed to a greater extent by international gambling companies rather than by a domestic gambling company and a Hong Kong gambling company (see Table 6.5).

Organizations in Macau's gambling industry seem to show weak normative pressures at the local level based on the institutional legitimacy literature (DiMaggio & Powell, 1983). RG developed by the University of Macau plays a vital role in shaping and promoting RG policies through working closely with the government of Macau (The Institute for the Study of Commercial Gaming, 2011). Professional power is largely assigned by the government of Macau (see DiMaggio & Powell, 1983). In other words, an academic institution can be inferred to have a similar professional understanding of what proper action is (see Boxenbaum & Jonsson, 2008) and can be viewed as an important center for the development of organizational norms and the standardization of the "skills and cognitive base" of managers and employees (DiMaggio & Power, 1983; Bondy et al., 2012). In particular, RG training courses organized by the University of Macau were for representatives of the gambling companies, who could receive practical RG training and then cascade these skills and practices to other team members. These organizations tend to express their support for RG training as well as the "Responsible Gambling Awareness Week" (RGAW). Such pressures are often related to education authorities, which as an external source directly or indirectly set standards for legitimate organizational practices (Matten & Moon, 2008). However, RG can be regarded as a guideline rather than a regulation, because the government of Macau appears to depend on the voluntary RG engagement of the gambling industry. Hence, it would be more effective if the government promoted mandatory, rather than voluntary, RG practices.

Conclusion

This analysis has attempted to provide a preliminary investigation of CSD and RGD in Macau's gambling industry. The results indicate that the volume of CSD provided by all the sampled companies appears to be relatively low. There are four major findings in this study. First, not surprisingly, disclosures are dominated by mandatory director disclosure and mandatory employee disclosure. These findings are consistent with those of previous CSD studies. Second, the role of RGD, concerning customer protection, is not seen as an important issue in the annual reports. However, the findings indicate that with no and low RGD, it cannot be considered a proactive legitimizing strategy. Arguably, the gambling industry attempts to remain silent in relation to sensitive information, notably gambling problems, gambling addiction and health-related issues. Thus, the gambling industry appears not to develop symbols, namely RGD, to maintain social legitimacy. Third, there is no relationship between corporate size and the volume of disclosure; although it can be explained that the composition and the selection of the sample might affect this result. Fourth, these organizations are likely to lack coercive pressures from the global, industry and local levels. There is not only a weak mimetic process of CSR and RGD in these international gambling companies, but also a weak normative pressure at the local level.

This initial exploration of CSD in Macau's gambling industry is not conclusive and is limited to a specific period of time (2007–2009). Further research could extend the sample period and the sample countries. Furthermore, widening the forms of media, to stand-alone reports and corporate websites, for example, should be considered. Such approaches could offer a persuasive, reliable and objective representation of trends and patterns of CSD in this industry over time.

The gambling operators tend to disclose positive CSR engagement, namely corporate sponsorships. However, they seem to be reluctant to open discussions in relation to gambling problems. Corporate transparency in this way remains unsatisfactory. It is fair to suggest that these organizations might have little self-critique. The local community should question their motivations for ongoing CSR engagement. These organizations need to develop a form of transparency and responsibility to show the integrity of their business operations (see Soriano et al., 2012).

Given the relatively low volume of voluntary RGD, this study asks whether some form of legal requirement for RGD is necessary in Macau's gambling industry. There appears to be a necessity for coercion, rather than voluntary RG reporting practices. The establishment of more stringent regulations by the government of Macau and greater pressure from stakeholders are needed. These organizations will then be more accountable and responsible. Such an approach tends to avoid a number of grey areas, such as gambling problems, health-related issues and collaborations with junket operators. Failure to do so could jeopardize customer health, their family members and the welfare of the local community. Thus, the government of Macau should play an important role in putting more pressure on the gambling industry to improve the addressing of ethical and social concerns in its business practices.

APPENDIX 6.1: Summary of primary disclosure categories of analysis

Total CSR:	Economic + Environment + Consumer + Community + Employee + Director + Corporate Governance + Others
Economic Disclosure	Economic Performance Beyond Tax + Market Presence + Indirect Economic Impact
Environmental Disclosure	Environment Policy + Environment Audit + Waste, Pack, Pollution + Financial Data and Provision + Sustainability + Energy + Environmental Other
Consumer Disclosure	Consumer/Customers + Responsible Gambling Protection
Community Disclosure	Charity and Political Donation + Community + Dialogue and Consultation
Employee Disclosure	Employee Data + Pension Commit + Disabled + Health and Safety + Shares Employees + Equal opportunities + Employee Others
Directors	Directors
Corporate Governance	Corporate Governance
Others	Others

APPENDIX 6.2: Descriptions of mandatory and voluntary disclosure

Total mandatory disclosure	Employee (Pension Commit + Shares Employees + Employee Others + Employee Benefits) + Directors + Corporate Governance
Total voluntary disclosure	Economic + Environment + Consumer + Community + Employee (Employee Data + Disable + Health and Safety + Equal Opportunities + Employee Others) + General Other

Notes

1. The Commission of the European Communities (2001: 6) defines CSR as "A concept whereby companies integrate social and environmental concerns

in the business operation and in their interactions with their stakeholders on voluntary basis".

2. Fong et al. (2011: 45) define the social cost of gambling as "(1) the cost has to be social, rather than private or personal; (2) the cost has to result in a real decrease in societal wealth; and (3) the cost has to result exclusively from gambling."
3. Soft law means "their effectiveness depends on the extent to which the inherent norms are understood and spread among business" (Moon et al., 2011).
4. Berelson (1952: 18) defines content analysis as "a research technique for the objective, systematic and quantitative description of the manifest content of communication". This method can be viewed as a quantitative and qualitative method (Unerman, 2002 cited in Belal, 2008). Quantitative content analysis (Gray et al., 1995a; 1995b; Krippendorff, 1980; 2012) measures volume of disclosure to signify the importance of the text, while qualitative content analysis (Bennington, 1999 cited in Belal, 2008) attempts to focus on the meaning and implication of disclosure. This study follows the former one.
5. The researcher started to collect all the annual reports at the end of 2009 and examined them at the beginning of 2010. It was not possible to obtain a subsidiary annual report for the whole period from 2009 to 2011. Wynn Macau Limited and Sands China Limited, for example, did not publish a subsidiary annual report until 2009 and MGM China Holdings Limited did not publish their subsidiary annual report until 2011.
6. If you are interested in the coding schedule, please contact the editor or the author.
7. Companies with a "higher public" profile – the most vulnerable to change in social opinion – tend to undertake community disclosure, and these types of companies are likely to relate to consumers and the general public (Campbell et al., 2006).
8. Companies with a "lower public" profile are less well known to the general public and produce very few products sold directly to consumers (Campbell et al., 2006).
9. Wynn Macau, Limited, Sands China Limited, and MGM China Holdings Limited were also traded on the mainboard of the Hong Kong Stock Exchange on 9 September 2009, 30 November 2009 and 3 June 2011, respectively (The Hong Kong Stock Exchange, 2012a; 2012b; 2012c). These three gambling companies are also subsidiaries of NASDAQ-listed Wynn Resorts, Limited, Las Vegas Sands Corp., and MGM Mirage.
10. Asia-Pacific region – Australia, Singapore, Hong Kong, the Philippines, Thailand, Indonesia and Malaysia.
11. The Framework Convention on Tobacco Control (FCTC) is an international standard on issues, for example tobacco production, advertising, marketing and prevention of smuggling.
12. The AA1000 guidelines from AccountAbility provides guidance on how to establish a systematic stakeholder engagement process that generates the indicators, targets and reporting systems needed to ensure its effectiveness in impacting on decisions, activities and overall organizational performance (KPMG, 2005: 43).

References

Abbott, W.F. & Monsen, R.J. (1979). On the measurement of corporate social responsibility: Self-reported disclosures as a method of measuring corporate social involvement. *Academy of Management Journal*, 22, (3), 501–515.

Adams, C.A. & Harte, G. (1998). The changing portrayal of the employment of women in British banks' and retail companies corporate annual report. *Accounting, Organizations and Society*, 23, (8), 781–812.

Adams, C.A., Coutts, A. & Harte, G. (1995). Corporate equal opportunities (non-) disclosure. *British Accounting Review*, 27, 87–108.

Adams, C.A., Hill, W-Y. & Roberts, C.B. (1998). Corporate social reporting practices in western Europe: Legitimating corporate behaviour. *British Accounting Review*, 30, (1), 1–21.

Andrews, B.H., Gul, F.A., Guthrie, J.E. & Teoh, H.Y. (1989). A note on corporate social disclosure practices in developing countries: The case of Malaysia and Singapore. *British Accounting Review*, 21, 371–376.

Ashforth, B.E. & Gibbs, B.W. (1990). The double-edge of organizational legitimation. *Organization Science*, 1, 177–194.

Austrin, T. & West, J. (2005). Skills and surveillance in casino gaming: Work, consumption and regulation. *Work, Employment and Society*, 19, (2), 305–326.

BBC (2009). *Bets are off for Macau gambling boom*. Available at http://news.bbc.co.uk/1/hi/world/asia-pacific/7807899.stm

Beattie, V. & Jones, M.T. (1992). The use and abuse of graphs in annual reports: Theoretical framework and empirical study. *Accounting and Business Research*, 22, (88), 291–303.

Beattie, V. & Jones, M. (1994). An empirical study of graphical format choices in charity annual reports. *Financial Accountability and Management*, 10, (3), 215–236.

Beattie, V., Mcinnes, B. & Fearnley, S. (2004). A methodology for analysing and evaluating narratives in annual reports: A comprehensive description profile and metrics for disclosure quality attributes. *Critical Perspectives on Accounting*, 28, 205–236.

Beattie, V. & Thomson, S.J. (2007). Lifting the lid on the use of content analysis to investigate intellectual capital disclosures. *Accounting Forum*, 31, 129–163.

Beem, B. & Mikler, J. (2011). National regulations for a borderless industry: US versus UK approaches to online gambling. *Policy and Society*, 30, 161–174.

Belal, A.R. (2008). *Corporate Social Responsibility Reporting in Developing Countries: The Case of Bangladesh*. Hampshire: Ashgate Publishing Limited.

Berelson, R. (1952). *Content Analysis in Communication Research*. New York: Free Press.

Bitektine, A. (2011). Toward a theory of social judgments of organizations: The case of legitimacy, reputation and status. *Academy of Management Review*, 36, 151–179.

Blaszczynski, A., Ladouceur, R. & Shaffer, H.J. (2004). A science-based framework for responsible gambling: The Reno model. *Journal of Gambling Studies*, 20, (3), 301–317.

Blaszczynski, A., Collins, P., Fong, D., Ladouceur, R., Nower, L., Shaffer, H. J., Tavares, H. & Venise, J. (2011). Responsible gambling: General principles and minimal requirements. *Journal of Gambling Studies*, DOI 10.1007/s10899-010-9214-0.

Bondy, K., Moon, J. & Matten, D. (2012). An institution of corporate social responsibility (CSR) in multi-national corporations (MNCs): Form and implications. *Journal of Business Ethics*, 111, 281–299.

Borrell, J. (2008). The public accountability approach: Suggestions for a framework to characterize, compare, inform, and evaluate gambling regulation. *International Journal of Mental Health Addiction*, 6, 265–281.

Bouten, L., Everaert, P. & Roberts, R.W. (2012). How a two-step approach discloses different determinants of voluntary social and environmental reporting. *Journal of Business Finance and Accounting*, 39, 567–605.

Boxenbaum, E. & Jonsson, S. (2008). Isomorphism, diffusion and decoupling. In: Greenwood, R., Oliver, C., Sahlin, K. & Suddaby, R. (eds.) *The SAGE Handbook of Organizational Institutionalism*. Thousand Oak, CA: Sage.

Brammer, S. & Pavelin, S. (2004). Voluntary social disclosures by large UK companies. *Business Ethics: A European Review*, 13, 86–99.

Breen, H., Buultjens, J. & Hing, N. (2005). The responsible gambling code in Queensland, Australia: implementation and venue assessment. *UNLV Gaming Research and Review Journal*, 9, (1), 43–60.

Bryman, A. & Bell, E. (2007). *Business Research Methods. 2nd ed.* New York: Oxford University Press, Inc.

Bryman, A. & Bell, E. (2011). *Business Research Methods. 3rd ed.* New York: Oxford University Press, Inc.

Buhr, H. (1998). Environmental performance, legislation and annual report disclosure: The case of acid rain and Falconbridge. *Accounting, Auditing and Accountability Journal*, 11, (2), 163–190.

Cai, Y., Jo, H. & Pan, C. (2012). Doing well while doing bad? CSR in controversial industry sectors. *Journal of Business Ethics*, 108, 467–480.

Campbell, D., Craven, B. and Shrives, P. (2006) Voluntary social reporting in three FTSE sectors: a comment on perception and legitimacy. *Accounting, Auditing and Accountability Journal*, 16(4), 558–581

Campbell, D. (2000). Legitimacy theory or managerial reality construction? Corporate social disclosure in Marks and Spencer Plc corporate reports, 1969–1997. *Accounting Forum*, 24, 80–100.

Campbell, D., Moore, G. & Shrives, P. (2006). Cross-sectional effects in community disclosure. *Accounting, Auditing and Accountability Journal*, 19, 96–111.

Campbell, J.L. (2007). Why would corporations behave in socially responsible ways? An institutional theory of corporate social responsibility. *Academy of Management Review*, 32, 946–967.

Cheng, T.J. (2009). *Introduction to Sociology of Gambling*. Beijing: Social Sciences Academic Press (China).

Cho, C.H., Roberts, R.W. & Patten, D.M. (2010). The language of US corporate environmental disclosure. *Accounting, Organizations and Society*, 35, (4), 431–443.

Chapple, W. & Moon, J. (2005). Corporate social responsibility (CSR) in Asia. A seven-country study of CSR web site reporting. *Business and Society*, 44, (4), 415–441.

Christiansen, E.M. (1998). Gambling and the American economy. *Annals of the American Academy of Political and Social Science*, 556, 36–52.

Collins, D. & Lapsley, H. (2003). The social costs and benefits of gambling: An introduction to the economic issues. *Journal of Gambling Studies,* 19, (2), 123–148.

Cormier, D. & Magnan, M. (2003). Environmental reporting management: A European perspective. *Journal of Accounting and Public Policy,* 22, (1), 43–62.

Cowen, S.S., Ferreri, L.B. & Parker, L.D. (1987). The impact of corporate characteristics on social responsibility disclosure: A typology and frequency-based analysis. *Accounting, Organizations and Society,* 12, (2), 111–122.

CSEAR (2011). *The Decision Rules for the Categories of Social and Environmental Disclosure.* Available at http:www.st-andrews.ac.uk/~csearweb/researchresources/csrdbaserules.htm

Dacin, T. (1997). Isomorphism in context: The power and prescription of institutional norms. *Academy of Management Journal,* 40, 46–81.

Day, R. & Woodward, T. (2004). Disclosure of information about employees in the Director's Report of UK published financial statements: substantive or symbolic. *Accounting Forum,* 28, (1), 43–59.

De Villiers, C. & Van Staden, C. J. (2006). Can less environmental disclosure have a legitimising effect? Evidence from Africa. *Accounting, Organizations and Society,*31, 765–781.

Deegan, C. & Gordon, B. (1996). A study of the environmental disclosure practices of Australian corporations. *Accounting and Business Research,* 26, 187–199.

Deegan, C. & Rankin, M. (1996). Do Australian companies report environmental new objectively? An analysis of environmental disclosures by firms prosecuted successfully by the Environmental Protection Authority. *Accounting, Auditing and Accountability Journal,* 9, 50–67.

Deegan, C. & Rankin, M. (1997). The materiality of environmental information to users of annual reports. *Accounting, Auditing and Accountability Journal,* 10, (4), 562–583.

Deegan, C., Rankin, M. & Voght, P. (2000). Firms disclosure reactions to major social incidents: Australian evidence. *Accounting Forum,* 24, (1), 101–130.

Deegan, C. (2002). The legitimizing effect of social and environmental disclosures – A theoretical foundation. *Accounting, Auditing and Accountability Journal,* 15, (3), 282–311.

Deegan, C., Rankin, M. & Tobin, J. (2002). An examination of the corporate social and environmental disclosures of BHP from 1983–1997: A test of legitimacy theory. *Accounting, Auditing and Accountability Journal,* 15, 312–343.

Deegan, C. & Blomquist, C. (2006). Stakeholder influence on corporate reporting: An exploration of the interaction between WWF-Australia and the Australian minerals industry. *Accounting, Organizations and Society,* 31, 343–372.

Deegan, C. (2007). Organizational legitimacy as a motive for sustainability reporting. In Unerman, J., Bebbington, J. & O' Dwyer, B. (eds.) *Sustainability Accounting and Accountability.* Oxon: Routledge.

Delfabbro, P. & King, D. (2012). Gambling in Australia: Experiences, problems, research and policy. *Addiction,* 107, 1556–1561.

DiMaggio, P.J. & Powell, W.W. (1983). The iron cage revisited: Institutional isomorphism and collective rationality in organizational fields. *American Sociological Review,* 489, 147–160.

Dowling, J. & Pfeffer, J. (1975). Organizational legitimacy: Social values and organizational behavior. *The Pacific Sociological Review*, 18, 122–136.

Eadington, W. & Siu, C.S. (2007). Between law and custom – Examining the interaction between legislative change and the evolution of Macau's casino industry. *International Gambling Studies*, 7, 1–28.

Elsbach, K.D. & Sutton, R.L. (1992). Acquiring organizational legitimacy through illegitimate actions: A marriage of institutional and impression management theories. *Academy of Management Journal*, 35, (4), 699–738.

Elsbach, K.D. (1994). Managing organizational legitimacy in the California cattle industry: The construction and effectiveness of verbal accounts. *Administrative Science Quarterly*, 39, 57–88.

Fallows, J. (2009). *Postcard from Tomorrow Square: Reports from China.* New York: Vintage.

Felsenstein, D., Littlepage, L. & Klacik, D. (1999). Casino gambling as local growth generation: Playing the economic development game in reverse? *Journal of Urban Affairs*, 21, (4), 409–421.

Fong, K.C., Fong, H.N. & Li, S.Z. (2011). The social cost of gambling in Macau: Before and after the liberalization of the gaming industry. *International Gambling Studies*, 11, 43–56.

Galvin, T.L., Ventresca, M.J. & Hudson, B.A. (2004–2005). Contested industry dynamics: New directions in the study of legitimacy. *International Studies of Management and Organization*, 34, (4), 56–82.

Gao, S., Heravi, S. & Xiao, J.Z. (2005). Determinants of corporate social and environmental reporting in Hong Kong: A research note. *Accounting Forum*, 29, 233–242.

Gaylord, M.S. (2008). The Banco Delta Asia affair: The USA patriot act and allegations of money laundering in Macau. *Crime Law Social Change*, 50, (4–5), 293–305.

Giroux, I., Boutin, C., Ladouceur, R., Lachance, S. & Dufour, M. (2008). Awareness training programme on responsible gambling for casino employees. *International Journal of Mental Health and Addiction*, 6, (4), 594–601.

Government of Macau Special Administrative Region Statistics and Census Service (2012a). *Yearbook of Statistic 2011.* Macau: Statistics and Census Service.

Gray, R., Kouhy, R. & Lavers, S. (1995a). Corporate social and environmental reporting: A review of the literature and longitudinal study of UK disclosure. *Accounting, Auditing and Accountability Journal*, 8, (2), 47–77.

Gray, R., Kouhy, R. & Lavers, S. (1995b). Methodological themes. Constructing a research database of social and environmental reporting by UK companies. *Accounting, Auditing and Accountability Journal*, 8, (2), 78–101.

Gray, R.H., Owen, D.L. & Adams, C. (1996). *Accounting and Accountability: Changes and Challenges in Corporate Social and Environmental Reporting*. London: Prentice Hall.

Gray, R. (2001). Thirty years of social accounting, reporting and auditing: What (if anything) have we learnt. *Business Ethics: A European Review*, 10, (1), 9–15.

Gray, R. & Bebbington, J. (2001). *Accounting for the Environment*. London: Sage.

Graves, O., Flesher, D.L. & Jordan, R.E. (1996). Pictures and the bottom line: The television epistemology of US annual reports. *Accounting, Organizations and Society*, 12, (1), 57–88.

Gu, X.H. & Tam, P.S. (2011). Casino taxation in Macau: An economic perspective. *Journal of Gambling Studies*, 27, 587–605.

Guthrie, J.E. & Parker, L.D. (1989). Corporate social reporting: A rebuttal of legitimacy theory. *Accounting and Business Research*, 19, 343–352.

Guthrie, J.E. & Parker, L.D. (1990). Corporate social disclosure practice: A comparative international analysis. *Advances in Public Interest Accounting*, 3, 159–176.

Hackston, D. & Milne, M.J. (1996). Some determinants of social and environmental disclosures in New Zealand companies. *Accounting, Auditing and Accountability Journal*, 9, (1), 77–108.

Hannigan, J. (2007). Casino cities. *Geography Compass*, 1, (4), 959–975.

Haveman, H.A. (1993). Follow the leader: Mimetic isomorphism and entry into new markets. *Administrative Science Quarterly*, 38, 593–627.

Hines, R.D. (1988). Financial accounting: In communicating reality, we construct reality. *Accounting, Organizations and Society*, 13, (3), 251–261.

Hing, N. (2003). Principles, process and practices in responsible provision of gambling: A conceptual discussion. *UNLV Gaming Research and Review Journal*, 7, 33–47.

Hing, N. & Nuske, E. (2011). Assisting problem gamblers in the gaming venue: As assessment of practices and procedures followed by frontline hospitality staff. *International Journal of Hospitality Management*, 30, 459–467.

Hobson, J.S.P. (1995). Macau: Gambling on its future? *Tourism Management*, 16, (3), 237–246.

Islam, M.A. & Deegan, C. (2008). Motivations for an organization within a developing country to report social responsibility information: Evidence from Bangladesh. *Accounting, Auditing and Accountability Journal*, 21, 850–874.

Islam, M.A. & Deegan, C. (2010). Media pressures and corporate disclosure of social responsibility performance information: A study of two global clothing and sports retail companies. *Accounting and Business Research*, 40, 131–148.

Jo, H. & Na, H. (2012). Does CSR reduce firm risk? Evidence from controversial industry sectors. *Journal of Business Ethics*, 110, 441–456.

Johnson, J. & Holub, M. J. (2003). Questioning organizational legitimacy: The case of U.S. expatriates. *Journal of Business Ethics*, 47, 269–293.

Jones, P., Hillier, D. & Comfort, D. (2009). Corporate social responsibility in the UK gambling industry. *Corporate Governance*, 9, (2), 189–201.

Kolk, A. (2003). Trends in sustainability reporting by the Fortune Global 250. *Business Strategy and the Environment*, 12, 279–291.

Korn, D.A. & Shaffer, H.J. (1999). Gambling and the health of the public: Adopting a public health perspective. *Journal of Gambling Studies*, 15, (4), 290–364.

KPMG (2005). *KPMG International Survey of Corporate Sustainability Reporting 2005*. Netherlands: KPMG.

KPMG (2008). *KPMG International Survey of Corporate Social Reporting 2008*. UK: KPMG International.

KPMG (2011). *KPMG International Survey of Corporate Social Reporting 2008*. Netherlands: KPMG International.

Krippendorff, K. (1980). *Content Analysis: An Introduction to its Methodology*. New York: Sage.

Krippendorff, K. (2012). *Content Analysis: An Introduction to its Methodology, 3rd ed.*, Thousand Oaks, CA: Sage.

LaPlante, D.A., Nelson, S.E., LaBrie, R.A. & Shaffer, H J. (2008). Stability and progression of disordered gambling: Lessons from longitudinal studies. *Canadian Journal of Psychiatry*, 53, (1), 52–60.

LaPlante, D.A., Gray, H M., LaBrie, R.A., Kleschinsky, J.H. & Shaffer, H.J. (2011). Gaming industry employee responses to responsible gambling training: A public health imperative. *Journal of Gambling Studies*, DOI 10.1007/s10899-011-9255-z

Lee, S. & Park, S.Y. (2009). Do socially responsible activities help hotels and casinos achieve their financial goals? *International Journal of Hospitality Management*, 28, 105–112.

Li, H., Zhang, J.J., Mao, L.L. & Min, D. (2011). Assessing corporate social responsibility in China's sports lottery administration and its influence on consumption behavior. *Journal of Gambling Studies*, DOI:10.1007/s10899-011-9270-0.

Lindblom, C.E. (1993). *The implications of organizational legitimacy for corporate social performance and disclosure*. Paper presented at the Critical Perspectives on Accounting Conference, New York.

Loo, J.M.Y., Raylu, N. & Oei, T.P.S. (2008). Gambling among the Chinese: A comprehensive review. *Clinical Psychology Review*, 28, 1152–1166.

Lynn, M. (1992). A note on corporate social disclosure in Hong Kong. *The British Accounting Review*, 2, (2), 105–110.

Macau Special Administrative Region Gaming Inspection and Coordination Bureau (2013). *Number of casinos in 2007–2012* (*Gaming statistics*). Available at http://www.dicj.gov.mo/web/en/information/DadosEstat/2012/content.html#n4

MarketLine (2013a). *Industry Profile: Global Casinos and Gaming*. London: MarketLine, Datamonitor.

MarketLine (2013b). *MarketLine Industry Profile: Casinos and Gaming in China*. London: MarketLine, Datamonitor.

MarketLine (2013c). *MarketLine Industry Profile: Global Investment Banking and Brokerage*. London: MarketLine.

MarketLine (2013d). *MarketLine Industry Profile: Global Oil and Gas*. London: MarketLine.

Matten, D. & Moon, J. (2008). Implicit and explicit CSR: A conceptual framework for a comparative understanding of corporate social responsibility. *Academy of Management Review*, 33, 404–424.

McMillen, J. (1996). Understanding gambling: History, concepts and theories. In McMillen, J. (ed.) *Gambling Cultures: Studies in History and Interpretation*. Oxon: Routledge.

Melco International Development Limited (2008). *Annual Report 2007*. Hong Kong: Melco International Development Limited.

Meyer, J. & Rowan, B. (1991). Institutionalized organizations: Formal structure as myth and ceremony. In Powell, W. & DiMaggio, P. (eds.) *The New Institutionalism in Organizational Analysis*. Chicago, IL: University of Chicago Press.

MGM China Holdings Limited (2012). *MGM China Holdings Limited 2011 Annual Report*. Hong Kong: MGM China Holdings Limited.

Miers, D. (2008). Gambling in Great Britain: Implementing a social responsibility agenda. *Gaming Law Review and Economics*, 12, 583–598.

Miller, R. & Michelson, G. (2012). Fixing the game? Legitimacy, morality policy and research in gambling. *Journal of Business Ethics*, 116, (3), 601–614.

Milne, M. and Adler, R. W. (1999). Exploring the reliability of social and environmental disclosures content analysis. *Accounting, Auditing and Accountability*, 12, (2), 237–256.

Milne, M.J. & Patten, D.M. (2002). Securing organizational legitimacy: An experimental decision case examining the impact of environmental disclosures. *Accounting, Auditing and Accountability Journal*, 15, 372–405.

Mizruchi, M. & Fein, L.C. (1999). The social construction of organizational knowledge: A study of the uses of coercive, mimetic and normative isomorphism. *Administrative Science Quarterly*, 44, 653–683.

Moerman, L.C. & Van Der Laan, S. (2005). Social reporting in the tobacco industry: All smoke and mirrors? *Accounting, Auditing and Accountability Journal*, 18, 374–389.

Moon, J., Kang, N. & Gond, J.P. (2010). Corporate social responsibility and government. In Coen, D., Grant, W. & Wilson, G. (eds.) *Oxford Handbook of Business and* Government. Oxford: Oxford University Press.

Moon, J., Crane, A. & Matten, D. (2011). Corporations and citizenship in new institutions of global governance. In Crouch, C. & Maclean, C. (eds.) *The Responsible Corporation in a Global Economy*. Oxford: Oxford University Press.

Neimark, M.D. (1992). *The Hidden Dimensions of Annual Reports: Sixty Years of Social Conflict at General Motors*. London: Paul Chapman Publishing Limited.

Newson, M. & Deegan, C. (2002). Global expectations and their association with corporate social disclosure practices in Australia, Singapore, and South Korea. *The International Journal of Accounting*, 37, 183–213.

Neu, D., Warsame, H. & Pedwell, K. (1998). Managing public impressions: Environmental disclosures in annual reports. *Accounting, Organizations and Society*, 23, (3), 265–282.

Oliver, L.C. (1988). The collective strategy framework: An application to competing predictions of isomorphism. *Administrative Science Quarterly*, 33, 543–561.

O'Donovan, G. (2002). Environmental disclosures in the annual report: Extending the applicability and predictive power of legitimacy theory. *Accounting, Auditing and Accountability Journal*, 15, (3), 344–371.

Parker, L. (2008/2009). Editorial notes: Addressing a broad scope SEA research agenda. *Issues in Social and Environmental Accounting*, 2, 155–157.

Patten, D.M. (1991). Exposure, legitimacy and social disclosure. *Journal of Accounting and Public Policy*, 10, 297–308.

Patten, D.M. (1992). Intra-industry environmental disclosures in response to the Alaskan oil spill: A note on legitimacy theory. *Accounting, Organizations and Society*, 17, (5), 471–475.

Patten, D.M. (2002). The relation between environmental performance and environmental disclosure: A research note. *Accounting, Organizations and Society*, 27, 263–773.

Patten, D.M. & Crampton, W. (2004). Legitimacy and the Internet: An examination of corporate website environmental disclosure. *Advances in Environmental Accounting and Management*, 2, 31–57.

Pfeffer, J. & Salancik, G.R. (1978). *The External Control of Organizations: A Resource Dependence Perspective*. New York: Harper and Row.

Preston, A.M., Wright, C. & Young, J.J. (1996). Imaging annual reports. *Accounting, Organizations and Society*, 21, (1), 113–137.

Quinn, F.L. (2001). First do no harm: What could be done by casinos to limit pathological gambling. *Managerial and Decision Economics*, 22, (1–3), 133–142.

Raylu, N. & Oei, T P.S. (2004). Role of culture in gambling and problem gambling. *Clinical Psychology Review*, 23, (8), 1807–1114.

Reast, J., Maon, F., Lindgreen, A. & Vanhamme, J. (2012). Legitimacy-seeking organisational strategies in controversial industries: A case study analysis and a bidimensional model. *Journal of Business Ethics*. DOI 10.1007/s10551-012-1571-4

Reith, G. (2007). Situating gambling studies. In Smith, G., Hodgins, D.C. & Williams, R.J. (eds.) *Research and Measurement Issues in Gambling Studies*. London: Elsevier.

Roberts, R.W. (1992). Determinants of corporate social responsibility disclosure. *Accounting, Organizations and Society*, 17, (6), 595–612.

Ruef, M. & Scott, R.W. (1998). A multidimensional model of organizational legitimacy: Hospital survival in changing institutional environments. *Administrative Science Quarterly*, 43, 877–904.

Sands China, Limited. (2010). *Annual Report 2009*. Available at http://www.hkexnews.hk/listedco/listconews/advancedsearch/search_active_main.asp

Scherer, A.G. & Palazzo, G. (2011). The new political role of business in a globalized world – A review of a new perspective on CSR and its implications for the firm, governance and democracy. *Journal of Management Studies*, 48, 899–931.

Sethi, S.P. (1978). Advocacy advertising – The American experiment. *California Management Review*, Fall, 58–64.

Smith, G. (2009). *Accountability and Social Responsibility in Ontario's Legal Gambling Regime*. Ottawa: Alberta Gaming Research Institute Dan Rubenstein.

Spar, D.L. & La Mure, L.T. (2003). The power of activism: Assessing the impact of NGOs on global business. *California Management Review*, 45, (3), 78–101.

Soriano, M.Y.D., Javed, U. & Yousafzai, S. (2012). Can an industry be socially responsible if its products harm consumers? The case of online gambling. *Journal of Business Ethics*, 110, 481–497.

Stern, R.N. & Barley, S.R. (1996). Organizations and social systems: Organization theory's neglected mandate. *Administrative Science Quarterly*, 41, 146–162.

Suchman, M.C. (1995). Managing legitimacy: Strategic and institutional approaches. *Academy of Management Review*, 20, 571–610.

Tilling, M.V. & Tilt, C.A. (2010). The edge of legitimacy: Voluntary social and environmental reporting in Rothmans' 1956–1999 annual reports. *Accounting, Auditing and Accountability* Journal, 23, 55–81.

Tilt, C.A. (1994). The influence of external pressure groups on corporate social disclosure: Some empirical evidence. *Accounting, Auditing and Accountability Journal*, 7, (4), 47–72.

The Economist (2013). The rise of the low-roll. Available at http://www.economist.com/news/business/21584995-although-it-has-growing-number-rivals-macau-worlds-casino-capital-set-new

The Macao Government Information Bureau (2010). *Macao Year Book 2010*. Macao: Government Information Bureau of the Macao Special Administrative Region.

The Institute for the Study of Commercial Gaming (2009). *Responsible Gambling Awareness Week*. Macau: University of Macau.

Tolbert, P.S. & Zucker, L.G. (1983). Institutional sources of change in the formal structure of organizations: The diffusion of civil service reform, 1880–1935. *Administrative Science Quarterly*, 30, 22–39.

Trotman, K.T. & Bradley, G.W. (1981). Associations between social responsibility disclosure and characteristics of companies. *Accounting, Organizations and Society*, 6, (4), 355–362.

Tyawa, B. (2012). Regulating gaming in the New South Africa. *UNLV Gaming Research and Review Journal*, 16, 93–96.

Unerman, J. (2000). Methodological issues: Reflections on quantification in corporate social reporting content analysis. *Accounting, Auditing and Accountability Journal*, 13, 667–680.

Vong, C.K. (2004). Gambling attitudes and gambling behaviour of residents of Macao: the Monte Carlo of the orient. *Journal of Travel Research*, 42, 271–278.

Vong, F. (2010). Perception of Macau teachers and students regarding gaming operators' social responsibility. *UNLV Gaming Research & Review Journal*, 14, 1–13.

Waller, D.S., Fam, K.S. & Erdogan, A.Z. (2005). Advertising of controversial products: A cross-cultural study. *Journal of Consumer Marketing*, 22, 6–13.

Weber, R.P., 1990. *Basic Content Analysis*. 2nd ed. California: SAGE Publications, Inc.

Williams, S.M. (1999). Voluntary environmental and social accounting disclosure practices in the Asia-Pacific region: An international empirical test of political economy theory. *The International Journal of Accounting*, 34, (2), 209–238.

Williams, S.M. & Pei, C.H.W. (1999). Corporate social disclosures by listed companies on their web sites: An international comparison. *The International Journal of Accounting*, 34, 389–419.

Wilmshurst, T. & Frost, G. (2000). The adoption of environment related management accounting, an analysis of corporate environment sensitivity. *Accounting Forum*, 24, (4), 344–265.

Wilson, A. & West, C. (1981). The marketing of "unmentionables". *Harvard Business Review*, 50, 91–102.

Wynn Macau, Limited (2010). *2009 Annual Report*. Hong Kong: Wynn Macau, Limited.

Part II

Corporate Social Disclosure in Japan

7

Revisiting Corporate Social Disclosure in Japan

Mohobbot Ali, Mohammad Badrul Haider and Mohammad Tazul Islam

Introduction

A corporation has a responsibility to contribute toward the economic development of society by creating added value and generating employment through fair competition; it should also make its existence useful to society at large. A corporation is expected to respect human rights, comply with relevant laws and regulations, observe the spirit of international rules, discharge social responsibility with a strong sense of ethical values and contribute toward sustainable development of society by acting in line with CSR principles (METI, 2012). Similarly, the disclosure of such corporate activities becomes an important part of corporate accountability (Gray et al., 1996; Deegan & Unerman, 2011). Although the origin of CSR disclosure is largely linked with the dawn of the modern corporation (Buhr, 2007), more systematic and standardized systems of CSR reporting only emerged in practice in the late 1980s and early 1990s (World Bank, 2004: 11). Over the last two decades, there has been substantial improvement in the number of companies around the world publishing such kind of non-financial reports, although these remain largely voluntary (KPMG, 2008, 2011). Japan is one of the leading countries in the world in CSR reporting (MOE & JICPA, 2007). According to the KPMG International Survey of Corporate Responsibility Reporting 2011, 99% of Japanese companies report on their impacts on society and environment. While the Japanese government is strongly in favor of CSR, social awareness about corporate activities has also increased over the years (Fukukawa & Moon, 2004). The Japan Business Federation (Keidanren) also emphasizes CSR reporting as a tool to link the market, consumers and investors with corporations, and it encourages its member companies and groups to actively establish and disclose the report (METI, 2012). All these have contributed to the development of corporate social disclosure (CSD) in Japan.

While a number of previous studies have investigated the different aspects of CSD in Japan ranging from descriptive studies to empirical analyses (Kokubu & Kurasaka, 2001; Kokubu & Kurasaka, 2002; Kokubu et al., 2003; Kokubu & Hirayama, 2004; Kokubu & Nashioka, 2005; Tanimoto & Suzuki, 2005; Fukukawa & Teramoto, 2009; Fukukawa, 2010; Haider, 2012), those of Yamagami and Kokubu (1991) and Fukukawa and Moon (2004) focused on the extent and nature of CSD in 1985 and 2002, respectively. The study of Fukukawa and Moon basically improved the work of Yamagami and Kokubu through comparing the disclosure during the two periods. The objective of this chapter is to report on the recent trend in CSD practices in Japan. To update the previous literature on Japanese CSD, we examine CSR reporting of the top 100 (based on revenues) companies in 2012. A comprehensive disclosure check list was prepared mainly based on the ISO 26000 (ISO, 2010) for this purpose. The rest of the chapter proceeds as follows. Firstly, the CSR reporting context in Japan is briefly explained. Then the research method is elaborated. The penultimate section includes findings and analysis before conclusions are drawn.

The context of Japanese CSR reporting

Historically, the notion of social responsibility has been deeply rooted in Japanese business practices (Wokutch, 1990; Lewin et al., 1995; Wokutch & Shepard, 1999; Kawamura, 2003; Fukukawa & Teramoto, 2009). However, disclosure on such corporate initiatives is a relatively new phenomenon that has obtained momentum during the early years of the new millennium. In one of the earliest studies, Yamagami and Kokubu (1991) investigated the social disclosure practice of the mid-1980s and found that there was no disclosure in the mandatory annual reports although some social information was seen in voluntary reports such as the "Operating Reports", "English Version of the Annual Reports" and "Public Relations Reports". They noted extensive disclosure on research and development and international activities but a relatively low level of disclosure on employee relations, community involvement and environment; although there were variations in disclosure according to industry characteristics. The study concluded that the development of social disclosure was slow in Japan compared with the US and European countries. Later, Fukukawa and Moon (2004) updated the study of Yamagami and Kokubu (1991) and found remarkable growth in disclosure of all categories, especially in environmental responsibility. Over 90% of the companies studied had environmental disclosure compared with only 11% during the 1980s. They identified a number of domestic and global factors that were mutually reinforcing as the key drivers for this improved disclosure. These included increased social awareness about public health and the environment, governmental guidelines and laws, initiatives by *Keidanren* (Japan Business Federation), adoption of ISO 14001 and other international reporting guidelines and commitment to the Kyoto Protocol. The study also noted that environmental disclosure has been institutionalized through guidelines, policies and use of external standards. However, disclosure in other aspects such as community involvement, employee relations and consumers was relatively poor with a minority of companies providing regular information and only a few institutionalizing the practice by stating guidelines and policies. They concluded that the clear difference in disclosure between environment and other aspects of CSR is due to the absence of explicit government guidelines.

The Japanese government has significant influence on the development of both CSR and CSD. Instead of specific rules and regulations, the government uses voluntary guidelines and suggestions to control CSR activities to ensure a cooperative relationship between the companies and government (Lewin et al., 1995). This approach gives much flexibility to companies in interpreting and adopting governmental guidelines and thereby providing a favorable business environment (Choi & Aguilera, 2009). Active participation of the industries in developing the guidelines also creates success in application. Kokubu and his colleagues, in a series of studies, (Kokubu & Kurasaka, 2002; Kokubu et al., 2003; Kokubu & Nashioka, 2005) investigated the role of such governmental initiatives in environmental accounting practices. They showed that environmental accounting in Japan has been led by MOE's (Ministry of Environment) Environmental Accounting Guidelines 2000 which emphasized on external reporting and METI's (Ministry of Economy, Trade and Industry) Environmental Management Accounting Workbook that focused exclusively on the internal management function of environmental accounting. Kokubu et al. (2003) indicated that there has been substantial improvement not only in the incidence of reporting but also in the content and format of the environmental disclosure since the issuance of MOE's guidelines. They also noted that environmental management accounting in Japan was lagging behind, as compared with external reporting, and that this was due to the delay in METI's guideline in comparison with MOE's initiatives. Later, Kokubu and Nashioka (2005) updated the previous findings and concluded that, although environmental disclosure was dominant for external reporting purposes, accounting for internal management has been increasing steadily mainly due to the ministry's guidelines.

The impact of globalization is another frequently cited reason in various studies for improved CSR practices of businesses (Fukukawa & Teramoto, 2009). Tanimoto and Suzuki (2005) examined the adoption of the Western approach of CSR in the Japanese context. They argued that the adoption of GRI guidelines by the Japanese companies can be explained by the globalization of corporate practices through foreign ownership or foreign sales rather than the traditional corporate governance system. The study thus concluded that foreign pressures are playing a significant role in spreading sustainability reporting in Japan. However, with respect to scope (title and content) of the reports, they observed a sharp difference between global and Japanese companies, where the former capture the broader concept of sustainability and the latter are more concerned with environmental disclosure.

A recent KPMG (2011) survey showed that 99% of the top 100 companies (in terms of revenues) in Japan have social responsibility disclosure either in stand-alone reports or in annual report. In 2008, over 88% of the companies published stand-alone reports, making the country leader in sustainability reporting. As 95% of the companies had some disclosure in their annual reports, KPMG (2008) argued that CSR is regarded a key issue for shareholders, investors and other stakeholders. It also observed that almost 100% of the companies from high environmental impact industries such as manufacturing, transportation, energy and utilities have published reports; while industries such as trade and retail, finance, insurance and securities, communication and media, and construction and building materials have relatively fewer reports, although the rate was also high. In terms of the number of reporting there is little room for improvement among the leading companies. However, key challenges for CSR reporting in Japan include development in the social aspect of reporting, linking CSR activities with mainstream business decisions and incorporating global activities into CSR reporting (Yamaguchi, 2010).

Research method

Sampling and data collection

The sample of this study consists of the top 100 companies (based on annual revenues) listed in Tokyo Stock Exchange. Individual company's website is accessed to collect the CSR report. In total 90 companies publish English version of the CSR reports that are analyzed and reported in this study. The sample represents a wide range of industries. For analysis, the companies are categorized into seven industry groups. These include food, fisheries, forest and rubber (FFFR); real estate and construction (REC); chemical and pharmaceutical (CP); power, mining and oil (PMO); non-manufacturing (retail trade and service) (NM); steel, machinery and metal (SMM); and transport and automobiles (TA) The number of companies analyzed in each category is given in Appendix 7.A.

There are different ways by which an organization can disclose CSR initiatives – for example, through an annual report, website, noticeboard, sending letters to shareholders and the various media such as television, radio and newspaper. Most of the previous studies have focused on the disclosure that organizations made in their annual reports, either as a proxy for social and environmental responsibility activities, or as an item of more direct interest (Milne & Adler, 1999). Such studies asserted that the most commonly used research method in this aspect is content analysis. Content analysis is a method of codifying the text or content of a piece of writing into various groups or categories according to the selected criteria (Weber, 1988). Thus, the essential stage of content analysis is to decide which documents are to be used (Krippendorff, 2004). Prior studies emphasized the annual report as an important document in CSR due to the high degree of credibility of the information it provides (Cowen et al., 1987; Guthrie & Parker, 1990; Adams et al., 1995, 1998; Gray et al., 1995; Deegan & Gordon, 1996; Deegan & Rankin, 1996; Hackston & Milne, 1996; Adams & Harte, 1998; Neu et al., 1998; Tsang, 1998; Unerman, 2000; Tilt, 2001). However, recent studies also focused on stand-alone CSR reports as the publication of such reports has increased (Clarkson et al., 2011; Thorne et al., 2014). Since stand-alone reports contain detailed disclosure on CSR and the prevalence of such reports is higher in Japan, this study considers the coding of stand-alone CSR reports of the top 100 companies.

Coding was mainly carried out by Mohammad Tazul Islam under the supervision of Mohammad Badrul Haider. The coder was adequately trained during his PhD dissertation project. Initially, a sample of annual reports was coded independently by Mohammad Islam and Mohammad Haider. Differences were then reconciled before proceeding with the full blown coding. Sufficient breaks were taken at regular intervals to avoid the danger of "coder fatigue" (Neuendorf, 2002) which might affect the high level of attention required in this type of work. This process was conceived to increase the reliability of the content analysis method.

Data analysis

We employ ISO 26000 (Guidance on Social Responsibility) as the framework to analyze the CSR reports, with some modifications. ISO 26000 was developed through a multi-stakeholder process and is widely accepted as a standard for CSR management (ISO, 2010). It defines the scope of CSR into seven broad categories. These include organizational governance (OG), human rights (HR), labor practices (LP), the environment (E), fair operating practices (FOP), consumer issue (CI), and community involvement and development (CID). In total, 44 variables were selected under these seven thematic variables to prepare our disclosure check list (Appendix 7.B). While 36 items were chosen from the ISO 26000, we added an additional eight variables under OG from the extant literature and also based on our pilot survey to make the disclosure list more comprehensive. The additional eight issues are basic policy for CSR management, top level commitment/message from CEO/President, corporate governance, compliance/commitment with external initiatives, risk management, internal control system, stakeholder engagement and assurance provision in CSR reporting.

Moreover, the study constructs a CSR disclosure index. In this case, an item which is disclosed by the company was coded "1" and coded "0" if it is not disclosed or irrelevant to the study. In other words, the study considered that if the company discloses the item of CSR reporting (e.g. corporate governance), it was awarded "1" and ifit did not disclose the item it was awarded "0". The scores of the items were then added up to obtain the ultimate score for the company. The CSR disclosure model for the CSR reporting thus measures the Total Disclosure (TD) for the company as follows:

$$\text{CSRDI} = \Sigma d_i^{44} / n_j \tag{i}$$

Where, CSRDI is Corporate Social Responsibility Disclosure Index, d_i is "1", if the item is disclosed and "0", if the item is not disclosed. n_j is the maximum number of items disclosed for the jth company where n_j equals to 44. To get a CSR disclosure score for a company, the score of items is added and then the total is divided by the maximum likely score (44), multiplied by 100 to obtain a percentage score. For example, if a company discloses an item (1) out of 44 items, the disclosure score will be 2.27 (approximately).

Again, the aggregate CSR disclosure was calculated for the seven thematic variables – organizational governance (OG), human rights (HR), labor practices (LP), the environment (E), fair operating practices (FOP), consumer Issue (CI), and community involvement and development

(CID) – by first adding the items disclosed by each of the company under the same thematic areas then adding the total items disclosed under the same thematic variable by all of the company (90), followed by dividing the maximum likely score.

Furthermore, an aggregated all-industries disclosure score, aggregated industry cluster disclosure score and the aggregated thematic variables disclosure score based on industry using the same equation (equation-i) were prepared. In this aspect, descriptive statistics have been used for data analysis and interpretation.

Findings and analysis

Title of the reports

Firstly, the title of the stand-alone reports of the sampled companies was analyzed (Figure 7.1). It shows that about 63% of the sampled companies have entitled their report "*CSR Report*" followed by 20% using "*Sustainability Report* (SR)". Around 8% of the companies used the term "*Social and Environmental Report* (SER)". A similar percentage of companies have claimed their report as "*Integrated Report* (IR)". The finding implies some improvement in terms of the title of the reports over the last decade. Tanimoto and Suzuki (2005) found that Japanese companies were more likely to use the term *Environment* rather than the broader term *Sustainability* during the early years of this century. It seems that the companies have enhanced their focus on reporting by embracing titles like *CSR* and *Sustainability*.

Standards/guidelines used in reporting

Adopting standards/guidelines in preparing CSR reports can assist an organization to become more accountable, responsible and sustainable

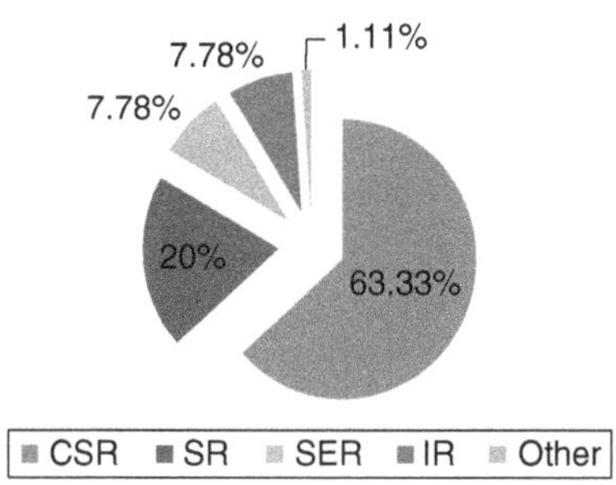

Figure 7.1 Reporting title

Table 7.1 Standards/guidelines used in preparing CSR reports

Standards/guidelines	Number of companies	Percentage of companies
MOE, Japan	58	64.44
ISO-26000	46	51.11
GRI guideline	53	58.89
Others	3	3.33
None	13	14.44

(AccountAbility, 2014; GRI, 2014). As a number of voluntary standards, codes and principles are available for such reporting, companies must decide which are most appropriate for their strategies (Epstein, 2008). As noted earlier, Japanese reporting practice, especially environmental disclosure, is largely influenced by local and international standards and guidelines. Therefore, we checked the guidelines or standards used by our sampled companies (see Table 7.1). The majority of the companies (64.44%) are seen to embrace the voluntary Environmental Reporting Guideline of the Ministry of Environment (MOE), which implies the co-operative relationship between companies and the government in developing the reporting system. Companies' adherence to both GRI guidelines and ISO standards is also clearly demonstrated. As the entire sample is made up of large multinational companies it is expected that they understand the internal benefits and external legitimacy which these global standards can bring for them. This gives the reporting practice an international flavor. Considering the extant literature, we can argue that CSR reporting in Japan has been driven by both local and international forces (Kokubu et al., 2003; Fukukawa & Moon, 2004; Kokubu & Nashioka, 2005; Tanimoto & Suzuki, 2005).

Overall CSR disclosure and industry variation

Previous studies observed significant variations in CSD between environmentally sensitive industries and non-environmentally sensitive industries (Patten, 1991; Deegan & Gordon, 1996; Adams et al., 1998; Cormier & Magnan, 1999). Environmentally sensitive industries such as manufacturing firms are more visible than others because of their high pollution intensity, greater regulatory burden, intense media scrutiny and public concern (Brammer & Pavelin, 2006). As a result, it is expected that such environmentally sensitive industries will have more incentives to disclose social and environmental information in order to reassure stakeholders about their activities and to project a positive social image. Fifka's review (2013) reveals that around 90% of the studies that utilize industry classification to explain disclosure practices have shown the

Table 7.2 Industry disclosure score

Industries	Aggregate Industry Disclosure Score	Ranking
Food, Fisheries, Forest and Rubber (FFFR)	78.18	3
Real Estate and Construction (REC)	78.90	1
Chemical and Pharmaceutical (CP)	75.57	5
Power, Mining and Oil (PMO)	74.83	6
Non-Manufacturing (Retail Trade and Service) (NM)	77.27	4
Steel, Machinery and Metal (SMM)	78.31	2
Transport and Automobiles (TA)	71.26	7
Aggregate Disclosure Score by the Industries	76.33	

influence of such classification. Table 7.2 shows the aggregate disclosure scores of all the sampled companies based on industry. This study finds that the highest CSR disclosure is scored by the real estate and construction (REC) industry at around 79%, followed by the steel, machinery and metal (SMM) industry at about 78%. Moreover, the food, fisheries, forest and rubber (FFFR) industry shows approximately with the same proportion of disclosure as SMM. On the other hand, non-manufacturing (NM) industry scored fourth by disclosing around 77% and chemical and pharmaceutical (CP) industry is ranked fifth at roughly 76%. Finally, the transport and automobiles (TA) industry scored at the bottom in the industry group by around 71% after the power, mining and oil (PMO) industry which is ranked sixth with approximately a 75% disclosure. In general, all the industries showed strong commitment to CSR disclosure and there are no significant differences among the industries with regard to the volume of disclosure. This is in contrast to many international studies which have found that environmentally sensitive industries are often seen to have more disclosure than non-environmentally sensitive industries (Patten, 1991; Brammer & Pavelin, 2006).

As noted in Table 7.3, all companies placed the highest importance on environmental disclosure (disclosure score 98.44%) among the seven disclosure categories of ISO 26000, followed by community involvement and development (disclosure score 90.17%). Disclosure on organizational governance and labor practices is also high (disclosure score of about 85% and 82%, respectively). In comparison to Fukukawa and Moon (2004), our study reconfirms Japanese companies' strong preference for the environment on one hand, and shows significant improvement on disclosure in community involvement and labor practices on

Table 7.3 Aggregate disclosure by the industry

	Organizational Governance (OG)	Human Rights (HR)	Labor Practices (LP)	The Environment (E)	Fair Operating Practices (FOP)	Consumer Issue (CI)	Community Involvement and Development (CID)
Food, Fisheries, Forest and Rubber (FFFR)	90.00	55	84	100	60	77.14	88.57
Real Estate and Construction (REC)	83.93	51.79	80	*100*	60	83.67	83.93
Chemical and Pharmaceutical (CP)	82.21	53.13	90	96.88	52.50	76.79	85.71
Power, Mining and Oil (PMO)	77.88	51.92	83.08	*96.15*	63.08	73.63	89.01
Non-Manufacturing (Retail Trade and Service) (NM)	87.5	52.34	78.75	*100*	53.75	77.68	*96.43*
Steel, Machinery and Metal (SMM)	91.15	55.21	80.83	98.96	58.33	75.60	93.45
Transport and Automobiles (TA)	79.41	44.12	75.29	97.06	48.88	70.59	94.12
Average disclosure score	84.67	51.93	81.71	98.44	56.22	76.44	90.17
Ranking	3	7	4	1	6	5	2

the other hand. Although previous studies (Yamagami & Kokubu, 1991; Fukukawa & Moon, 2004) did not focus on organizational governance, we consider it as an important issue for CSR management. The lowest disclosure is seen on the human rights category with a disclosure score of 51.93%. This is an important finding considering little is known about corporate disclosure on human rights (Islam & McPhail, 2011).

However, from the environmental disclosure point of view – which is the highest disclosure rate among all other categories – FFFR, REC, and NM disclosed all the subcategories, namely prevention of pollution, sustainable resource use, climate change mitigation and adaptation, protection and restoration of the natural environment. PMO disclosed the lowest in the environment although the disclosure score is over 96%. Community involvement and development is the second highest category of sustainability disclosure by the Japanese companies, where NM disclosed more than 96%, followed by TA at around 94%. In all other industries, the community involvement and development category was disclosed at between around 84% and 90%, which is remarkable. Again, in the organizational governance category, which is ranked as third by disclosure among all seven categories, SMM disclosed the highest at around 91% followed by FFFR at 90%. However, in this category, PMO disclosed the lowest, about 78%, after the TA industry at more than 79%. The disclosure of labor practices is quite satisfactory and higher than that in the fair operating practices and human rights categories. The disclosure score of labor practices is more than 75–90%, which is also remarkable for fair and transparent HR-related issues disclosure. Among the seven categories, human rights disclosure is the lowest at around 52%, followed by the disclosure of fair operating practices at more than 56%, which is a little higher than the human rights disclosure (see Table 7.3). Moreover, TA disclosed only around 44%, which is the lowest among all other industries in Japan. However, all other industries are roughly between 51% and 55%. The second lowest category of disclosure by the Japanese industries is fair operating practices (around 56%) in which TA scored lowest at around 49% where all other industries are approximately 52–63% (see Table 7.3).

Disclosure on organizational governance

Corporate governance has become an important issue over the last decade especially after the high profile accounting and ethical scandals around the world including Japan (Brucksch & Grünschlob, 2008;

Kolk, 2008; KPMG, 2008; Kolk & Pinkse, 2010). Corporations are also seen to disclose more on this issue in order to meet social expectations,. For example, Kolk and Pinkse (2010) observed that more than half of Fortune 225 companies have a separate corporate governance section in their CSR reports and/or explicitly link corporate governance and CSR issues. For in-depth analysis, our study in this chapter focuses on eight organizational governance items including basic policy for CSR management, top management commitment, corporate governance, compliance/commitment with external initiatives, risk management, internal control system, stakeholder engagement, and assurance/third party opinion (see Appendix 7.C).

The disclosure score on organizational governance is shown in Table 7.4. About 98% of Japanese companies are seen to adhere to external initiatives for CSR such as guidelines/standards issued either by Japan's Ministry of Environment or international standard setting bodies like ISO and GRI. Similarly, more than 95% of the companies have disclosure on risk management and stakeholder engagement for CSR. Information on corporate governance, top management commitment and internal control are also common for most of the sampled companies. Surprisingly, only two-thirds of the companies have disclosed their policies for CSR management in stand-alone CSR reports although Fukukawa and Moon (2004) observed that environmental policies or guidelines were available on the internet for 88% of their investigated companies. Finally, a relatively low adoption of assurance on CSR reports in Japan is consistent with the previous findings of Haider (2012) and Haider and Kokubu (2014). Table 7.4 also shows that there is minimum variation in the disclosure of organizational governance among the industries. However, it is noteworthy to mention that Food, Fisheries, Forest, Rubber; Non-Manufacturing industry, and still, Machinery and Metal have significantly higher disclosure rates even on basic policy for CSR management and adoption of assurance, the two lowest disclosed items on average.

Disclosure on Human Rights

Human rights is the second CSR disclosure item in ISO 26000. This regulation explains that organizations should show respect for human rights and recognize both their importance and their universality. Yamagami and Kokubu (1991) and Fukukawa and Moon (2004) did not consider the human rights issue in their analyses. However, with the increasing power of corporations to impact human rights both positively and negatively, corporate responsibility to protect human rights has become a

Table 7.4 Core subject: Organizational governance

Key issues	FFFR	REC	CP	PMO	NM	SMM	TA	Average disclosure score	Ranking
Basic policy for CSR management	80	57.14	50	61.54	81.25	79.17	58.82	66.85	7
Top level commitment/ Message from CEO/MD	100	85.71	87.50	76.92	100	95.83	88.24	90.60	5
Corporate Governance	100	100	100	92.31	87.50	95.83	88.24	94.84	4
Compliance/ commitment with external initiatives	100	100	100	92.31	93.75	100	100	98.01	1
Risk management	100	100	100	92.31	93.75	95.83	88.24	95.73	2
Internal control system	80	100	87.50	92.31	87.50	91.67	76.47	87.92	6
Stakeholder engagement	100	100	87.50	92.31	100	100	88.24	95.44	3
Assurance/third party opinion	60	28.57	50	23.08	56.25	70.83	47.06	47.97	8

serious global concern over the past decades (Islam, 2011; McPhail & McKernan, 2011). For this study, we consider eight issues under the thematic variable *human rights*. These are due diligence, human rights risk situation, avoidance of complicity, resolving grievances, discrimination and vulnerable groups, civil and political rights, economic, social and cultural rights, and fundamental rights at work. The coding rule for human rights disclosure is given in Appendix 7.D. Table 7.5 contains the disclosure score for human rights.

As mentioned earlier, human rights is the lowest disclosed item by the Japanese companies. However, over 90% of the companies sampled have disclosure on avoidance of complicity and economic, social and cultural rights. Avoidance of complicity implies that companies are not involved either directly or indirectly in any human rights abuses. Similarly, Japanese companies support education and life-long learning for community members and engage with other organizations and governmental institutions to ensure the economic, social and cultural rights of the people. Disclosure of information on discrimination and vulnerable groups is also significant (83.51%). However, only half the companies have information on fundamental rights at work. This implies that companies are reluctant to disclose important issues like freedom of association and effective collective bargaining, elimination of forced or compulsory labor, abolition of child labor, elimination of discrimination in respect of employment and occupation at the workplace. Similarly, human rights grievance-resolution mechanisms and civil and political rights are also largely ignored by the Japanese companies. Finally, for human rights disclosure we do not see any significant variation among the different types of industry.

Disclosure on labor practices

Harmonious relationship between employees and the company is a distinctive feature of Japanese corporate culture (Wokutch & Shepard 1999; Tanimoto & Suzuki 2005). Recent studies (Haider, 2012; Haider & Kokubu, 2013) have also observed employees as important stakeholders for CSR reporting in Japan. Such reporting is seen in Japan as an important CSR education tool for employees (Yamaguchi, 2010). Therefore, it is expected that corporations will provide extensive information on labor practices.

ISO 26000 explains that the labor practices of an organization should encompass all policies and practices relating to work performed within, by or on behalf of the organization. We consider five labor practice

Table 7.5 Core subject: Human rights

Key Issues	FFFR	REC	CP	PMO	NM	SMM	TA	Average disclosure score	Ranking
Issue 1: Due diligence	60	42.86	50	46.15	56.25	37.50	5.88	42.66	5
Issue 2: Human rights risk situations	20	28.57	62.5	15.38	31.25	45.83	35.29	34.12	6
Issue 3: Avoidance of complicity	100	100	87.5	100	87.50	100	94.12	95.59	1
Issue 4: Resolving grievances	0	0	0	7.69	0	12.50	0	2.88	8
Issue 5: Discrimination and vulnerable groups	80	100	75	92.31	87.50	79.17	70.59	83.51	3
Issue 6: Civil and political right	0	0	12.5	15.38	18.75	12.50	11.76	10.13	7
Issue 7: Economic, social and cultural right	100	85.71	87.5	92.31	93.75	100	94.12	93.34	2
Issue 8: Fundamental right at work	80	57.14	50	46.15	43.75	54.17	41.18	53.20	4

Table 7.6 Core subject: Labor practices

Key Issues	FFFR	REC	CP	PMO	NM	SMM	TA	Average disclosure score	Ranking
Issue 1: Employment and employment relationships	60	100	100	92.31	81.25	83.33	70.59	83.93	4
Issue 2: Conditions of work and social protection	100	100	100	100	93.75	100	94.12	98.27	3
Issue 3: Social dialogue	60	0	50	23.08	18.75	25	17.65	27.78	5
Issue 4: Health and safety at work	100	100	100	100	100	95.83	94.12	98.56	2
Issue 5: Human development and training in the workplace	100	100	100	100	100	100	100	100	1

issues for our coding purpose, and these are shown in Appendix 7.E. The disclosure score is given in Table 7.6. Consistent with Fukukawa and Moon (2004), this study finds that all the companies are enthusiastic in providing information on employee training and development, health and safety at work, and condition of work and social protection. A closer look at the sample also reveals that the majority of the companies now disclose information on employment and working conditions policies and guidelines which were seen as insignificant a decade ago. However, only around 28% of the companies identified the presence of some kind of social dialogue with their employees.

Disclosure on the environment

The state of the natural environment has worsened over the last hundred years (Zadek, 2007). Society is now facing a number of environmental challenges including depletion of natural resources, pollution, climate change, destruction of habitats, loss of species and the collapse of entire ecosystems and the degradation of urban and rural human settlements (ISO, 2010). Massive industrialization all over the world is considered to be an important factor in such environmental degradation. As organizations are a part of the broader social system, it is expected that they will take measures to protect the environment and disclose such information to the stakeholders.

This study uses four issues including prevention of pollution, sustainable resource use, climate change mitigation and adaptation, and protection and restoration of the natural environment under the broad thematic variable *the environment*. Explanations of these items are given in Appendix 7.F.

There has been a significant improvement in environmental disclosure in Japan over the last two decades. While Yamagami and Kokubu (1991) found that environmental responsibility was disclosed less frequently than any other CSR issues, the study of Fukukawa and Moon (2004) revealed that more than 90% of companies were committed to publish information on this issue. Considering the nature of disclosure, the latter study argued that "environmental responsibility is well institutionalized within Japanese CSR" (p. 52). As noted earlier, a number of local and international forces, including social awareness about public health and environment, governmental co-operation through guidelines/standards, initiatives by business associations, and international pressure, have contributed to the increased attention to environmental disclosure. Table 7.7 displays the coding result of environmental disclosure in the current study. It shows that information disclosure on

Table 7.7 Core subject: The environment

Key issues	FFFR	REC	CP	PMO	NM	SMM	TA	Average	Ranking
Issue 1: Prevention of pollution	100	100	100	100	100	100	100	100	1
Issue 2: Sustainable resource use	100	100	100	100	100	100	100	100	1
Issue 3: Climate change mitigation and adaptation	100	100	100	92.31	100	95.83	94.12	97.47	2
Issue 4: Protection and restoration of the natural environment	100	100	87.5	92.31	100	100	94.12	96.28	3

environmental issues is close to saturation. Companies in Japan are also enthusiastic about the protection and restoration of the natural environment along with issues such as the prevention of pollution, sustainable resource use, climate change mitigation and adaptation,. In a recent comparative study, Kokubu et al. (2014) also found that biodiversity, which receives relatively little attention in international reporting entities, is also closely managed by Japanese companies. They identified the role of the government through formulating guidelines and initiatives by the *Keidanren* for improved attention on biodiversity. Finally, Table 7.7 does not indicate any significant differences among the industries with regard to environmental disclosure.

Disclosure on fair operating practices

Fair operating practices concern ethical conduct in an organization's dealings with other organizations and individuals such as relationships between organizations and government agencies, as well as between organizations and their partners, suppliers, contractors, competitors and business association (ISO, 2010). Specific issues considered for this study include anti-corruption, responsible political involvement, fair competition, socially responsible behaviors in the sphere of influence and respect for property right. The coding rule is given in Appendix 7.G.

Table 7.8 shows that more than 89% of Japanese companies have disclose on promotion of social responsibility in the sphere of their influence. For example, the majority of the companies explain the influence of their purchase and procurement decisions on other organizations. The second highest disclosed item is fair competition, which is scored at 66.76%. A good number of companies also provide information on their policies and practices regarding property rights and anti-corruption. The lowest disclosed item is responsible political involvement, which is marked at 21.48%.

Disclosure on consumer issues

Consumer issue is another hardcore issue in CSR disclosure, as explained by ISO 26000. The extant literature also noted consumers as an important stakeholder for CSR in Japan (Kokubu et al., 2002; Higashida et al., 2005; Kokubu et al., 2012). Companies are increasingly focusing on general consumers to show their commitment to sustainable activities that will ultimately enhance their reputation and market share. Therefore, it is expected that companies will disclose extensive information about goods and services and other consumer-related matters. We

Table 7.8 Core subject: Fair operating practices

Key issues	FFFR	REC	CP	PMO	NM	SMM	TA	Average disclosure score	Ranking
Issue 1: Anti – corruption	60	28.57	62.5	53.85	62.5	50	23.53	46.83	4
Issue 2: Responsible political involvement	20	28.57	12.5	46.15	25	16.67	0	21.48	5
Issue 3: Fair competition	80	85.71	37.5	69.23	62.5	75	70.59	66.76	2
Issue 4: Promoting social responsibility in the sphere of influence	100	85.71	87.5	92.31	81.25	95.83	94.12	89.45	1
Issue 5: Respect for property right	40	71.43	62.5	53.85	37.5	54.17	41.18	53.44	3

considered a total of seven consumer issues in the coding rule outlined in Appendix 7.H.

Table 7.9 shows the disclosure rate on consumer issues. As expected, almost all the companies provided information on fair marketing, sustainable consumption and consumer education and awareness. Disclosure on consumers' health and safety and consumer service and support also increased substantially compared with Fukukawa and Moon's (2004) findings. However, companies are still unwilling to provide information on consumer data protection and privacy, a similar scenario that prevailed in the early 2000s. Table 7.9 does not show any significant variation between disclosure on consumer issues and industry classifications. However, real estate and construction, and steel, machinery and metal industries are seen to be more active in this matter.

Disclosure on community involvement and development

The last issue in CSR discourse is *community involvement and development*, which includes seven subcategories, namely community involvement, education and culture, employment creation and skills development, technology development, wealth and income creation, health and social investment (ISO, 2010). The coding rule for this category is given in Appendix 7.I.

Corporations in Japan have a long history of contributing to community development (Wokutch & Shepard 1999; Fukukawa & Moon, 2004). Therefore, it is expected that corporations will report such social contributions to their stakeholders. In this regard, Fukukawa and Moon (2004) pointed out that community involvement is the less institutionalized dimension of CSR in Japan, although they noted remarkable improvement in the number of companies making such disclosure.

The current study finds that all the companies disclose information on their community involvement (see Table 7.10). Similarly, nearly all the companies are eager to show commitment to education and culture, social investment, employment, and wealth and income creation. We do not observe any significant variations in community involvement disclosure among the different types of industry. However, the real estate and construction industry is found to have disclosed all items of community involvement and development.

Conclusion

The objective of the study in this chapter has been to understand the recent development of CSR reporting among leading Japanese

Table 7.9 Core subject: Consumer issues

Key issues	FFFR	REC	CP	PMO	NM	SMM	TA	Average disclosure score	Ranking
Issue 1: Fair marketing, information and contractual practices	100	100	100	100	100	95.83	100	99.4	1
Issue 2: Protecting consumers' health and safety	100	85.71	100	84.62	68.75	91.67	82.35	87.59	4
Issue 3: Sustainable consumption	80	100	100	100	93.75	100	100	96.25	3
Issue 4: Consumer service, support, and dispute resolution	80	85.71	87.5	84.62	75	70.83	82.35	80.86	5
Issue 5: Consumer data protection and privacy	20	57.14	25	23.08	43.75	54.17	17.65	34.4	7
Issue 6: Access to essential services	60	57.14	50	23.08	62.5	16.67	11.76	40.16	6
Issue 7: Education and awareness	100	100	75	100	100	100	100	96.43	2

Table 7.10 Core subject: Community involvement and development

Key Issues	FFFR	REC	CP	PMO	NM	SMM	TA	Average disclosure score	Ranking
Issue 1: Community involvement	100	100	100	100	100	100	100	100	1
Issue 2: Education and culture	100	100	87.5	100	100	100	100	98.21	2
Issue 3: Employment creation and skills development	100	100	87.5	84.62	100	100	88.24	94.34	4
Issue 4: Technology development	40	100	75	69.23	81.25	75	76.47	73.85	6
Issue 5: Wealth and income creation	100	100	75	76.92	93.75	95.83	94.12	90.80	5
Issue 6: Health	80	100	87.5	92.31	100	83.33	100	91.88	3
Issue 7: Social investment	100	100	87.5	100	100	100	100	98.21	2

companies. We focused particularly on the nature and extent of disclosure in order to update the extant literature. The study revealed that CSR reporting by Japanese companies is remarkable as measured in terms of organizational governance, human rights, labor practices, the environment, fair operating practices, consumer issues and community involvement and development. Consistent with previous studies, Japanese companies' strong commitment to the environment was confirmed. Moreover, a significant improvement in information disclosure on community involvement, labor practices, and consumer issues is also observed. Relatively less emphasis is given to the disclosure of human rights. As corporations have the power to influence human rights, companies should focus on this issue in the future. Given the companies' extensive disclosure, it is surprising that only two-thirds of them have stated their basic policy for CSR management in stand-alone reports. Although companies are committed to external initiatives such as standards and guidelines, it is important that they have their own CSR policies, principles and codes and to make them publicly available. While the real estate and construction industry is the leader in CSR reporting, we did not find any significant differences among different types of industry. In contrast to the literature, non-manufacturing industries were also seen to provide detail information on their CSR performance. The study also noted the influence of international organizations such as the GRI and ISO in shaping Japanese CSR practices. While a decade ago companies were seen to focus narrowly on the *environment* only, recently they have broadened their scope of reporting by embracing *CSR* and *sustainability*. However, the concept of *integrated reporting* is still at an emerging stage.

This descriptive study can benefit a number of audiences including researchers, practitioners and regulators. The comprehensive check list captures the detailed CSR information on seven core areas which can be used to advance the current study. Future research, for example, can focus on in-depth analysis of specific CSR issues. A limited number of studies have already been conducted on climate change (Haque & Deegan, 2010), human rights (Islam & McPhail, 2011), corporate governance (Kamal & Deegan, 2013). Management can assess their own performance and identify areas for improvement. The information revealed can assist regulators to monitor and supervise the companies.

Appendix 7.A

Cluster of sample industries

Industry	**Number of companies**	**Companies analyzed (analysis in %)**
Food, Fisheries, Forest and Rubber	8	5 (62.5)
Real Estate and Construction	7	7 (100)
Chemical and Pharmaceutical	9	8 (88.89)
Power, Mining and Oil; Glass and Ceramic	16	13 (81.25)
Non-Manufacturing (Retail Trade and Service)	17	16 (94.12)
Steel, Machinery and Metal	25	24 (96)
Transport and Automobiles	18	17 (94.44)
Total	**100**	**90 (90)**

Note: figure in the parentheses indicate the percentages of companies analyzed.

Appendix 7.B

List of CSR disclosure items

Core subject: Organizational governance
Issue 1: Basic policy for CSR management
Issue 2: Top level commitment/Message from CEO/MD
Issue 3: Corporate Governance
Issue 4: Compliance/commitment with external initiatives
Issue 5: Risk management
Issue 6: Internal control system
Issue 7: Stakeholder engagement
Issue 8: Assurance/third party opinion

Core subject: Human rights
Issue 1: Due diligence
Issue 2: Human rights risk situations
Issue 3: Avoidance of complicity
Issue 4: Resolving grievances
Issue 5: Discrimination and vulnerable groups
Issue 6: Civil and political right
Issue 7: Economic, social and cultural right
Issue 8: Fundamental right at work

Core subject: Labor practices
Issue 1: Employment and employment relationships
Issue 2: Conditions of work and social protection
Issue 3: Social dialogue

(Continued)

Issue 4: Health and safety at work
Issue 5: Human development and training in the workplace

Core subject: The environment
Issue 1: Prevention of pollution
Issue 2: Sustainable resource use
Issue 3: Climate change mitigation and adaptation
Issue 4: Protection and restoration of the natural environment

Core subject: Fair operating practices
Issue 1: Anti – corruption
Issue 2: Responsible political involvement
Issue 3: Fair competition
Issue 4: Promoting social responsibility in the sphere of influence
Issue 5: Respect for property right

Core subject: Consumer issues
Issue 1: Fair marketing, information and contractual practices
Issue 2: Protecting consumers' health and safety
Issue 3: Sustainable consumption
Issue 4: Consumer service, support, and dispute resolution
Issue 5: Consumer data protection and privacy
Issue 6: Access to essential services
Issue 7: Education and awareness

Core subject: Community involvement and development
Issue 1: Community involvement
Issue 2: Education and culture
Issue 3: Employment creation and skills development
Issue 4: Technology development
Issue 5: Wealth and income creation
Issue 6: Health
Issue 7: Social investment

Appendix 7.C

Core subject: Organizational governance
Basic policy for CSR management, top level commitment/message from CEO/ President, corporate governance, compliance/commitment with external initiatives, risk management, internal control system, stakeholder engagement and assurance/third party opinion are used to code and analyze organizational governance.

Appendix 7.D

Core subject: Human rights

Issue 1: Due diligence
Includes human rights policy, means of assessing how existing and proposed activities affect human rights, integrating human rights policy throughout the organization, and means of tracking performance over time.

Issue 2: Human rights risk situations
Specific care in circumstances and environments where organizations are more likely to face challenges and dilemmas relating to human rights and the risk of human rights abuse may be exacerbated such as political instability; poverty, drought, natural disasters; extractive activities that affect natural resources; proximity of operation of indigenous people, can affect children; value chain; extensive measure to secure premises.

Issue 3: Avoidance of complicity
Security arrangements respect human rights and are consistent with international norms and standards for law enforcement; training to security personnel; complaints about the security procedure; not provide goods/service that harm human rights; not enter into a formal partnership that commit human rights abuses; inform about the social and environmental conditions for goods/service produced; consider making public.

Issue 4: Resolving grievances
Human rights grievance resolving mechanism

Issue 5: Discrimination and vulnerable groups
Action to ensure equal opportunity and respect for all, not discrimination to stakeholders, examine its own operation and within its sphere of influence about discrimination, raising awareness about human rights, redressing past discrimination, take positive and conducive view of diversity among people.

Note: Vulnerable group includes women and girls, people with disabilities, children, indigenous people, migrants and migrants workers, people discriminated on the basis of descent including caste, others such as poor, illiterate, minority and religious group.

Issue 6: Civil and political right
Respect civil and political right that include life of individuals; freedom of opinion and expression; freedom of peaceful assembly/association; freedom to seek receive and impart information and ideas through any means regardless boarder.

Issue 7: Economic, social and cultural right
Support/facilitate education and life-long learning; joining organization/governmental institutions supporting respect; ways to adapt goods/service to purchasing poor people; making facilities/resources available to occasional cultural activities.

Issue 8: Fundamental right at work
Freedom of association and effective collective bargaining; elimination of forced/compulsory labor; abolition of child labor; elimination of discrimination in respect of employment and occupation.

Appendix 7.E

Core subject: Labor practices
Issue 1: Employment and employment relationships Confidence in work performed, not seek to avoid *obligation by law*, active *workforce planning*, provide reasonable *notice/time* that affect employment, ensure equal opportunities, eliminate arbitrary/discriminator dismissal practices, protect employee data and privacy, contracted or sub-contracted organization's has decent working condition, no benefit from unfair/exploitative or abusive labor practices and promotion & advancement of nations of host country of multinational company.
Issue 2: Conditions of work and social protection *Condition of work* with national laws and regulations consistent with international standard, collective agreement, observe minimum provision of ILO, provide decent condition of work, provide equal pay for work, pay direct to the workers, respect to normal working hour, compensate overtime works, observe national/religious traditions and customs. Note: Condition of works includes wages and other forms of compensation, working time, rest periods, holidays, disciplinary and dismissal practices, maternity and welfare maters; and social protection includes all legal guarantees and organizational policies and practices to mitigate the reduction or loss of incase in injury, illness, maternity, parenthood, old age, unemployment, disability or any other hardship.
Issue 3: Social dialogue *Collective bargaining* structure, right to join/form CB organization, reasonable notice to the government for major employment impact, workers representative with access to authorized decisionmaker, refrain from encouraging government to restrict social dialogue. Note: Social dialogue includes all types of negotiation, consultation or exchange of information between or among representatives of governments, employers and workers, or matters of common interest relating to economic and social concern.
Issue 4: Health and safety at work *Health, safety and working environment policy*; understand and apply principles of health and safety management; analyze and control the health and safety risk; communicate information, provide safety equipment; record and investigate all health and safety incidents; address Occupational Safety and Health (OSH); equal health and safety to part-time/temporary/subcontracted workers; eliminate psychosocial hazard; join labor-management health and safety committee.
Issue 5: Human development and training in the workplace Skills *development, training and apprenticeship*, career advancement, help to transition to new employment through skills recognition, respect family responsibilities, joint labor-management programs.

Appendix 7.F

Core subject: The environment

Issue 1: Prevention of pollution
Emission to air, discharge to water, waste, release to toxic and hazardous chemicals, other identifiable forms.

Issue 2: Sustainable resource use
Energy efficiency *programs, water conservation* and access to water, efficiency in the use of materials.

Issue 3: Climate change mitigation and adaptation
Source, measure, record and report *GHG emission*; programs to reduce GHG emissions, reduce to use of fossil fuels.

Consider opportunities for emission trading under UN Framework Convention on Climate Change (UNFCCC), future global and local projects to mitigate climate risk; and identify opportunities to avoid/minimize climate change risk.

Issue 4: Protection and restoration of the natural environment
Valuing, protecting and restoring *ecosystem* service; valuing and protecting *biodiversity*; using land and natural resources sustainably; advancing environmentally sound urban and rural development.

Appendix 7.G

Core subject: Fair operating practices

Issue 1: Anti-corruption
Policy and practices to counter corruption, bribery and extortion; ensure leadership to implement anti-corruption policy; support employees and representative to eradicate; train and raise awareness; ensure remuneration is appropriate; effective internal control; encourage report violations; bringing violation to law; work to oppose corruption.

Issue 2: Responsible political involvement
Train and raise awareness among employees and representatives; *transparent policy* in lobbying, political contribution and involvement; policies and guidelines to manage people to retain on the organization behalf; avoid political contribution that in favor of a specific cause; prohibit activities in misinformation, misrepresentation, threat or compulsion.

Issue 3: Fair competition
Manner consistent with *competition laws and regulations*; procedure and other safeguard to *prevent anti-competitive* behavior; promote employee awareness; support anti-trust and anti-dumping practices; encourage public policy; not take advantage in social condition.

(Continued)

Core subject: Fair operating practices
Issue 4: Promoting social responsibility in the sphere of influence *Influence other organizations* through the exercise of its procure and purchasing decisions; consider potential impact/unintended consequences of it procurement decision on other organization.
Issue 5: Respect for property right *Policy and practices* to promote respect property right and traditional knowledge; lawful title permitting use or disposal; not engage in activities that violate; pay fair compensation; consider the expectations of society, human rights.

Appendix 7.H

Core subject: Consumer issues
Issue 1: Fair marketing, information and contractual practices Not engage in *deceptive, misleading, fraudulent or unfair information*; clearly identify *advertising and marketing*; openly disclose total prices and taxes, terms and conditions; substantiate claims or assertions; not use text/image that perpetuate stereotyping; not unfairly target vulnerable groups; language in the point of sale; contracts in written and clear.
Issue 2: Protecting consumers' health and safety Reasonably foreseeable condition to use; assess the adequacy of *health and safety laws*, regulations and standards; minimize risks in design; avoid use of harmful chemicals in development; perform human health risk assessment; convey safety information; adopt safety measures in handling/storage; withdraw all products when against consumers' health and safety.
Issue 3: Sustainable consumption Offer socially and *environmentally beneficial products and services considering the full life cycle* and reduce adverse impacts on the environment and society.
Issue 4: Consumer service, support, and dispute resolution Warranties and guarantees, technical support regarding use, provision for return, repair and maintenance; measures to prevent, review, improve practice to response to complaints; dispute resolution (ISO-1001,1002,1003) and redress mechanism.
Issue 5: Consumer data protection and privacy *Rigorous system* for obtaining, using and protecting data
Issue 6: Access to essential services Contribute to the fulfilment of right of essential services such as electricity, gas, water, waste water services, drainage, sewerage and telephone.
Issue 7: Education and awareness *Education and awareness* initiatives to enable consumers to be well informed, conscious of their right and responsibilities, assume an active role and be able to knowledgeable purchasing decision and consumption, skills in assessing products and services, and making comparison.

Appendix 7.I

Core subject: Community involvement and development

Issue 1: Community involvement
Consult representative *community groups* in determining priorities for social investment and community development activities; developments that can affect them; participate *local association*; maintain transparent relationship with local *government officials* and *political representatives*; contribute to policy formulation.

Issue 2: Education and culture
Promote and support *education at all levels*, learning opportunities to vulnerable/discriminate group, encourage the enrollment of children education, facilitating human rights to education and awareness rising; conserve and protect *cultural heritage*, promote traditional knowledge and technologies.

Issue 3: Employment creation and skills development
Impact of investment decision on *employment creation*; consider the impact of technology choice and outsourcing; participating local and national skill development programs; attention to vulnerable group in employment and capacity building; framework condition to create employment.

Issue 4: Technology development
Contributing to the development of *low-cost*, economically feasible with developing *potential local and traditional* knowledge and skills technologies; engaging in partnership with local organization such as universities; adopt practices that allow technology transfer and diffuse.

Issue 5: Wealth and income creation
Contribute positively to wealth and income creation through *entrepreneurship programs*, development of local suppliers, employment of local community members, empowering women, meeting *tax obligation*, value chain, compliance with laws and regulations to alleviate poverty.

Issue 6: Health
Minimize or eliminate negative health impact of any production processes, product/services; contributing to access *to medicine and vaccination*; raising awareness *HIV/AIDS*, cancer, heart disease malaria, tuberculosis, and obesity; access to health care services, clean water and sanitation.

Issue 7: Social investment
Social investments include projects to *education, training, culture, healthcare, income generation, infrastructure* development, and access to information; *philanthropic (e.g. grants, volunteering and donation)*, prioritize projects that viable in the long-run and contribute sustainable development.

References

AccountAbility (2014). Setting the standard. Available at http://www.accountability.org/standards/index.html

Adams, C.A. & Harte, G. (1998). The changing portrayal of the employment of women in British banks' and retail companies' corporate annual reports. *Accounting, Organizations and Society*, 23, (8), 781–812.

Adams, C.A., Coutts, A. & Harte, G. (1995). Corporate equal opportunities (non-) disclosure. *The British Accounting Review*, 27, (2), 87–108.

Adams, C.A., Hill, W.Y. & Roberts, C.B. (1998). Corporate social reporting practices in western Europe: Legitimating corporate behavior? *The British Accounting Review*, 30, (1), 1–21.

Buhr, N. (2007). Histories of and rationales for sustainability reporting. In Unerman, J., O'Dwyer, B. & Bebbington, J. (eds.) *Sustainability Accounting and Accountability*. London: Routledge.

Brammer, S. & Pavelin, S. (2006). Voluntary environmental disclosure by large UK companies. *Journal of Business Finance and Accounting*, 33, (7–8), 1168–1188.

Brucksch, S. & Grünschlob, C. (2008). From environmental accountability to corporate social responsibility? Reflections on the CSR boom in Japan from the perspective of business management and civil society groups. In Volker, E. & Lützeler, R. (eds.) *Regionalentwicklung und regionale Disparitäten (Japanstudien, 20)*. München: Iudicium Verlag.

Choi, S. & Aguilera, R.V. (2009). Corporate social responsibility dynamics in South Korea and Japan: A comparative analysis. In Mallin, C.A. (ed.) *Corporate Social Responsibility: A Case Study Approach*. Cheltenham: Edward Elgar.

Clarkson, P., Overell, M. & Chapple, L. (2011). Environmental reporting and its relation to corporate environmental performance, *Abacus*, 47, (1), 27–60.

Cormier, D. & Magnan, M. (1999). Corporate environmental disclosure strategies: Determinants, costs and benefits. *Journal of Accounting, Auditing and Finance*, 14, (3), 429–451.

Cowen, S.S., Ferreri, L.B. & Parker, L.D. (1987). The impact of corporate characteristics on social responsibility disclosure: A typology and frequency-based analysis. *Accounting, Organizations and Society*, 12, (2), 111–122.

Deegan, C. & Gordon, B. (1996). A study of the environmental disclosure practices of Australian corporations. *Accounting and Business Research*, 26, (3), 187–199.

Deegan, C. & Rankin, M. (1996). Do Australian companies report environmental news objectively? An analysis of environmental disclosures by firms prosecuted successfully by the Environmental Protection Authority. *Accounting, Auditing & Accountability Journal*, 9, (2), 50–67.

Deegan, C. & Unerman, J. (2011). *Financial Accounting Theory*. Berhshire: McGraw-Hill Higher Education.

Epstein, M.J. (2008). *Making Sustainability Work: Best Practices in Managing and Measuring Corporate Social, Environmental and Economic Impacts*. San Francisco, CA: Berrett-Koehler.

Fifka, M.S. (2013). Corporate responsibility reporting and its determinants in comparative perspective – A Review of the empirical literature and a meta-analysis. *Business Strategy and the Environment*, 22, (1), 1–35.

Fukukawa, K. (2010). Corporate social responsibility in Japan: A local-global perspective. Working Paper No. 10/03, Bradford University School of Management.

Fukukawa, K. & Moon, J. (2004). A Japanese model of corporate social responsibility? A study of website reporting. *Journal of Corporate Citizenship*, 14, 45–59.

Fukukawa, K. & Teramoto, Y. (2009). Understanding Japanese CSR: The reflections of managers in the field of global operations. *Journal of Business Ethics*, 85, 133–146.

Global Reporting Initiative (GRI) (2014). Available at https://www.globalreporting.org/Pages/default.aspx

Gray, R., Owen, D. & Adams, C.A. (1996). *Accounting and Accountability: Changes and Challenges in Corporate Social and Environmental Reporting*. London: Prentice-Hall.

Gray, R., Kouhy, R. & Levers, S. (1995). Methodological themes: Constructing a research database of social and environmental reporting by UK companies. *Accounting Audit and Accountability Journal*, 8, (2), 78–101.

Guthrie, J. & Parker, L.D. (1990). Corporate social disclosure practice: A comparative international analysis. *Advances in Public Interest Accounting*, 3, 159–175.

Hackston, D. & Milne, M.J. (1996). Some determinants of social and environmental disclosures in New Zealand companies. *Accounting, Auditing & Accountability Journal*, 9, (1), 77–108.

Haider, M.B. (2012). Assurance in sustainability reporting and its legitimacy: Evidence from Japan. Unpublished PhD thesis, Kobe University, Japan.

Haider, M.B. & Kokubu, K. (2013). Managerial motivation on adoption of assurance in sustainability reporting: Evidence from Japan. Paper presented at the European Accounting Association 36th Annual Congress, Paris.

Haider, M.B., & Kokubu, K. (2014). Assurance and third-party comment on sustainability reporting in Japan: A descriptive study. *International Journal of Environment and Sustainable Development*. Accepted and forthcoming.

Higashida, A., Kokubu, K. & Kawahara, C. (2005). A study of the environmental disclosure in environmental report and its determinants in Japanese firms (in Japanese). *Shakai Kanren Kaikei Kenkyu*, 17, 29–38.

Haque, S. & Deegan, C. (2010). An exploration of corporate climate change-related governance practices and related disclosures: Evidence from Australia. *Australian Accounting Review*, 20, (4), 317–333.

International Organization for Standardization (ISO), (2010), ISO 26000:2010, Guidance on social responsibility, Switzerland: ISO.

Islam, A. (2011). Human right performance reporting: A study of corporations within Australian financial sector. Paper presented at the Critical Perspectives on Accounting Conference 2011, Clearwater, Florida.

Islam, A. & McPhail, K. (2011). Regulating for corporate human right abuses: The emergence of corporate reporting on the ILO's human right standards within the global garment manufacturing and retail industry. *Critical Perspectives on Accounting*, 22, (8), 790–810.

Kamal, Y. & Deegan, C. (2013). Motivation of corporate managers for social responsibility related governance disclosure: Evidence from Bangladesh Paper presented at the Seventh Asia Pacific Interdisciplinary Research in Accounting Conference, Kobe.

Kawamura, M. (2003). Japanese companies launch new era of CSR management in 2003. *NLI Research*, 1–12.

Kokubu, K. & Kurasaka, T. (2001). Corporate environmental accounting: A Japanese perspective. Discussion Paper No. 2001–8, Graduate School of Business Administration, Kobe University.

Kokubu, K. & Kurasaka, T. (2002). Corporate environmental accounting: A Japanese perspective. In Bennett, M., Bouma, J.J. & Wolters, T. (eds.) *Environmental Management Accounting: Purpose and Progress*. Dordrecht: Kluwer Academic Publishers.

Kokubu, K. & Hirayama, K. (2004). *Environmental Reporting in Japan*. The Energy Conservation Centre, Japan.

Kokubu, K. & Nashioka, E. (2005). Environmental management accounting practices in Japan. In Rikhardsson, P.M., Bennett, M., Bouma, J.J. & Schaltegger, S. (eds.) *Implementing Environmental Management Accounting: Status and Challenges*. Berlin: Springer.

Kokubu, K., Kitada, H. & Haider, M.B. (2014). Corporate sustainability barometer in Japan. In Schaltegger, S., Windolf, S.E., Harms, D. & Horisch, J. (eds.) *Corporate Sustainability in International Comparison: Eco-Efficiency in Industry and Science 31*. Springer International Publishing.

Kokubu, K., Nashioka, E., Saio, K. & Imai, S. (2003). Two governmental initiatives on environmental management accounting and corporate practices in Japan. In Bennett, M., Rikhardsson, P. & Schaltegger, S. (eds.) *Environmental Management Accounting: Purpose and Progress*. Dordrecht: Kluwer Academic Publishers.

Kokubu, K., Nishitani, K., Kitada, H. & Shinohara, A (2012). Corporate environmental disclosure practices in Japan's environmental reports: Stakeholder influence and information needs. *Sangyo-Keiri*. Accepted and forthcoming.

Kokubu, K., Shinabe, T., Higashida, A., Onishi, Y. & Noda, A. (2002). Analysis of environmental reports by Japanese companies: Content analysis and determinants. *Society for Environmental Economics and Policy Studies, Annual Report*, Vol. 7.

Kolk, A. (2008). Sustainability, accountability and corporate governance: Exploring multinationals' reporting practices. *Business Strategy and the Environment*, 17, (1), 1–15.

Kolk, A. & Pinkse J. (2010). The integration of corporate governance in corporate social responsibility disclosures. *Corporate Social Responsibility and Environmental Management*, 17, 15–26.

Krippendorff, K. (2004). *Content Analysis: An Introduction to its Methodology*. Thousand Oaks, CA: Sage.

KPMG (2008). *International Survey of Corporate Responsibility Reporting 2008*. Amsterdam.

KPMG (2011). *International Survey of Corporate Responsibility Reporting 2011*. Amsterdam.

Lewin, A.Y., Sakano, T., Stephens, C.U. & Victor, B. (1995). Corporate citizenship in Japan: Survey results from Japanese firms. *Journal of Business Ethics*, 14, (2), 83–101.

McPhail, K. & McKernan, J. (2011). Accounting for human right: An overview and introduction. *Critical Perspectives on Accounting*, 22, (8), 733–737.

Ministry of Economy, Trade and Industry (METI) (2012). Japan's policy for CSR. Available at http://www.meti.go.jp/english/policy/economy/corporate_accounting/pdf/121114_11.pdf

Ministry of Environment (MOE) & Japanese Institute of Certified Public Accountants (JICPA) (2007). *Report on CSR Information Assurance Research*. Tokyo.

Milne, M.J. & Adler, R.W. (1999). Exploring the reliability of social and environmental disclosures content analysis. *Accounting Audit and Accountability Journal*, 12, (2), 237–256.

Neu, D., Warsame, H. & Pedwell, K. (1998). Managing public impressions: Environmental disclosures in annual reports. *Accounting, Organizations and Society*, 23, (3), 265–282.

Neuendorf, K.A. (2002). *The Content Analysis Guidebook*. London: Sage.

Patten, D. (1991). 'Exposure, legitimacy, and social disclosure', *Journal of Accounting and Public Policy*, 10, 297–308.

Tanimoto, K. & Suzuki, K. (2005). Corporate social responsibility in Japan: Analyzing the participating companies in global reporting initiative. European Institute of Japanese Studies, Working Paper 208, Stockholm: European Institute of Japanese Studies.

Thorne, L., Mahoney, L.S. & Manetti, G., (2014). Motivations for Issuing Standalone CSR Reports: A Survey of Canadian Firms. *Accounting, Auditing and Accountability Journal*, 27, (4), 1–32.

Tilt, C.A. (2001). The content and disclosure of Australian corporate environmental policies. *Accounting, Auditing and Accountability Journal*, 14, (2), 190–212.

Tsang, E.W.K. (1998). A longitudinal study of corporate social reporting in Singapore: The case of the banking, food and beverage and hotel industries. *Accounting, Auditing and Accountability Journal*, 11, (5), 624–635.

Unerman, J. (2000). Methodological issues: Reflection on quantification in corporate social reporting content analysis. *Accounting, Auditing and Accountability Journal*, 13, (5), 667–680.

Weber, R.P. (1988). *Basic Content Analysis*. Beverly Hills, CA: Sage.

World Bank (2004). Opportunities and obstacles for corporate social responsibility reporting in developing countries. Report prepared by Corporate Social Responsibility Practice of the World Bank Group.

Yamagami, T. & Kokubu, K. (1991). A note on corporate social disclosure in Japan. *Accounting, Auditing and Accountability Journal*, 4, (4), 32–39.

Yamaguchi, A. (2010). CSR reporting in Japan. Paper presented at the 2010 Global Compact CJK Researchers Meeting, Discussion on CJK CSR Report Research. Tokyo.

Wokutch, R.E. (1990). Corporate social responsibility Japanese style. *Academy of Management Executive*, 4, (2), 56–74.

Wokutch, R.E., & Shepard, J.M. (1999). The maturing of the Japanese economy: corporate social responsibility implications. *Business Ethics Quarterly*, 9, (3), 527–545.

Zadek, S. (2007). *The Civil Corporation*. London: Earthscan.

8

Global Compact Corporations in Japan and Their Reporting: Trends and Issues

Mari Kondo

Intoduction

Launched in 2000, the UN Global Compact has expanded throughout the world, providing global standards for sustainable and responsible reporting. It is considered to be one of the prime organizations in the world to promote corporate social responsibility (CSR), especially among multinational corporations. Its principles can be understood as soft laws which bind the activities of businesses around the world. The UN Global Compact itself is a unit within the United Nations (UN) in New York, but it has many local organizations to promote its principles and activities at the country level. In Japan, the Global Compact Japan Network, hereafter referred to as GC-JN, is the organization established as the local network.

This chapter discusses the experiences of GC-JN and the signatory corporations in Japan. Through the efforts of the local network, many top-tier companies in Japan have become members. This chapter focuses on the development of GC-JN within the context of CSR development in Japan. It discusses the activities and characteristics of the signatory companies. The chapter also elaborates the recent development in reporting, particularly, in terms of Integrated Reporting, and thereby attempts to illustrate the emerging trend of CSR reporting practices in Japan.

There are various reasons why GC-JN will be a topic of interest to the readers of this book. Firstly, in spite of the volume of literature that exists on the UN Global Compact, there is relatively little literature on the activities of its local networks. In particular, the activities of GC-JN have not been reported in any English language scholarly paper, making this chapter the first to do so.

Secondly, GC-JN serves as a good reference for other local networks as it demonstrates the activities of a good model. This is because GC-JN has been considered to be one of the best ten UN Global Compact local networks, and recognized as such in 2013 and 2014. We are therefore interested in learning which of GC-JN's activities make it one of the best local networks in the world. Thirdly, this chapter addresses some comparative aspects of GC-JN in the East Asian context. Local networks differ from country to country. Based on a survey (Global Compact Network China, Global Compact Network Japan & Global Compact Network Korea, 2010) and other literature available, this chapter also discusses the differences between GC-JN and the local networks in Korea and China.

Lastly, this chapter also discusses the significant impact that Integrated Reporting will have on the CSR activities of Japanese corporations.

Aside from GC-JN-related websites, there are various literature and research papers available in Japanese. These are not necessarily directly related to GC-JN, but many are related to Japanese CSR and reporting. In particular, attention has been paid to a report issued by the Ministry of Economics, Trade and Industry (METI) concerning CSR, which was published in Japanese in May 2014. The report clearly indicates the new direction that Japanese business should take concerning CSR. GC-JN is also sending the same message to its members.

Besides literature and research papers, from 2010 until the present the author has been fortunate to have been personally involved in certain GC-JN activities. These include a series of presentations of GC-JN signatory companies from 2010 onward, the Doshisha University joining GC-JN in 2011, the China-Japan-Korea Roundtable Conference session in 2011, an invitation to an international symposium from GC-JN in 2012, their annual seminar in 2013 and their information seminars in 2014, and consultation on their new strategies which actively seek partnerships with academics. Furthermore, a former administrative head of GC-JN was invited to conduct a course on sustainability and new technologies for Doshisha MBA students. Substantial insights have been gained from such experiences.

Following this introductory section, the UN Global Compact and a brief history of Japanese CSR are introduced. These sections are meant to provide the context in which GC-JN has emerged, before a discussion of this local network is presented. Following a description of the development of GC-JN, its activities will be introduced, and then the working groups and Communication of Progress, or COP, are described in detail. These are the two very strong aspects of GC-JN. Thereafter, its characteristics will be compared with Chinese and Korean local networks, based on the three-country member survey results published in 2010.

The latter parts of the chapter will introduce the METI report published in 2014. METI studied leading multinationals including GC-JN members, and concluded that Japanese businesses need to view CSR more strategically by integrating global issues. There is a clear awareness that CSR offers a way of building the international competitiveness of Japanese business. Ajinomoto is one of the leading GC-JN companies, which will be introduced in this chapter. The final part of the chapter concludes with a discussion of the issues presented so far, including an introduction to some challenges that GC-JN may face.

The UN Global Compact

In this section, a brief overview of the UN Global Compact is provided, so that the development and activities of GC-JN can be put in context.

The birth of the UN Global Compact can be understood as a response to the current globalization phenomenon. Ongoing globalization comes with all the benefits of a global movement of capital, transportation, the World Wide Web, and communication technologies. The boundaries between societies seem to have been drastically reduced. However, in spite of the euphoria of the 1990s in line with the expectation that globalization would bring peace and prosperity to all the countries of the world, by the turn of the century, the shadow of globalization has become apparent.

The statement by Kofi Annan, Secretary-General of the United Nations in 1999, illustrates the urgent need faced by corporations to focus more on universal values.

> Globalization is a fact of life. But I believe we have underestimated its fragility. The problem is this. The spread of markets outpaces the ability of societies and their political systems to adjust to them, let alone to guide the course they take.
>
> (United Nations, 1999)

As Annan declared, growing worldwide has repercussions on inequality, environmental pollution, labor exploitation, corruption, making it necessary for corporations to invest their resources in implementing universal values based on human rights or other values that the Unites Nations has promoted. Annan's address also illustrates a development analogous to economic expansion in the postwar era. After explaining the then failure of industrial countries during the Great Depression, Annan states,

> In order to restore social harmony and political stability, they adopted social safety nets and other measures, designed to limit economic volatility and compensate the victims of market failures. That consensus made possible successive moves towards liberalization, which brought about the long post-war period of expansion. Our challenge today is to devise a similar compact on the global scale, to underpin the new global economy.
>
> (United Nations, 1999)

As this address shows, the UN Global Compact engages in creating "a set of core values in the areas of human rights, labor standards, and environmental practices" (United Nations, 1999) to bring about a new global economy.

The UN Global Compact encourages corporations to initiate their responsibility toward societies that have common values. In other words, the Compact aims to create one global society for which all companies should take responsibility. What kind of society does the Compact have in mind? As a guideline, it has set ten principles (UN Global Compact, undated) that corporations must follow in order to gain membership. Businesses should:

- Principle 1: support and respect the protection of internationally proclaimed human rights; and
- Principle 2: make sure that they are not complicit with human rights abuses.
- Principle 3: uphold the freedom of association and the effective recognition of the right to collective bargaining;
- Principle 4: eliminate all forms of forced and compulsory labor;
- Principle 5: abolish child labor; and
- Principle 6: eliminate discrimination in respect of employment and occupation.
- Principle 7: support a precautionary approach to environmental challenges;
- Principle 8: undertake initiatives to promote greater environmental responsibility; and

- Principle 9: encourage the development and diffusion of environmentally friendly technologies.
- Principle 10: work against corruption in all its forms, including extortion and bribery.

These ten principles are made up of four pillars, namely human rights, labor, the environment and anti-corruption. Following the ten principles is easier said than done. In order to reinforce their implementation and the education of these principles to businesses, the UN Global Compact encourages the establishment of local networks among companies within particular geographical areas. These networks can tackle different national, cultural and language contexts more closely and succeed as one society that the Compact aims to establish for corporations to grow in tandem with.

The development or CSR In Japan

While the UN Global Compact has made efforts to increase participants all over the world and strengthen its local networks so as to implement their values more effectively, Japan has nurtured its own development of CSR. This evolution can be traced back from a period long before the Compact was established. By illustrating a brief history of CRS activities in Japan, we can understand more clearly the kind of cultural context in which GC-JN is embedded.

According to Mizuo (2004), the concept of CSR was discussed in Japan as early as 1949. Akira Yamashiro (1949), a pioneering business management scholar in Japan, introduced his article "Social responsibility in business (*Keiei no Shakaiteki Sekinin*)" to Harvard students. Keizai Doyukai (Japan Association of Corporate Executives), a private, non-profit, non-partisan organization designed to invigorate Japan's economy after the World War II, followed his philosophy. The organization approved the principle of "Awareness and Implementation of Social Responsibility of Business Managers (*Keieisha no Shakaiteki Sekinin no Jikaku to Jissen*)" as its purpose in 1956. This aimed to reinforce checks and balances and fair competition among corporations. The concept highlighted the idea that the profits of corporations should benefit society as a whole. Furthermore, these ideas and concepts also helped to tackle environmental issues that had seriously emerged in Japan during the 1960s (Mizuo, 2004).

Since then, Japanese corporations have developed ways in which they can contribute their profits to society. But their emphasis on responsibilities did not include issues which we can now classify as core issues. Instead, when a certain crisis or social issue came up, companies set great store on this issue; but when the need disappeared, they moved on to other, more urgent issues. A good example is that involving the oil shock that hit Japan in 1973. Companies then debated how to tackle the distribution of toilet paper, of which there was a shortage both within corporations and society at large. When scandals involving corporate relations and anti-social groups occurred, serious debates on company ethics surfaced (Mizuo, 2004). From this we can see that corporations were simply responding to the social issues or crises as they emerged: there were no concrete core values or principles for them to follow. However, from the late 1990s, issues around corporate responsibility began to consolidate among Japanese corporations.

What propelled the consolidation of CSR values and principles was ISO 14001 in 1996. The issuing of these regulations triggered the articulation of environmental management practices among Japanese corporations. It was also in the 1990s when global environmental concerns became heated issues. For example, the UN-led Earth Summit in 1992 was unprecedented in terms of its size and the issues focused on (United Nations, 1997). The summit discussed the growing problems of poverty, the developed countries' excessive consumption and damage to the environment. Followed by ISO 14001, Japanese corporations further raised their concern for environmental issues from a global perspective when the Kyoto Protocol (COP3) was promulgated in 1997. This allowed the strengthening of environmental management among Japanese corporations. Gradually, CSR was considered a tool of environmental protection in Japan, although it was not yet been considered as a part of business strategy. Nevertheless, the first stage of CSR in Japan had especially focused on environmental protection.

The second stage of Japanese CSR was the inclusion of corporate ethics and compliance within the concept of CSR around the year 2000. Many corporate scandals emerged during that time. For example, food companies in Japan were criticized for malpractices involving production and food safety. It was also at this time when Enron and other scandals among overseas companies gained attention.

The year 2003 is often considered as the birth year of CSR in Japan, in terms of the current appreciation of the term globally. This was the time when socially responsible investment (SRI) also received attention. The SRI companies sent questionnaires which included questions concerning human rights and labor issues that made Japanese corporations become aware of the important components of CSR. Triggered in 2003, the third stage of Japanese CSR activities highlighting human rights and labor issues thus started. Furthermore, Japanese corporations had to consider also their supply chains.

The year 2003 was an eye-opener for many Japanese corporations. Previously they tended to exercise their power to contribute socially only when society accused them of wrongdoing or malpractice. However, in contrast, issues focusing on human rights and labor problems were much more deeply related to daily corporate practices. Businesses were also asked about their responsibilities to their supply chains. On top of environmental issues, they were asked to be responsible for their work-life styles; that is, the cultural contexts where business practices are exercised.

Recently, Japan's CSR has been widening its scope further. More specifically, there are several new topics that have emerged. Among corporations, women's empowerment has become a hot topic since 2005. Although the progress of gender mainstreaming has been slow, this has been a topic of the Abe administration since 2013. Sustainable consumption is another new topic, which has not yet been talked about much. Community development is also a new issue for Japanese companies, and is now gaining attention. Japanese CSR has for long focused on the environmental and sustainability areas which have become a mainstream business opportunity, including smart cities and green energies, especially after the Tohoku earthquake and the nuclear power crisis in Fukushima in 2011.

Development of the global compact Japan network

The above are the current developments pertaining to CSR in Japan. GC-JN was established during the third stage of CSR in Japan.

Among Japanese corporations, Kikkoman was the first to sign up with Global Compact. This was in 2001 when there were only a few local networks in the world. Kikkoman is one of the leading soy sauce companies in Japan. It is known to be heavily engaged in global business. It introduced soy sauce to many kitchens in the world outside Japan. It is involved in manufacturing, marketing, wholesale, the health food business and research and development worldwide. Furthermore, Kikkoman has business relations with Del Monte, so it is very much aware of the importance of UN activities (Global Compact Japan Network, 2012). According to Kikkoman's CEO, Yuzaburo Mogi, Global Compact's principles match Kikkoman's three corporate themes on social responsibility: being responsible in business activities, contributing to a healthy diet and living together with global society

(Kikkoman, 2014). Mogi states that taking these responsibilities to heart is the company's business philosophy.

Following Kikkoman's participation in the Compact, five other companies signed up in 2002. In December 2003, with 11 companies already signed up with the Compact, GC-JN was established. Initially, GC-JN was merely a part of the United Nations Public Relations Center in Tokyo. Thereafter, the number of member companies increased constantly. Having starting out with one member in 2001, the number of members increased to six in 2002, 11 in 2003, 27 in 2004, 39 in 2005, 47 in 2006 and 57 in 2007.

Seeking further growth, Global Compact became an independent private organization in April 2008. By then, the signatory companies had grown to 76. It should be noted that GC-JN is not a subsidiary of UN Global Compact. Each local network is independent and autonomous vis-à-vis UN Global Compact. It also has its own governance structure. The requirement is that every local network and its members should support the ten principles of the Compact.

The number of members has increased further since, from 108 in 2009, to 133 in 2010 and 155 in 2011. This increasing number enabled the organization to be incorporated in October 2011. Membership continued to increase thereafter, to 170 in 2012 and then to 183 by the end of 2013. Members are involved in all kinds of businesses and come from various municipalities and prefectures. They also include such entities as universities and NGOs.

GC-JN offers a platform for the signatory companies to learn from, collaborate with and disseminate activities that allow it to put UN Global Compact's ten principles into practice. For example, GC-JN offers workshops to disseminate current CSR philosophy that follows the Compact's principles, and encourages other companies and groups to sign and promote collaboration with different businesses and groups so as to implement CSR philosophy. Since signatories come from a wide range of businesses and organizations, they are able to take advantage of the networks of other companies in implementing their CSR activities.

Activities of the global compact Japan network

GC-JN conducts various activities for its members. One is the provision of support for reporting to the UN Global Compact, and this is discussed in the following section. Another activity is education. UN Global Compact provides a platform for active working committees arranged according to issues, thereby allowing members to exchange information. These active working committees will be discussed in a subsequent section.

In line with its education focus, GC-JN conducts annual seminars and symposiums. The topics discussed thus far include: "Changing Japan through CSR – After the 3.11 Tohoku Earthquake" (2011), "Development of Human Rights for Sustainability" (2012) and "Post 2015 CSR" (2013). Starting 2008, GC-JN has been conducting special seminars for executives annually, entitled "Seminar for Future Management (*Asuno Keiei wo Kangaeru Kai*, or AKK)". About 85 executives participated in the program between 2008 and 2013.

GC-JN serves as a link between Japanese businesses and the UN Global Compact. While GC-JN has been increasing its membership, the number of local networks under the UN Global Compact has also increased, totaling more than 100 at present. Local networks have been organized into regional networks. GC-JN participates not only in UN Global Compact's activities in New York, but also in regional activities in Asia. Also, GC-JN and local Korean and Chinese networks have banded together to form the China-Japan-Korea Roundtable. They meet every year, rotating venues. The roundtable activities will be further discussed in the following section.

Communication on progress (COP)

To join the UN Global Compact as a signatory is not difficult but is a commitment for corporate leaders. However, to stay as a member, annual reporting is indispensable. For the UN Global Compact, reporting has a special meaning. Companies are required to disclose COP to the public, including investors, consumers, civil societies and governments. COP discloses how much progress they have made in implementing the ten principles of the UN Global Compact and in accomplishing the UN development goals. COP is an extremely important part of being a member of the Global Compact because it tells the public how much society can trust a company in terms of its transparency, how much a company tries to improve itself and how a company helps reinforce values and education that the UN Global Compact and the United Nations disseminate to educate non-participants and civil societies (UN Global Compact, undated).

One important feature of GC-JN is that no member has ever failed to submit the COP to the UN Global Compact headquarters. The 100% reporting record is amazing remarkable achievement. In practice, Japanese corporations understand that reporting means turning their annual CSR report or environment report into COP. For the UN Global Compact, turning in the COP is considered to be the statement of a company's commitment to society. If all the companies in GC-JN submit their reports fully, it would be safe to assume that there are many Japanese companies committing their operations and profits to the goodwill of society; thus society can trust them as well. And this means that this is a form of society that the United Nations aims to achieve, namely a truly global society. The 100% submission in reporting might enhance the reputation of Japanese companies globally. This is the main reason why GC-JN could receive awards from the UN, for being one of the top ten superior local networks around the world.

However, it should be noted that the number of signatories of UN Global Compact from Japan suddenly increased in 2012–2013 and suddenly decreased in 2013–2014. This has nothing to do with GC-JN or its member corporations. The sudden increase was a result of the promotion of certain business associations in Japan, of which the majority of members are small and medium-sized companies. They were asked to join UN Global Compact as signatories without understanding what the Compact was all about. Most of them are local businesses, not interested in reporting annually. Therefore, after one year, they withdrew from the membership. It was nothing but a one-time phenomenon; but this leaves GC-JN wondering how it should approach SMEs to extend their membership. This issue – the expansion of GC-JN to SMEs – will be discussed toward the end of this chapter.

Working groups

Perhaps one of the salient characteristics of GC-JN is the up-do-date activities of its working groups. In 2013, working groups were asked to focus on one of ten issues. The groups generally met once a month or once every two months. They invited experts and participants discussed and exchanged ideas around specific issues concerning CSR, includingoperational issues, difficulties, solutions and joint actions, among others.

The number of working groups organized varies year to year, reflecting the interests and issues that member companies face. Generally speaking, there has been an increasing trend involving more companies and more issues. This reflects the increase in the number of issues and the number of member companies. Some working groups have been operating for years. Others are new. Some are merged or transformed bodies, developed alongside the evolution of CSR topics. The groups usually have one organizing champion, supported by several participants who become core supporters of the champion participants. GC-JN office staff help out during their meetings and activities; however, the working groups are run in a highly autonomous manner.

In 2008, the working groups were divided along these topics: CSR Case Studies, Climate Change, and Asian Supply Chain and Procurement. At that time, the 15 corporations involved in the Case Study group met 11 times a year, and discussed what would be included in the COP report, the internalization of Global Compact principles in their own organizations, and the like. Because different corporations from different industries could meet, in-depth learning could be facilitated. Likewise, for the Climate Change group, the best practices of domestic corporations were presented and studied. On behalf of the working group, Fuji Xerox presented a report during the international conference on caring for climate change.

By 2011, the number of working groups had increased to 13, indicating how more topics had grabbed members' attention. In 2011, the working groups were as follows: Supply Chain Management, Climate Change, In-house Awareness on the Global Compact, Biodiversity, CSR Reporting Study, Regional Working Group in Western Japan, Millennium Development Goals (MDGs), Human Rights, Study of CSR Activities for SMEs, Water, Bottom of the Pyramid (BOP) Business and Social Business, ISO 26000, and Socially Responsible Investment (SRI). These were the times when there was increasing awareness of ISO 26000, the water crisis, human rights and MDGs.

Various trendy issues were raised in working group discussions, to the level of all members of GC-JN. For example, in 2012, ISO 26000 was emphasized and discussed during the 2012 GC-JN Symposium. Presenters introduced the development of ISO 26000, the corporations which applied for ISO 26000, the seven core subjects of social responsibility. However, as we know, ISO 26000 is different from the other ISO standards such as ISO 9000 and ISO 14000, which grant certifications. There are no particular strong requirements or measurements for the corporations which apply for the standards. ISO 26000's regulating power is limited and can be abused. So, among GC-JN members, the positive and the negative aspects of ISO 26000 were shared, and they decided to pay attention to how the ISO 26000 should be utilized.

In 2013, GC-JN had working groups for ISO 26000, Environmental Management, Western Japan Area (Kansai area), Supply Chains, CSR Reporting, Global Compact within companies, BOP Business and Social Business, Human Rights and Due Diligence and Anti-corruption. Some working groups in 2012 were merged; thus their number was decreased. For the coming years, there are plans to set up working groups around issues including Post-2015, Creating Shared Values

Figure 8.1 Social responsibility: Seven core subjects

(CSV), SRI/Environment, Society and Governance (ESG) and Disaster Management.

Among the achievements of 2013 in terms of the GC-JN working groups, two elements should be pointed out: the formation of the Anti-corruption working group and the publication of a booklet by the Supply Chain group. First, in 2013, the Anti-corruption working group was established. Among the ten principles of the Global Compact, this issue is one of the most sensitive areas for corporations to discuss. For many Japanese companies, this is also an area with which they are not very familiar. Ten companies joined the Anti-corruption group, which is a very encouraging development, indicating that GC-JN provides a platform for Japanese companies to tackle issues that they may not be able to work on alone and are not familiar with.

Second is the publication. One of the most active working groups has been the working group on supply chains. They came up with a booklet in August 2013 entitled "*Appropriate CSR Supply Chain Activities*". Twenty-five member corporations involved in the supply chain working group jointly became authors of the booklet. This booklet will soon be available in English. It serves as a practical handbook for corporations to work on with regard to supply chain issues and aims to make triple win relationships among buyers, suppliers and society. It provides suggestions on activities concerning purchasing, supplier guidance and supplier auditing, among others. Following the supply chain working group, other working groups are also aiming to create their own publications.

As has been discussed, GC-JN provides an excellent infrastructure for Japanese corporations to jointly study important issues, exchange ideas and come up with solutions among themselves.

The China-Japan-Korea roundtable conference and GC-JN in comparative terms

The Global Compact functions as a global soft law to regulate businesses. Yet since the Compact is perceived as a product of the West, there are certain concerns expressed by local networks in Asia. In the case of East Asia, the economies of China, Korea and Japan account for a considerable portion of the global economy. In order to gain a voice in the global arena and also to share their own experiences, local networks in China, Japan and Korea have organized a roundtable. The first roundtable conference was held in Seoul, Korea, in 2009. In 2011, some of the academics who participated conducted questionnaire surveys among the members of each local network.

The UN Global Compact allows local networks to be organized as they please. Therefore, the characteristics of the local networks in the three countries are quite different from each other. Though this may be a very much simplified and generalized statement, Korea's local network can be considered as being under the strong influence of the government's Foreign Service, from where the UN Secretary General came. Because the Korean government takes development strategies to markets outside the country, the soft laws of UN Global Compact may have some impact on Korean business activities. In the case of China, the local network arrangements are just evolving. Both government and state enterprises regards CSR as important. The relationship of China's local network with the government is strong, as in Korea, when compared with the local network in Japan.

Hereafter, the summaries of the joint surveys of the three countries show that certain characteristics of the local networks have become apparent. The joint survey asked questions concerning five elements, including: Global Compact participation, CSR engagement, communication with stakeholders, COP and expectations of Global Compact local networks. The sample was taken from among the 151 Global Compact member companies in China, Japan and Korea in 2010–2011. Fifty-three out of 99 members from Japan responded, while from China the figures are 59 of the 143 members and, for Korea, 39 members responded from among 94.

In Korea, members said that they learned about UN Global Compact from the UN office or the local network. Their reason for joining is to actively participate in Global Compact's international conferences and international events. They have thus far been participating in the various initiatives of the Compact. This participation has activated their CSR activities; and support from the government is expected to promote CSR. Korean companies receive some assistance from the government, including financial subsidies.

For Korean companies, the most important stakeholders are ranked as follows: customers (1st), government (2nd), local communities (3rd) and employees (4th). Korean awareness of CSR linked to corporate strategies is high. The companies believe communication with the customers on CSR is important. COP is considered important in enhancing their corporate brands. Some companies use CSR reports for COP, but some prepare independent COPs for reporting purposes to the UN. To communicate their CSR activities, besides annual reports, Korean companies use COP less than the companies of Japan or China do. Some Korean companies use teleconferencing and web chats to communicate their CSR activities instead.

Korean companies think that the local network is helpful as a venue for communicating to various stakeholders. The network has helped in making partnership with the UN a reality. It is also a venue for policy recommendations.

In China, before joining the local network, members learned about UN Global Compact from their trade partners, the UN office or the local network. They joined the UN Global Compact to understand CSR from a global perspective. They were also attracted by the possibility of utilizing the management tools and guidelines provided by the Compact. Participation was mostly initiated by top executives. Upon joining, almost all the members set specific goals to achieve the UN principles, although they think these principles need improvement. China has actively participated in Global Compact meetings. It has a particularly high interest in environmental issues and concerns. China sends several delegates to the working groups, especially those that concern the environment. Joining the Compact has impacted Chinese companies in the "creation of new businesses". Moreover, their participation has enhanced the image of Chinese companies, especially as "sustainable companies", and has considerably invigorated their CSR activities. Chinese companies expect support from the Chinese government. About half of the companies responded that they have received such support, including financial assistance. They have shown scant interest in ISO 14000, FTSE4Good Index, Dow Jones Sustainability Index, on the other hand.

Asked to rank stakeholders according to their importance, Chinese companies revealed the following: most important are the employees, followed by customers, government, and shareholders. Chinese companies think communication with stakeholders is important to "improve performance". Besides CSR reports, they frequently rely on annual and quarterly meetings to communicate to stakeholders. COP is considered important to demonstrate their commitment toward environment, society and governance issues, and to enhance their corporate brands.

For Chinese companies, the local network serves as a venue for communicating with various stakeholders, for realizing their partnership with the UN and for policy recommendations. When the survey was conducted, the members of the local network were the smaller companies. Therefore, they responded that they wanted to learn about CSR education and training, but were not interested in pioneering CSR activities by large companies.

As to the responses of Japanese members, unlike China or Korea, Japanese members learned of UN Global Compact from the media and other sources (perhaps, a network of executives). In joining the Compact, it was the CSR office which played an important role, followed by top executives. Upon joining, only a few participating companies set goals specific to the UN principles, since they already had their own CSR programs running when they joined the Compact. Compared with their Chinese and Korean counterparts, Japanese firms' participation in the Compact did not activate their CSR activities.

Compared with Korean and Chinese members, the participation of Japanese companies in UN Global Compact's international meetings and events was limited. Likewise, the participation of Japanese companies in UN projects, such as MDGs, is minimal. The participation of Japanese companies comes in such forms as promoting their employees' volunteerism in the community and in international development projects for MDGs. It should be noted that they do not strategically utilize UN projects to promote their own businesses.

"Difficulties in organization-wide recognition of CSR" is very strongly felt in promoting CSR within Japanese companies. ISO 14000 is popular and the Japanese companies also participate in the FTSE4Good and Dow Jones Sustainability Indexes. CSR reports, sustainability reports and COP are heavily used to communicate to stakeholders. CSR reports are used as COP tools.

Japanese companies do not receive government support, a "practice" remarkably different from Korea and China. Japanese companies want to learn about the "best CSR practices of the industry or of similar sized companies" and "pioneering CSR activities" upon joining the local network. For Japanese companies, the stakeholders ranked in order of importance are as follows: customers, followed by employees, shareholders, and finally, local communities. Unlike the rankings made by Chinese or Korean companies, Japanese companies did not mention government at all.

The local network is for information gathering, that is, networking with other members and organizations and acquiring knowledge on how to realize UN Global Compact principles. There is almost no interest in using the local network for policy recommendations or rule-making in the global arena.

In summary, unlike Chinese or Korean Global Compact signatories, Japanese members have the following four characteristics:

1) They already had CSR programs running when they joined, and GC-JN is only for further information gathering.
2) In spite of the fact that the UN Global Compact has certain international political economy related aspects, Japanese participants are not interested in voicing their ideas internationally.
3) In relation to (2), Japanese companies do not expect any support or interference from the government. For them, CSR has nothing to do with the government.
4) Global issues, such as MDGs, are "studied" by CSR specialists of the member companies through GC-JN. However, those issues are not well reflected in their mainstream businesses. There is lack of strategic consideration on how global issues are to be used in their mainstream business.

Integrated reporting and the METI report

Globally speaking, reporting practice has witnessed a new trend lately. This has created a challenge for participants in GC-JN, who have had an excellent reputation in reporting. Until recently, as mentioned in the last section, a company submitted its CSR report as a COP report to the public. However, under the recent trend, there is discussion that a company should integrate its annual report with its CSR report. In other words, a company should conceive CSR activities as part of its strategic management. In this section, discussions on recent CSR reporting trends and how Japanese corporations will face the new challenges are explored. What exactly does this Integrated Reporting procedure mean in terms of a company's operation and strategy? How does it affect the positive reputation of Japan's reliable performance in the Global Compact?

Since 2005 a growing number of corporations have started to integrate their annual reports with their CSR report, according to the Global Reporting Initiative (GRI), a non-profit organization which supports sustainability (Nikkei, 2012). This trend began in Europe where many investors started to get involved in SRIs. The European states' unique national pension systems helped to develop this type of investment. Some reviews of Integrated Reporting could be said to serve the state-influenced social systems among European countries. To function as a social system, businesses need to respond seriously to their societies. Merely to combine CSR reports with annual reports and then refer to them as Integrated Reporting does not work. To use Integrated Reporting with integrity requires a company to transform its mainstream business operations to socially responsible ones.

The UN Global Compact has been a pioneer in promoting Integrated Reporting since 2011. Although many Japanese members are new to Integrated Reporting, they are now seriously studying its impacts (CGGVeritas, 2010; IIRC, 2011).

It is not only businesses that are taking this shift seriously; so, too, is the Japanese government, as witnessed in the report on corporate global activities and CSR published by the Minister of Economy, Trade and Industry (METI, 2014). This report aims to study the current CSR practices of leading Japanese corporations as well as multinational corporations in the US, Europe and Korea. The report focused especially on their response toward the trend of Integrated Reporting. There are concerns on the part of the government that Japanese corporations need to revisit their CSR activities and to try to integrate CSR as the mainstream strategy of their business. The report proposed five suggestions, which are summarized below.

The first thing that the METI report pointed out was the importance of a strategic view toward CSR. It presented cases of companies that gain competitiveness by responding seriously to social issues. Those companies actually became stronger after engaging in CSR. The report also pointed out that leading companies in the West enhance corporate value by foreseeing CSR issues and managing them strategically. So METI urges Japanese corporations to see CSR issues not merely as risks but as strategic opportunities. In this, CSR should be considered a strategic management issue, rather than as mere philanthropy.

The METI report also suggested that companies should conduct effective materiality analysis. It recommended that corporations should not try to tackle all problems equally, but, rather, should prioritize issues. The report further suggested that companies make good use of different kinds of platform and their connections with other companies to identify issues important to the company's business. Thereafter, they should deal with those issues in order of priority, based on risk management criteria.

One of the important findings of the METI report, which is why the government has alerted Japanese corporations, is their appreciation of CSR as a license to operate. This is the second point. Dealing with CSR issues, such as managing relationship with local communities in large-scale projects overseas and responding to water risks in high water-stressed areas, has become a precondition of doing successful business. The impacts of social issues on business operations are much stronger than before; and CSR activities affect businesses' license to operate in the future. Therefore, for Japanese companies, strategically managing CSR issues related to the company's business is crucial to maintain their current level of operations.

The METI report pointed out a third point. Japanese corporations need to be aware of the importance of the "industry by industry" approach in dealing with social issues. The research pointed out how different industries may face different important social issues. Therefore, in many countries, the trend has been to develop different CSR guidelines by industries. For example, industry sub-guidelines are developed within the Sustainability Accounting Standards Board (SASB) guidelines in the US; industry-by-industry risk analysis is being conducted in the Netherlands within the OECD guideline framework and industry guidelines based on the EU's directives. In contrast, many Japanese companies have been managing issues by referring to ISO 26000. METI expressed its concern that ISO 26000 issues are general issues. Few companies are conducting analyses of issues which are material to their operations. In other words, METI urged Japanese corporations to conduct materiality analysis based on the situation of the company in relation to its industry's situation.

The fourth recommendation is that the METI urged Japanese corporations to take into consideration the view point of the value chain. Japanese corporations are not necessarily well attuned to the issues of emerging countries. Yet there are important social issues, such as water risk in high water-stressed countries, food supply chain and conflict metals, and so on. In order to tackle such issues, a viewpoint of the value chain as a whole is critical. The report urged Japanese corporations to widen their policies with perspectives that are based on the value chain, even outside their group of companies, beyond focusing only within their own group companies.

As to the fifth recommendation, the report highlighted the importance of collaboration among corporations. Social issues are broad and many companies in the same industries may face the same social issues that have to be dealt with. In other words, social issues are too broad for just one company to tackle. This is especially true for small and medium-sized corporations. Therefore, alliances among corporations have become important in tackling these issues. For instance, industry-wide collaborations such as the Electronic Industry Citizenship Coalition (EICC) in the electronics industry and the Sustainable Apparel Coalition (SAC) in the clothing industry are already in existence. Such alliances are not necessarily within an industry. There are broader alliances for particular social issues. For example, the Fair Labor Association (FLA) for labor issues and the Ethical Trading Initiative (ETI) for ethical supply chain issues have a broader focus of crossed boundaries between industries. The METI report urged Japanese corporations to utilize not only within-industry collaborations but also broad, across-industries collaborations to efficiently and effectively tackle important social and so CSR issues.

Case study of Ajinomoto's CSR/CSV (from the METI report)

So how do leading Japanese companies respond to the need to shift their CSR to become a more strategic one which addresses social concerns? Here, Ajinomoto's case, as discussed in the METI report, is introduced.

Ajinomoto is one of the top Japanese food companies. It celebrated its 100th anniversary in 2009. When the company was established 100 years ago, nutritional deficiency was an issue; but the situation is quite different now. To commemorate its longevity in society, Ajinomoto identified three global issues that humanity faces in the 21st century, namely sustainability, food resources and healthy living. Ajinomoto has a medium-term strategic plan covering 2014 to 2016. The plan sets the Ajinomoto Group's shared values. These shared values aim to generate economic value through business contribution to society and the earth.

Ajinomoto worked on the identification of materiality. It defined global issues in three aspects, as follows:

a) Global sustainability including abnormal weather conditions and other challenges of climate change; destruction of ecosystems and biodiversity through overfishing, overhunting and pollution; increasing demand for water from growing, populations, and so on.

b) Food resources including increasing demand for food from growing populations; higher grain demand caused by greater demand for meat; yield per unit of arable land has not been keeping up with crop demand, and so on.
c) Healthy living conditions including the emergence of more people with nutritional problems, among them, hunger and obesity; greater healthcare needs due to aging populations, and so on.

As a Global Compact signatory member, Ajinomoto thought about its materiality issues in relation to the United Nations MDGs. The company identified that Ajinomoto's business is related to maternal and child health and reducing child mortality goals of the MDGs. Ajinomoto used dialogues with intellectuals to identify important themes. Along with the CSR department, other departments including environment and safety, corporate planning, public relations, food business and bioscience also participate in the management meetings during the process to decide its CSR goals. Then, these global issues are linked to the company's medium-term plan drafted in 2014. (The company is also creating a long-term plan for up to 2020.) Ajinomoto's executives had training in CSV and also collected external opinions. And Ajinomoto plans to communicate its CSR activities in a simple but efficient way to outside stakeholders.

In order to implement CSR, Ajinomoto uses its CSR department, together with the environment and safety, HR, procurement and risk management departments or sections. For each group company, Ajinomoto HQ allows that each should have its own opinion about CSR management and should incorporate CSR in its medium-term corporate plan. With that purpose in mind, information exchange on "Ajinomoto's Shared Value" is conducted among domestic group companies during CSR meetings. Ajinomoto found out that it is beneficial to participate in the GC-JN's working group meetings. For example, one of the reasons why the company has decided to strengthen its food supply chain is due to the influence of the GC-JN.

So what is Ajinomoto doing? As agricultural products are the main raw materials of Ajinomoto's goods, a stable supply of agricultural products becomes a major objective of the business. Since food traceability is indispensible for food safety, even though the cost of traceability is high, Ajinomoto initiated direct transactions with suppliers and stepped up efforts to realize traceability.

Ajinomoto sets great store by its supplier relationships. In the autumn of 2013, the company drafted the"Supplier CSR Guideline" and had it approved by corporate executives. The guideline is based on the

UN Global Compact and ISO 26000, clarifying expectations for the suppliers. While the "Ajinomoto Group Principles" indicate the main direction of CSR, the "Supplier CSR Guideline" gives the direction concerning suppliers in more detail. The company organized a supplier seminar and started a self-assessment test. Ajinomoto has prepared an English version of the guidelines and plans to apply them overseas in the future. Ajinomoto is also creating the "Policy/Guideline for Sustainable Supply of Agricultural Products, Livestock and Fisheries".

In fact, Ajinomoto is already working toward the sustainable supply of agriculture, livestock and fisheries. Here are some examples. To maintain the stable supply of bonito, which is the raw material of the company's main product of fish-based seasoning broth powder, Ajinomoto implemented ecological monitoring by means of a discharge survey (500 days) of bonitoes. Ajinomoto also sells edible oils and uses oils in its various products. The company's annual consumption of palm oil is currently 3,000 tons, so it tries to use certified palm oil by joining the Roundtable for Sustainable Palm Oil (RSPO), thereby making a roadmap for sustainable palm oil supply and receiving authentication for the supply chain. The company's goal is 100% use of authenticated palm oil by 2018. Ajinomoto has an alliance with AGF in the coffee business. The AGF group is trying to raise the percentage of coffee beans authenticated by the Rainforest Alliance and 4C Association to 30%. As water resources are critical to agriculture, Ajinomoto also conducted an investigation on water resources.

In terms of their CSR to emerging countries, Ajinomoto has been conducting the Ghana Nutrition Improvement Project since 2009. This is a social business project with three goals in mind: a) development of new market; b) innovation – the project involves the manufacture and sale of KOKO Plus, a supplement containing amino acids which is mixed with baby food to fortify nutrition for weaning children; and networking with new partners with local universities in Ghana, international NGOs, government, the UN and other entities. Through the leaders of microfinance agencies, Ajinomoto is aiming to come up with new sales methods and to build a new sales network. Ajinomoto realized that multi-sector partnerships with government, local governments and international organizations are very important to new social business development. In addition to the project in Ghana, Ajinomoto also launched a nutrition Bachelor of Science program in Vietnam, at Hanoi's medical university, in October 2013. This is a Japan International Cooperation Agency (JICA) funded project. Ajinomoto hopes to cultivate long-term business overseas in partnership with JICA, the UN, NGOs and the like, to overcome the limitations of what one company can do alone.

Conclusion

This chapter has discussed the GC-JN, which is regarded as one of the best local networks by the UN Global Compact. The network enjoys a 100% submission of COP and is very active in using working groups to study new issues. However, unlike the Chinese or Korean local networks, its members do not form close links with the government, nor are they very active in showing their presence in the global political economy arena. Nevertheless, a new trend has recently emerged.

As of 2014, a new topic, namely the trend toward Integrate Reporting, has emerged among members of the GC-JN. Leading corporations have started to integrate their CSR reports with their annual reports. This trend in reporting appears to hold the key for GC-JN's future. Integrated Reporting has affected Japanese companies' ways of thinking and conducting business, enabling corporations to understand the concept of materiality. Materiality explains what is strategically important to a particular company. A company needs to understand the unique areas that it should pay attention to in terms of CSR (often those areas can be particularly due to the kinds of business it is conducting or the industries it is in). If this understanding is lacking the company cannot submit a substantial Integrated Report, and failing to do so can lead to failure to attract investors. Analyzing materiality is a key to adopting strategic ways of integrating global issues into a company's business.

Materiality matters to a company's way of doing business. It also matters with regard to how far a company reports its social responsibility. Here the concept of boundaries becomes important, although traditional reporting can do away with boundary issues. In previous eras, if a company's CSR report said it had reduced CO_2 emissions by a certain amount, stakeholders were inclined to believe the statement. This is because the company could just report the amount of CO_2 that it had emitted, without further verification. This is the case of the narrow boundary. However, in reality, the company's supply chain companies might have been responsible for even more CO_2 emissions. Therefore, to substantiate Integrated Reporting, a company should explain why it has chosen its supply chains and how it has contributed to environmental protection through its relationship with suppliers. Perhaps, for that purpose, a company should present its suppliers with a detailed account of the activities that they have jointly conducted for a better environment. In this way, materiality intertwines with the issues of boundary in reporting.

Today, in contrast to earlier periods, the Japanese government (METI) cooperates with GC-JN to alert its members on this important shift. Nowadays, collaboration with METI is discussed among GC-JN members. Furthermore, GC-JN tries to work as a catalyst to change the nature of the CSR of Japanese businesses to that of CSV. The GC-JN journey continues.

References

CGGVeritas (2010). 2nd Communication on Progress. Available at http://www.unglobalcompact.org/system/attachments/7906/original/10B-QH-273-V1_COP2010_English_Version.pdf?1285159314

Global Compact Japan Network (2012). Message from the board members (in Japanese). Available at http://www.ungcjn.org/gcjn/state/board.html

Global Compact Network China, Global Compact Network Japan and Global Compact Network Korea (2010). China-Japan-Korea Joint Survey. UN Global Compact Leaders Summit 2010.

IIRC (2011). Towards Integrated Reporting: Communicating Value in the 21st Century. International Integrated Reporting Committee. Available at http://www.theiirc.org/wp-content/uploads/2011/11/IIRC-Discussion-Paper_Japanese.pdf

Kikkoman (2014). Top commitment (in Japanese). Available at http://www.kikkoman.co.jp/corporate/csr/commitment.html

METI (2014). Research Paper on CSR Issues and Management among International Corporate Activities (in Japanese). Ministry of Economics, Trade and Industry.

Mizuo, S. (2004). Strategic CSR management and business operation (in Japanese). Available at http://www.nikkei.co.jp/csr/pdf/enquiry/enquiry_n_csr_report01.pdf

Nikkei (2012). 350 companies in the world are issuing Integrated Reports (in Japanese). Available at http://business.nikkeibp.co.jp/article/report/20130614/249684/?rt=nocnt

UN Global Compact (undated). The ten principles. Available at http://www.unglobalcompact.org/AboutTheGC/TheTenPrinciples/index.html

UN Global Compact (undated). What is a COP? Available at http://www.unglobalcompact.org/COP/

United Nations (1997). UN Conference on Environment and Development (1992). Available at http://www.un.org/geninfo/bp/enviro.html

United Nations (1999). Secretary-General proposes Global Compact on human rights, labor, environment, in address to World Economic Forum, Davos. Press Release SG/SM/6881. Available at http://www.un.org/News/Press/docs/1999/19990201.sgsm6881.html

Yamashiro, A. (1949). Social responsibility in business (in Japanese). Keiei Hakusho, December.

9

Assurance in Sustainability Reporting: Evidence from Japan

Mohammad Badrul Haider and Katsuhiko Kokubu

Introduction

The last two decades have witnessed significant improvement in sustainability reporting (SR) around the world (KPMG, 2013). While accountability to the external stakeholders should be the basic premise of SR, a number of observers have criticized the credibility and completeness of such reporting to ensure transparency and accountability (O'Dwyer & Owen, 2005; Adams, 2004; Adams & Evans, 2004). SR is observed as an important tool to manage the powerful stakeholders and ensure corporate legitimacy (Deegan & Unerman, 2011). The provision of assurance[1] in SR can enhance the credibility of reporting and thereby can ensure the accountability and transparency to the stakeholders (Dando & Swift, 2003). In fact, there has been a steady increase in third-party assurance in SR in the last ten years. While in 2002, only 29% of leading global companies had purchased such assurance service, the adoption rate was increased to 59% in 2013 (KPMG, 2013[2]).

The extant literature has already explained the different aspects of this emerging audit practice. Studies by Ball et al. (2000), O'Dwyer and Owen (2005), and Deegan et al. (2006) analyzed the quality of assurance statements from accountability perspective and questioned the value of the current assurance service for external stakeholders. A number of studies were also conducted based on interviews of corporate managers and assurance providers (Jones & Solomon, 2010; O'Dwyer, 2011; O'Dwyer et al., 2011; Edgley et al., 2010; O'Dwyer et al., 2011; Park & Brorson, 2005). These studies mainly examined the importance, development process, obstacles and legitimacy of sustainability assurance. Another strand of literature empirically examined the relationship between a number of company and country level variables and adoption of assurance in SR (Kolk & Perego, 2010; Simnett et al., 2009). In contrast to European contexts that are largely examined in the above literature, this study investigates the assurance provision in SR of Japanese companies. Although Japan is one of the leaders in the world to publish corporate SR, the adoption of assurance in such reporting is low compared with European countries. For example, while in 2011, 99% of leading Japanese companies issued SR, only 23% of these purchased assurance provision (KPMG, 2011). On the other hand, more than 60% of companies in Denmark, Spain, Italy, and France adopted assurance in 2011. The Japanese trend is aligned with Asian practices where approximately 20% of reports were externally assured in 2007 (CorporateRegister.com, 2008). The objective of this exploratory study is to analyze the assurance statements attached to SR in Japan. The study is primarily motivated by prior studies such as Ball et al. (2000), O'Dwyer and Owen (2005, 2007) and Deegan et al. (2006). This is the first known study to examine assurance statements from the Japanese context.

Literature Review

As noted above, a number of previous studies have examined the quality of assurance statements in SR. Ball et al. (2000) analyzed the verification statements attached to 'leading edge' or 'best practice' environmental reports of 1990s. They raised questions about the independence of this verification and observed management control over the whole verification process. They also identified variations and inconsistencies in the nature of the verification work undertaken by the auditors and the verification reports issued by them. Finally they argued that the current form of verification can only enhance organizational legitimacy rather than ensuring accountability to external stakeholders.

O'Dwyer and Owen (2005, 2007) in two consecutive studies reviewed the assurance statements of 'best practice' among European companies. Although their content analysis showed some improvements in the assurance statements (i.e., disclosure on independence of assuror and assurance work undertaken were increased in the assurance statements), they were also concerned about the independence of the assurance provision and management control of the assurance process. They also highlighted the variations in assurance approaches among accountants and consultant assurors.

In a similar study, Deegan et al. (2006) compared the UK and the European assurance statements. They examined the completeness of these statements as against the key elements of assurance statements recommended by internationally accepted guidelines/standards. Consistent with previous studies, they also found ambiguities and inadequacies in assurance statements within and across the countries. They emphasized the development of guidance and regulation to overcome the uncertainties in sustainability assurance. However, in another study Al-Hamadeen (2007) observed improved disclosure in UK assurance statements with regard to materiality, completeness, responsiveness, independence, and competency of the assurance providers.

Two recent studies in this vein were conducted in France and Canada. However, again they failed to show any real improvements in SR assurance. Gillet (2010) from France argued that assurance statements lack precision and explanation as to the verification process and conclusion and were therefore incomplete, even though all the statements examined included the nature, scope, procedures applied and opinion of the assurance process. Fonseca (2010) analyzed the SR assurance practices of mining companies in Canada and mirrored several quality problems highlighted in previous studies, such as low levels of stakeholder involvement in the assurance engagement, management-related addressees, few disclosures of assurance level and few conclusions on the principles of materiality, inclusiveness and responsiveness to stakeholders.

The analysis of Mock et al. (2007) was based on the assurance statements of global companies issued in 2002–2004. While companies from the European Union and environmental sensitive industries were more likely to adopt such practices, the study also confirmed the findings of previous research regarding the variation in SR assurance (Ball et al., 2000; O'Dwyer & Owen, 2005; Deegan et al., 2006). In addition, they found that the characteristics of assurance statement differed significantly between assurance provided by Big 4 accounting firms and others. Big 4 accounting firms were more likely to use Global Reporting Initiative (GRI) guidelines (GRI, 2002; 2006) and to disclose the assurance framework and assurance symbols used. However, these firms were less likely to give positive assurance and recommendations in the assurance statements. This implies that big accounting firms are seen to prefer a "cautionary" and "standardized" approach to assurance. Perego (2009) also concluded that Big 4 accounting firms were better when assurance quality was measured by reporting format and assurance procedures. However, non-accounting firms provided better services when quality was measured by assurance recommendations and opinions.

Using a sample of the Fortune Global 250 firms, Smith et al. (2011) revisited the evolution of SR assurance. They also found considerable variability in the adoption pattern and adherence to the assurance standards. Companies were seen to project a decoupled or symbolic image of accountability through assurance, thereby undermining the credibility of these verification practices.

In their study, Haider and Kokubu (forthcoming) investigated SR assurance in Japan. They observed a low level of assurance adoption over the years, with only 17.5% of the Nikkei 225 companies having such services in 2010. Consistent with prior studies, it was seen that large and environmentally sensitive industries were more likely to adopt assurance in their sustainability reports. As with other countries, the assurance market in Japan is also dominated by the accounting firms followed by non-governmental organizations/non-profit organizations (NGOs/NPOs) and certification firms. However, their study did not focus on the quality of the assurance practice. Therefore, the current study attempts to unveil the quality of assurance statements in SR of Japanese companies.

Methodology and sampling

Content analysis was widely used in previous studies on the quality of assurance in SR (Ball et al., 2000; Wilson, 2003; O'Dwyer & Owen, 2005; 2007; Mock et al., 2007). This method is particularly helpful in evaluating the content of assurance statement using some disclosure instruments. The evaluative frameworks used in previous studies were based on the recommended minimum contents of assurance statements specified in recognized assurance standards and guidelines. The assurance statements were analyzed based on the presence or absence of the predefined characteristics.

Following the trend, this study is also based on content analysis of assurance statements attached to SR of Nikkei 225 companies. The Nikkei Stock Average, publicly known as the Nikkei 225, is Japan's most widely watched index of stock market activities. It is a simple price-weighted arithmetic average of the 225 component stocks that are among the most actively traded issues on the first section of the Tokyo Stock Exchange. The study is interested in observing the development of assurance practice over the years. Therefore, considering time and labor limitation, it analyzes the assurance practice of five years, 2006–2010. The focus is on the most recent phenomena, as assurance practice gains attention from a number of international/national standard setting bodies, voluntary organizations and civil society groups during this period (O'Dwyer et al., 2011).

Although a number of guidelines and standards are available, there is no universal or authoritative framework to govern the SR assurance practice. At present, ISEA 3000 and AA 1000AS are widely used globally in providing such service. The International Auditing and Assurance Standard Board (IAASB), the issuing agency of the International Federation of Accountants (IFAC), issued the International Standard on Assurance Engagements (ISAE 3000), also known as "Assurance Engagements other than Audits or Reviews of Historical Financial Information". All professional accountants have had to comply with ISEA 3000 for assurance of non-financial matters since 2005. The AA 1000 Assurance Standard, on the other hand, was launched by the Institute of Social and Ethical Accountability (AccountAbility) in 2003. In Japan, a high-profile initiative was undertaken by the Japanese Association of Assurance Organizations for Sustainability (J-SUS), which issued "Practical Guidelines for the Assurance of Sustainability Information" in 2007. The content of the assurance statement recommended by all these standards is summarized in Table 9.1 below. The evaluative framework for this study is based on these three standards/guidelines, which is similar to the earlier studies. The study investigates only the English version of the SR of the Nikkei 225 companies. Therefore, we investigated in total 131 assurance statements issued in 2006–2010, the yearly breakdown of which is given in Table 9.2.

Findings: Characteristics of the assurance statements

Title of the statement

In the context of SR, different terminologies such as assurance, verification, validation and audit are used interchangeably to describe the fairly similar work being undertaken by the external third party (Deegan et al., 2006: 331). However, using different titles in the statement may confuse the users and make the comparison difficult. Both ISAE 3000 and J-SUS guidelines require that the title should clearly indicate the report as an independent assurance report. The titles of the statements used by the sampled companies are given in Table 9.3. As seen in this table, "independent review report" and "independent assurance report" are mostly used by the accounting firms, whereas "third party verification" and "independent verification" are frequently used by other assurance providers. The finding is consistent with the recent study by Frost and Martinov-Bennie (2010), where 50% of the Australian samples

Table 9.1 Evaluative framework

Content of report	J-SUS Guideline	ISAE 3000	AA 1000
Title of the report	✓	✓	
Addressee	✓	✓	✓
Scope and purpose/objective of the engagement	✓	✓	✓
Respective responsibility of reporter and assuror	✓	✓	✓
Criteria used to assess evidence and conclusion	✓	✓	✓
Assurance standards used	✓	✓	✓
Parties and purpose for which the report is restricted (if any)		✓	✓
Significant inherent limitation in evaluation (if any) of subject matter		✓	✓
Summary of work performed	✓	✓	✓
Conclusion	✓	✓	✓
Competencies of assuror			✓
Impartiality of assuror toward stakeholders/conflict of interests/ independence	✓		✓
Additional comments/ recommendations			✓
The report date	✓	✓	✓
Name and location of assuror	✓	✓	✓

Adapted from O'Dwyer & Owen (2005).

Table 9.2 Number of assurance statements analyzed

	2006		2007		2008		2009		2010	
	Acc. Firms	Others[3]	Acc. Firms	Others	Acc. Firms	Others	Acc. Firms	Others	Acc. Firms	Others
Number of statements issued	20	16	23	14	18	17	19	12	23	13
Number of statements analyzed[4]	14	9	19	7	18	9	17	9	21	8

Table 9.3 Title of the statements

	2006		2007		2008		2009		2010		Total	
	Acc. Firms	Others	Acc. Firms	Others	Acc. Firms	Others	Acc. Firms	Others	Acc. Firms	Others	Acc. Firms	Others
Independent review	10 (71.43)	3 (33.33)	12 (63.16)	2 (28.57)	12 (66.67)	1 (11.11)	7 (41.18)	1 (11.11)	4 (19.05)	1 (12.50)	45 (50.56)	8 (19.05)
Independent assurance	4 (28.57)		5 (26.31)		6 (33.33)	1 (11.11)	10 (58.82)	2 (22.22)	17 (80.95)	1 (12.5)	42 (47.19)	4 (9.52)
Third party review			2 (10.53)								2 (2.25)	0
Third party verification		3 (33.33)		3 (42.86)		3 (33.33)		4 (44.44)		3 (37.50)		16 (38.10)
Independent verification		2 (22.22)		2 (28.57)		1 (11.11)		2 (22.22)		3 (37.50)		10 (23.81)
Verification report						1 (11.11)						1 (2.38)
Assurance statement						1 (11.11)						1 (2.38)
Third party statement						1 (11.11)						1 (2.38)
Responsible care verification		1 (11.11)									0	1 (2.38)

used the term "assurance statement" followed by "verification statement and review". It is important to note that almost all the statements issued by accounting firms and over 52% of the statements by other assurors use the phrase "independent" in their titles. Accounting firms' utilization of review or assurance statement can be argued from their cautious approach in providing the services, as review and assurance engagement is for providing relatively low level assurance compared to audit (Deegan et al., 2006; Al-Hamadeen, 2007).

Addressee of the statement

In financial reporting, the audit report addresses the "shareholders" exclusively. However, no such legal requirement exists for assurance statements in SR. ISEA 3000 states that "whenever practical, the assurance report is addressed to all the intended users, but in some cases there may be other intended users". Similarly, AA 1000AS recommends addressing "intended users", while J-SUS guidelines use the "CEO or representative director or Board of Directors" as the addressee. Table 9.4 shows the addressees used in the sample statements. All the assurance statements other than seven by the consulting and certification firms identify an addressee who is significantly more highly placed than in the previous studies (O'Dwyer & Owen, 2005; 2007; Deegan et al., 2006). However, all the addressees are internal parties. Only two statements by consultants and certification firms recognize broader stakeholder groups or readers. In this regard, researchers have long been arguing for the inclusion of a wider range of constituencies in the assurance statement, since the SR itself is generally addressed to these stakeholder groups (O'Dwyer & Owen, 2005; Adams & Evans, 2004).

Statement on responsibility of the management and assuror

One of the important aspects of assuror independence is that the responsibility of the management and the assuror should be clearly stated in the assurance statement, in order to avoid a possible "expectations gap" among the users (Deegan et al., 2006). Similarly, ISAE 3000 and voluntary guidelines (such as GRI) also recommend the demarcation of responsibilities of management and assuror in the statement. Guided by applicable standards, it is not surprising that all the assurance statements provided by accounting firms have such declarations, whereas other assurors are lagging behind, with more than 60% not focusing on this issue (see Table 9.5).

Table 9.4 Addressee of the statements

	2006		2007		2008		2009		2010		Total	
	Ac. Firms	Others	Ac. Firms	Others	Ac. Firms	Others	Ac. Firms	Others	Ac. Firms	Others	Ac. Firms	Others
Board of Directors	4 (28.57)		5 (26.32)		7 (38.89)		8 (47.06)		9 (42.86)		33 (37.08)	
Director, chairman, president, CEO	10 (71.43)	6 (66.67)	14 (73.68)	5 (71.43)	11 (61.11)	6 (66.67)	9 (52.94)	5 (55.56)	12 (57.14)	5 (62.50)	56 (62.92)	27 (64.29)
Senior management and stakeholders						1 (11.11)						1 (2.38)
The company		2 (22.22)		2 (28.57)				1 (11.11)		1 (12.50)		6 (14.29)
All the readers						1 (11.11)						1 (2.38)
None		1 (11.11)				1 (11.11)		3 (33.33)		2 (25.00)		7 (16.67)

Table 9.5 Statement on responsibility of the management and assuror

	2006		2007		2008		2009		2010		Total	
	Ac. Firms	Others	Ac. Firms	Others	Ac. Firms	Others	Ac. Firms	Others	Ac. Firms	Others	Ac. Firms	Others
Yes	14 (100)	3 (33.33)	19 (100)	3 (42.86)	18 (100)	4 (44.44)	17 (100)	3 (33.33)	21 (100)	3 (37.50)	89 (100)	16 (38.10)
No		6 (66.67)		4 (57.14)		5 (55.56)		6 (66.67)		5 (62.50)		26 (61.90)

Objectives of assurance engagements

Unlike a financial audit there is no generally agreed-upon or uniform objective of assurance in SR, which results in a wide range of objectives defined by the assurors in the assurance statements from all over the world (Al-Hamadeen, 2007; Deegan et al., 2006). It is important to read these statements carefully as objectives vary from engagement to engagement. In the current context, all the assurors clearly state the objectives of the engagement as seen in Table 9.6. It is seen that in almost all the cases accounting firms focus on the evaluation of reported indicators/data. This is related to whether indicators are prepared in compliance with criteria and determining the accuracy or credibility of the reported information. Similarly, certification firms also focus on the verification of the reported data, whereas industry specialist Responsible Care Verification Center (Responsible Care Japan, 2010) emphasizes the evaluation of responsible care activities along with accuracy of the numeric and non-numeric information.

Levels of assurance

All the standards/guidelines (ISAE 3000, AccountAbility 1000AS or J-SUS) differentiate between reasonable and limited/moderate level of assurance based on the assurance engagement risk borrowed from the financial audit literature (CorporateRegister.com, 2008). It is important to declare the level as this will determine the nature, timing, extent of audit procedure and the related conclusion. Table 9.7 presents the levels of assurance identified by the sampled statements. While more than 60% of the statements provided by accounting firms clearly state that the engagement is for limited assurance, only 16.7% by other assurors specified the level of assurance. However, there is no incidence of reasonable assurance. In this regard, AccountAbility explained that assurance levels may depend on the extent and quality of information available, sufficiency of evidence, underlying systems and processes, internal assurance systems, existing assurance for specific aspects of performance reporting, resources allocated for assurance by the reporting company, legal or commercial constraints and competencies of the assurance provider.

Scope of assurance

All the assurance statements analyzed clearly state the scope of the assurance engagement as seen in Table 9.8. However, a deeper look at the assurance statements evidenced limitation in the scope of assurance, as the majority of the cases only verified certain aspects of SR,

Table 9.6 Objectives of assurance engagements

	2006		2007		2008		2009		2010		Total	
	Ac. Firms	Others	Ac. Firms	Others	Ac. Firms	Others	Ac. Firms	Others	Ac. Firms	Others	Ac. Firms	Others
To evaluate indicators prepared/reported according to criteria or accurately	13 (92.86)		19 (100)		18 (100)		17 (100)		21 (100)		88 (98.88)	
Assess completeness defined by J-SUS (The Japanese Association of Assurance Organizations for Sustainability Information)/ J-AOEI (The Japanese Association of Assurance Organizations for Environmental Information)	1 (7.14)		2 (10.53)		6 (33.33)		6 (35.29)		9 (42.86)		24 (26.97)	
AA 1000APS (The AccountAbility Principles Standard) application check									1 (4.76)		1 (1.12)	
GRI application check			1 (5.26)		1 (5.56)		2 (11.76)		4 (19.04)		8 (8.99)	
ICMM's (The International Council on Mining and Metals) 10 sustainable development check							1 (5.88)		2 (9.52)		3 (3.37)	
Evaluate materiality identification and management process									2 (9.52)		2 (2.25)	
Information cover all material aspects without omission/significant items disclosed without omission/completeness of disclosure	3 (21.43)	1 (11.11)	3 (15.79)								6 (6.74)	1 (2.38)
To give assurance based on AA 1000AS		1 (11.11)				2 (22.22)				1 (12.50)		4 (9.52)
To verify the reliability and consistency of data		4 (44.44)		3 (42.86)		1 (11.11)		2 (22.22)		3 (37.50)		13 (30.95)
To conduct independent assurance of report								2 (22.22)		1 (12.5)		3 (7.14)
To provide assurance on agreed terms of reference						1 (11.11)						1 (2.38)
To perform responsible care report verification		3 (33.33)		4 (57.14)		4 (44.44)		4 (44.44)		4 (50.00)		19 (45.24)
To verify the CSR report						1 (11.11)		1 (11.11)		1 (12.50)		3 (7.14)
To express opinion for ensuring credibility		1										1 (2.38)

Table 9.7 Level of assurance provided

	2006		2007		2008		2009		2010		Total	
	Ac. Firms	**Others**	**Ac. Firms**	**Others**	**Ac. Firms**	**Others**	**Ac. Firms**	**Others**	**Ac. Firms**	**Others**	**Ac. Firms**	**Others**
Reasonable												
Limited/moderate	7 (50.00)		8 (42.11)		8 (44.44)	2 (22.22)	11 (64.71)	1 (11.11)	21 (100)	4 (50.00)	55 (61.80)	7 (16.67)
Not mentioned	7 (50.00)	9 (100)	11 (57.89)	7 (100)	10 (55.56)	7 (77.78)	6 (35.29)	8 (88.89)	0	4 (50.50)	34 (38.20)	35 (83.33)

Table 9.8 Scope of assurance

	2006		2007		2008		2009		2010		Total	
	Acc. Firms	**Others**	**Acc. Firms**	**Others**	**Acc. Firms**	**Others**	**Acc. Firms**	**Others**	**Acc. Firms**	**Others**	**Acc. Firms**	**Others**
Clearly stated	14 (100)	9 (100)	19 (100)	6 (85.71)	18 (100)	9 (100)	17 (100)	9 (100)	21 (100)	8 (100)	89 (100)	41 (97.62)
Describe areas not reviewed		1 (11.11)		1 (14.29)		2 (22.22)		2 (22.22)		1 (12.5)		7 (16.67)
Not clear				1 (14.29)								1 (2.38)

and this confirms the findings of earlier studies in the UK and Europe (O'Dwyer & Owen, 2005; 2007). Different performance data such as environmental performance indicators or environmental accounting data are commonly verified by all the assurors. In contrast to accounting firms, other assurors (consultants or NGOs) also evaluate qualitative information and responsible care initiatives (for chemical companies), thereby widening the scope of their assurance engagements. A small number of statements by certification firms also identify the areas that are not covered in the assurance assignment. It is important to analyze how the scope of assurance is determined. However, in our sample only two assurance statements by certification firms explain the scope determination process.

Reporting criteria against which the reports were assessed

Standards used in assurance process

Information on the standards or guidelines used to govern the assurance process may help interested users to understand whether appropriate standards or guidelines are applied as well as the nature of the assurance provided (Deegan et al., 2006; Al-Hamadeen, 2007). Table 9.10 displays the standard/guideline specified by the sampled assurance statements. Similar to the identification of reporting criteria, almost all the accounting firms mention some kind of standards or guidelines that are used to provide assurance service. However, more than two-thirds (69%) of the assurance statements by other assurors do not recognize any standard or guideline. Along with the mandatory professional standard (ISAE 3000), the influence of J-SUS can be seen in framing the sustainability assurance practice in Japan. In contrast to the UK or Australia, where AccountAbility standards are mostly used (Owen et al., 2000; Frost & Martinov-Bennie, 2010), we have only six assurance statements based on these standards, and they are issued mainly by consultants or certification firms (out of six only one is issued by an accounting firm).

Nature, timing and extent of procedures employed by the assurance provider

Both the GRI guideline and ISAE 3000 require that the assurance statement should include a summary of work performed; that is the nature, timing and extent of procedures employed by the assuror. Table 9.11 shows the audit procedures explained in the assurance statements by the sampled assurors. It can be seen that a wide range of procedures is employed both by the accounting firms and other assurors. Only in

Table 9.9 Reporting criteria to evaluate the reports

	2006		2007		2008		2009		2010		Total	
	Ac. Firms	Others	Ac. Firms	Others	Ac. Firms	Others	Ac. Firms	Others	Ac. Firms	Others	Ac. Firms	Others
Environmental reporting guidelines- Ministry of Environment (MOE, Japan)	8 (57.14)	1 (11.11)	11 (57.89)		11 (61.11)	1 (11.11)	10 (58.82)		14 (66.67)		54 (60.67)	2 (4.76)
GRI sustainability reporting guidelines	5 (35.71)	1 (11.11)	10 (52.63)		12 (66.67)	1 (11.11)	10 (58.82)		13 (61.90)		50 (56.18)	2 (4.76)
Environmental reporting assurance and registration criteria of the J-SUS					4 (22.22)		7 (41.18)		9 (42.86)		20 (22.47)	
Environmental accounting guidelines- (MOE, Japan)	2 (14.29)		4 (21.05)		2 (11.11)	1 (11.11)	4 (23.53)				12 (13.48)	1 (2.38)
Code of the J-SUS			4 (21.05)		2 (11.11)						6 (6.74)	
Company's own policies and standards	13 (92.86)		19 (100)		14 (77.78)		14 (82.35)		15 (71.43)		75 (84.27)	
Criteria for environmental information certification and registration- J-AOEI/ (The Japanese Association of Assurance Organizations for Environmental Information)	1 (7.14)										1 (1.12)	
The Natural Step's Sustainability Analysis						1 (11.11)						1 (2.38)
Establish methods adopted by co.									1 (4.76)		1 (1.12)	
AccountAbility 1000APS									1 (4.76)		1 (1.12)	
Act on the Rational Use of Energy									1 (4.76)		1 (1.12)	
Act on promotion of the global warming countermeasure									1 (4.76)		1 (1.12)	
Manual for calculating and reporting greenhouse gas emission									1 (4.76)		1 (1.12)	
The greenhouse gas protocol: a corporate accounting and reporting standard									1 (4.76)		1 (1.12)	
Not mentioned		8 (88.89)		7 (100)		6 (66.67)		9 (100)		8 (100)		38 (90.48)

Table 9.10 Standards for assurance practice

	2006		2007		2008		2009		2010		Total	
	Ac. Firms	Others	Ac. Firms	Others	Ac. Firms	Others	Ac. Firms	Others	Ac. Firms	Others	Ac. Firms	Others
Assurance standard for environmental reporting (MOE, Japan-2004)	3 (21.43)		4 (21.05)		7 (38.89)		8 (47.10)		3 (14.29)		25 (28.09)	
Practical guidelines of sustainability information assurance 2008-(J-SUS)					13 (72.22)		13 (76.47)		16 (76.19)		42 (47.19)	
International standards on assurance engagements (ISAE)-3000 (IFAC)	11 (78.57)		13 (68.42)		15 (83.33)		11 (64.71)	1 (11.11)	21 (100)	3 (37.5)	71 (79.78)	4 (9.52)
Proposed Environmental report review standard- (MOE Japan)	5 (35.71)		5 (26.32)		4 (22.22)		1 (5.88)		3 (14.29)		18 (20.22)	
Practical guidelines for the assurance of environmental information- J-AOEI	12 85.71		9 (47.37)								21 (23.60)	
Practical guidelines for the assurance of non-financial information- JICPA (The Japanese Institute of Certified Public Accountants)	2 14.29		3 (15.79)								5 (5.62)	
Environmental report assurance engagements guidelines-JICPA	2 (14.29)										2 (2.25)	
AccountAbility 1000 AS		1 (11.11)				2 (22.22)		1 (11.11)	1 (4.76)	1 (12.50)	1 (1.12)	5 (11.90)
SGS Sustainability Report Assurance Methodology								2 (22.22)		1 (12.50)		3 (7.14)
DNV protocol for verification of sustainability reporting						1 (11.11)						1 (2.38)
Bureau Veritas standard procedures and guidelines								1 11.11		3 37.5		4 (9.52)
Responsible Care code										1 12.50		1 (2.38)
Emerging good practices and guidance		1 11.11		1 14.29								2 (4.76)
Not mention any standard		8 (88.89)	2 (10.53)	6 (85.71)		6 (66.67)		6 (66.67)		3 (37.50)	2 (2.25)	29 (69.05)

Table 9.11 Audit procedure employed

	2006		2007		2008		2009		2010		Total	
	Acc. Firms	Others	Acc. Firms	Others	Acc. Firms	Others	Acc. Firms	Others	Acc. Firms	Others	Acc. Firms	Others
Review of documents/standards/systems/ process	9 (64.29)	6 (66.67)	18 (94.74)	5 (71.43)	18 (100)	6 (66.67)	16 (94.11)	7 (77.78)	21 (100)	5 (62.50)	82 (92.13)	29 (69.05)
Site Inspection	9 (64.29)	3 (33.33)	18 (94.74)		15 (83.33)	2 (22.22)	14 (82.35)	4 (44.44)	17 (80.95)	3 (37.50)	73 (82.02)	12 (28.57)
Recalculation/reconciliation	9 (64.29)		19 (100)		18 (100)		17 (100)		19 (90.48)	3 (37.50)	82 (92.13)	3 (7.14)
Analytical procedure	1 (7.14)		2 (10.53)		2 (11.11)		10 (58.82)		16 (76.19)		31 (34.83)	
Interview of management	10 (71.43)	(88.89)	15 (78.95)	5 (71.43)	18 (100)	7 (77.78)	17 (100)	6 (66.67)	21 (100)	5 (62.50)	81 (91.01)	31 (73.81)
Evaluate overall statement	4 (28.57)		7 (36.84)		8 (44.44)		8 (47.06)		1 (4.76)		28 (31.45)	
Review stakeholder engagement process									1 (4.76)		1 (1.12)	
Evaluate materiality identification and management									2 (9.52)		2 (2.25)	
Media analysis									1 (4.76)		1 (1.12)	
Attending stakeholder dialogue						1 (11.11)		1 (11.11)				2 (4.76)
Verification of data/data collection/data management system		8 (88. 89)		7 (100)		8 (88.89)		9 (100)		8 (100)		36 (85.71)
Pre assurance research								2 (22.22)		1 (12.5)		3 (7.14)
Based on financial audit procedure		1 (11.11)										1 (2.38)
Not mention specifically	6 (42.86)										6 (6.74)	

six instances of 2006 was such description not included in the statements. This finding resembles that of Deegan et al. (2006), where most of the UK and European statements included some description of work performed. However, O'Dwyer and Owen (2005) found that 10% of their samples interviewed stakeholders other than internal management, which are totally absent in Japan. Among other things, the nature of work performed is influenced by the level of assurance (limited or reasonable assurance). Future studies should focus on the determination on the nature, timing and extent of audit procedure.

Discussion

Accounting firm assurors are seen to standardize their conclusion by using the phrase "nothing has come to our attention that causes us to believe that the indicators in the report are not prepared, in all material respects, based on company's reporting criteria" for limited assurance engagement, which may mean that the data are accurately reflected in reports. The type of assurance opinion/conclusion used by the sampled statements is shown in Table 9.12. The negative form of conclusion given by all the accounting firm assurors is consistent with the limited level of assurance given by them. Other assurors are not seen to provide standardized opinion/conclusion, as close to 60% issued opinion both in positive and negative forms. A closer look reveals that these assurors (consultants/certification firms/NGOs) give importance on the accuracy and reliability in their opinion, and also use some general praiseworthy words such as "evaluate highly", "excellent", "proactive", "impressed", "well balanced", "satisfied" and "reasonable", the exact meaning of which, according to O'Dwyer and Owen (2005; 2007), is difficult to understand in the absence of any generally accepted assurance standard.

Additional comments/improvements identified by assurance provider

Deegan et al. (2006) noted that strictly speaking, identifying areas for improvements or giving praise for good performance are not part of providing assurance. This may hamper the perceived independence of the assurors. AA 1000AS requires that assurance statement must include additional comments which could cover progress as well as suggestions for improvements in the future. ISAE 3000, however, states that the assuror may include recommendations in the statement if these are significant for the intended users – but they should be clearly separated from the practitioner's conclusion and should not affect the conclusion.

Table 9.12 Conclusion/opinion of assurance engagement

	2006		2007		2008		2009		2010		Total	
	Ac. Firms	Others	Ac. Firms	Others	Ac. Firms	Others	Ac. Firms	Others	Ac. Firms	Others	Ac. Firms	Others
Positive		4 (44.44)		1 (14.29)		3 (33.33)		4 (44.44)		3 (37.50)		15 (35.71)
Negative	14 (100)	1 (11.11)	19 (100)	1 (14.29)	18 (100)		17 (100)		21 (100)		89 (100)	2 (4.76)
Both		4 (44.44)		5 (71.42)		6 (66.67)		5 (55.56)		5 (62.50)		25 (59.52)

Table 9.13 shows the frequency of such additional comments identified by the sampled assurance statements. Accounting firm assurors clearly adhere to the ISAE 3000 in this respect, with only one statement including recommendations for future improvement. This particular assurance statement is based on the AA 1000AS. Another 28% have additional comments that are separated from the assurance statement. Consultant assurors are positive in this respect, with more than 54% having identified the areas for further improvement which are noted under the same heading of conclusion or opinion.

Declaration of independence of assurance providers

J-SUS guideline and AA 1000AS require the assurance provider to make information publicly available about its independence from the reporting organization and impartiality toward its stakeholders. Declaration of such independence by the sampled statements is included in Table 9.14. In total, about 69% of the assurance statements have some references to the assuror's independence from the reporting organization. Accounting firms (more than 90%) are more likely to disclose information on independence than the other assurors (9%). This is in contrast with the European finding, where consulting and other assurors are more likely to give details of their competencies and independence (O'Dwyer & Owen, 2005).

Conclusion

Through content analysis of assurance statements, this study examines the quality of SR assurance of Japanese companies. Previous studies that investigated the assurance practice largely from European countries have observed wide variations and ambiguity and have raised the question of value addition of such practice for external stakeholders (Ball et al., 2000, O'Dwyer & Owen, 2005; 2007; Deegan et al., 2006). Although comparing with those studies will be very general because of time difference, it can provide important perspectives that will be used to assess the assurance quality from the Japanese viewpoint. In most of the areas of our analyzing protocol which are similar to earlier studies, we do observe some improvements, particularly with respect to the "title of the statement", "statement on responsibility of the management and assuror", "standard/guidelines used for evaluation of SR as well for assurance process", "procedure of the assurance work performed" and "declaration of assuror interest and independence". Similar to a financial audit, independence is the most debatable issue. In our

Table 9.13 Additional comments in assurance statements

	2006		2007		2008		2009		2010		Total	
	Ac. Firms	Others	Ac. Firms	Others	Ac. Firms	Others	Ac. Firms	Others	Ac. Firms	Others	Ac. Firms	Others
Yes		5 (55.56)		4 (57.14)		5 (55.56)		5 (55.56)	1 (4.76)	4 (50.00)	1 (1.12)	23 (54.76)
No	14 100	4 (44.44)	19 (100)	3 (42.86)	18 (100)	4 (44.44)	17 (100)	4 (44.44)	20 (95.24)	4 (50.00)	88 (98.88)	19 (45.24)
Separately	6 (42.86)		5 (26.32)		4 (22.22)	2 (22.22)	4 (23.53)		6 (28.57)	2 (25.00)	25 (28.09)	4 (9.52)

Table 9.14 Declaration about independence of assuror

	2006		2007		2008		2009		2010		Total	
	Acc. Firms	Others	Acc. Firms	Others	Acc. Firms	Others	Acc. Firms	Others	Acc. Firms	Others	Acc. Firms	Others
Yes	13 (92.86)	1 (11.11)	18 (94.74)		16 (88.89)	3 (33.33)	16 (94.12)	3 (33.33)	18 (85.71)	3 (37.50)	81 (91.01)	10 (23.81)
No	1 (7.14)	8 (88.89)	1 (5.26)	7 (100)	2 (11.11)	6 (66.37)	1 (5.88)	6 (66.67)	3 (14.29)	5 (62.50)	8 (8.99)	32 (76.19)

case, while more than 95% of the sample clearly separates management and assurors' responsibility, over 60% of the sample provides explanations of their interest with the company. Arguably these enhance the independence of the assurors.

From the accountability perspective, there are still concerns with regard to the addressee, purpose, and scope of the assurance provision. Majority of the assurance statements are addressed to the internal management. All the cases are examples of limited assurance for some selected data/information such as environmental indicators and environmental accounting data for their accuracy. None of the assurance is for complete SR or for reasonable assurance. In this regard studies have already identified the barriers to adopt assurance in SR (Park & Brorson, 2005; Jones & Solomon, 2010; Haider, 2012). Management may consider the benefits of assurance provision against the cost and time required for such voluntary service. However, over 70% of the statement clearly state that they are giving limited assurance which may help the users to minimize the 'expectation gap'.

When we compared the approaches of different assurors, accounting firms are seen to standardize their practices based on applicable guideline/standard (such as ISAE 3000). However, examples show they only provide limited assurance or review level engagement with emphasis on data accuracy or compliance with guidelines/standards rather than providing a 'strategic' or 'value added' approach. In contrast, when compared with applicable standards or guidelines, assurance statements issued by other assurors lack quality in certain respects. For example, in many cases statements were provided without any addressee or explanation of the audit procedure. Identification of reporting criteria to prepare SR, specifying assurance standards or guidelines to govern assurance services, stating the level of assurance provided, and declaration of independence are also rare in these assurance statements. Similar to accounting assurors, consultants/certification firms also emphasize on the reliability and accuracy of the reported information. In contrast, assurance provided by NGOs/NPOs has a relatively wider scope of assurance. They also provide recommendations for future improvement, thereby can be treated as 'strategic' and 'value added' for the management as well as for the stakeholders.

Acknowledgments

This research was supported by the Environmental Research and Technology Development Fund (1E-1106) from the Ministry of

Environment, Japan and Grand-in-Aid for Scientific Research (B) Grant Number 25285138 and Grant-in-Aid for Young Scientists (Start-up) Grant Number 24830088 from Japan Society for the Promotion of Science (JSPS).

Notes

1. IAASB (International Auditing and Assurance Standard Board) (2006) defines assurance as "an engagement in which a practitioner expresses a conclusion designed to enhance the degree of confidence that intended users can have about the evaluation or measurement of subject matter that is the responsibility of a party, other than the intended users or the practitioner, against criteria".
2. The first survey was published in 1993 by KPGM International. Since then, in total six surveys have been issued, with the latest one in 2008. This survey has been conducted by KPMG in association with the University of Amsterdam.
3. The study categorizes assurance providers broadly into two groups: accounting firms and others. Others include certification firms, consultants and NGOs/NPOs. Only for analysis we classified them in the same group.
4. Only the English version of assurance statements was analyzed. The scanned copies of a few assurance statements were so small in size that we could not read them. These were excluded from coding.

References

Adams, C. (2004). The ethical, social and environmental reporting – Performance portrayal gap. *Accounting, Auditing and Accountability Journal*, 17, (5), 731–757.

Adams, C. & Evans, R. (2004). Accountability, completeness, credibility and the audit expectations gap. *Journal of Corporate Citizenship*, 14, 97–115.

Al-Hamadeen, R.H. (2007). *Assurance of Corporate Stand-Alone Reporting: Evidence from the UK*. Unpublished PhD thesis, University of St. Andrews, UK.

Ball, A., Owen, D.L. & Gray, R.H. (2000). External transparency or internal capture? The role of third party statements in adding value to corporate environmental reports. *Business Strategy and the Environment*, 9, (1), 1–23.

CorporateRegister.com (2008). *Assure View: The CSR Assurance Statement Report*. London: CorporateRegister.com.

Dando, N. & Swift, T. (2003). Transparency and assurance: Minding the credibility gap. *Journal of Business Ethics*, 44, (2–3), 195–200.

Deegan, C., Cooper, B.J. & Shelly, M. (2006). An investigation of TBL report assurance statements: UK and European evidence. *Managerial Auditing Journal*, 21, (4), 329–371.

Deegan, C. & Unerman, J. (2011). *Financial Accounting Theory*. London: McGraw-Hill Higher Education.

Edgley, C.R., Jones, M.J. & Solomon, J.F. (2010). Stakeholder inclusivity in social and environmental report assurance. *Accounting, Auditing and Accountability Journal*, 23, (4), 532–557.

Fonseca, A. (2010). How credible are mining companies' sustainability reports? A critical analysis of external assurance under the requirement of the International Council on Mining and Metals. *Corporate Social Responsibility and Environmental Management*, 17, (6), 355–370.

Free, C., Salterio, S.E. & Shearer, T. (2009). The construction of auditability: MBA rankings and assurance in practice. *Accounting, Organizations and Society*, 34, 119–140.

Frost, G. & Martinov-Bennie, N. (2010). *Sustainability Reporting Assurance: Market Trends and Information Content*. Melbourne: CPA Australia.

Gillet, C. (2010). *A Study of Sustainability Verification Practices: The French Case*. Paper presented at the European Accounting Conference, Istanbul.

GRI (Global Reporting Initiative) (2002). *Sustainability Reporting Guidelines*. Boston, MA: The Global Reporting Initiative, Boston.

GRI (Global Reporting Initiative) (2006). *RG Sustainability Reporting Guidelines – Version 3 (G3)*. Amsterdam: The Global Reporting Initiative.

Haider, M.B. (2012). *Assurance in Sustainability Reporting and its Legitimacy: Evidence from Japan*. Unpublished PhD thesis, Kobe University, Japan.

Haider, M.B. & Kokubu, K. (forthcoming). Assurance and third-party comment on sustainability reporting in Japan: A descriptive study. *International Journal of Environment and Sustainable Development*.

International Auditing and Assurance Standards Board (IAASB) (2006). *Handbook of International Auditing, Assurance, and Ethics Pronouncements 2006 Edition*. New York: The International Federation of Accountants.

Jones, M.J. & Solomon, J.F. (2010). Social and environmental report assurance: Some interview evidence. *Accounting Forum*, 34, (1), 20–31.

Kolk, A. & Perego, P. (2010). Determinants of the adoption of sustainability assurance statements: An international investigation. *Business Strategy and the Environment*, 19, (3), 182–198.

KPMG (2008). *International Survey of Corporate Responsibility Reporting 2008*, Amsterdam: KPMG.

KPMG (2011). *International Survey of Corporate Responsibility Reporting*. Amsterdam: KPMG.

KPMG (2011). *KPMG International Survey of Corporate Responsibility Reporting 2011*. Amsterdam: KPMG.

KPMG (2013). *The KPMG Survey of Corporate Responsibility Reporting 2013*. Amsterdam: KPMG.

Mock, T.J., Strohm, C. & Swartz, K.M. (2007). An examination of worldwide assured sustainability reporting. *Australian Accounting Review*, 17, (1), 67–77.

O'Dwyer, B. (2011). The case of sustainability assurance: Constructing a new assurance service. *Contemporary Accounting Research*, 28, (4), 1230–1266.

O'Dwyer, B. & Owen, D.L. (2005). Assurance statement practice in environmental, social and sustainability reporting: A critical evaluation. *British Accounting Review*, 37, (2), 205–229.

O'Dwyer B. & Owen D.L. (2007). Seeking stakeholder-centric sustainability assurance: An examination of recent sustainability assurance practice. *Journal of Corporate Citizenship*, 25, 77–94.

O'Dwyer, B., Owen, D. & Unerman, J. (2011). Seeking legitimacy for new assurance forms: The case of assurance on sustainability reporting. *Accounting, Organizations and Society*, 36, (1), 31–52.

Owen, D., Swift, T.A., Humphrey, C. & Bowerman, M. (2000). The new social audits: Accountability, managerial capture or the agenda of social champions? *European Accounting Review*, 9, (1), 81–98.

Park, J., & Brorson, T. (2005). Experiences of and views on third party assurance of corporate environmental and sustainability reports. *Journal of Cleaner Production*, 13, (10–11), 1095–1106.

Perego, P.M. (2009). Causes and consequences of assurance provider choice for sustainability reporting: An international study. *International Journal of Management*, 26, (3), 412–425.

Responsible Care Japan (2010). *Responsible Care Report 2010*. Responsible Care Japan.

Power, M. (1999). *The Audit Society: Rituals of Verification*. Oxford: Oxford University Press.

Simnett, R., Vanstraelen, A. & Chua, W.F. (2009). Assurance on sustainability reports: An international comparison. *Accounting Review*, 84, (3), 937–967.

Smith, J., Haniffa, R. & Fairbrass, J. (2011). A conceptual framework for investigating "capture" in corporate sustainability reporting assurance. *Journal of Business Ethics*, 99, (3), 425–439.

Wilson, M.J. (2003). *Independent Assurance on Corporate Sustainability Reports*. Unpublished PhD thesis, University of Calgary, Canada.

10

The Growing Acceptance of Global Standards by Japanese Companies and Its Implication in Terms of Disclosure

Philippe Debroux

Introduction

Modern Japan was built on a strong linkage between government, business and society. But it did not proceed without fight, claims or revolts, as exemplified by the history of peasants and industrial workers' protests, the rise of environmentalist movements and the instability of the business and political system for long periods of time. The Japanese economic and business system, including the employment relations framework, is the result of an interaction between interests and ideologies that sometimes clashed and sometimes compromised in specific political, social and economic contexts. Ideas about the roles of business in society and the concepts of corporate social responsibility (CSR) that have emerged and evolved in Japan since the Edo period derive from these complex influences.

Philosophically, concepts of CSR in Japan share core permanent elements that are related to human relationships and the relations of Japanese people with nature; these are recurrent in the architecture, policies and practices of the whole modern period. In this regard, the cultural heritage, and particularly spiritual traditions coming from Buddhism, Confucianism and Shintoism, have significantly and consistently shaped the underlying assumptions and values concerning the role of business in society. But a long-standing Marxist tradition, Christianity and social liberalism have also played a significant role since the Meiji era. Thus, the evolution of thought about the place of business in society represents a mix between Japanese traditional wisdom and the Western ideal of equality and social justice, based on individual rights.

Therefore, in order to understand CSR performance, one must delve into the historical background and try to understand the origin of Japanese companies' perception of CSR and how it has been integrated into their management system up until now. It is also crucial to observe how the institutions have operated over time, and how they have led business to cope with the successive stages of CSR development. Since the *shonindo*[1] in the Edo era, Eichi Shibusawa[2] in the prewar period, and leading business figures such as Konosuke Matsushita and Akio Morita (respectively, founder of Panasonic and co-founder of Sony) in the postwar era, the mantra of humanistic management, protection of the environment and emphasis on the quality of products and services has been deeply engrained in Japanese business culture and a constant source of inspiration that has defined the expected roles of business and the key success factor of prosperity. Long-term success in business comes when the objective is not only to make profit but also to serve society's needs and aspirations.

But at several historical junctures society reacted against business, which was perceived as not responding to social and economic expectations anymore. Gaps and contradictions appeared between the proclaimed CSR-related values and reality on the ground. Nurtured by increasingly varied domestic and foreign sources, the business world had to construct new compacts to respond to the new needs and expectations of key stakeholders. But this was only temporary, as CSR constantly entered new phases, demanding new behaviors and attitudes from business in a changing institutional environment.

It may be argued that we are at the beginning of a paradigmatic change in the world with regard to the roles of business in society; more precisely, with regard to what are now called ESG terms: social, environmental and governance-related terms. External stakeholders such as national and international non-governmental organizations (NGOs) and consumer groups are emerging as powerful societal voices. Based on wider universal principles, the regulatory environment becomes more constraining. Because of the different nature of relationships with the stakeholders that this implies, the carefully circumscribed business case trade-off between profit and contribution to society that has been the cornerstone of Japanese companies' CSR strategy during the last three decades may be put into question.

The new challenge of CSR

The successful shift of Japanese CSR in the neo-liberal framework

As pointed out by Kinderman (2012), modern CSR emerged from the dominance of the neo-liberal paradigm in economic and business systems. The breaking down of the traditional social compact in the Anglo-Saxon world (and subsequently in continental Europe), the immense power acquired by large companies in a deregulated and globalized world and the concomitant weakening of the state requested a stronger simultaneous involvement with ESG-related aspects of management.

The Japanese regulatory system and business philosophies and practices have also been strongly influenced by the neo-liberal paradigm since the 1980s, putting in question the traditional business order, including the social compact. In order to keep the traditional balance between traditions and the new paradigm in an uncertain environment, the last 25 years have seen Japan's and Japanese organizations' constant oscillation between being receptive and resistant to the "global standards" argument of converging philosophies and practices of management.

Because CSR was first developed in the Anglo-Saxon institutional setting, it may be pointed out that the main CSR criteria are biased toward the measurement of explicit CSR. Therefore, they tend to be mainly reflected in market-oriented disclosure of information and branded programs in order to satisfy key stakeholders (Brammer et al., 2012). At government, intermediate organizations and business levels Japanese organizations have understood that the Western concept of CSR could be a threat to their traditional practices, but that it also offered opportunities. As in Western countries and for the same reasons, that is, in order to protect organizations against backlashes resulting from environmentally and socially related scandals that could cause liabilities, Japanese companies have adopted Western-style CSR as a risk management policy.

Adaptation and differentiation

Since the 1970s, however, Japanese companies have evolved toward a wider utilitarian "business case" viewpoint of CSR. They have tried in traditional fashion to make the most of the "Western concepts" of CSR, carefully selecting those aspects that are identified as suitable for adoption while preserving their self-contained and self-sustained identity. This gives rise to today's institutional mix, where they attempt to maintain close cooperation with employees yet concurrently give more importance to shareholder value; remain committed to lifetime employment of permanent employees yet offer performance-based pay and stock options and use more non-permanent employees; engage with external stakeholders in Japan and abroad in ESG-related matters while keeping relationships at arm's length; give importance to international certification while remaining cautious and selective in the global CSR-related rule-making process.

Without denying the need for a change in management practices, public authorities, intermediate bodies and companies believe that the traditional Japanese CSR philosophies and practices, especially the concern (and thus expertise) for environment and quality, embedded in the diligence, sense of responsibility and high skill of Japanese workers, are potential sources of new competitive advantages based on differentiation (Keidanren, 2009). With the backup of the state since the 1970s, Japanese companies have been developing products and services that they present as contributing to humanity's well-being in ESG terms. Since the 1990s, embracing the concepts of enlightened shareholder value and creating shared values (Porter & Kramer, 2011), they have started to engage with stakeholders, not only in Japan but also in the rest of the world in projects that go beyond their traditional premises (Mizuo, 2014).

The challenge of the sustainability-based concept of CSR

However, having accepted the premises of explicit CSR they are not immune from new trends in CSR. As has been pointed out (Brammer et al., 2012), at issue in the current CSR trend are the regulatory, normative and cognitive pillars that underlie the question of the extent to which and to whom a company should be accountable. Encompassing a broader, deeper notion of corporate responsibility, CSR moves toward a more ambitious but also more ambiguous and subjective approach. The process is still incomplete but it has already created a mix of soft and hard law-based pressure on companies.

Arguments about the role of business in society have gradually been put forward regarding sustainable development, mixing all ESG elements (The United Nations, 1987). International public organizations such as the United Nations (Global Compact, Millennium Development Goals), the International Labor Organization (Core labor standards – concept of decent work) and also individual companies, NGOs, business groups such as Ethical Trade Initiative (ETI) and organizations such as ISO and Transparency International, are promoting an ever broadening and deepening concept of CSR.

It rests on the idea that company behaviors must aim at the most effective and efficient possible use of the resources that assure their existence, but also protect the interest of other stakeholders. It supposes that ESG objectives are integrated on the same footing as economic objectives in the core activities of the company and are not detached or semi-detached in externalized entities (Roper, 2012). The sustainability-based concept of CSR goes beyond stakeholder models that typically place the organization as the center of a wheel with stakeholders forming the spokes. Therefore, it changes the set of expectations, behaviors and attitudes that stakeholders have vis-à-vis companies (Roper, 2012).

As a consequence, to the extent that it empowers stakeholders, corporations may face stronger pressures to adopt CSR measures to legitimize their activities. Recent evidence of this direction is the emergence of mandatory rules on social or environmental disclosure in some countries. So far, despite the deepening and enlarging of their CSR activities, Japanese companies have not changed their mind fundamentally concerning their priorities. They have continued to be a locus for the realization of the economic and social needs of those with which they have a direct relationship; that is to say, permanent employees, customers, business partners, lenders and government officials (Wokutch & Shepard, 1999).

The limit of the Japanese explicit CSR model

However, skillfully blending explicit CSR strategy with traditional management features may not be good enough in the new context. It may even lead to contradictions that lead to management dysfunction. On the one hand, the contribution to global society welfare and well-being of Japanese organizations during the last three decades has been significant, and it could be argued that the achievements can be linked to some extent to cultural heritage and traditional wisdom. Indeed, the world benefits from the organizational expertise, high skill and dedication of Japanese organizations and workers, their sense of responsibility and their action-oriented and practical approach to ESG-related issues.

But it can also be said that these positive traditional characteristics of Japanese management can also have negative consequences for a number of stakeholders. To some extent, it could even be argued that these negative consequences have been exacerbated by the superposition of neo-liberal performance norms to socio-cultural behaviors and attitudes. It might be the case, for instance, that work patterns linked to customer satisfaction and criteria of profitability impose norms that are extremely stringent. But it may also be said that the traditional split between insiders and outsiders in a group-oriented society such as Japan (Sugimoto, 2010) and the hierarchical characteristics of Japanese social order between organizations (large versus small companies) and between categories of workers (permanent versus non-permanent) explain the growing social inequality in a business system that is submitted to more intense competition than before.

The sustainability-based concept of CSR requires a more inclusive type of multi-stakeholders' framework and a higher and broader level of adaptation to global ESG standards that apply to all stakeholders. Trade-offs and priorities are unavoidable, but maintaining management policies that create or retain structurally unfair treatment of any stakeholder, and restricting CSR policy to a narrowly defined set of stakeholders, is unsustainable whatever the intrinsic value of the current CSR activities of Japanese companies and their impact in improving specific social and environmental situations.

CSR as the new avatar of industrial democracy?

Japanese companies are under pressure to engage in a dialogue on societal issues that they have considered irrelevant up until now in terms of stakeholders' priorities or too intrusive in terms of managerial prerogatives to be discussed with outsiders. Quoting Brammer et al. (2012),

> a key focal point for any analysis of CSR should be: the societal checks and balances on the exercise of corporate power. The effectiveness of explicit CSR in the form of voluntarism, and its effectiveness in reaching social, environmental or other objectives are likely to depend strongly on its linkages to other institutionalized forms of governance. CSR at the company level must be understood within the wider dynamics of business and trade associations, social networks and state regulation.

In the institutional view of CSR that the authors adopt, the latent historical alternative of bringing public interest back into the private domain of the corporation could come again to the fore.

In an American and European context, from the 1920s to the 1970s, there was a putting forward of corporate values linked to public social interest and industrial democracy. Berle (1954) referred to the

American business system as one of "People's Capitalism". Managers were expected to balance the interests of the key stakeholders and to manage what were expected to be socially responsible corporations (Galbraith, 1956). In Europe it was argued that it would be normal that not only the shareholders, but also the employees, consumers and the community, be represented to ensure that all social interests had a voice in the decision-making process (Ireland & Pillay, 2010). Eventually, because of the change in stakeholders' relative influence in favor of shareholders in the dominant neo-liberal framework those transformational ideas have been replaced since the 1970s by ameliorative schemes that are promoted by the CSR concept. But they have never fully gone away, and the emergence of the sustainability-based concept of CSR might be a foretaste of changes in that direction, this time in a globalized institutional framework.

The postwar CSR environment

CSR in the golden age of the company-centered business system

The company, seen as a place of social solidarity, seemed to have lost ideological ground in the immediate postwar period. But prewar and postwar CSR concepts shared a strong belief in the key intermediary role of companies between the family and the state. The message, constantly reinforced by public and private instances, was that the two pillars of social policy had to be the company, where human capital was preserved, and the family, where it was reproduced.

Corporate laws enacted after the war clearly put shareholders at the center of the corporate governance system. There is nothing in law that gives any kind of privileged position to labor (Wolff, 2010). Nevertheless, business continued to be considered a fundamental source of power and cohesion in the social fabric. The opinion that large companies are "public goods", *Gemeinschaft* types of community organizations responsible for creating jobs and maintaining standards of living, has remained strongly engrained in the minds of Japanese people until now (Dore, 1987). The Japanese-style welfare system, from family and unemployment allowances to the vocational education (and acquisition of skills in general) and the pension system, has been built around companies in the postwar period.

In such a welfare corporatist system, CSR norms and values have been legitimized, supported and/or imposed through economic, societal, legal and political instruments of power. Lifetime employment and the difficulty of laying off permanent employees were social norms, but the courts' precedents have consistently reinforced them during the whole postwar period (Araki, 2002). An explicit type of CSR was not considered necessary because of the constant exchanges between management and permanent employees and between companies and the state in order to adjust to socio-economic changes.

The mantra of the humanistic management approach emphasizing stakeholders' solidarity (as opposed to the instrumental approach presented as typical of Anglo-Saxon management philosophy) was brought to the fore again. Under this social compact, horizontal class-based solidarity that had peaked in the immediate postwar period declined significantly. It assured the long-lasting development of a company-centered system that rejected class struggle, in line with the prewar ideas promoted by Eichi Shibusawa through the *Kyochokai*.[3] The strength of traditional values as a key inspirational factor that differentiated Japanese management in terms of CSR philosophy was defended, among others, by the founder of Matsushita Electric, Konosuke Matsushita (Matsushita Electric, 2014) and by the co-founder of Sony, Akio Morita (Morita et al., 1986). Nowadays, traditional Japanese management principles are under severe challenge and are often considered impediments to the adaptation of Japanese companies to globalization (Schaede, 2008). Nevertheless, prominent business leaders such as Mitarai (Canon) and Inamori (Kyocera) still defend the same motto of humanistic management based on traditional wisdom.

This humanistic management appears in the philosophical and spiritual overtones, based on the *kyozon kyoei* principle, that propound a holistic coexistence and co-prosperity among stakeholders. This is to be found in many Japanese CSR and sustainability reports, and is a phenomenon that is seldom observed in the Western world, where the spiritual connotation of management philosophy almost disappeared with the separation of management and ownership in the 1930s. As in the precepts of the *zaibatsu* in the Meiji era, the reports reiterate the professed social and environmental concern of business and the culturally engrained strong love and respect of Japanese people for nature (Yamanaka, 2006).

The continuous impact of traditional management values on CSR

The philosophical overtone of Japanese CSR reporting is mixed with an extremely down-to-earth (business case-centered) approach and presentation of the CSR issues that may look paradoxical at first glance. However, this reflects the engrained field-oriented philosophy that underlies Japanese management practices. The idea that problems must be explored through multidimensional approaches underlines the organizational flexibility that is characteristic of Japanese organizations (Dore, 1987). It attunes them to societal needs. As stated by Konosuke Matsushita (2014), the responsibility of a company to society requires that it has to explore all types of possibilities, even remote, in order to make the best product in terms of convenience, cost and variety of features.

The focus of learning in Japan was always directed at practical applications, that is, embedding knowledge through practice. This epistemology, originating from the high scholarship and ideals of the Bushido code, still prevails in many management practices (Miyamoto & Grainger, 2007). In Zen Buddhism practices, which are at the heart of Bushido, basic human qualities such as trust, simplicity, feeling and understanding of the self are at work. They are not presented as special behavioral features that can only be mastered by enlightened elites and are useless in day-to-day private and business life. They are emotionally grounded in the minds and hearts of average people and systems, and are expected to appear in the values of organizations. The sense of responsibility, loyalty, commitment, work ethics and discipline of the workforce that comes from this heritage is reflected in Japanese products and services, and in workplace practices (Dore, 1987).

The clash between proclaimed ideals and the reality

However, the multi-stakeholder framework remained highly skewed toward permanent employees and customers during the heyday of Japanese management, despite the projected harmonious image of labor–management collaboration and respect for the environment. Japanese companies started to lose a great deal of their legitimacy among key stakeholders in the 1970s because of environmental problems, the growing assertiveness of consumer groups and pressure from women to get fair treatment in the workplace. The image of *kyozon kyoei*-based "society friendliness" took a turn for the worse in the 1980s and 1990s. Scandals occurred that were linked to environment and product quality-related failures and workplace physical and mental pathologies.[4]

The stable corporate governance environment that has assured the sustainability of the social compact accordingly changed with financial deregulation and the shift toward direct financing (Schaede, 2008). Stable ownership began to decline and nowadays, traditional industrial group (*keiretsu*)-linked shareholding accounts for no more than around 20% of the total of outstanding shares in most large companies. Many of them, such as Canon, Sony, Orix or Hoya, have more than 50% foreign ownership (Nikkei Weekly, 2011).

Leading Japanese companies have succeeded up until now in gathering a core of domestic and foreign shareholders who accept the basic tenets of the welfare corporatist system. So far, they do not seem to be under strong pressure from shareholders to drop it or to change it radically, provided it is streamlined to make it more efficient. Intensive use of non-permanent labor, adoption of performance related pay systems and tighter control of human capital costs go alongside a compensation differential that remains relatively low among permanent employees and a long-term job guarantee for a pool (albeit shrinking) of permanent workers (Debroux, 2013). But the new shareholders (domestic and foreign) privilege EVA (economic value added), ROI (return on investment) and ROE (return on equity) as ratios of performance, and expect higher financial return than the traditional shareholders. This put investor relations much higher up management priorities. Financial markets ask for more precise and broader disclosure of information than before, for example on business results, risk and identification of the shareholders, on a par with Western (especially US) companies.

The shift toward utilitarian and explicit CSR strategy

The institutionalization of CSR

The stronger pressure for disclosure from stakeholders has triggered a shift toward a more explicit type of CSR strategy, initiated by public authorities and the leading employer associations, such as Keidanren (Japan Business Federation) and Keizai Doyukai. The traditional method of disseminating practices through imitation starting from the top, through leading employer and labor associations, and through *gyosei shido* (government and bureaucracy administrative guidance), continues to be the key driver of CSR activity. Guidance should be provided that does not impose formal rules on large companies but induces them to become de facto models for smaller companies.

As a result, the concepts of competitive social performance, license to operate and business case have become almost the official doctrine in Japanese officialdom and companies since the 1990s. The ambition is to promote Japanese CSR standards that reflect the peculiarities of Japanese CSR traditions, so that they could even become de facto CSR world standards. Japanese companies have developed sophisticated quality control architecture in production processes for decades. They know how to balance short-term containment measures and long-term policy. Because they have also mastered the methodology and techniques required for the analysis of quality issues, the idea is that they have the right experience and knowledge to implement similar approaches in order to solve social issues, for instance in relation to supply chain management.

Keidanren and Keizai Doyukai have taken concrete initiatives since the 1990s, such as the announcement of charters and guidelines for CSR activities. In 2003 Keizai Doyukai released its 15th White Paper entitled *Market Evolution and Socially Responsible Management – Moving Towards the Building of Trust and Industry and the Continuous Creation of Value* (Keizai Doyukai, 2009). After the *Earth Environment Charter* in 1991, Keidanren (Nippon Keidanren at the time) enacted the *Keidanren Charter for Corporate Behavior"* the same year. The charter became the *"Charter of Good Corporate Behavior – Nippon Keidanren –* in 2002 and in 2010 was revised again with the incorporation of core elements of ISO 26000 (ISO/IR Mirror Committee, 2012). In 2011, in line with the policy of boosting new types of competitive advantages, Keidanren created the "Japan Inclusive Business Support Center" in order to promote Japanese expertise in environmental matters in the developing world (WBCSD, 2014).[5]

Since the end of the 1990s, the Fair Trade Commission, under the authority of the Ministry of Economy, Trade and Industry (METI), assesses and provides guidance to companies about misconduct in domestic and international markets. Already, in 2002, the Cabinet Office had formed the Exploratory Committee of Self-Imposed Codes of Conduct. In addition, in 2005, the Japanese government enacted the Law Concerning the Promotion of Business Activities with Environmental Consideration by Specified Corporations by Facilitating Access to Environmental Information. The aim of this is to encourage companies to disclose environmental information to the public. Typically, it requires designated organizations, including national universities, the Japan Post, the Japan Broadcasting Corporation (NHK), the Nippon Telegraph and Telephone Corporation (NTT), Japan Railways companies, and the Japan Highway Public Corporation, to prepare environmental reports and act as role models for other organizations (Ministry of Environment, 2014a).

In 2009 the government launched the "Multi-Stakeholder Forum on Social Responsibility for a Sustainable Future" in line with the European Commission's initiative. The forum gathered representatives from businesses, consumers groups, labor unions, the financial sector and the government. Each of the relevant authorities, such as the Ministry of the Environment and the Ministry of Health, Labor and Welfare, engage in disseminating guidance on CSR issues. For instance, since the beginning of the previous decade the Ministry of Environment has published a guidebook entitled *Environmental Performance Indicators for Business and Environmental Accounting* and a white paper on recycling (Ministry of Environment, 2014a).

Broadening and deepening of CSR activities

In their search for new markets in emerging countries, Japanese companies' activities have gradually shifted away from traditional philanthropy performed through external foundations. They devote more directly technical and managerial resources to projects (education, health, energy, water supply, environment protection) linked to all markets but also, more specifically, to the nurturing of the so-called "base of pyramid" (BOP) markets (Nomura Soken Kenkyujo, 2011). For instance, Yakult is now involved in many projects related to the development of products specifically for the BOP markets. They have at the same time a social dimension because they are linked to the nurturing of female entrepreneurship (Mizuo, 2014).

But even in the case of activities unrelated to business, stakeholder engagement in projects managed jointly with NGOs and international organizations is not precluded. For example, Toyota's participation in reforestation projects in China is outside its main activities. However, the projects involve a number of NGOs and employees, and they require managerial decisions and technological transfers. As a result they have led to the development of specific techniques to achieve results, and have an impact on the level of skills and knowledge of employees, locally involved manpower and local communities (Toyota, 2006), in line with the concept of "creating shared values" promoted by Porter and Kramer (2011).

Since the 1980s companies have started to work to improve the performance of management systems in both socio-efficiency and eco-efficiency terms. The objectives of socio-efficiency were to make companies more profitable through the adoption of performance-driven human resource practices while maintaining the tenets of the welfare corporatist system, namely long-term labor–management mutual commitment leading to high workforce motivation, constant nurturing of skills and acceptance of change management.[6]

In terms of eco-efficiency, the public's growing awareness of environmental issues has induced companies to develop products with specifications that go beyond regulations. With the backup of the state, large companies such as Toyota, Toshiba, Panasonic, Hitachi and Sony have invested in the development of environmentally friendly products such as low energy housing, freon-free and low-energy refrigerators, low-water-consuming toilets and washing machines. They have also started to work on pollution prevention, reduction in carbon dioxide emissions, green procurement and recycling. Toyota and Honda have begun to sell hybrid cars responding to environmental concern. In the financial sector, all main banks have been offering loans for environmentally friendly houses since the mid-1990s (*The Economist*, 2005).

In the framework of branding strategy, community involvement started to link with cause-related marketing. Although success remains limited, it gave opportunities to companies to nurture their image and reputation in establishing links with other organizations and causes (Cheron et al., 2012). The eco-town program (Ministry of the Environment, 2014b) is an example of putting policy into action in order to develop industrial and technical infrastructures to sustain the development of a sound material cycle society. An effective approach to improving the capacity of local governments is networking between cities for knowledge sharing and mutual learning. The Kitakyushu initiative for a clean environment (CITYNET) is one example of such schemes. In 2008, 13 award-winning eco-model cities, with other cities and ministries, research institutions and private companies, formed the Promotion Council for the Low-Carbon Cities. They are now committed to becoming low carbon, sustainable cities. Businesses actively work with national and prefectural governments and the general population in those projects (Global Environment Centre Foundation, 2005).

Most large Japanese companies proceed to an environmental assessment of their products during the planning and R&D stages. For about two decades they have trained their employees on conservation issues and worked with their suppliers (in sending engineers and technicians and welcoming trainees to their premises in Japan and to their facilities abroad), to upgrade their environmental expertise (Holtschneider, 2007). The expertise of Japanese companies (engineering and construction) in disaster management leads them to local engagement with public authorities, citizens and NGOs in many projects in Japan and abroad (Shimizu, 2013).[7]

CSR certification and international involvement

Modern CSR is characterized not only by the adoption of specific standards, but also by the emergence of accredited third-party agents entrusted with examining whether a company's CSR effort meets the agreed standards. With the caveat that will be explained later, Japanese companies now tend to believe that the best way to evaluate a company's CSR effort is through adoption of official standards, despite the fact that this requires increased transparency and accountability to stakeholders at large.

Nationally, they observe the guidance standards developed by Keidanren and Keizai Doyukai (although at the time of writing only a relatively small percentage, 16%, of Japanese companies tell us that they have actively adopted ISO 26000 into their CSR activities in the entire organization) (ISO, 2014). Internationally, the importance given to certification explains the attractiveness of the ISO 14000 environmental norm (the number of registered Japanese companies is the highest in the world) (ISO, 2014). An increasing number of companies adopt the guidelines of the Global Reporting Initiative (GRI), which is the world's most widely used sustainability-reporting framework (GRI, 2014). Reluctant to participate at first, a growing number of Japanese companies now adhere to the United Nation's Global Compact project (220 Japanese members by the end of 2013) (Global Compact, 2014). Top leaders also participate more actively in the activities of the World Business Council for Sustainable Development (WBCSD), an organization that plays a growing role in international negotiations linked to environmental issues, notably in terms of climate change (WBCSD, 2014). At last, alongside public authorities, Japanese companies, employers and labor associations are increasingly involved in the International Labor Organization (ILO) Better Work and Green Growth projects (ILO, 2014).

A high standard of reporting

Japanese companies have opened themselves to the world in focusing their CSR strategies on environmental issues, customer satisfaction and strategic philanthropy. In so doing they have been able to keep pace with the worldwide CSR trend. As in the West, Japanese non-financial reporting focused on environmental issues in the 1990s because of the high level of public awareness and stronger regulatory measures, namely the Environmental Consideration Promoting Law (2006) and Environmental Reports Guideline (2007). In the 2000s, with a lead-time of about five years compared to Western companies, Japanese companies have started to enlarge their reporting to include social issues (Yamaguchi, 2010).

Today, most listed Japanese companies publish annual environmental reports, and much more information is available that is directly relevant to CSR issues. It may be observed that Japan is the highest corporate responsibility reporting country, with about 88% of companies producing corporate responsibility reports (KMPG, 2008). Japanese CSR and sustainability reports are of high quality in term of details and accuracy of information. They reveal in details the stages of the plan-do-check-act (PDCA) process.

The uncertain shift to CSR centered on sustainability

A strong utilitarian way of thinking

In a similar manner to Western companies, Japanese companies pick and choose aspects that they believe fit with their strengths and could boost competitiveness. Customer satisfaction and brand image continue to be the two priority CSR issues (Yamaguchi, 2010). Japanese companies place high priority on product safety and quality assurance, and use CSR reports to communicate with their suppliers and buyers to that effect. The reason why the ISO 14001 norm is widely adopted is that government encourages enrollment as a way of providing customer assurance and boosting international competitiveness.

Japanese companies remain more inclined to meet quantifiable objectives with clear international standards (as in the case of environmental norms) rather than changing the internal dynamics of the company by opening it up to outsiders. Their interest in certification and norms remains closely linked to the business case mindset. Eco-labeling is promoted because customers' environmental (and food-related) concern is high. Conversely, Japanese people remain relatively unconcerned by most social issues outside Japan or issues that do not influence product quality. Fair Trade products' share of the market is growing, but it is still very small compared to the development in some European countries (Matsutani, 2012). Few companies (the large retailer Aeon, for example) actively promote the concept, and the range of products on the market is limited. The same can be said of certifications such as Rug Mark (social standards on rugs and carpets), UTZ Kupa (a standard for coffee, cocoa, tea and beans that are sustainably grown) and Marine Stewardship Council (standard for fish caught in a way that reduces overfishing), which are almost completely unknown in Japan.

The first Socially Responsible Fund (SRI) trust was set up in 1999. Since then, there have been many cases of SRI that focus on environmental issues but few on social issues (SIF Japan, 2013). The SRI market was boosted by investments coming from public pension funds as in several European countries (SIF Europe, 2013), but this is not the case now. Public pension funds are reluctant to move in that direction as long as the definitions of SRI funds and investment criteria are not clarified. They insist on their fiduciary obligation to invest and manage optimally risk and return for Japanese pensioners. It is unlikely their stance will significantly change in the coming years. For an economy the size of Japan, SRI is likely to remain relatively small and driven by environmental issues (SIF Japan, 2013).

The challenge of the shift to sustainability-based CSR

It is argued that the stronger the reciprocal involvement with stakeholders the richer the results of the CSR strategy will be, and the more convincing the message conveyed by companies (Roper, 2012). However, it means that dialogues with stakeholders may, for instance, include challenges to current CSR policies. The CSR philosophy proclaimed by Japanese companies is based on traditional production-driven economic and business practices to assure the well-being of stakeholders. The idea of economic growth as the engine of social and economic progress has never been seriously challenged as it is now in the Western world, where alternative development patterns are being debated in earnest (Alcott, 2005).

This means that eco- and socio-efficient products such as hybrid cars and low energy and non-polluting electronic appliances could be challenged by environmental groups because they are considered not effective in the use of natural and human resources, whatever their merits for some stakeholders (Dyllick & Hockerts, 2002). A green growth strategy, if pursued with only eco- and socio-efficiency in mind, can run foul of Jevon's Paradox (Alcott, 2005), which states that as the efficiency with which a given resource is used increases, the use of the resource tends to increase as well, because consumers find that they can afford more of it. Accordingly, a high level of customer service may lead to overconsumption of products and services (and thus waste of resource and potential health hazard) and overuse of energy. It can be linked to burnout, mental disease and even death by overwork (*karoshi*). Imposing too stringent performance criteria in order to satisfy cost and time imperatives can lead to lethal accidents involving trains, buses or trucks (Chikudate, 2012).

The overtime culture, the severe performance norms imposed on permanent employees and the poor working conditions of many non-permanent workers are the reverse side of the values underlying a corporate culture that is considered "society friendly" because dedicated employees and companies deliver high-quality products and services at a reasonable price. Whatever the efforts to integrate female employees, such a mindset creates problems that are difficult to overcome. Most married women cannot easily cope with working norms that take overtime as expected because they make it almost impossible to combine work and family life, except for the small number of high-flyers who may get support from their employers. Eventually, it leads to the perpetuation of recruitment, training and career development practices that disadvantage women (Nakakubo, 2007).

The attitude of many companies at the time of the 2011 earthquake and tsunami disaster has been much appraised for good reasons. Participation of businesses in bringing first aid and contributing to the economic revival of the devastated Tohoku region was significant. But the fact that thousands of non-permanent workers (and also some permanent workers of Tokyo Electric) work in Fukushima nuclear facilities to clean up sites in conditions that are claimed to put their life in danger does not seem to be socially unacceptable, in view of the indifference to their fate not only of the media and public opinion but also of the Tokyo Electric in-house union (Saito & Slodkowski, 2014). It shows that the in-out mentality nurtured by a hierarchically organized society can have negative consequences for those at the base of the social pyramid (Sugimoto, 2010).

Japanese companies' performance in terms of energy control and material recycling is impressive. But it goes alongside Japan being one of the worst offenders in advanced economies in terms of waste of energy and food (Brazor, 2009). This is the natural result of the need to satisfy customers who expect to find vending machines everywhere, shops to be open all the time and very fast delivery of a wide variety of new products that all have to be fresh. As a consequence of the insatiable need for energy, Japan may be forced to reactivate nuclear facilities in conditions that are suboptimal in terms of risk.

Likewise, pursuing this line of thought, whatever its CSR contribution, a company cannot be considered as having an appropriate CSR strategy if it flouts the ILO convention on the right of workers to organize, for example in attempting to curtail the right to have a union in some foreign subsidiaries, or treat unfairly some categories of workers (non-permanent workers, women, minorities, foreign workers in the subsidiaries and supply chain). Many Japanese companies may consider a number of issues irrelevant, such as those linked to the place of visible minorities in management or in respect of diversity criteria in recruitment and career management. They may not give priority to working conditions in the supply chain because Japanese customers and NGOs do not put this issue high on their agenda. But it is not true of external stakeholders in the world. International NGOs are likely to protest and may call for boycotts. Rating agencies and SRIs may sanction the company.

Growing awareness of external stakeholders but limited dialogue

Among Japanese people, as consumers but also as concerned citizens, there has been an increase in the level of consciousness regarding public welfare and interest in community issues. Since 1998, non-profit organizations (NPOs) and NGOs have played a growing role in social life in Japan, and their number has increased dramatically (Tanimoto, 2010). For a while there were fewer NGOs acting in Japan and they exerted almost no pressure. Although it can be considered as subdued by Western standards (Hoffschneider, 2007), the situation is changing. Foreign NGOs have strengthened their network in Japan, and they are backed up by more assertive Japanese NGOs in their requests.[8]

Most Japanese companies mention stakeholder dialogue in their CSR reports. But with complete outsiders the main objective is limited. This is especially the case with the dialogue between the media and advocacy-type NGOs (although companies often collaborate with NGOs involved in community projects). Companies have no intention of involving them in important decisions or even to negotiate if it is not absolutely necessary. But to gain access to fresh points of view on societal and market evolution is crucial. Stakeholder dialogue is considered a way in which to achieve this objective without responding to requests that would create business constraints.

Achievements and remaining uncertainties

Japanese companies place the same general emphasis on business ethics as Western companies. Some of them have internal social audit mechanisms (Tanimoto, 2010). The Whistleblower Protection Act was passed in 2004, which aims to encourage insiders to disclose wrongdoings. Japanese companies have started to work on developing comprehensive compliance systems in recent years and they have put in place mechanisms in order to facilitate the flow of information up the chain of command. Points of contact within the overall structure of the company have been established to help employees express their opinions and complaints. It could be argued that the new developments indicate a departure from the traditional sense of loyalty and a shift toward more open practices based on universal CSR principles. But to change the mindset inside large organizations regarding external and internal disclosure requires changes in corporate culture that are likely to take time to become fully rooted at all levels (The Economist Unit, 2005).

Many Japanese companies have a comprehensive welfare policy in their subsidiaries and partnership activities in developing countries. They engage with local personnel and community in miscellaneous welfare-related projects that focus on energy, education, housing and other areas (Asian Institute of Technology, 2012). But it has been pointed out that practices remain weak concerning human rights, labor practices and corporate governance in overseas activities. It has been observed, for instance, that Japanese companies have shown little interest so far in signing industrial codes of conduct, for example the Global Electronic Industry Code of Conduct, despite the fact that they manage supply chains in developing countries with a high risk of social and human rights violations. Moreover, few of them are said to incorporate social concerns into strategic planning, decision-making mechanisms, compliance and risk-assessment functions in supply chains (EIRIS, 2007).

However, the reality may be more nuanced. First of all, it is observed by Japanese companies (and other countries' multinational corporations as well) and local suppliers that the GRI approach and many other types of social audits are often purely formal exercises. There is little or no real dialogue between the parties between the yearly assessments (Debroux, 2014). Local suppliers argue that the mainstream approach of CSR procurement only takes into account the buyer's interest and is de facto an obligation imposed on them by external stakeholders. It does not induce them to engage further with other stakeholders over the long term.

The business risk of such insufficient monitoring explains why Japanese companies set up initiatives among themselves. The Global Compact Japan Network (GC-JN) has launched the Triple Win Procurement system based on the *sampo-yoshi* concept[9] in their report titled *A Vision of Desirable CSR Activity in the Supply Chain* (Global Compact Japan Network Supply Chain Working Group, 2013).[10] This concept explains effective and efficient CSR procurement that should achieve benefits for buyers, suppliers and subsequently society.

Buyers and suppliers are expected to collaborate to improve their products and services in giving equal consideration to quality, price, environment, human rights and other social concerns. This approach is based on a constant dialogue and follow-up of CSR policies and practices, and is in line with what is practiced by the ILO under its Better Work schemes (ILO-Better Work, 2014). This type of engagement is more demanding for all parties. It requires capability and trust building and the mobilization of more human and financial resources. It also adds layers to the decision-making process, making it slower and more cumbersome. However, it is argued by the proponents that it reduces business risks because it enhances the corporate value of all players and boosts competitiveness, once again in the line of Porter and Kramer's (2011) concept of "shared value creation" (Debroux, 2014).

Likewise, the Japanese Electronics and Information Technology Association (JEITA) established its own code of conduct of supply-chain management in 2005. To date, 12 companies, led by NEC, are participating in the working group that has been created to deal specifically with CSR in supply chain management. They have identified seven main issues: human rights and labor issues, occupational health and safety (OHS), environment, fair trade, product quality and safety, information security and contribution to society (JEITA, 2006).

The increase in the percentage of non-permanent workers is a deep concern because of the key role of Japanese companies in the acquisition of skills. The large discrepancy between the treatment of permanent and non-permanent employees in Japan has been stigmatized for a long time (OECD, 2012). The growing number of non-permanent workers, including many young people, is an important source of worry because it is an unaffordable under-use of human capital in an ageing society. But it is also bound to lead to structural socio-economic inequality in a country where equality is considered a key element of the legitimacy of the business system, and full employment has been the cornerstone of the social compact for the last 60 years. A number of companies have programs to shift non-permanent workers to permanent status. Besides improving their economic situation, it gives them a unique chance to acquire skills and experience. But it is unlikely that the majority of non-permanent workers will be included in such programs soon, and the issue is bound to remain a lingering problem in the foreseeable future (Debroux, 2013).

Likewise, a growing number of Japanese companies have advanced gender equal opportunity policies. In general, large companies offer more career opportunities to female university graduates than before (OECD, 2012). Nevertheless, obstacles remain to women's promotion above middle management (McKinsey, 2012). Moreover, companies show little interest in the issue of gender diversity at board level. In the absence of any legislative encouragement in this respect, contrary to what has happened in countries such as Norway and Sweden, representation of women on the board continues to be extremely low (less than 1% overall), making Japan an outlier in this respect (McKinsey, 2012).

At the opposite end of the employment spectrum, few programs are devised to cope with the problems of average female employees. They remain concentrated in the lowest segments of the labor market in small companies with low pay and little access to corporate welfare (Debroux, 2013), and have difficulties in maintaining a healthy work-life balance. Some improvements can be attributed to the revised 2010 Childcare Leave Law, which requires companies to allow shorter working hours for women with children. Although it is a positive step forward, only 40% of women continue working after the birth of their first child, a rate that has remained steady for years. Although it also reflects the cultural attitude toward mother-child relations (the perceived need of the mother's permanent presence with her child during the first three to four years after birth), clearly women need more support from companies if they are going to work in good conditions as well as to have children. This is necessary to fulfill the twin objectives of the Japanese government's optimization of female talent and a boost of the fertility rate (*The Japan Times*, 2013).

The difficult reconciliation of conflicting interests

On the one hand, neglect of the interests of outside stakeholders is likely to have negative business consequences. Loss of reputation may lead to disaffection of shareholders and customers. Strikes may damage the supply chain and hinder further recruitment. Low motivation may cause quality control problems. Low-paid non-permanent workers can hardly be expected to show high "quality spirit". Under-par treatment of female talent is unaffordable in a rapidly ageing society. On the other hand, attempts to satisfy outside stakeholders may challenge relationships with the three most important stakeholders, namely permanent employees, shareholders and customers.

The difficulties that in-house unions have in organizing non-permanent employees comes partly from the unease that permanent employees feel in sharing the benefits of permanent status, all the more in a period of low (no) wage increase and decline of welfare corporatism (Nitta, 2009). The same conflict of interest is likely to occur with customers and shareholders. Additional costs that would result from the inclusiveness of neglected human resources would necessarily have to be transferred to consumer prices. As indicated earlier, shareholders expect a higher financial return than before from Japanese companies. So, higher wages and extension of welfare corporatist benefits to a larger number of workers would not be acceptable if this is not justified by commensurately higher labor productivity and lower costs that maintain a high financial return. However, this can lead to yet more stringent work patterns and may potentially destroy permanent jobs.

Ultimately, a more inclusive approach of the welfare corporatist framework could have crucial consequences for the competitive advantages of many companies, if they can no longer rely on structural (and largely unpaid) overtime culture and low wages paid to non-permanent employees. Those factors explain the uneasiness to deal with those issues and the paucity of communication channels with outside stakeholders in this regard.

Conclusion

Japanese companies are often genuinely baffled by the intensity of the CSR debate in Western companies. It is even more true that they (wrongly in many respects) perceive Western companies as inherently oriented toward short-term financial gain, and thus not being likely to give importance to stakeholder dialogue. But the point is that Western companies face a much more heterogeneous and conflict-prone socio-political and business environment. It has forced them willy-nilly to develop and integrate dialogue in their mechanisms and to nurture more open corporate cultures in order to improve their accountability to stakeholders at large.

All the examples in the Japanese context exemplify contradictions that arise from a systematically nurtured inward-looking corporate culture that has shown a remarkable capacity to adapt to change over time, including to Western-inspired CSR practices during the last three decades. But if companies are indeed not only in the market but also in society, it is not sufficient any longer just to inform, control or influence the stakeholders.

Previously neglected stakeholders may exert pressure on the company but they may also be useful in terms of business collaboration. This is exemplified by the growing engagement between Western multinationals and advocacy-type NGOs. This means that companies must accept the possibility of being influenced by them. They must be ready to negotiate and tackle issues that result from a conflict of interests among stakeholders, including the possible negative effects of current CSR policies on some of them. Fundamentally, to do so and to create an original universalistic CSR culture with Japanese characteristics creates a higher level of diversity of corporate culture.

The examples given in the chapter show that for many Japanese companies, CSR policies go far beyond compliance and risk management, and have already separated from Japanese socio-cultural practices. The innovative part of the Japanese Charter of Corporate Behavior, revised in 2010, is its direct reference to ISO 26000, and its emphasis on the diversification of social issues and the globalization of business activities. The next challenge is how to fully integrate social policies and management systems. Change can come from outside but eventually momentum has to come from within, from a greater exposure of Japanese society to the world. This could lead to a new challenge, by Japanese people themselves, to existing CSR concepts.

Notes

1. The *shonindo* business ethics drew on early 18th-century Shintoism, Confucianism and Buddhism (Miyamoto & Grainger, 2007). This led to a business culture where companies were expected to bear a benevolent responsibility toward those with whom they had direct relations: employees, subsidiaries, business partners and customers, and the community surrounding the workplace, shopkeepers as well as service providers; that is, the stakeholders in modern CSR.
2. Eichii Shibusawa (1840–1931) was a Japanese industrialist who spearheaded the introduction of Western capitalism to Japan after the Meiji Restoration. He founded the first modern bank based on joint-stock ownership in Japan, as well as the Japanese Chamber of Commerce and Industry. He was also involved in the foundation of hospitals, schools, universities (including the first women's university) and charitable organizations, including the Japan Red Cross.
3. Government-sponsored associations such as the Society for the Study of Social Policy (Shakai Seisaku Gakkai) and the Society for the Cooperation (Kyochokai), created by Eiichi Shibusawa, promoted such ideas. It put the company as the main intermediary entity, responsible for the social and political integration of the workers in a hierarchical model based on labor–capital cooperation (Humbert, 2014).
4. Families started to sue companies for death from overwork (*karoshi*) (Furuya, 2007); women challenged companies about their rights to proper training and fair career treatment (Debroux, 2003); sexual harassment began to be treated seriously as a fundamental breach of human rights (Wolff, 1996).
5. Other intermediate organizations are active in the dissemination of standards. The largest labor confederation, RENGO (Japanese Trade Union Confederation), has launched a movement for promoting "environmentally friendly" lifestyle to their members and their family called RENGO ECOLIFE 21. RENGO is promoting "Union Social Responsibility" and has also been engaged with promotion of the ISO 26000. Currently, 36 social and environmental organizations and non-profit network/intermediary organizations throughout Japan are members of "NGO Network for SR Initiatives Japan" They also promote ISO 26000 and more generally social responsibility through booklets, seminars and workshops (Japan NPO Center, 2014).

6. On the shop floor, companies have adopted work patterns such as cell-based production and socio-technical schemes, providing a more motivational (more empowering) working environment to production workers, even in utilizing non-permanent workers (Debroux, 2003). Then, after the enactment of the Equal Employment Opportunity Law (EEOL) in 1986, the number of female employees entering the managerial track began to increase, albeit slowly and starting from a low basis (Debroux, 2003).
7. It was exemplified at the time of the 2011 Tohoku earthquake and tsunami and also in other instances, such as the typhoon in the Philippines in 2013. Working with Japanese and local authorities, Japanese companies have significantly contributed to life saving and damage control. But prevention is also high on the agenda. Companies acknowledge that close contacts with local civil societies are instrumental in the building of facilities that will assure a better level of protection in case of earthquakes (Taisei, 2013).
8. It is all the more true that the growing influence of NGOs is linked to their greater cooperation with the Japanese government, which needs to be seen in the context of a more proactive public involvement in developing countries. Japanese official development aid policy was concentrated for a long time on the building of infrastructure. It is shifting now toward a softer approach, with involvement in education, health, family planning, food, housing and energy projects that aim to cultivate a more people-friendly image of Japan and Japanese organizations. In many cases it requires collaboration with NGOs at grass-roots level.
9. The Omi merchants are considered the archetypal proponents of the traditional CSR concept in the Edo period. Their mindset has worked to anchor capitalistic behavior in ethical and social ideals. In doing so, they have engrained in the minds of generations of businesspeople values and assumptions that constitute an important element of the permanent fabric that is found in the successive avatars of CSR policies and practices of Japanese organizations. Their motto of *sanpo-yoshi*, "good for the seller", "good for the buyer" and "good for society", is a concept of management close to the multi-stakeholder concept (Hirschmeyer & Yui, 2006).
10. The members of the Supply Chain Working Group of GC-JN include corporate buyers and suppliers.

References

Alcott, B. (2005). Jevon's paradox. *Ecological Economics*, 54, 9–21.

Araki, T. (2002). *Labor and Employment Law in Japan*. Tokyo: The Japan Institute of Labor.

Asian Institute of Technology (2012). *Workshop on CSR in Asia: Case Studies of Community Engagement in Japanese Companies in Thailand*. Bangkok: AIT.

Berle, A. (1954). *The Twentieth Century Capitalist Revolution*. New York: Harcourt Brace.

Brammer, S., Jackson, G. & Matten, D. (2012). Corporate social responsibility and institutional theory: New perspectives on private governance. *Socio-Economic Review*, 10, 3–28.

Brazor, P. (2009). Japan loves wasting food. *The Japan Times*, 1 March, 5.

Cheron, E., Kohlbacher. F. & Kusuma K. (2012). The effects of brand-cause fit and campaign duration on consumer perception of cause-related marketing in Japan. *Journal of Consumer Marketing*, 29, (5), 357–368.
Chikudate, N. (2012). Toyota's inadequate CSR and corporate apologia. Paper presented at the 29th Euro-Asia Management Studies Association Annual Conference. 31 October-3 November, Singapore: National University of Singapore.
Debroux, P. (2003). *Human Resource Management in Japan: Changes and Uncertainties*. Aldershot: Ashgate Publishers.
Debroux, P. (2013). Human resource management in Japan. In Varma, A. & Budhwar, P. (eds.) *Managing Human Resources in Asia-Pacific*. London: Routledge.
Debroux, P. (2014). Field survey on supply chain management in Japanese companies in Southeast Asia (Vietnam and Malaysia). Unpublished manuscript.
Dore, R. (1987). *Taking Japan Seriously: A Confucian Perspective on Leading Economic Issues*. Redwood City, CA: Stanford University Press.
Dyllick, T. & Hockerts, K. (2002). Beyond the business case for corporate sustainability. *Business Strategy and the Environment*, 11, 130–141.
Ethical Investment Research Service (EIRIS). (2007) *The State of Responsible Business*. Available at http://www.eiris.org/media/statistics/
Furuya, S. (2007). Karoshi and Karojisatsu in Japan. Asia Monitor Resource Centre. Available at http://www.amrc.org.hk/alu_article/multifibrearrangement/karoshji_and_karoshijisatsu_in_japan.
Galbraith, J.K. (1956). *American Capitalism*. Oxford: Blackwell.
Global Compact (2014). Available at www.unglobalcompact.org
Global Environment Centre Foundation (2005). *Eco-Towns in Japan*. Available at www.gec.jp/
Global Reporting Initiative (2014). Available at http://www.globalreporting.org
Hirschmeyer, J. & Yui, T. (2006) *Development of Japanese Business*. London: Taylor and Francis.
Holtschneider, U. (2007). Safeguarding CSR in global supply chain in Japanese MNCs and compliance in China. East Asia Economic Studies Japan/Korea, University of Duisburg-Essen.
Humbert, M. (2014). The outstanding Japanese success in business and society, without CSR. *Soka Keiei Ronshu*, 38, 2–3.
International Labor Organization (2014). Available at www.ilo.org/japantc
Ireland, P. & Pillay, R. (2010). Corporate social responsibility in a neoliberal age. In Utting, P. & Marques, J.C. (eds.) *Corporate Responsibility and Regulatory Governance: Towards Inclusive Development?* Basingstoke: Palgrave.
ISO/IR Mirror Committee (2012). Use of ISO26000 by different stakeholders in Japan. ISO26000 International Workshop. 7–8 November, Geneva.
International Organization for Standardization (ISO). (2014). Available at www.iso.org.
Japan NPO Center (2014). Available at www.jnpoc.ne.jp/en
Japan Electronic and Information Technology Association (JEITA). (2006). Supply Chain CSR Deployment Guidebook (Tutorial of CSR Items).
Keidanren (2009). *Charter of Corporate Behavior*. Available at http://www.keidanren.or.jp
Keizai Doyukai (2009) *Evolution of Market and Social Responsibility Management – Make Toward Reliance Construction of a Company and Continuous Value Creation – 15th White Paper*, March. Available at http://www.douyukai.or.jp.

KMPG (2008). *KPMG International Survey of Corporate Responsibility Reporting Trends*. Available at www.econtext.co.uk.

Kinderman, D. (2012). Free us up so we can be responsible: The co-evolution of CSR and neo-liberalism in the UK, 1997–2010. *Socio-Economic Review*, 10, 29–57.

Matsushita Electric (2014). Matsushita Konosuke monogatari (Stories of Konosuke Matsushita). Available at http://panasonic.co.jp/company/person/story/part3/story3-3.html.

Matsutani, M. (2012). Fair trade slowly catching on here. *The Japan Times*, 1 November, 4

McKinsey & Company (2012). *Women Matter 2012: Making the Breakthrough*. McKinsey & Company

Ministry of Environment (2014a). Law Concerning the Promotion of Business Activities with Environmental Consideration by Specified Corporations by Facilitating Access to Environmental Information. Available at https://www.env.go.jp/en/laws/policy/business.pdf

Ministry of Environment (2014b). *Eco-Town Program*. Available at http://www.env.go.jp/en/recycle/manage/eco_town/index.html

Miyamoto, T & Grainger, R. (2007). Management in Japan: Contemporary issues. In Chatterjee, S. & Nankervis, A. (eds.) *Asian Management in Transition*. Basingstoke: Palgrave Macmillan.

Mizuo, J. (2014). A discussion of CSV centered global CSR: Learning about corporate sustainability activities mainly from studying Yakult (in Japanese). *Keiei Kyoiku Kenkyu*, 17, (1), 28–45.

Morita, A., Reingold, E.M. & Shimomura, M. (1986). *Made in Japan: Akio Morita and Sony*. New York: Dutton.

Nakakubo, H. (2007). Phase III of the Japanese Equal Employment Opportunity Act. *Japan Labor Review*, 4, (3), 6–27.

Nitta, M. (2009). *Nihonteki Koyo System (Japanese-Style Employment System)*. Tokyo: Nakanishiya Shuppan.

Nomura Soken Kenkyujo (2011). *BOP Business Senryaku* (*Strategy for BOP Business*). Tokyo: Toyo Keizai Shinposha.

Porter, M.E. & Kramer, M.R. (2011). Creating shared value: How to reinvent capitalism and unleash a wave of innovation and growth. *Harvard Business Review*, January-February, 2–17.

RENGO (2014). Action Policies 2012–2013. Available at http://www.jtuc-rengo.org/12th_biennial_convention/data/action_policies2012-2013.pdf.

Roper, J. (2012). Stakeholder engagement: Concepts, practices, and complexities. In Japan Forum of Business and Society (ed.) *Jisokukano na Hatten to Multi-Stakeholder* (*Sustainable Development and Multi-stakeholders*). Tokyo: Chikura-shobo.

OECD (2012). *Employment Outlook*. Paris: OECD.

Saito, M. & Slodkowshi, A. (2014). Special report: Japan's homeless recruited for murky Fukushima clean-up. Available at http://www.reuters.com/article/2013/12/30/us-fukushima-workers-idUSBRE9BT00520131230.

Schaede, U. (2008). *Choose and Focus, Japanese Business Strategies for the 21st Century*. Ithaca, NY: Cornell University Press.

Shimizu House Kabushiki Gaisha (2013). Kigyo gaiyo to CSR katsudo no tokuchou (Outline of company and characteristics of CSR activities). In Japan

Forum of Business and Society (ed.) *Jisokukano na Hatten to Multi-Stakeholder (Sustainable Development and Multi-stakeholders)*. Tokyo: Chikura-shobo.

SIF-Europe (2013). 2012 Review of Socially Responsible Investment in Europe.

SIF-Japan (2013). 2011 Review of Socially Responsible Investment in Japan.

Sugimoto, Y. (2010). *An Introduction to Japanese Society*. Cambridge: Cambridge University Press.

Taisei Corporation (2013). Corporate Report 2013.

Tanimoto, K. (2010). Structural change in corporate society and CSR in Japan. In Fukukawa, K (ed.) *Corporate Social Responsibility in Asia*. London: Routledge.

The Economist Intelligence Unit (2005) *The Way of the Merchant*. London: The Economist Intelligence Unit.

The Japan Times (2013). More women working for less. 13 December, 5.

The Nikkei Weekly (2011). Foreign ownership in Japanese companies. 17 June, 3.

The United Nations (1987). *Our Common Future, World Commission on Environment and Development*. New York: United Nations.

Toyota Motor Corporation Limited (2006). *Toyota Jidosha Kabushiki Gaisha (Toyota Motor Corporation), Sustainability Report*.

World Business Council for Sustainable Development (2014). Available at www.wbcsd.org.

Yamaguchi, A. (2010). *CSR Reporting in Japan. 2010 Global Compact CJK Researchers: Meeting Discussion on CJK Report Research*. Hosei Research Center for the Support of the Global Compact.

Wokutch, R. & Shepard, J.M. (1999). The maturing of the Japanese economy: Corporate social responsibility implications. *Business Ethics Quarterly*, 9, (3), 527–540.

Wolff, L. (1996). Eastern twists on Western concepts: Equality jurisprudence and sexual harassment in Japan. *Pacific Rim Law and Policy Journal*, 5, (3), 510–537.

Wolff, L. (2010). Lifelong employment, labor law and the lost decade: The end of a job for life in Japan. In Haghirian, P. (ed.) *Innovation and Change in Japanese Management*. Basingstoke: Palgrave Macmillan.

Yamanaka, K. (2006). Importance of leaders in CSR and humanism (in Japanese). *Soka Keiei Ronshu*, 30, (1), 1–16.

11
Corporate Social Disclosure Practices in Japanese Corporations: The Case of Meiko Electronics

Gustavo Tanaka

Introduction

Japan is regarded for a high degree of accuracy in corporate social disclosure (CSD) practices among its corporations. However, concerns have been raised about the practices of Japanese companies in the electronics industry, particularly among suppliers of Apple Inc. This chapter aims at analyzing CSD practices in Japan by looking at a Japanese corporation that has operations in China – Meiko Electronics Company Limited. This company was selected since some environmental problems at Meiko have been investigated. This chapter uses content analysis to compare the corporate social responsibility (CSR) and environmental practices of the company (disclosed in Meiko's CSR reports and website) with the perceptions of stakeholders on these practices. Public data in three languages, Chinese, English and Japanese, are analyzed and interpreted. The chapter aims to analyze the factors that influence a Japanese corporation's CSR policies and decisions on disclosure, specifically on environmental issues. The chapter also addresses the following questions: How and in what ways do stakeholders influence the company's CSR practices and disclosure? Are there any gaps between Meiko's CSR disclosures and the perceptions of its stakeholders on social and environmental matters? Does Meiko's CSD comply with CSR reporting standards? How can a company improve its CSR disclosure practices?

Definitions and fundamentals

Definitions of CSR and CSD

Although the concept of CSR can be traced back to the 1930s (Carroll, 1999), currently there is no consensus on its definition. However, for this chapter, two of the most widely accepted definitions (those of the European Commission and the Ministry of Economy, Trade and Industry (METI)) are used.

The European Commission defines CSR as "the responsibility of enterprises for their impacts on society". To fully meet their social responsibility, enterprises "should have in place a process to integrate social, environmental, ethical human rights and consumer concerns into their business operations and core strategy in close collaboration with their stakeholders" (European Commission, 2011).

METI, which conducts activities to promote CSR, adds in its definition that CSR "not only complies with laws/regulations and risk management, but encourages the improvement of corporate brands/human resources in the same way as corporate competitiveness" (METI, 2012).

However, no matter the definition, a strategic approach to CSR is increasingly important to a company's competitiveness. According to the European Commission (2011), CSR can bring benefits in terms of risk management, cost savings, access to capital, customer relationships, human resource management and innovation capacity.

On the other hand, for this chapter a definition of CSD or CSR/environmental reporting will be used. According to Japan's Ministry of the Environment (MOE), CSD is any reporting that includes information about corporate social responsibility or sustainability (MOE, 2007).

CSR in Japan

Although some Japanese business commentators name 2003 as the CSR "*gannen*" (the first year of CSR) (Fukukawa, 2010), the fundamentals of the CSR concept have actually been applied in Japan for decades. CSR in Japan originated from the philosophy of *sampo yoshi*, which refers to the triple satisfaction concept: "good for the seller, the buyer and the society" (METI, 2012). In present day Japan, a commonly understood rule derived from traditional strategy for corporate longevity is that managers who pursue their own interests but do not consider the interests of others have no right to talk about CSR (Teramoto, 2006). Moreover, Fukukawa (2010) argues that the driving factors for contemporary Japanese corporations engaging in CSR practices lie behind the thinking that companies are members of society, and without society's trust they cannot exist.

Will et al. (2013) argue that Japan's business model has conventionally been regarded as comparatively "society-friendly", with high-performance corporate governance, close coordination with government economic policy, teamwork and life-long employment.

Regarding the adoption of the CSR concept in Japan, a survey of management awareness of CSR by the Japan Association of Corporate Executives found that the concept is very well received. Indeed, 86% of managers of Japanese companies think that "companies should play a role in solving social issues from social contribution through philanthropy and *mécénat* activities to CSR that deals with social issues through business activities" (METI, 2012: 3).

CSD in Japan

Saka and Noda (2013) posit that the disclosure of CSR information began in the 1980s. Although Japanese companies have been widely adopting the CSR and CSD concepts (Japanese corporations had the second highest percentage of companies reporting CSR performance by country between 2008 and 2011) (KPMG, 2011), the process has not been simple because of cultural reasons. As Fukukawa (2010: 8) states, there has been some hesitancy toward CSR amongst Japanese businesses that fear being seen as "walking the talk" (*yu-gen jikko*). There is still a strong belief in "good karma" (*intokuyo – ho-*), whereby if you keep to good practices without expecting any type of reciprocity, the returns are more rewarding. There is, then, a perceived problem with CSR reporting itself, as it can be taken as an unnecessary or even vulgar marketing tool.

However, the globalization process and the competitive environment were key reasons for beginning CSD in many companies. Williams and Aguilera (2008) argue that Japanese companies might have followed Western ideologies on CSD owing to their growing business expansion into the Western world.

Moreover, when institutions such as the Global Reporting Initiative (GRI) or the International Organization for Standardization (ISO) started to develop regulations and guidelines regarding CSR information disclosure, the number of firms disclosing CSR information increased substantially (Saka & Noda, 2013). Later, the MOE issued the Environmental Reporting Guidelines 2000 in February 2001, and METI also published the Environmental Reporting Guidelines 2001 – with –Focus on Stakeholders in order to improve environmental reporting. Around this period, Japanese firms started to change from environmental reports to more holistic CSR reports. As a result, more companies referred to the GRI guidelines. In 2003, the Nippon Keidanren established the Subcommittee on Socially Responsible Management, a union of two committees (Corporate Behavior Committee and the Committee for the Promotion of Contribution to Society). In 2004, the CSR Forum Japan, a business initiative for corporate social responsibility with support from METI, was founded. The CSR Forum Japan is composed of highly motivated individuals from leading multinational corporations, and is regarded as one of the most outstanding networks in Japan. In 2005 the Companion for Combined Application of Environmental Reporting Guidelines and GRI Guidelines was published. Later, the Environmental Reporting Guidelines were revised twice (in 2007 and 2012), and they now require firms to disclose information on the social and economic aspects of their operations, apart from their environmental information. Moreover, Nippon Keidanren has released the CSR Matrix, which provides guidelines to Japanese companies for complying with social and environmental issues. Keidanren's CSR Matrix content is based on the Charter of Corporate Behavior (Keidanren, 2010) and the Implementation Guidance for the Charter of Corporate Behavior.

Yamaguchi (2010) posits that the main audiences of CSR reports in Japan are shareholders, suppliers and buyers, employees, investors and students (as future employees). Moreover, Yamaguchi (2010) mentions six distinctive elements in the CSR reports in Japan, namely the (1) boundary of CSR reporting, including the integration of CSR activities of overseas offices and subsidiaries, group companies and suppliers; (2) clear linkage between CSR and core business; (3) PDCA (plan–do–check–act) (management) cycle; (4) accuracy and confidentiality; (5) stakeholder-dialogue; and (6) focus on materiality.

Among the challenges of CSR reporting in Japan, Yamaguchi (2010) mentions the following: strong focus on environmental field and poor focus on social field; poor linkage between CSR activities and business strategy; poor information on performance of social field for several years; no information on social impact of CSR activities; and strong focus on local activities and poor focus on global activities. Yamagami and Kokubu (1991) suggest that one of the reasons for the lack of disclosure is that information regarding employee relations is considered to be classified, presumably because the employee is taken to be an extremely important stakeholder.

Most applied CSD standards in Japan

Sun et al. (2011) classify CSR reporting standards in the following categories: (1) comprehensive CSR standards (GRI, UN Global Compact and the ISO 26000, etc.); (2) CSR standards with emphasis on people (the Universal Declaration of Human Rights (UN), Social Accountability 8000, etc.); (3) standards with emphasis on environmental responsibility (ISO 14000, Environmental Reporting Guidelines-Japan, etc.); and (4) CSR for specific industries or substances (Electronic Industry Code of Conduct – EICC, Restriction of Hazardous Substances Directive in Electrical and Electronic Equipment, etc.).

In Japan, CSR disclosure is voluntary. Moreover, the contents of sustainability reports, as well as the stakeholders targeted as preferential readers, vary according to the issues addressed in the report. For example, environmental reporting is designed to handle waste material management, and social reporting to address employees' issues (Nakao et al., 2013). In the next paragraphs the most widely used CSD standards in Japan are presented.

GRI

GRI refers to the global network of many thousands worldwide that create a reporting framework in the sustainability field. GRI promotes the use of sustainability reporting as a way for organizations to become more sustainable and to contribute to sustainable development (GRI, 2006). In May 2013, the fourth generation of Sustainability Reporting Guidelines (G4) was released. G4 was developed to increase emphasis on the need for organizations to focus their reporting process and final reports on those topics that are material to their business and their key stakeholders. This "materiality" focus will make reports more relevant, more credible and more user-friendly.

Environmental Reporting Guidelines (Japan's Ministry of the Environment)

These guidelines summarize the preferred directions and contents, based on current domestic and international trends of environmental reporting. When engaging in environmental reporting the following general reporting principles should be used: relevance (materiality and timeliness); reliability (complete, accurate, impartial and verifiable); clarity; and comparability. Moreover, the information and indicators that should be included in environmental reporting can be classified into the following five categories: basic information; status of environmental management; status of activities for reduction of the negative environmental impacts; status of relationship between environmental considerations and management; and status of social initiatives.

ISOs

ISO 14000

The ISO 14000 family addresses various aspects of environmental management. It provides practical tools for companies and organizations looking to identify and control their environmental impact and constantly improve their environmental performance. ISO 14001 and ISO 14004 focus on environmental management systems. The other standards in the family focus on specific environmental aspects, such as life cycle assessment (ISO 14040), material flow cost accounting (ISO 14051), greenhouse gas (GHG) Accounting (ISO 14064) and carbon footprint of products (ISO 14067), among others.

ISO 26000

ISO 26000 provides guidance rather than requirements, so it cannot be certified like other well-known ISO standards. The CSR content required under ISO 26000 reflects the demands of international as well as Japanese stakeholders, and will be useful for appreciating the effect of stakeholder behavior on CSR information disclosure. ISO 26000 is divided into seven core subjects: organizational governance, human rights, labor practices, environment, fair operating practices, consumer issues and community involvement and development (Saka & Noda, 2013).

UN Global Compact

Launched in 2000, the Global Compact (GC) has expanded throughout the world, providing global standards for sustainable and responsible reporting. In Japan, through the efforts of the Global Compact Japan Network, which is a local arm of the GC, many top tier companies have become members of this international institution. Managerial practice of voluntary environmental and social activities is based on ten principles that fall into four categories, namely human rights, labor, environment and anti-corruption (Nakao et al., 2013).

According to Saka and Noda (2013), most Japanese firms prepare their CSR reports based on the MOE's Environmental Reporting Guidelines and the GRI's Sustainability Reporting Guidelines (although some firms such as Toyota or Takeda provide a comparison table with ISO 26000). In the case of Meiko, CSR reports will be analyzed taking into consideration the standards applied by the company (its own Environmental Action Guidelines, MOE's Environmental Reporting Guidelines 2007, GRI 2006 and ISO 26000).

Variables which affect CSD in Japan

A number of variables affect CSD in corporate Japan. The analysis of these variables can explain the behavior of some Japanese corporations with respect to CSD.

Stakeholders

Diverse groups of stakeholders have some impact on the decisions of Japanese corporations to disclose their CSR practices.

On one hand, intermediary stakeholders, such as environmental conservation groups and lobby groups, have an influence on Japanese corporations' CSD. Saka and Noda (2013) concluded that firms in industries with a significant environmental impact and those with a close connection with NPOs, NGOs and lobby groups disclose more CSR information.

On the other hand, internal stakeholders such as employees and shareholders also influence CSR disclosure in Japan. In the case of employees and shareholders, the results showed that they have no effect on CSR information disclosure (Saka & Noda, 2013).

Finally, external stakeholders also have some impact on the CSD of Japanese companies. Saka and Noda (2013) concluded that firms under scrutiny from governments and/or politicians and those that are exposed to political costs through the political process disclose more CSR information voluntarily, as a means of avoiding political costs. However, the effect of the government on CSR for environmental issues is low. Consistent with findings by Huang and Kung (2010) regarding financial leverage, Saka and Noda (2013) state that firms with high default risk tend to disclose additional CSR information. When a firm faces high financial risks, creditors will demand that more information be disclosed in order to stay informed about the latest corporate developments, and to be prepared to make economic decisions accordingly.

Other variables

A number of additional factors may influence Japanese corporations' CSD practices.

The size of the company

Large firms generally disclose higher-quality CSR information since they receive more attention from the government, unions and consumers and thus face higher political costs. Those firms will disclose more of their environmental information under such scrutiny (Huang & Kung, 2013).

Fines and penalties

Firms receiving fines and penalties tend to disclose more positive environmental information for the purpose of reversing the negative information associated with having received penalties (Huang & Kung, 2013).

Visibility in Media

Being targeted by the media is another important variable that influences CSD. Branco and Rodrigues (2008) explain that well-known firms that are close to their customers, or are targeted by the media, have higher social visibility. In this regard, a firm's CSR information disclosure is related to its distance from end customers and to the frequency at which it is targeted by the media.

Local subsidiaries

Subsidiaries have a tendency to adapt to local practices. With regards to CSD, if necessary, subsidiaries will legitimize their actions, or lack of actions, by arguing that local conditions, such as the institutional environment in the host countries, are very different from those in their home country (Yang & Rivers, 2009). These findings are consistent with Jamali (2010), who states that subsidiaries of multinational corporations tailor their CSR strategies to reflect characteristics of the subsidiary in question as well as the nature of the specific market environment encountered.

Governance information disclosure

Kamal and Deegan (2013) conclude that governance information disclosure by local supply companies is more focused on maintaining support from multinational buying companies than on securing legitimacy.

A good grasp of the above paragraphs together with an understanding of Meiko's characteristics ("relevant" stakeholders, size, probability of being penalized and subsidiaries/plants overseas) could explain why Meiko adopted some of its CSD practices.

Objective and methodology

The main objectives of this chapter are to investigate the compliance of Meiko's CSD (regarding environmental issues) to CSR reporting standards, and to find out whether there is a gap between Meiko's CSR disclosure and the perceptions of its stakeholders on CSR issues.

This chapter has used content analysis in order to collect information on CSR disclosure. According to Abbot and Monsen (1979), content analysis is a technique for gathering data that consists of codifying qualitative information in anecdotal and literal form into categories, in order to derive quantitative scales of varying levels of complexity.

Currently, Meiko discloses its CSR practices via its CSR reports and website in two languages – English and Japanese. Meiko first disclosed its CSR activities in Japanese in 2008, and the first English version was issued in 2010. The company has been disclosing its CSR activities steadily every year up until the time of writing. For this chapter, the Japanese versions of the CSR reports (from 2008 to 2013) and the English versions (from 2010 to 2013), as well as relevant information on Meiko's website (English and Japanese), were analyzed. Information from the annual reports (including financial statements and notes) was also taken into consideration, in order to gain a better grasp of the company's situation.

The CSR standards supposedly applied by Meiko (according to the company's public information) were first reviewed and then compared with Meiko's CSR reports in order to determine Meiko's compliance with CSR standards. Meiko publicly states that it uses the Environmental Reporting Guidelines (Japan's Ministry of the Environment) from 2007, and the Sustainability Reporting Guidelines (GRI) from 2006. Moreover, Meiko holds the ISO 9001, ISO 14001 as well as the ISO 27001 certifications. Meiko also uses ISO 26000 as a benchmark for its CSR practices and disclosure. Furthermore, Meiko's CSR reports were compared with information about the company that was obtained from external sources (in Chinese, English and Japanese), in order to determine whether or not there is a disclosure-performance gap between Meiko's CSR activities and the information disclosed by the firm.

Analysis and discussion

Description of the company

Meiko Electronics Company Limited, a Japanese corporation established in 1975, designs, manufactures and sells printed circuit boards (PCBs). Meiko is headquartered in Kanagawa prefecture. As for production plants, Meiko operates factories in three countries, Japan, China (Guangzhou and Wuhan) and Vietnam (Hanoi). Meiko constructed its Guangzhou plants in January 2001 (plant 1) and June 2004 (plant 2).

The Wuhan plant 1 was constructed in June 2006 and in July 2009 Wuhan plant 2 was completed and operations were launched.

Meiko provides state-of-the-art products, such as Any-Layer HDI, which offer free connection among all layers, adapted to the shrinking size of mobile phones and other handheld devices. Meiko also manufactures high heat dissipation PCBs and high electric current PCBs, capable of withstanding harsh environments such as the inside of car engines and solar power generators. PCBs pose many environmental concerns, such as toxic waste water, heavy metal contamination and contaminated sediments. The appendix includes more information about Meiko.

Analysis of Meiko's CSR reports

Meiko issued its first CSR reports in Japanese and English in 2008 and 2010, respectively. The reports were prepared by Meiko (without third-party opinion/assurance). Meiko's CSR reports are generally released in July and present data for the previous fiscal year. For example, the 2008 CSR report was released in July 2008 and covers activities from the 2007 fiscal year. One exception was the 2010 CSR report, which was released in June 2010.

The 2008 CSR report (in Japanese)

In this section, information regarding the Wuhan and Guangzhou plants will be emphasized.

Since environmental issues became a major theme at Toyako's G8 Summit (Hokkaido, Japan 2008) the firm has emphasized environmental issues in the report.

Meiko stated that its Guangzhou and Wuhan plants received the ISO 14001 certification in 2003 and 2007, respectively. Meiko reached an agreement with the Wuhan City Environmental Protection Bureau on drainage water quality. In addition, Meiko hired approximately 3,000 employees from the Wuhan city neighborhoods, trained its engineers in collaboration with local universities, and actively contributed to local communities.

In December 2006, the Wuhan City Environmental Protection Agency and the Agency for the Development of Zones and Protection of the Environment requested that Meiko deliver its waste water to a nearby paper mill. The paper mill uses around 20,000 tons of water per day. Meiko has 6,500 tons of waste water output. Consequently, the reuse of Meiko's waste water spares the Yangtze River contamination. In order to reuse its waste water Meiko mentioned that it had launched a reuse

Table 11.1 Structure of Meiko's 2008 CSR report

2008	Pages	Percentage
Meiko group business principles	1	2.3
In publishing the CSR report	1	2.3
Message from the president	2	4.7
Meiko's approach to CSR	2	4.7
Special features	6	14.0
1.Corporate activity rooted in community		
2.Management innovation toward zero emissions		
CSR activity	2	4.7
Management system	6	14.0
Sociality report	12	27.9
Environmental report	8	18.6
Communication tools	1	2.3
Financial performance	1	2.3
Corporate profile	1	2.3
Total	43	100.0

study committee that embarked on a drainage pipe installation project with an investment of RMB400,000 (about 6 million yen). The project was tested in August 2007 and was recognized by the Chinese media as a successful water recycling project.

Meiko also stated that in the Wuhan plant (located along the banks of the Yangtze River) the levels of copper pollution from industrial waste water are much lower than the standard in China. Moreover, Meiko stated that it contributed to maintaining the water quality of the Yangtze River. Meiko also mentioned that because of the waste water recycling system at its nearby Wuhan plant, the company received awards from the Wuhan authorities (Table 11.1).

The 2009 CSR report (in Japanese)

In its 2009 CSR report, Meiko celebrated its environmentally friendly Wuhan plant, and claimed that the achievement of coexistence and co-prosperity between Meiko and the local communities is the most advanced of its kind in the world. Meiko also stated that since manufacturing electronic circuit boards requires a large amount of water, co-processing of waste water is a big responsibility for the company. Some paragraphs from the previous CSR report were repeated, specifically the ones regarding the company's good practices in the Wuhan plant (Table 11.2).

Table 11.2 Structure of Meiko's 2009 CSR report

2009	Pages	Percentage
Meiko group business principles	1	2.4
In publishing the CSR report	1	2.4
Message from the president	2	4.9
Meiko's approach to CSR	2	4.9
Special feature	4	9.8
Efforts of each plant for environmental conservation		
CSR activity	2	4.9
Management system	6	14.6
Sociality report	12	29.3
Environmental report	8	19.5
Communication tools	1	2.4
Financial performance	1	2.4
Corporate profile	1	2.4
Total	42	100.0

The 2010 CSR report (in English)

In the message from the president section, following an introduction about the impacts of the global financial turndown, a list of environmental efforts was included. They are the company's goal of creating a low-carbon society, the effort to encourage each worker to promote CSR initiatives, and the establishment of a set of compliance regulations and a compliance manual in response to a pressing need.

In the environmental reporting section, Meiko presented its Green Society Initiatives, including the promotion of eco-friendly products such as light-emitting diode (LED) light and more powerful printed wiring boards (PWBs) to encourage the rise of photovoltaic power generation and eco-cars. Meiko also mentioned that its system for complying with environmental laws and regional ordinances allows the company to contribute to environmental protection in the local community, and to ensure full compliance. Other aspects covered in the environmental report were the company's initiatives to prevent global warming, reduce CO_2 emissions to zero, manufacture environmentally friendly products and measure a reduction of environmental burdens (Table 11.3).

The 2011 CSR report (in English)

The environmental report includes Meiko's basic environmental policy, its system for environmental management, prevention of global warming, cyclical use of resources, prevention of contamination

Table 11.3 Structure of Meiko's 2010 CSR report

2010	Pages	Percentage
Meiko group business principles	1	2.6
In publishing the CSR report	1	2.6
Message from the president	2	5.1
Meiko's approach to CSR	2	5.1
Special feature "Our Green Society Initiatives"	4	10.3
Management system	6	15.4
Sociality report	14	35.9
Environmental report	6	15.4
Communication tools	1	2.6
Financial performance	1	2.6
Corporate profile	1	2.6
Total	39	100.0

in ecosystems and measures for reducing environmental burdens. The communication tools section deals with communication to stakeholders.

In its approach to CSR section, Meiko stated that its main stakeholders are its employees, business partners, local communities, customers and shareholders. Meiko's CSR declaration stated that Meiko's business principles and activities align with its global social responsibilities and support an environmentally sustainable society.

The main topic in the message from the president section was the Great East Japan Earthquake that damaged the company's plants in Miyagi and Fukushima. Regarding environmental issues, the president stated that Meiko was actively involved in solving energy problems, preventing global warming, reducing environmental burdens and risks and enhancing resources efficiency.

The 2011 CSR report's special focus, "Our Green Society Initiatives", discusses Meiko's goal of cutting CO_2 emissions to counter global warming and help to create a green society. These initiatives include saving energy by autonomic cleaning of cooling water piping used for air conditioning at the Guangzhou plant and saving energy by replacing fluorescent lighting with LED lighting at the Wuhan plant.

In the "Environmental Report" section (p. 29), Meiko stated its basic environmental policy and commitment to clean air and water, and therefore its effective use of resources and its operation in a manner that is compatible with the living environment. Meiko showed its system for environmental management and mentioned that it established an ISO environmental system and had appointed a person responsible for controlling the environmental management system (EMS) at each of its plants in Japan and overseas. Meiko also mentioned its "Eco Project", which undertakes activities to reduce CO_2 emissions and achieve zero emissions.

Meiko also addressed the acquisition of the ISO 14001 certification and the list of certifications obtained and renewed in each plant (p. 30). The report mentioned that prompt actions had been taken in order to obtain ISO 14001 at its newly constructed and expanded plants, including the Wuhan plant. Meiko also mentioned that its environmental practices were in compliance with environmental laws and ordinances, including all the amended laws of individual regions. Consequently, it is stated that Meiko contributed to environmental protection in each local community and ensured full compliance (p. 31). Finally, various additional environmental initiatives, such as preventing global warming, reducing CO_2 emissions, a zero emissions target, environmental quality of products and measures for reducing environmental burdens, were shown.

Meiko mentioned the ISO 14001 standard for environmental management and its compliance with laws and ordinances. It includes many charts and environmental performance results in graphs and tables. The tone of the language in the report is general and very positive. There is no specific mentioning in any section of environmental problems or challenges that Meiko faced in the Guangzhou or Wuhan plants (Table 11.4).

The 2012 CSR report (in English)

In the message from the president, the president firstly addressed the suspension of operations at two domestic factories owing to the Great East Japan Earthquake and nuclear power plant disaster. Several issues were mentioned, such as effects on the supply chain's interruptions, power shortages, yen appreciation, increase in raw material prices, impact from the floods in Thailand and reduction in orders owing to intensifying global competition in the electronics industry. In addition, the president announced the suspension of the Wuhan plant: "During the fall we were forced to suspend operations at the second factory of the Wuhan Plant in China for three months due to an issue concerning environmental assessment licensing procedures. We are deeply sorry for any inconveniences or problems this may have caused our customers."

Table 11.4 Structure of Meiko's 2011 CSR report

2011	Pages	Percentage
Meiko group business principles	1	2.7
In publishing the CSR report	1	2.7
Message from the president	2	5.4
Meiko's approach to CSR	2	5.4
Special focus "Our Green Society Initiatives"	4	10.8
Management system	6	16.2
Sociality report	10	27.0
Environmental report	8	21.6
Communication tools	1	2.7
Financial performance	1	2.7
Corporate profile	1	2.7
Total	37	100.0

It was revealed in the environmental report (p. 25) that the suspension of the Wuhan plant operation was from 18 October 2011 until 19 January 2012. The reason behind the temporary suspension was "environmental assessment licensing procedures". Meiko stated that the corrective measures were taken immediately and that operations were resumed on 19 January 2012.

In the environmental report section (page 29), the manager of the Environment Preservation Department at the Wuhan plant mentioned various initiatives taken at the factory, including preservation activities through energy efficiency and water reduction, waste water management and air pollution prevention, and waste emissions management in accordance with rules and regulations. However, it was revealed that Meiko did experience a problem concerning "environmental assessment licensing procedures" in the fiscal year 2011.

The main problem with the CSD of Meiko is that it is not clear what "environmental assessment licensing procedures" means. For example, the city of Manitoba (2013) outlines in its Environment Act a procedure called environmental assessment and licensing process for those developments that may have the potential of significant environmental effects. All developments with significant environmental impact require a site-specific assessment and approval prior to construction or operation. However, in the case of Meiko's 2012 CSR disclosure there is no explanation of the "environmental assessment licensing procedures".

Since there is no explanation, a number of questions may be raised. Does this mean that Meiko was not able to complete its licensing procedures because of a document it did not submit, or that they were penalized for not meeting an environmental standard? Had Meiko met all minimum requirements for operation in the previous years? How was Meiko able to operate for several years without completing licensing procedures? Was this the first time Meiko was penalized (forced to suspend operations)? If so, is not the penalty too drastic (suspension for three months), assuming that it was suspended just because of an administrative issue, for example not submitting a document? If Meiko was forced to suspend operations just because of administrative issues, is the table on p. 28 (2012 CSR report) accurate (showing that they are meeting the standards)?

The fact is that the information provided is not clear. Companies must comply with standards regarding disclosure to provide information to their stakeholders. As Nakao et al. (2013) state, "companies that perform poorly with respect to governance tend to use expressions containing ambiguity and optimism in their environmental disclosures". It would thus seem better for Meiko to explain clearly what the issue was that cost the company large amounts of money (see below) in 2012 and 2013. If we complement this information (from the CSR report) with the information from the annual report, a better picture of the situation is obtained. Meiko presents the figures related to environmental issues in the income statement, and in the notes to the financial statements where it is mentioned that "the company was temporarily shut down due to a problem in the permitting process regarding environmental assessment". The figures of the expenses/losses become clear: 478 million yen for losses on abandonment of inventories in 2013, environmental expenses for 292 million yen and 219 million yen in 2013 and 2012, respectively, and a loss from suspension of plant operation of 243 million yen in 2013. To put the numbers in perspective, the expenses/losses related to the Wuhan suspension represent 32.7% of the net income of 2012 and 49.1% of the net loss of 2013.

There are a number of reasons that might explain the three-month suspension of Meiko's Wuhan plant. These may include: (1) political reasons such as the tense relations between China and Japan; (2) overproduction in China in response to the suspension of operations in the Tohoku region after the triple disaster (earthquake, tsunami and nuclear power plant failure) which affected Japan in March 2011; (3) the result of inefficiency in operations in the factory. However, the goal of this chapter is not to research the reasons for the Wuhan closure, but rather

Table 11.5 Structure of Meiko's 2012 CSR report

2012	Pages	Percentage
Meiko group business principles	2	5.6
Message from the president	2	5.6
Special focus	6	16.7
1. CSR activities at the Vietnam plant		
2. Improvement activities at the plants in China		
Sociality report	10	27.8
Environmental report	8	22.2
Management report	6	16.7
Corporate profile	2	5.6
Total	36	100.0

to analyze Meiko's CSD. Meiko was forced to suspend operations but did not disclose clearly and in an appropriate way (the operations in the Wuhan plant represent a substantial percentage of the total of the operations of the company) (Table 11.5).

The 2013 CSR report (in English)

Compared with the 2012 CSR report, the proportion of the environmental report has been reduced from 22.2% to 16.7% while the sociality report and management report sections have maintained almost the same size as in the previous year.

In the message from the president, Meiko mentioned its success in developing new technology that reduces the copper and energy needed to produce PCBs. It was also stated that all of Meiko's employees around the world recognize that CSR is central to every aspect of its business activities and that Meiko fulfills its responsibility at the local level as a member of society with the aim of establishing trust in the company.

On pages 11 and 12, Meiko showed the environmental assessment of its overseas factories. For Meiko Electronics (Wuhan) Company Limited, it was stated that the environmental assessment was certified by the Wuhan Environmental Protection Bureau for the first factory (in 2007) and second factory in December 2011. The second factory passed its opening environmental assessment in January 2013, and was currently operating as a mass-production facility. It was also mentioned that the Wuhan plant had reduced CO_2 emission through more efficient use of equipment. The Hubei National Development and Reform Commission consequently selected Meiko's Wuhan plant as the only corporate model for energy conservation in Wuhan City in December 2012. This

Table 11.6 Structure of Meiko's 2013 CSR report

2013	Pages	Percentage
Meiko's CSR	2	5.6
Message from the president	2	5.6
Special focus	8	22.2
1. Fukushima		
2. Environmental assessment of overseas factories		
Sociality report	10	27.8
Environmental report	6	16.7
Management report	6	16.7
Corporate profile	2	5.6
Total	36	100.0

was thanks to the deployment of an online monitoring system for preventing waste water pollution in March 2013. The environmental report section in the 2013 CSR report did not cover any information about the Wuhan plant. This section covers many environmental initiatives, such as energy saving improvements in the Fukushima and Yamagata factories, and waste exchange system in the Kanagawa factory (Table 11.6).

Meiko's website

The CSR section of Meiko's website has the following structure:

Message from the president
Meiko's approach to CSR
Special focus
Management system
Sociality report
Environmental report
CSR report

The website has basically the same content as the last CSR report (2013, when this chapter was written), so comments regarding the 2013 CSR report also apply to the website.

Meiko's opinion regarding compliance with reporting standards

For the 2011 to 2013 CSR reports, Meiko stated that it uses as references the Environmental Reporting Guideline (Fiscal year 2007 version,

Table 11.7 Environmental status by the Department of Environmental Protection of Guangdong Province on Meiko's Guangzhou plant

Year of the issue	Status (Year of reporting)
2008	Red "card" (2009)
2009	Yellow "card" (2010)
2010	Green "card" (2011) Still on the watch list
2011	Green "card" (2012) Still on the watch list

Source: Municipality of Guangzhou and CCTV http://www.gdep.gov.cn/

by Ministry of the Environment) and the Sustainability Reporting Guideline 2006 (presumably the GRI guideline).

Moreover, 2013 is the first year in which Meiko showed a comparison of ISO 26000's seven aspects matching its 2013 CSR report content listed by page. As mentioned before, this chapter focuses on the environmental part. Meiko shows that many environmental issues comply with the environmental aspect of ISO 26000. However, despite the company's efforts, the comparison between the requirements of ISO 26000 together with GRI guidelines and Meiko's CSR reports did not match (see Table 11.7). Moreover, in Meiko's case there is no assurance by a third party in the CSR report. This fact could probably be explained because Meiko does not deal with the final consumer directly. Haider et al. (2013) argue that consumer-oriented industries are more inclined to have social reporting.

Opinions of other stakeholders

Non-profit organizations (NPOs)

The Institute of Public and Environmental Affairs (IPE) is considered as one of the main NPOs that investigated Meiko's environmental issues. IPE was established in May 2006 and is based in Beijing. IPE's goal is to expand environmental information disclosure to allow communities to fully understand the hazards and risks in the surrounding environment and to promote widespread public participation in environmental governance. However, IPE was not the only NPO that investigated Meiko's issues. More than 30 organizations participated, including the NPOs Friends of Nature, Green Beagle and Envirofriends. According to the investigations of these NPOs there were some environmental issues in Meiko's plants in China which were summarized in a number of reports: *The Other Side of Apple*, *The Other Side of Apple II* and *Apple*

Opens Up – IT Industry Supply Chain Investigative Report – Phase VI, among others.

Issue 1: Meiko's Guangzhou plant

According to *The Other Side of Apple II* report by IPE (2011), the Guangdong Provincial Environmental Protection Bureau issued the 2008 assessment results for the Key Pollution Sources Environmental Protection Credit Management Plan that considered Meiko's Guangzhou plant as an "Enterprise under Strict Environmental Protection Supervision" (Rated Red). In 2009, Meiko Electronics was among the companies that must focus on complying with regulations on both high energy consumption and high levels of pollution. Meiko was listed as one of the "seven key violators needing special enforcement" and was required to finish all rectification work by 30 November 2009. On 27 January 2010, Meiko's Guangzhou plant was again listed owing to "secret or direct discharge of pollution, emissions that seriously exceeded authorized standards and acts relating to illegal construction projects, all with severity".

Issue 2: Meiko's Wuhan plant

According to IPE's report *Apple Opens Up* (2013), Meiko in Wuhan was not meeting standards for waste water treatment. The findings from the audit showed that Wuhan Meiko Electronics had problems with heavy metal waste water pollutants and total discharge amounts exceeded the authorized standards. This has polluted the Yangtze River, the water body into which the waste water flows. In 2011, between April and June, Meiko was found to have discharged waste water, and nearby Nantaizi Lake was seriously polluted with high levels of copper (IPE, 2013).

On 3 June 2011, an investigation was conducted by local NPOs near Meiko's Wuhan factory. The contamination content found was 4.8 times higher than the standards given by the Ministry of Environmental Protection of the People's Republic of China (http://tech.hexun.com/2011-08-31/132958458.html).

According to Green Choice Alliance (GCA) Supplier Audit (2012),

> on October 21, 2011, the online advisory column of the Wuhan Environmental Protection Bureau's website announced that Meiko Electronics (Wuhan) Company Limited has stopped production due to the fact that they have not obtained environmental impact assessment approval. The length of time that the production will be halted is still uncertain.

IPE and other NPOs stated in their report *Apple Opens Up* (2013) that Meiko Electronics had to fulfill the requirements of their clients and the Japanese Embassy, so it held several rounds of discussions with the Wuhan Branch of Friends of Nature and IPE in September 2011. On 23 and 24 September, Apple commissioned Golder, one of the auditing companies approved by the Green Choice Alliance (GCA), to carry out an environmental audit on Meiko Electronics. The audit confirmed that in order to target the problem of waste water being discharged through the storm water outlet, Meiko Electronics should adopt a waste water treatment facility for heavy metal sediment pollution (IPE, 2013).

Chinese Government

Issue 1: Meiko's Guangzhou plant

According to the Municipality of Guangzhou and CCTV (China Central Television), Meiko's Guangzhou plant was put on the environmental red list by the Department of Environmental Protection of Guangdong Province in 2008. The department pushed Meiko to improve its environmental condition. In 2009, Meiko was still on the red list, but improved and moved to the yellow list in 2010. In 2011, Meiko achieved the green list status, which means the company complies with all environmental responsibility requirements. Meiko remained on the green list in 2012.

Issue 2: Meiko's Wuhan plant

Meiko's plant was shut down because of environmental problems. On 24 January 2013, the Hubei Environmental Protection Bureau announced that after concluding its investigation of Meiko in Wuhan, the company complied with national standards for all relevant areas of environmental responsibilities, including air pollution and water waste. As a result the Wuhan plant received permission to operate again (see http://report.hbepb.gov.cn:8080/pub/root8/bgswj/201202/t20120209_50841.html).

Media

A number of documents can be found on the internet regarding issues in the Chinese plants of Meiko. As an example, one of the most significant documents with regards to content is presented.

On 4 June 2010, the program "Undercurrents" on CCTV2's regular economics and law segment exposed the specifics of Guangzhou Meiko Electronics' emissions discharge that exceeded the authorized standards. CCTV2 is the finance-focused channel of CCTV.

Client (Apple)

According to Apple's supplier list in 2012 and 2013, Apple purchased some of its parts from Meiko's Wuhan plant. This information was disclosed because of the pressure by stakeholders such as IPE on Apple to open up their transparency. According to IPE (2013), in 2010 Apple was pressured to reveal their suppliers' list, but Apple responded by claiming that in order to safeguard corporate secrets they had a "long-term policy of not disclosing supplier information". Apple was heavily criticized for not being transparent by NPOs such as IPE. Although Apple had begun to respond to two poisoning cases in their supplier responsibility report, it did not respond to the pollution cases raised by the NGOs.

NPOs continued to pressure Apple for transparency. Eventually, in February 2011, Apple released its first supplier responsibility progress report. However, it was observed that Apple paid relatively little attention to environmental issues. In the same year, as for the case of Wuhan's environmental issue, Apple was still resistant to the idea of accepting third-party audits under the supervision of NGOs (IPE, 2013).

According to IPE, on 27 January 2012, Apple finally agreed to carry out a pilot Green Choice Alliance audit under the supervision of environmental NGOs. Later on 26 April 2012, Meiko Electronics formally agreed to the third-party environmental audit (IPE, 2013). It is argued that Meiko received pressure not only from NPOs, but also from its suppliers and Apple.

Conclusions

This chapter has analyzed an Apple supplier (a Japanese corporation) and concluded that in general it has some good practices regarding environmental issues and has been improving its CSR disclosures in its CSR reports and website. However, when a stricter analysis of its CSD is conducted some issues can be revealed.

Comparison with stakeholders' versions

The reports from outside Meiko which included Chinese reports (central and local government data), media reports and independent investigation reports from NPOs indicated that Meiko has had some environmental problems in the surroundings of its factories in China, including the plant at Guangzhou but more severely in the plant at Wuhan (plant 2).

This information was not properly disclosed in Meiko's CSR reports. The issues regarding the Guangzhou plant were not disclosed in the CSR reports and the one regarding the Wuhan plant, which forced Meiko to close its factory for three months, was not clearly disclosed in the 2012 CSR report. The latter was only partially clarified in the 2013 CSR report.

Comparison with CSR standards

Some gaps can be found when comparing Meiko's CSR reports with CSR standards (see below for a comparison between Meiko's CSD and GRI and ISO 26000 in Tables 11.8 and 11.9).

Moreover, when comparing Meiko's CSR reports with the MOE's Environmental Reporting Guidelines, specifically the General Principles of Environmental Reporting, Relevance (materiality and timeliness), Reliability (complete, accurate, impartial, and must be verifiable), Clarity and Comparability, the following issues were found.

Relevance

Meiko did not disclose properly in several periods, regarding the issues in the Guangzhou and Wuhan plants. For example, as mentioned before, Meiko did not present properly the issue regarding the shutdown of the Wuhan plant in the 2012 CSR report. To analyze the materiality of the issue it is necessary to analyze the annual report (income statement) since not much information can be found in the CSR report. When the amounts of expenses/losses caused by the "shut down due to problems on permitting process regarding environmental assessment", 160 million yen (loss in valuation of inventories) and 219 million yen (environmental expenses), are analyzed in perspective it is clear that they are material. The total of both amounts represents almost one-third (exactly 32.7%) of the total net income (1,159 million yen). Meiko did not explain properly the reason of its shutdown. Moreover, Meiko presents in the 2013 CSR report and on its website (Special Focus/Feature II) the environmental assessment initiatives being carried out for its three overseas factories; but the issue is that Meiko did not disclose what had happened (why they were forced to suspend operations) before it passed its opening environmental assessment in January 2013. The same happened with the Guangzhou plant issue. No information regarding the red or yellow "card" issue was disclosed. In summary, material information must be disclosed in a timely fashion since it can affect stakeholders.

Reliability

Proper environmental reporting needs to be reliable (complete, accurate, impartial and verifiable). Meiko has been improving its environmental reporting in the last years. For example, the CSR reports of the first

Table 11.8 Non-compliance of Meiko's CSR report with the GRI principles

Reporting principles	Requirements	Non-compliance in Meiko's CSR reports
Materiality	The information should cover topics and indicators that reflect the organization's significant economic, environmental and social impacts or that would substantively influence the assessments and decisions of stakeholders.	IPE reports and local news had widely reported that Meiko's waste water (Wuhan plant) had caused serious pollution to the environment. According to the environmental status by the Department of Environmental Protection of Guangdong Province, Meiko had also violated the local government law and its Guangzhou plant was on the Environmental Black List. For the Wuhan plant, it was forced to suspend its operation by the Chinese government in fall 2011 for three months. However, none of these facts were disclosed in the CSR reports.
Stakeholder inclusiveness	The reporting organization should identify its stakeholders and explain in the report how it has responded to their reasonable expectations and interests.	Meiko was silent in the 2008–2012 CSR reports regarding opinions made by some of its stakeholders concerning environmental issues in China. No clear responses to their expectations and interests were found in the reports.
Completeness	Coverage of the material topics and indicators and definition of the report boundary should be sufficient to reflect significant economic, environmental and social impacts and enable stakeholders to assess the reporting organization's performance.	No negative information was found in the 2008–2012 CSR reports although Meiko had been reported badly in public news regarding its environmental management. Meiko disclosed more information in the 2012 report but the language used was ambiguous.

Table 11.8 (Continued)

Reporting principles	Requirements	Non-compliance in Meiko's CSR reports
		Also, no disclosure regarding external investigation reports which indicated that Meiko's plant in Guangzhou was rated in the environmental watch list by the local government.
Balance	The report should reflect positive and negative aspects of the organization's performance.	No disclosure of negative information could be found. Only positive aspects were elaborated in detail.
Timeliness	Reporting occurs on a regular schedule and information is available in time for stakeholders to make informed decisions.	Apparently there was a gap of around four months between a period's publications of CSR reports. The English electronic version was posted on Meiko's website in November 2013 while the Japanese version was issued in July 2013 (according to Meiko).

Table 11.9 Non-compliance of Meiko's CSR report with the GRI guidelines

Relevant GRI Guidelines Disclosures	ISO 26000 Core Social Responsibility Subjects and Themes	Requirement	Compliance level of 2013 CSR report
Materials	Environment/ Sustainable resource use	Materials used by weight or volume. Percentage of materials used that are recycled input materials. Direct energy consumption by primary energy source.	In the 2013 CSR report page 26, Meiko showed the changes in usage amount of environmental resources. Meiko presented the environmental burden of their business activities on page 28. However, the language and the information were not communicated clearly (whether the information refers to materials used or not since it was communicated as environmental burdens). Also, the list of input may not reflect the total input Meiko uses in its operation. Although the cyclical use of resources was mentioned (p. 26), the percentage of materials used that were recycled input materials was not revealed. Meiko did reveal the changes in usage amount of environmental resources (p. 26), but did not reveal the consumption amount.
Energy	Environment/ Sustainable resource use	Indirect energy consumption by primary source. Energy saved through conservation and efficiency improvements. Initiatives to provide energy-efficient or renewable energy based products and services, and reductions in energy requirements as a result of these initiatives.	There was no part about indirect energy consumption by primary sources. The energy saved owing to conservation and efficiency improvement was not shown although Meiko mentioned that it had implemented other power conservation measures (p. 23).

Table 11.9 (Continued)

Relevant GRI Guidelines Disclosures	ISO 26000 Core Social Responsibility Subjects and Themes	Requirement	Compliance level of 2013 CSR report
		Initiatives to reduce indirect energy consumption and reductions achieved.	Although Meiko listed their major activities in 2012 (p. 23) such as holding Energy Saving Committee meetings and adding hybrid vehicles to the company-owned vehicle fleet (six vehicles), there was no tangible measurement of the impact to the improvement. The future plans of environmental target also were very weak without a timeline that Meiko wished to achieve goals.
Water	Environment/ Sustainable resource use	Total water withdrawal by source. Water sources significantly affected by withdrawal of water. Percentage and total volume of water recycled and reused.	Although Meiko mentioned about its water consumption issue on page 26, there was no information regarding the total water withdrawal by source, water sources they draw from, nor the percentage and total volume of water recycled and reused. Water is particularly crucial for Meiko's production process
Biodiversity	Environment/ Protection of the environment and biodiversity, and restoration of natural habitats	Location and size of land owned, leased, managed in, or adjacent to, protected areas and areas of high biodiversity value outside protected areas.	There was no part in the report mentioning about biodiversity.

Source: Prepared based on https://www.globalreporting.org/resourcelibrary/How-To-Use-the-GRI-Guidelines-In-Conjunction-With-ISO26000.pdf

two years look very similar in content, and in the following periods it disclosed more information. Also, Meiko explained its environmental assessment in the 2013 CSR report (a year after it incurred material losses). However, some reporting issues, specifically selective disclosure, can be found.

Selective disclosure is a form of symbolic behavior whereby firms seek to gain or maintain legitimacy by disproportionately revealing beneficial or relatively benign performance indicators to obscure their less impressive overall performance (Marquis & Toffel, 2013). As can be deduced from the previous paragraphs, regretfully Meiko has not been impartial in disclosing CSR practices. Basically it has disclosed the positive practices but not those which could affect its reputation.

Clarity

In the 2012 CSR report, Meiko said "we were forced to suspend operations at the 2nd Factory of Wuhan Plant in China for three months due to an issue concerning environmental assessment licensing procedures". Is "disclosure issue" what "environmental assessment licensing procedures" means? Meiko repeats the same paragraph or mentions a "problem on permitting process regarding environmental assessment" in the annual report. Again, the issue is that the disclosed information is not clear for the average reader. Companies must use easy-to-understand expressions to avoid misunderstandings among stakeholders.

Comparability

In general, Meiko properly discloses some information which can be compared, for example, the "Changes in Usage Amount of Environmental Resources" and the "Measured Values for Discharged Water Quality and Atmospheric Measurements". However, as mentioned above in the 2012 CSR report, the value is missing for the Wuhan water quality item.

In summary, gaps between Meiko's CSD and CSR reporting standards, as well as between Meiko's CSD and external sources of information, were found.

Suggestions

Meiko should continue improving its CSD. Meiko has been disclosing mainly the positive aspects of its CSR environmental practices; thus this creates an opportunity. As Qian and Schaltegger (2013) suggest, the pattern may be that at first, poorer environmental performers try to achieve higher levels of environmental disclosure to legitimize and compensate their poor performance. Then, once their disclosure is improved, they are motivated to use disclosure as an "outside-in" opportunity to create change and improve their carbon performance. This implies environmental disclosure is used as a "legitimacy" as well as a "management" tool.

Moreover, even though Meiko is headquartered in Japan, it should balance better its CSD considering all its plants worldwide (in Japan, Vietnam and China). However, Meiko's behavior is the expected one, as stated by Guler et al. (2002). Headquarters location is likely to be the institutional environment with the most influence on corporate decisions.

Some reasons why Meiko should improve environmental performance and disclosure include:

a) Adequate CSR practices and disclosure (proper disclosure according to basic reporting principles) will help the company avoid being penalized.
b) A company with as high a level of financial leverage as Meiko could benefit from proper disclosure. Firms disclosing their efforts to improve as well as the actual improvement of their environmental performance experience a lower cost of capital (Cho et al., 2013; Dhaliwal et al., 2011). Moreover, companies with commitment to environmental reporting, measured in terms of the number of years of continuous reporting, seem to induce an additional decrease in the cost of capital.
c) As Nuzula and Kato (2011) stated, financial markets present positive reactions toward the publication of CSR reports in Japan marginally. The reactions are demonstrated over longer periods of time rather than over short periods.
d) Kitora (2010) concludes that companies with a better assessment of their disclosure on corporate websites significantly showed an improved assessment of corporate reputation.

However, in order to enjoy the benefits mentioned above, Meiko must actually incorporate CSR into the management processes and corporate governance. As Tanimoto (2013) argues, simply establishing the relevant institutions is not enough to ensure the automatic functioning of CSR.

Regarding the standards to be applied, Meiko should comply with the updated versions of the CSD standards, that is the Environmental Reporting Guidelines 2012 (MOE) and G4 Sustainability Reporting Guidelines.

Finally, Meiko should adopt third-party assurance. Gray and Gray (2000) define assurance as a generic concept which includes auditing, verification, review or other forms of checking. Assurance will enhance the credibility of sustainability reporting and can be seen as a way to manage public pressures (Patten, 1991). The main reason assurance is suggested is because Meiko is very closely scrutinized by several groups (especially intermediate stakeholders).

Concluding remarks

In this study the CSD practices of a Japanese corporation with operations in China (Meiko) were reviewed. Meiko, an Apple Inc. supplier with a capital of 12,888.47 million yen, designs, manufactures and sells PCBs. The company has plants in China and Vietnam.

Meiko's first CSR report was issued in 2008 (Japanese version), while its first CSR report in English was issued in 2010. Currently, Meiko uses its website and CSR reports in Japanese and English to disclose its CSR practices.

Although Meiko has been improving its CSD practices steadily, some gaps between the company's CSD and CSR reporting standards were found. Meiko publicly states that it uses the MOE's Environmental Reporting Guidelines 2007 and the Sustainability Reporting Guidelines (GRI) 2006. Meiko also uses ISO 26000 as a benchmark for its CSR practices and disclosure. However, a more detailed analysis shows that there are several non-compliances of these standards in the company's CSR reports and website.

Gaps were also found between information in Meiko's official CSD and information from external sources of information. While Meiko discloses positive aspects in its CSD and basically no negative information can be found, external sources show that this information is not totally accurate. NPOs disclosed some information that showed how Meiko's Guangzhou plant was not meeting pollution standards. Moreover, in 2011, Meiko's Wuhan second factory was forced by Chinese regulators to suspend operations for three months because it did not obtain environmental impact assessment approval. This issue was only mentioned in the company's CSD as an "issue concerning environmental assessment licensing procedures", which certainly can be considered confusing and unclear. Additionally, in 2009 and 2010 Meiko's Guangzhou plant was put on the red list and yellow list, respectively, by the Department of Environmental Protection of Guangdong Province, information which was not mentioned in the company's CSD. Therefore, it can be concluded that although Japanese companies have been widely adopting the CSR and CSD concepts, Meiko's case shows that there are still some problems with this process.

Finally, a number of suggestions to improve Meiko's CSD practices are offered.

1) Meiko is advised to aim for a better balance in its CSD, focusing on all its stakeholders, rather than only on stakeholders in Japan (especially stakeholders in Vietnam and China where Meiko has plants).
2) Meiko is advised to apply the most up-to-date versions of CSD standards (updated versions of its current standards, Environmental Reporting Guidelines 2012 (MOE) and G4 Sustainability Reporting Guidelines).
3) Meiko is advised to have third-party assurances for its CSD reports.

Appendix: Highlights of Meiko for the year 2012 captured from the Osiris Database

2012	Total assets	Operating revenue	Market capitalization	Number of employees
Meiko's figures in millions of yen except for number of employees	102,046	60,709	22,036	9.966
Meiko's ranking among the 3,134* companies in the sample	820	1,083	1,536	245

*Total number of Japanese companies in the Osiris Database with valid data.

References

Abbot, W.F. & Monsen, R.J. (1979). On the measurement of corporate social responsibility: Self-reported disclosures as a method of measuring corporate social involvement, *Academy of Management Journal*, 22, (3), 501–515.

Apple (2013). Supplier List 2013. Available at https://www.apple.com/br/supplier responsibility/pdf/Apple_Supplier_List_2013.pdf

Branco, M. & Rodrigues, L. (2008). Factors influencing social responsibility disclosure by Portuguese companies, *Journal of Business Ethics*, 83, 685–701.

Carroll, A. (1999). Corporate social responsibility: Evolution of a definitional construct. *Business & Society*, 38, (3), 268–295.

Cho, C., Michelon, G. & Tanaka, Y. (2013). Does environmental disclosure influence cost of capital? An empirical investigation of Japanese companies. In Kokubu, K., Sawabe, N. & Sakaue, M. (eds.) *Proceedings of the Seventh Asia Pacific Interdisciplinary Research in Accounting Conference*. Kobe: The APIRA Conference Committee.

Dhaliwal, D., Li, O., Tsang, A. & Yang, Y.G. (2011). Voluntary nonfinancial disclosure and the costs of equity capital: The initiation of corporate social responsibility reporting. *The Accounting Review*, 86, (1), 59–100.

European Commission (2011). Communication from the Commission to the European Parliament, the Council, the European Economic and Social Committee and Social Committee and the Committee of the regions.

Fukukawa, K. (2010). Corporate social responsibility in Japan: A local-global perspective (Working Paper No 10/03).

Global Reporting Initiative (GRI) (2006). *Sustainability Reporting Guidelines*. Version 3.0

Gray, G.L. & Gray, M.J. (2000). *Assurance Services: Implications for the Internal Audit Profession*. Altamonte Springs, FL: Institute for Internal Auditors Research Foundation.

Green Choice Alliance (GCA) (2012). Supplier Audit Explanations and Conclusions: Meiko Electronics (Wuhan) Co., Ltd. Available at http://www.ipe.org.cn/Upload/Audit-Meiko-Electronics-Wuhan-Co-Ltd-EN.pdf.

Guler, I., Guillén, M. & Macpherson, J. (2002). Global competition, institutions, and the diffusion of organizational practices: The international spread of ISO 9000 quality certificates. *Administrative Science Quarterly*, 47, (2), 207–232.

Haider, M., Kokubu, K. & Nishitani, K. (2013). Stakeholder influence on the adoption of assurance in sustainability reporting: Evidence from Japan. In Kokubu, K., Sawabe, N. & Sakaue, M. (eds.) *Proceedings of the Seventh Asia Pacific Interdisciplinary Research in Accounting Conference*. Kobe: The APIRA Conference Committee.

Huang, C. & Kung, F. (2010). Drivers of environmental disclosure and stakeholder expectation: Evidence from Taiwan. *Journal of Business Ethics*, 96, 435–451.

IPE, Friends of Nature and Green Beagle (2011). The Other Side of Apple. Available at http://www.ipe.org.cn/Upload/Report-IT-V-Apple-I-EN.pdf

IPE, Friends of Nature, Green Beagle Envirofriends & Green Stone Environmental Action Network (2011). The Other Side of Apple II, Pollution Spreads Through Apple's Supply Chain. Available at http://www.greenbiz.com/sites/default/files/63637255-Apple-II-Final-20-14.pdf.

IPE, Friends of Nature, Envirofriends, Nature University and Nanjing Greenstone (2013). Apple Opens Up: IT Industry Supply Chain Investigative Draft Report – Phase VI. Available at http://switchboard.nrdc.org/blogs/lgreer/Report-IT-Phase-VI-Draft-EN.pdf.

Jamali, D. (2010). The CSR of MNC subsidiaries in developing countries: Global, local, substantive or diluted? *Journal of Business Ethics*, 93, 181–200.

Kamal, Y. & Deegan, C. (2013). Motivation of corporate managers for social responsibility related governance disclosure: Evidence from Bangladesh. In Kokubu, K., Sawabe, N. & Sakaue, M. (eds.) *Proceedings of the Seventh Asia Pacific Interdisciplinary Research in Accounting Conference*. Kobe: The APIRA Conference Committee.

Keidanren (Japan Business Federation) (2010). Charter of Corporate Behavior. Available at http://www.keidanren.or.jp/english/policy/csr/charter2010.html

Kitora, Y. (2010). Corporate disclosure on corporate websites and its effect on corporate reputation: By controlling the respondents' attributes (in Japanese). *The Japan Society for Socio-Information Studies*, 14, (1), 33–45.

KPMG (2011). *KPMG International Responsibility Reporting 2011: The Definitive Snapshot of Corporate Responsibility Reporting*. KPMG International.

Manitoba City (2013). Information Bulletin – Environmental Assessment and Licensing under the Environment Act.

Marquis, C. & Toffel, M.W. (2013). Scrutiny, norms, and selective disclosure: A global study of greenwashing. Harvard Business School Organizational Behavior Working Paper No. 11–115.

Ministry of Economy, Trade and Industry (METI) (2012). *Japan's Policy for CSR*. METI.

Ministry of the Environment (MOE) (2007). *Environmental Reporting Guidelines*. MOE.

Nakao, Y., Nishitani, K. & Kokubu, K. (2013). Determinants of narrative content of sustainability reporting by Japanese companies. In Kokubu, K., Sawabe, N. & Sakaue, M. (eds.) *Proceedings of the Seventh Asia Pacific Interdisciplinary Research in Accounting Conference*. Kobe: The APIRA Conference Committee.

Nuzula, N. & Kato, M. (2011). Do Japanese capital markets respond to the publication of corporate social responsibility reports? *Journal of Accounting, Finance and Economics*, 1, (1), 48–60.

Patten, D. (1991). Exposure, legitimacy, and social disclosure. *Journal of Accounting and Public Policy*, 10, 297–308.

Qian, W. & Schaltegger, S. (2013). Perform to disclose or disclose to perform: Which drives which? In Kokubu, K., Sawabe, N. & Sakaue, M. (eds.) *Proceedings of the Seventh Asia Pacific Interdisciplinary Research in Accounting Conference*. Kobe: The APIRA Conference Committee.

Saka, C. & Noda, A. (2013). The effects of stakeholders on CSR disclosure: Evidence from Japan. In Kokubu, K., Sawabe, N. & Sakaue, M. (eds.) *Proceedings of the Seventh Asia Pacific Interdisciplinary Research in Accounting Conference*. Kobe: The APIRA Conference Committee.

Sun, M., Nagata, K. & Onoda, H. (2011). The current status and promotion of Chinese corporate social responsibility. *International Proceedings on Biology, Environment and Chemistry IPCBEE*, 1, 401–405.

Tanimoto, K. (2013). Corporate social responsibility and management process in Japanese corporations. *World Review of Entrepreneurship, Management and Sustainability. Development*, 9, (1), 10–25.

Teramoto, Y. (2006). Thought of honest fortune – The way of using personal fortune: Japanese practitioners, Edo period canto (in Japanese), *Nikkei Venture*, November, 128–131.

Will, M., Kumarasinghe, S. & Hoshino, Y. (2013). Corporate social responsibility disclosures and performance in Japanese companies. Available at http://www.bsec.canterbury.ac.nz/sars/documents/CSRD%20in%20Japanese%20companies(%20PaperforNZSARS).pdf.

Williams, C. & Aguilera, R. (2008). Corporate social responsibility in a comparative perspective. In McWilliams, A., Matten, D., Moon, J. & Siegel, D. (eds.) *The Oxford Handbook of Corporate Social Responsibility*. Oxford: Oxford University Press.

Yamagami, T. & Kokubu, K. (1991). A note on corporate social disclosure in Japan. *Accounting Auditing and Accountability Journal*, 4, (4), 32–39.

Yamaguchi, A. (2010). CSR reporting in Japan, 2010 Global Compact CJK Researchers Meeting Discussion on CJK CSR Report Research.

Yang, X. & Rivers, C. (2009). Antecedents of CSR practices in MNCs' subsidiaries: A stakeholder and institutional perspective, *Journal of Business Ethics*, 86, 155–169.

12
Corporate Social Disclosure in China and Japan: Concluding Remarks

Carlos Noronha

This book provides the readers with the latest observations of corporate social disclosure (CSD) in China and Japan, covering various issues such as disclosure trends, labor matters, product safety, state-owned enterprises, contentious industries, global corporate social responsibility (CSR) standards and organizations, and CSR audit and assurance. Through critical analyses, performance-disclosure gaps have been identified in some industries in China (e.g. Chapters 3 and 4) and Japan (e.g. Chapter 11). Furthermore, the CSD practices, from a more macro perspective, as influenced by the social, economic and political environment in China (e.g. Chapters 2 and 5) and Japan (e.g. Chapter 10) have also been surveyed. By this exercise, it is hoped that a modest contribution has been made to the research arena of CSR and CSD in China and Japan, especially to that of the former, the strongest developing country of all.

Also, through the comparison between China and Japan as two runners in a linear marathon, the development of CSR and CSD in these two countries has been explored in a lucid and vivid way by embracing perspectives of the political economy, stakeholder and legitimacy theories. Given China's important role in the global economy today, it is expected that this linear marathon will evolve into a genuine speed race in the near future; as long as institutional factors continue to improve in line with its economic advancement.

However, owing to the still rudimentary development of CSR in China, such performance-disclosure gaps are no surprise, and the use of CSD as a propaganda tool is also not unexpected given the current social, political and legal climate on the mainland. The "pragmatism versus idealism" dichotomy arising from a socio-cultural perspective suggested in Chapter 1 appears to apply well to the case of today's China. CSR and CSD remain largely at the instrumental level of responding to government directives and policies; for example, the government-led concept of the "harmonious society" (Wong, 2009; Wang & Juslin, 2011), where the society's resources are to be distributed in a balanced and sustainable manner, the CSR initiatives and guidelines issued by the Shanghai and Shenzhen Stock Exchanges (Noronha et al., 2013) as well as the launching of the CSR index (the *Blue Book*) by the Chinese Academy of Social Science (2009). This is notwithstanding the fact that customers' awareness of their own rights (Wong, 2009) and their demands for more corporate disclosure have been increasing in recent years. The time is right for CSR and CSD to be institutionalized in China. Through gradual improvement, especially by the betterment of institutional factors thanks to the lead of Central Government and state-owned enterprises as well as pressure from international organizations and counterparts, we shall look forward to the convergence of the pragmatism end and the idealism end of the continuum. That is to say, until a time when more and more businesses abide by socially responsible ways of conducting their operations and become more transparent in disclosing their corporate affairs; or in other words, when a more market-based CSR orientation can be seen in China.

On the other hand, while Japan continues to be much more sophisticated in terms of CSR than China and even many other developed countries (Wokutch, 1990), there are still structural problems to be overcome. The corporate governance system, corporate culture traits, labor issues such as work-life balance of employees (e.g. Chapter 10 of this volume and Kuriyama, 2009), overwhelming emphasis on disclosing environmental issues and the reluctance to embrace global standards and practices (e.g. Chapter 9 on Japan's limited assurance of sustainability reports) as well as language barriers are just some examples we have explored in this volume. Japanese businesses have been facing many challenges as to how to sustain their CSR and CSD ever since their inheritance of the notion of *sanpo-yoshi* by the Omi merchants from the Edo period.

Finally, in terms of avenues for new research directions, this volume has certainly helped to open up some intriguing opportunities. One area of further research is the application of the legitimacy theory in different social, political and economic settings. For example, the examination of the gaming industry as a contentious or controversial industry (Chapter 6) opens a challenging path to research into "sin industries", in addition to the current small but essential body of studies in related areas (e.g. Deegan et al., 2002; Campbell et al., 2003; Moerman & Van der Laan, 2005; Palazzo & Richter, 2005; Tilling & Tilt, 2010; Lindorff et al., 2012). Another suggestion for further research is the application of the legitimacy theory to the unique political setting in China, as in the case of state-owned enterprises. An interesting question to probe is "fundamentally speaking, why do state-owned enterprises 'have' to pursue CSR and CSD?" Although Chapter 5 has provided us with some hints from the perspectives of economic, legal, environmental, moral and political responsibilities, a much bigger picture and theoretical framework to relate China's institutional environment to the legitimacy theory is to be expected (see, e.g., Guan et al., 2013). In fact, a similar thought can also be applied to government-led industries which are controversial. For example, the Japanese government-led Japan Tobacco, which has an outstanding CSD record (Noronha et al., 2014), is a proper case worth investigating under the umbrella of the legitimacy theory, but in a unique setting.

Turning to the case of Japan, a suggestion for future research relates to the issue of cultural influence on accounting disclosure (Gray, 1988; Gray & Vint, 1995) as discussed in Chapter 1, which was unfortunately not touched on in detail in the other chapters in this volume. Given the advancement of Japan's experience in terms of CSD and the changes in its socio-cultural environment through rapid globalization, the state of Japan's disclosure practice (in terms of secrecy versus transparency) deserves to be revisited. Furthermore, as revealed in Chapters 8, 9 and 10, Japanese businesses' gradual acceptance of global accreditation and verification of CSD warrants more in-depth studies. Also, structural changes in the Japanese economic and social systems call for corresponding tactics in terms of CSR practices. For instance, how does Japan's opening of full-time employment to females and "part-timers" relate to global CSR issues, such as equal rights and opportunities? In a related aspect, Suzuki et al. (2008) have pointed out the issue of falling birth rate and working parent support in Japanese firms. Also, how does corporate Japan cope with the issues of long working hours, employee benefits and well-being in view of CSR expectations? These are issues to be pondered upon. In particular, Japanese corporations' willingness to engage with environmental disclosure (Tanimoto, 2004) but avoid disclosing human rights issues (e.g. risks, complicity, civil and political rights) (Kokubo, 2011) is very much related to profound changes in the social system.

The present volume closes with this concluding remark, which hopes to shed light on research ideas that are of course not exhaustive. The area of CSR and CSD remains one of the most interesting, challenging and compelling research topics in contemporary accounting studies. It is hoped that the chapters in this volume may stimulate the further exploration of corporate disclosure behaviors, especially by employing a critical, qualitative and multidisciplinary approach, so as to enrich the ever emerging study of CSR and CSD.

References

Campbell, D., Craven, B. & Shrives, P. (2003). Voluntary reporting in three FTSE sectors: A comment on perception and legitimacy. *Accounting, Auditing and Accountability Journal*, 16, (4), 558–581.

Chinese Academy of Social Science (2009). *Research Report on Corporate Social Responsibility of China (2009): Blue Book of Corporate Social Responsibility*. Social Sciences Academic Press.

Deegan, C., Rankin, M. & Tobin, J. (2002). An examination of the corporate social and environmental disclosures of BHP from 1983–1997: A test of legitimacy theory. *Accounting, Auditing and Accountability Journal*, 15, (3), 312–343.

Gray, S.J. (1988). Towards a theory of cultural influence on the development of accounting systems internationally. *Abacus*, 24, (1), 1–15.

Gray, S.J. & Vint, H.M. (1995). The impact of culture on accounting disclosure: *Asia Pacific Journal of Accounting*, 21, 33–44.

Guan, J., Noronha, C. & Tayles, M.E. (2013). Explaining social reporting of state-owned enterprises in China: A market economy with socialist characteristics. In Proceedings of the 7th Asia Pacific Interdisciplinary Research in Accounting Conference, Kobe, 26–28 July 2013.

Kokubo, K. (2011). CSR in Japan. What is social responsibility in Japan? Presentation at the European Economic and Social Committee (EESC), Brussels. Availabel at http://www.eesc.europa.eu/resources/docs/kokubu.pdf

Kuriyama, N. (2009). The role of business in Asian living and working conditions. In Hasegawa, H. & Noronha, C. (eds.) *Asian Business and Management: Theory, Practice and Perspectives 1st edition*. Basingstoke: Palgrave.

Lindorff, M., Jonson, E. & McGuire, L. (2012). Strategic corporate social responsibility in controversial industry sectors: The social value of harm minimization. *Journal of Business Ethics*, 110, 457–467.

Moerman, L. & Van der Laan, S.L. (2005). Social reporting in the tobacco industry: All smokes and mirrors? *Accounting, Auditing and Accountability Journal*, 13, (8), 374–389.

Noronha, C., Si Tou, M.I. & Guan, J. (2013). Corporate social responsibility reporting in China: An overview and comparison with major trends. *Corporate Social Responsibility and Environmental Management*, 20, (1), 29–42.

Noronha, C., Guan, J.J. & Leung, T.C.H. (2014). Further challenges to the legitimacy theory: Corporate social disclosure of the Chinese and Japanese tobacco industries. Working Paper.

Palazzo, G. & Richter, U. (2005). CSR business as usual? The case of the tobacco industry. *Journal of Business Ethics*, 61, (4), 387–401.

Suzuki, K., Tanimoto, K. & Atsumi, N. (2008). Support for working parents: Government policies and corporate responses in Japan. *Asian Business and Management*, 7, (3), 297–319.

Tanimoto, K. (2004). Changes in the market society and corporate social responsibility. *Asian Business and Management*, 3, (2), 157–172.

Tilling, M.V. & Tilt, C.A. (2010). The edge of legitimacy: Voluntary social and environmental reporting in Rothmans' 1956–1999 annual reports. *Accounting, Auditing and Accountability Journal*, 23, 55–81.

Wang, L. & Juslin, H. (2011). The effects of value on the perception of corporate social responsibility implementation: A study of Chinese youths. *Corporate Social Responsibility and Environmental Management*, 18, 246–262.

Wokutch, R.E. (1990). Corporate social responsibility Japanese style. *Academy of Management Executive*, 4, (2), 57–74.

Wong, L. (2009). Corporate social responsibility in China: Between the market and the search for a sustainable growth development. *Asian Business and Management*, 8, (2), 129–148.

Index

Printed and bound by CPI Group (UK) Ltd, Croydon, CR0 4YY